6

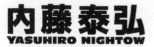

TRIGUN MAXIMUM
YASUHIRO NIGHTOW
DEEP SPACE PLANET FUTURE GUN ACTION!!

YASUHIRO NIGHTOW

TRANSLATION JUSTIN BURNS

LETTERING STUDIO CUTIE

DARK HORSE MANGA

DMP Digital Manga Publishing

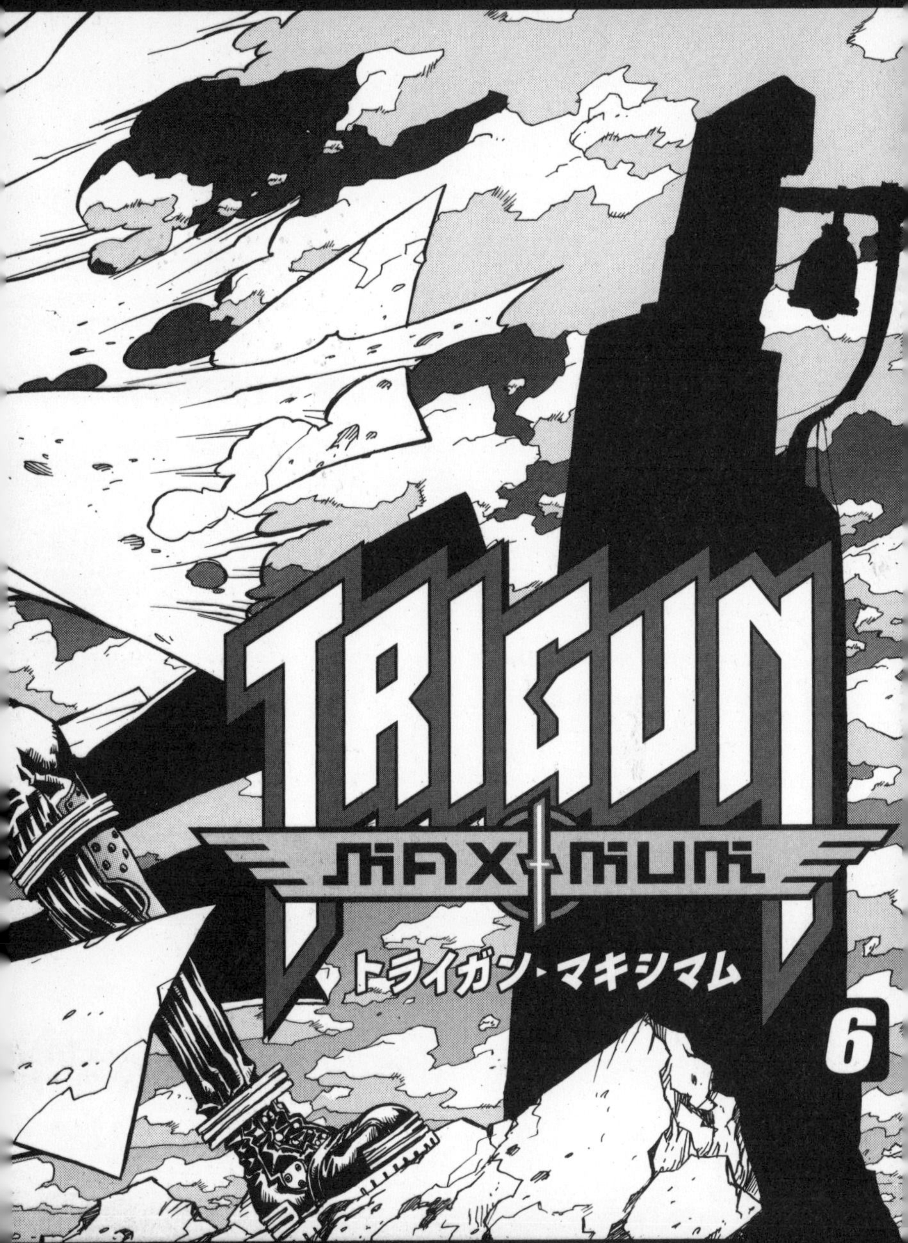
TRIGUN
MAXIMUM
トライガン・マキシマム
6

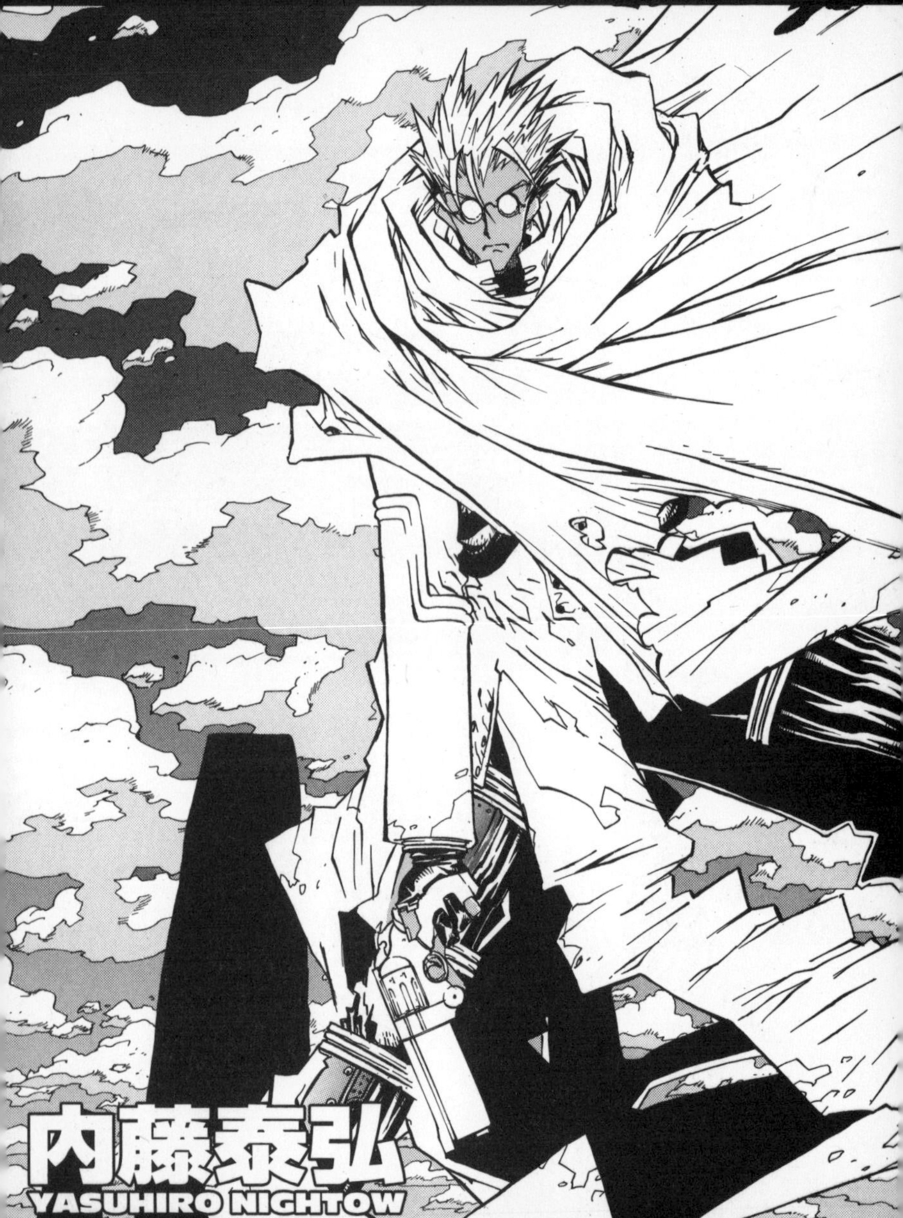
内藤泰弘
YASUHIRO NIGHTOW

TRIGUN MAXIMUM
YASUHIRO NIGHTOW
DEEP SPACE PLANET FUTURE GUN ACTION!!
CONTENTS

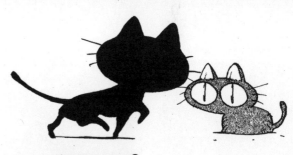

TRIGUN MAXIMUM 6
THE GUNSLINGER

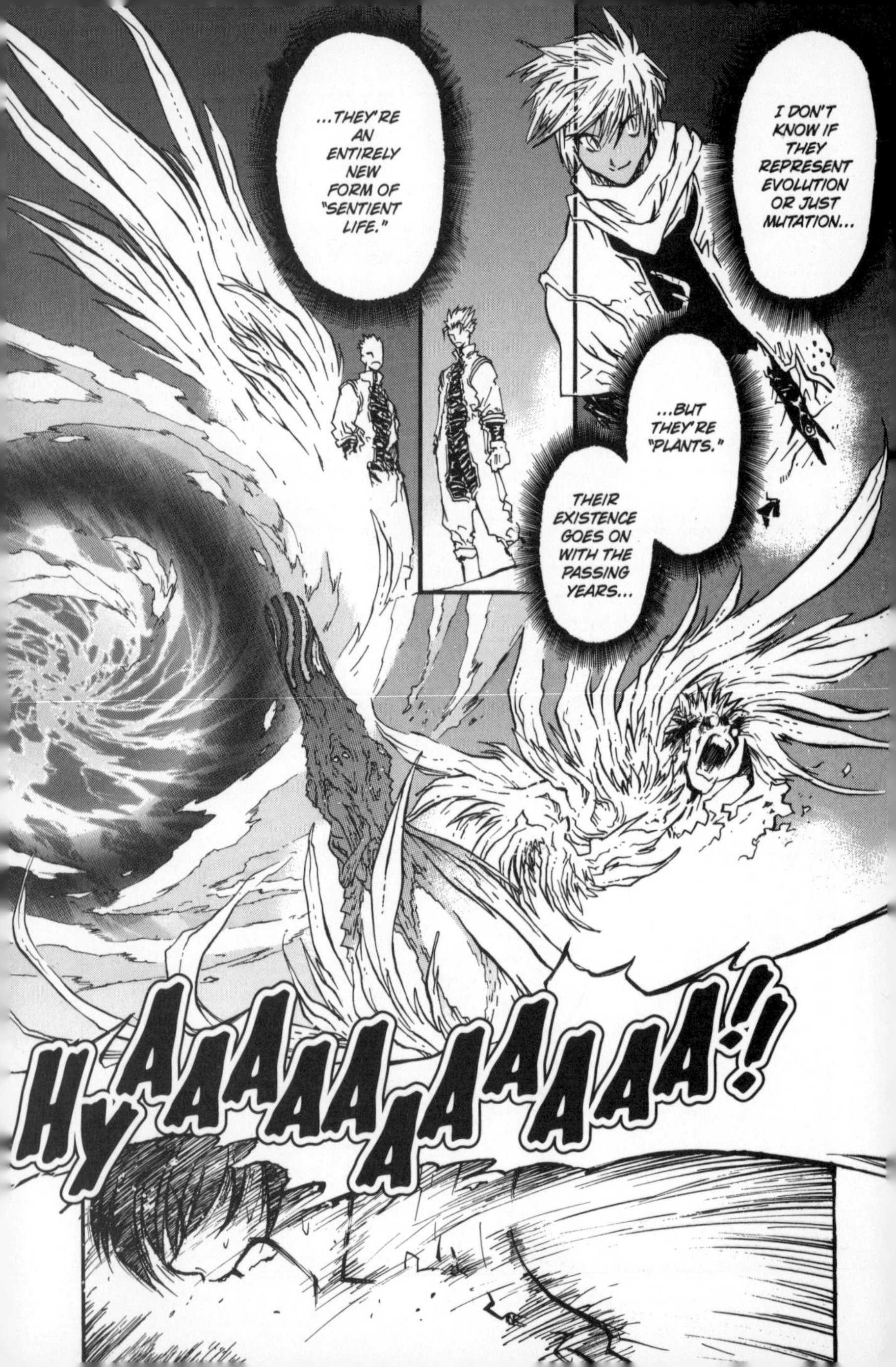
I DON'T KNOW IF THEY REPRESENT EVOLUTION OR JUST MUTATION...
...BUT THEY'RE "PLANTS."
THEIR EXISTENCE GOES ON WITH THE PASSING YEARS...
...THEY'RE AN ENTIRELY NEW FORM OF "SENTIENT LIFE."
HYAAAAAAAAAAA!

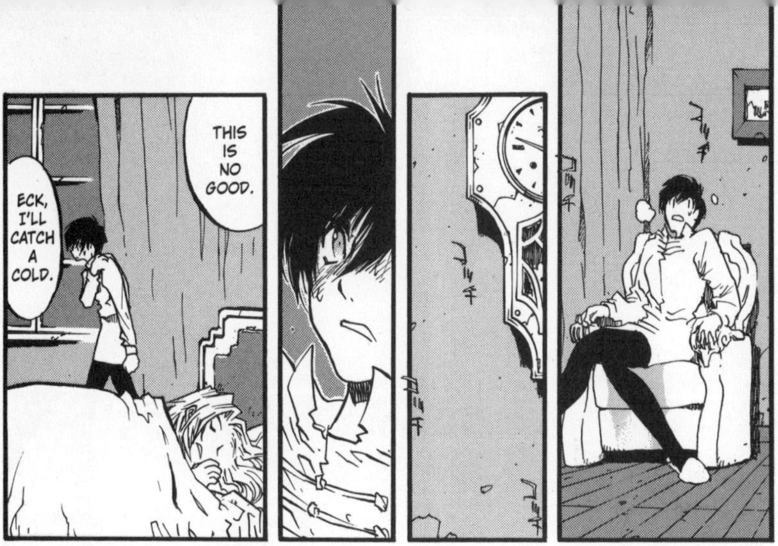
THIS IS NO GOOD.
ECK, I'LL CATCH A COLD.

#1. THE GUNSLINGER

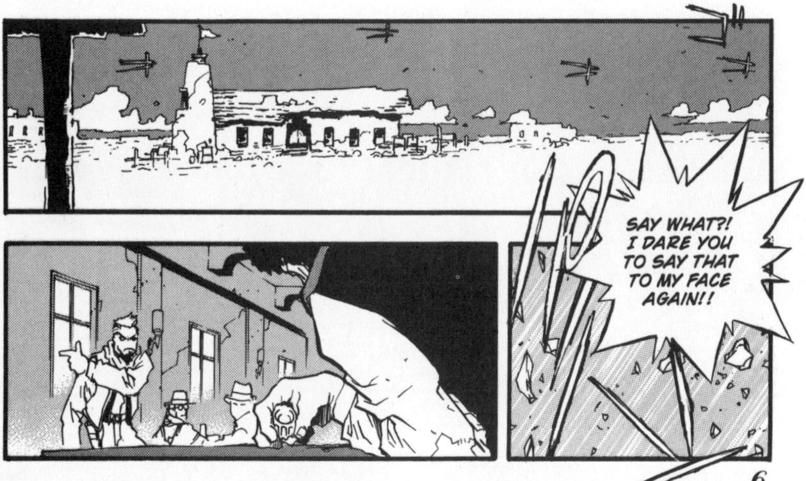
SAY WHAT?! I DARE YOU TO SAY THAT TO MY FACE AGAIN!!

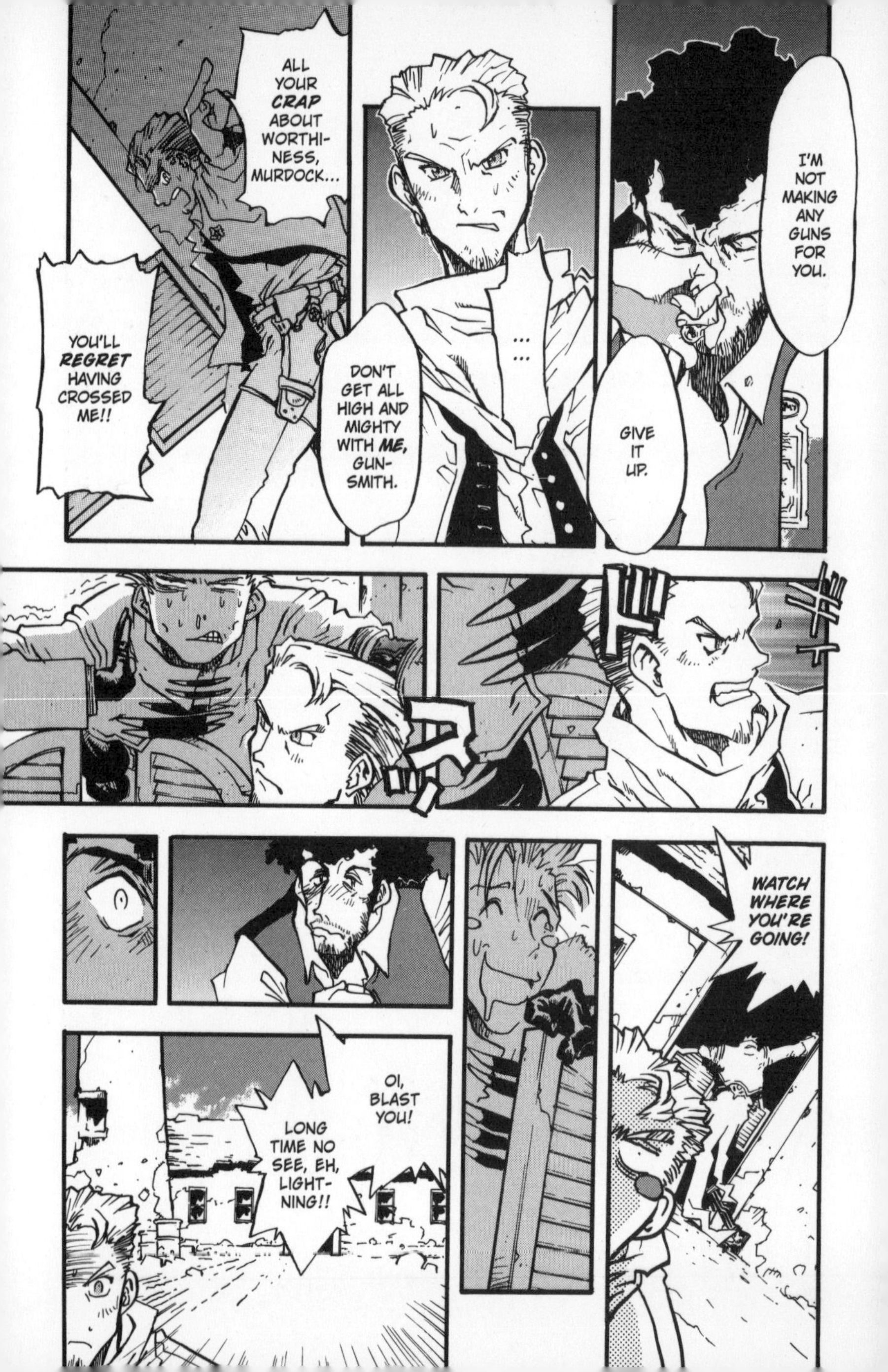
I'M NOT MAKING ANY GUNS FOR YOU.
GIVE IT UP.
...
...
DON'T GET ALL HIGH AND MIGHTY WITH ME, GUNSMITH.
ALL YOUR CRAP ABOUT WORTHINESS, MURDOCK...
YOU'LL REGRET HAVING CROSSED ME!!
WATCH WHERE YOU'RE GOING!
OI, BLAST YOU!
LONG TIME NO SEE, EH, LIGHTNING!!

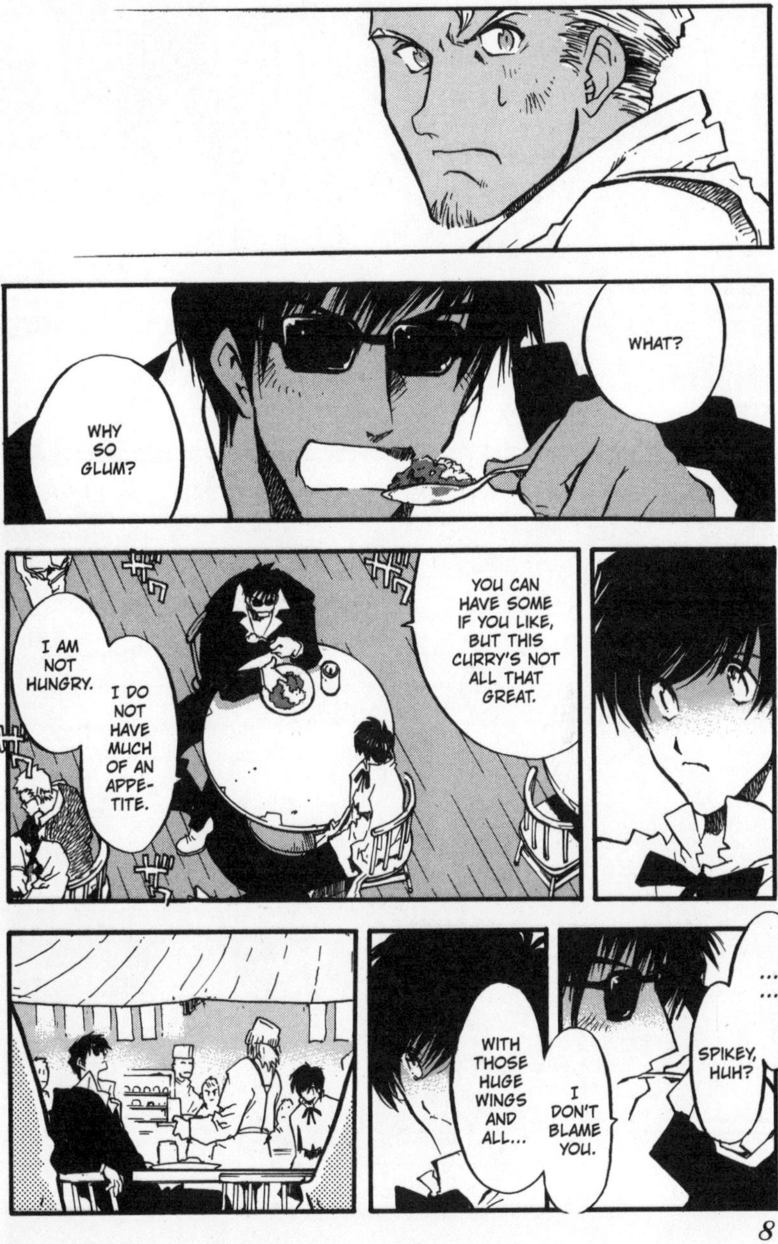
WHAT?
WHY SO GLUM?
YOU CAN HAVE SOME IF YOU LIKE, BUT THIS CURRY'S NOT ALL THAT GREAT.
I AM NOT HUNGRY.
I DO NOT HAVE MUCH OF AN APPE-TITE.
......
SPIKEY, HUH?
WITH THOSE HUGE WINGS AND ALL...
I DON'T BLAME YOU.

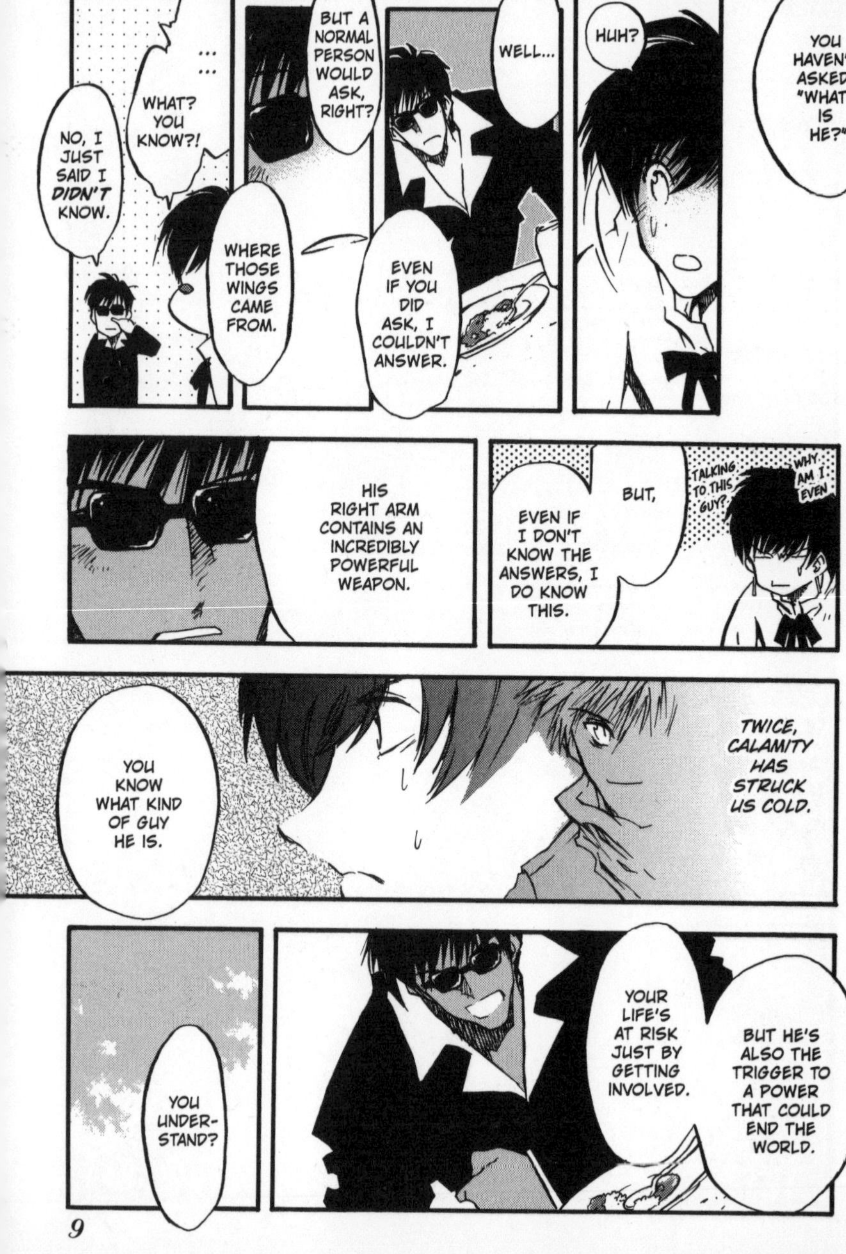
YOU HAVEN'T ASKED, "WHAT IS HE?"
HUH?
WELL...
BUT A NORMAL PERSON WOULD ASK, RIGHT?
EVEN IF YOU DID ASK, I COULDN'T ANSWER.
WHERE THOSE WINGS CAME FROM.
... ...
WHAT? YOU KNOW?!
NO, I JUST SAID I *DIDN'T* KNOW.
WHY AM I EVEN TALKING TO THIS GUY?
BUT,
EVEN IF I DON'T KNOW THE ANSWERS, I DO KNOW THIS.
HIS RIGHT ARM CONTAINS AN INCREDIBLY POWERFUL WEAPON.
TWICE, CALAMITY HAS STRUCK US COLD.
YOU KNOW WHAT KIND OF GUY HE IS.
BUT HE'S ALSO THE TRIGGER TO A POWER THAT COULD END THE WORLD.
YOUR LIFE'S AT RISK JUST BY GETTING INVOLVED.
YOU UNDERSTAND?

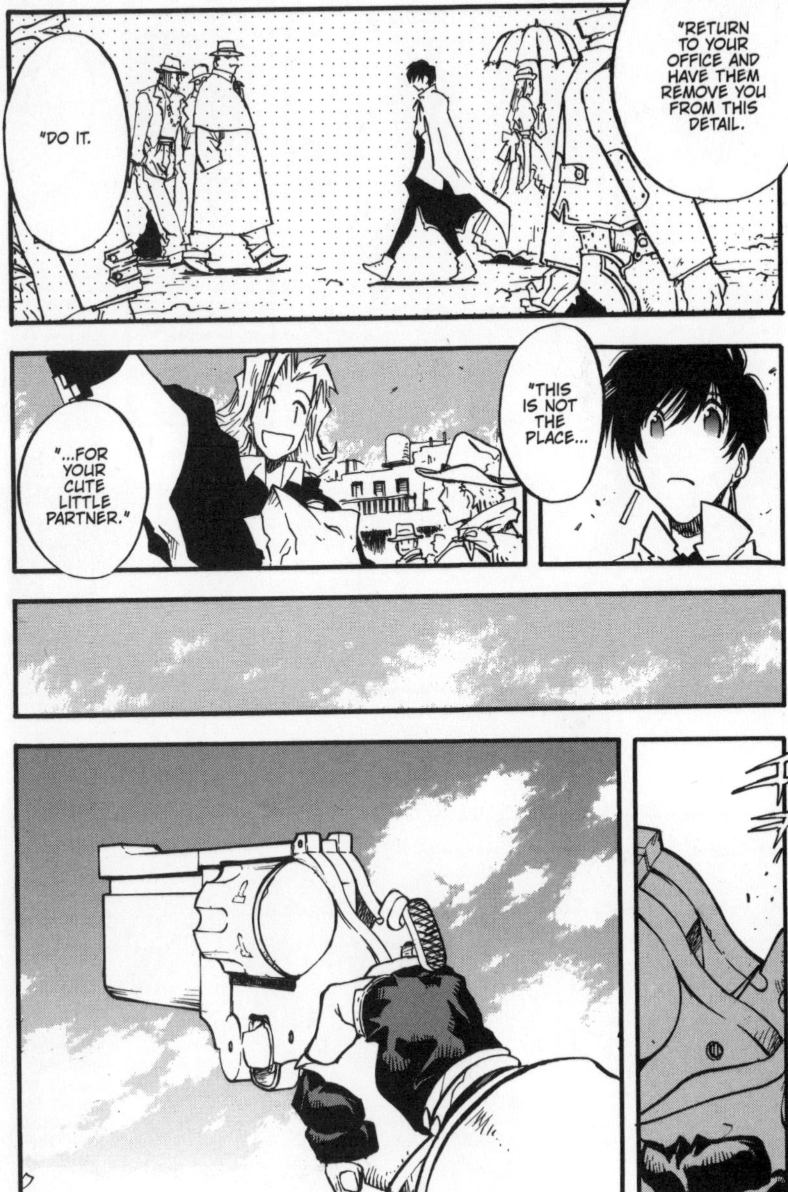
"RETURN TO YOUR OFFICE AND HAVE THEM REMOVE YOU FROM THIS DETAIL.
"DO IT.
"THIS IS NOT THE PLACE...
"...FOR YOUR CUTE LITTLE PARTNER."

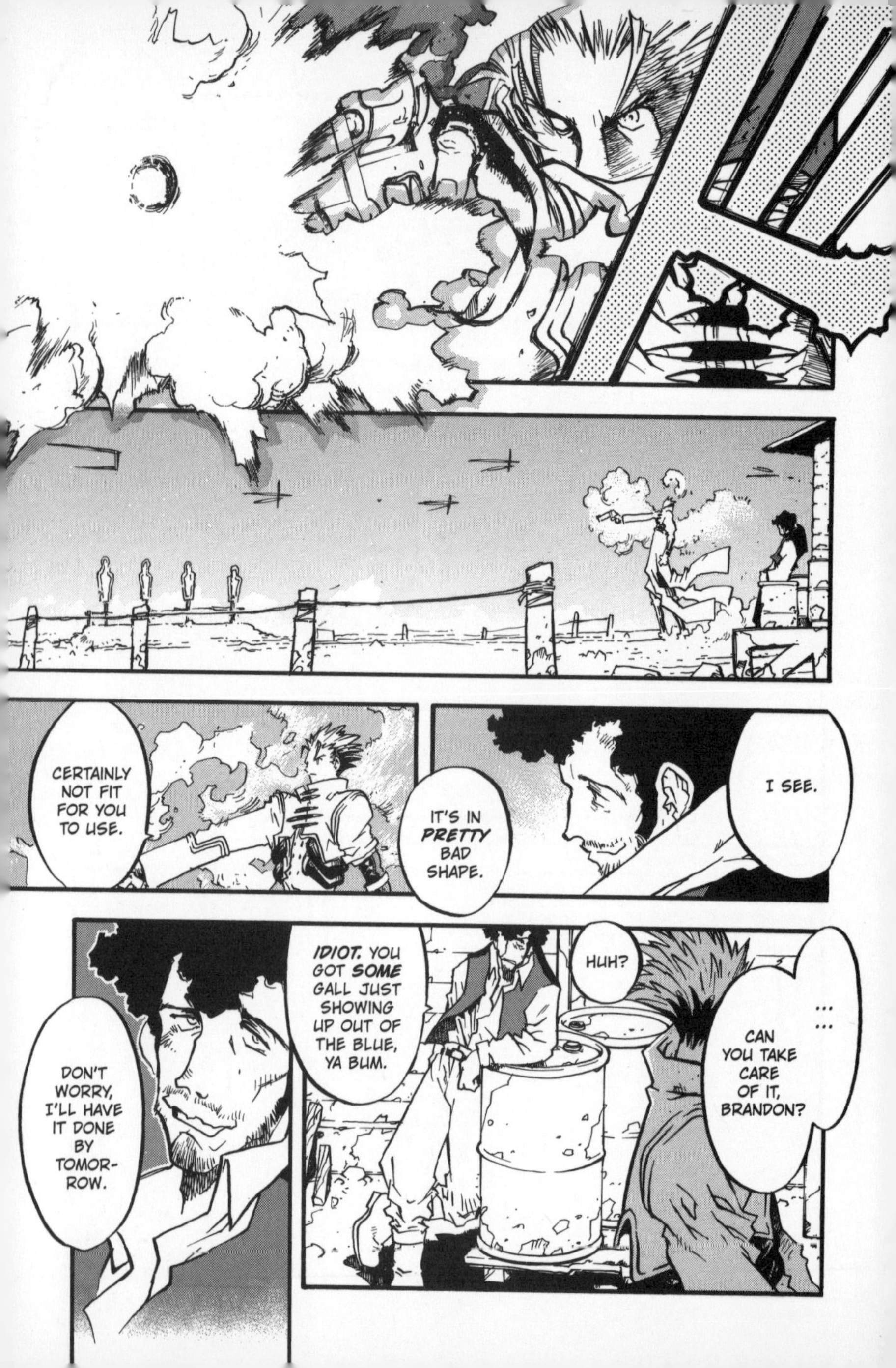

I SEE.
IT'S IN *PRETTY* BAD SHAPE.
CERTAINLY NOT FIT FOR YOU TO USE.
...... CAN YOU TAKE CARE OF IT, BRANDON?
HUH?
IDIOT. YOU GOT **SOME** GALL JUST SHOWING UP OUT OF THE BLUE, YA BUM.
DON'T WORRY, I'LL HAVE IT DONE BY TOMOR-ROW.

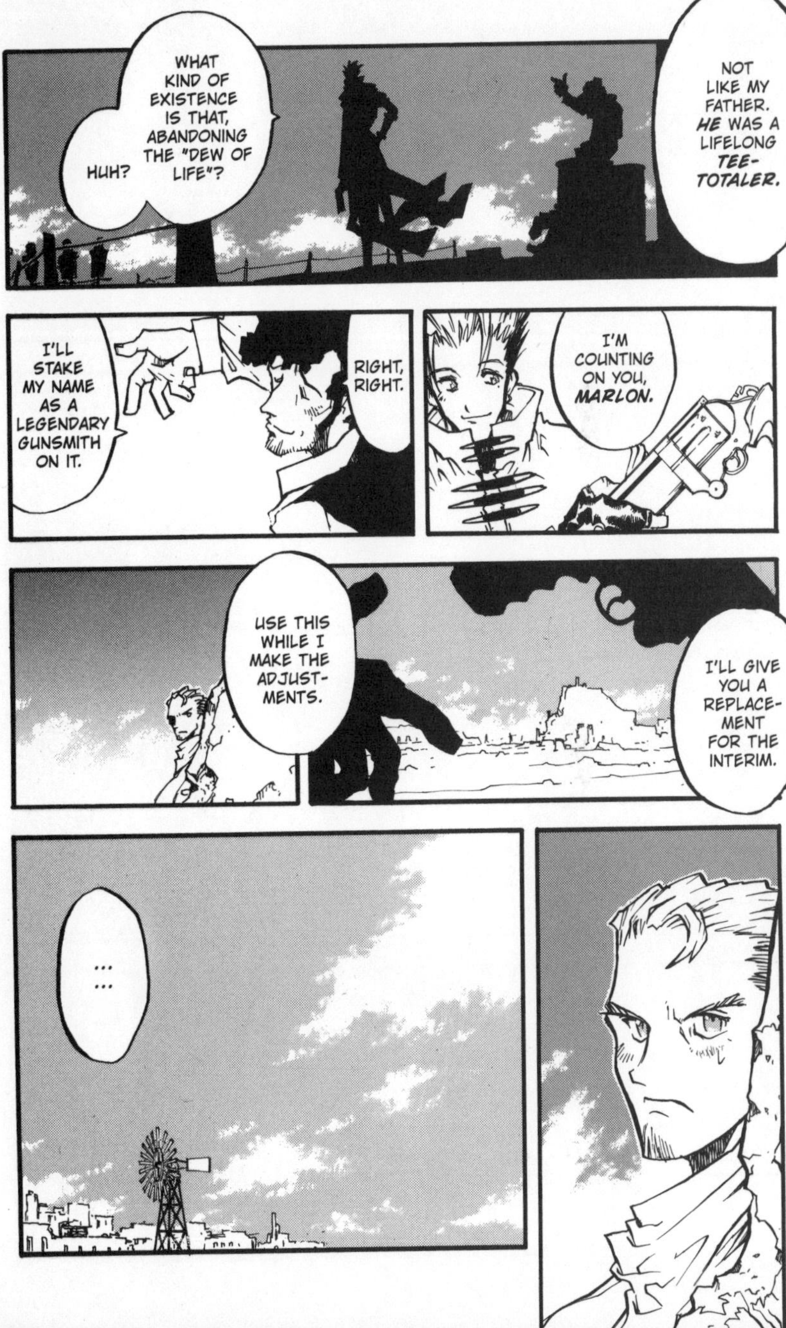
NOT LIKE MY FATHER. *HE* WAS A LIFELONG *TEE-TOTALER.*
WHAT KIND OF EXISTENCE IS THAT, ABANDONING THE "DEW OF LIFE"?
HUH?
I'M COUNTING ON YOU, *MARLON.*
RIGHT, RIGHT.
I'LL STAKE MY NAME AS A LEGENDARY GUNSMITH ON IT.
I'LL GIVE YOU A REPLACE-MENT FOR THE INTERIM.
USE THIS WHILE I MAKE THE ADJUST-MENTS.
... ...

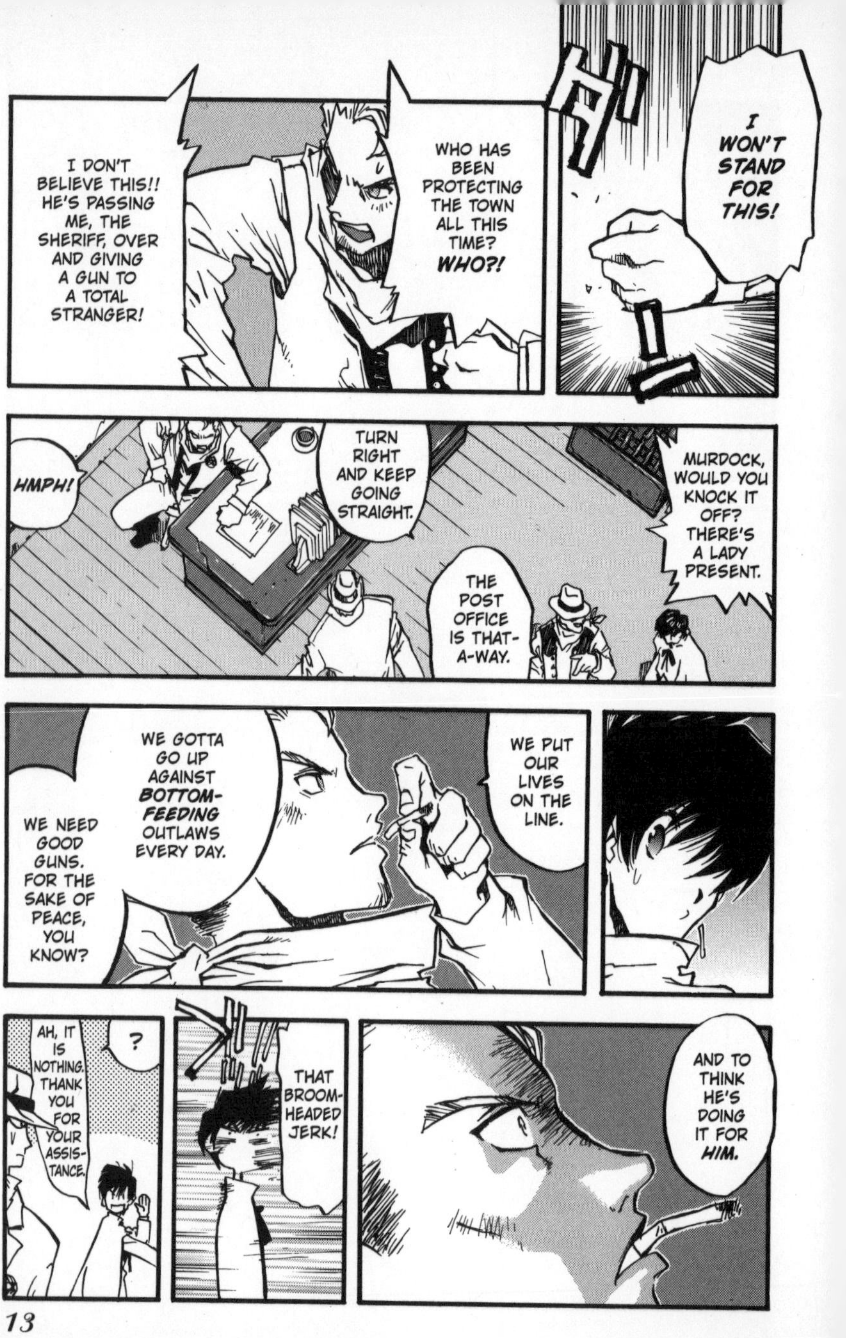
I WON'T STAND FOR THIS!
WHO HAS BEEN PROTECTING THE TOWN ALL THIS TIME? WHO?!
I DON'T BELIEVE THIS!! HE'S PASSING ME, THE SHERIFF, OVER AND GIVING A GUN TO A TOTAL STRANGER!
MURDOCK, WOULD YOU KNOCK IT OFF? THERE'S A LADY PRESENT.
TURN RIGHT AND KEEP GOING STRAIGHT.
THE POST OFFICE IS THAT-A-WAY.
HMPH!
WE PUT OUR LIVES ON THE LINE.
WE GOTTA GO UP AGAINST BOTTOM-FEEDING OUTLAWS EVERY DAY.
WE NEED GOOD GUNS. FOR THE SAKE OF PEACE, YOU KNOW?
AND TO THINK HE'S DOING IT FOR HIM.
THAT BROOM-HEADED JERK!
?
AH, IT IS NOTHING. THANK YOU FOR YOUR ASSISTANCE.

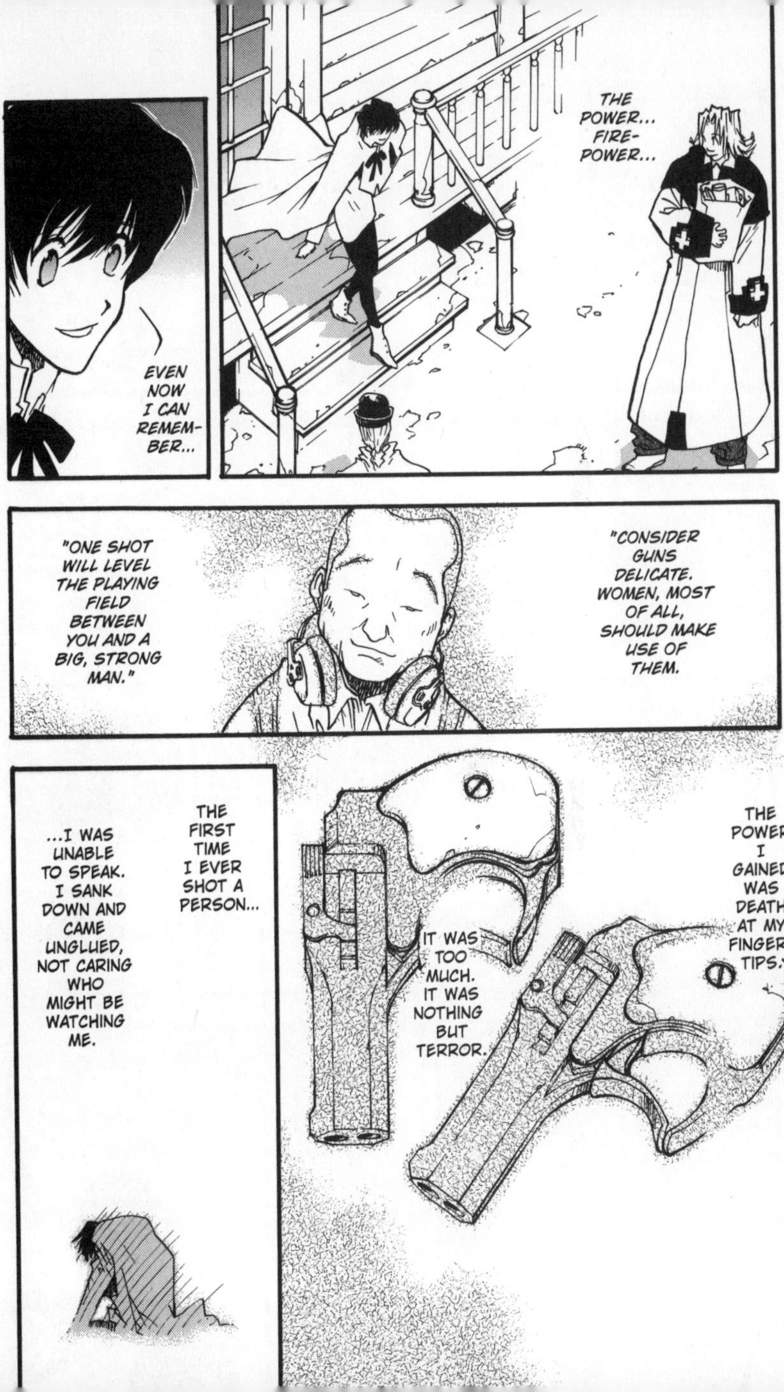
THE POWER... FIRE-POWER...
EVEN NOW I CAN REMEMBER...
"CONSIDER GUNS DELICATE. WOMEN, MOST OF ALL, SHOULD MAKE USE OF THEM.
"ONE SHOT WILL LEVEL THE PLAYING FIELD BETWEEN YOU AND A BIG, STRONG MAN."
THE POWER I GAINED WAS DEATH AT MY FINGER-TIPS.
IT WAS TOO MUCH. IT WAS NOTHING BUT TERROR.
THE FIRST TIME I EVER SHOT A PERSON...
...I WAS UNABLE TO SPEAK. I SANK DOWN AND CAME UNGLUED, NOT CARING WHO MIGHT BE WATCHING ME.

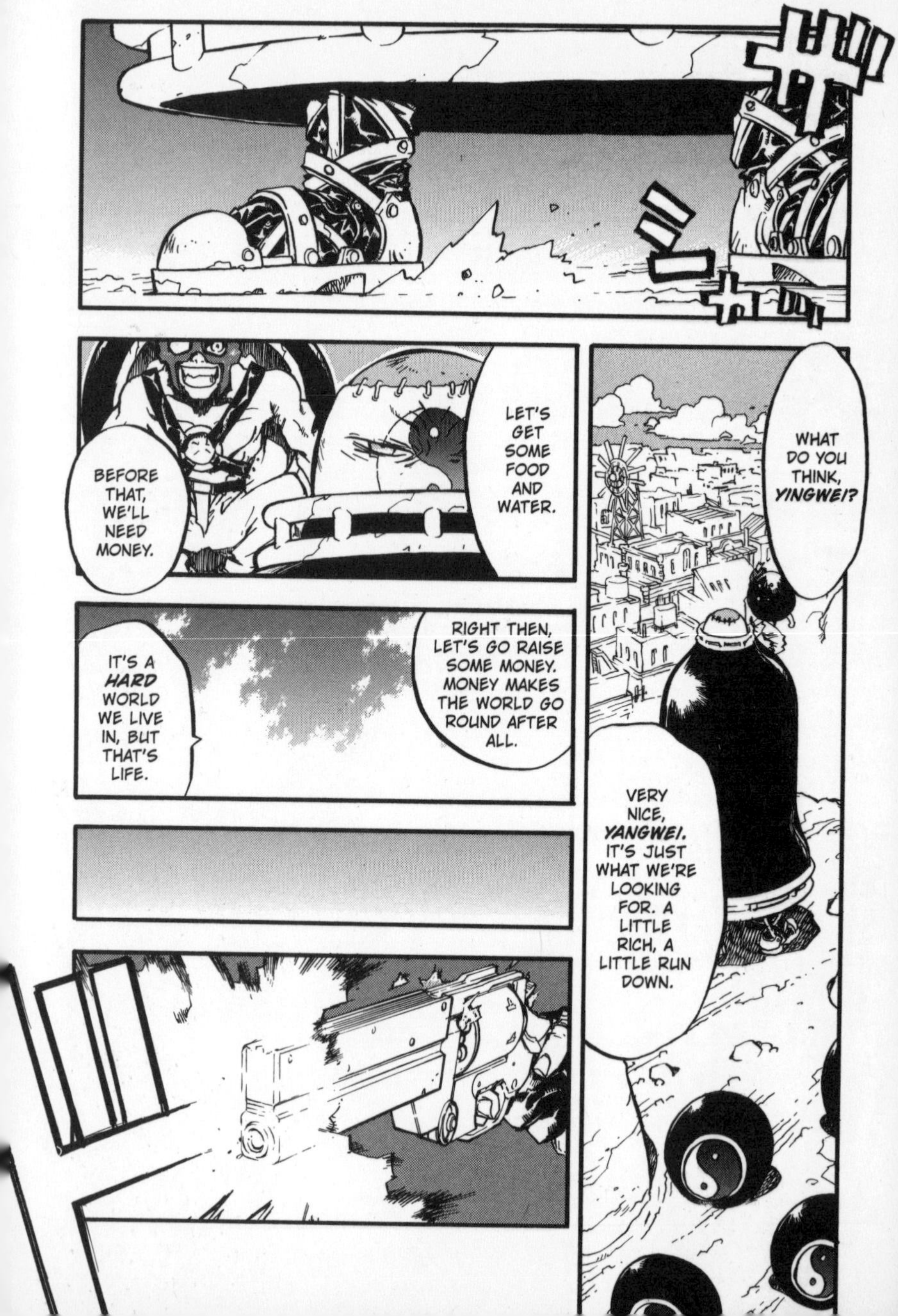
WHAT DO YOU THINK, *YINGWEI?*
VERY NICE, *YANGWEI.* IT'S JUST WHAT WE'RE LOOKING FOR. A LITTLE RICH, A LITTLE RUN DOWN.
LET'S GET SOME FOOD AND WATER.
BEFORE THAT, WE'LL NEED MONEY.
RIGHT THEN, LET'S GO RAISE SOME MONEY. MONEY MAKES THE WORLD GO ROUND AFTER ALL.
IT'S A *HARD* WORLD WE LIVE IN, BUT THAT'S LIFE.

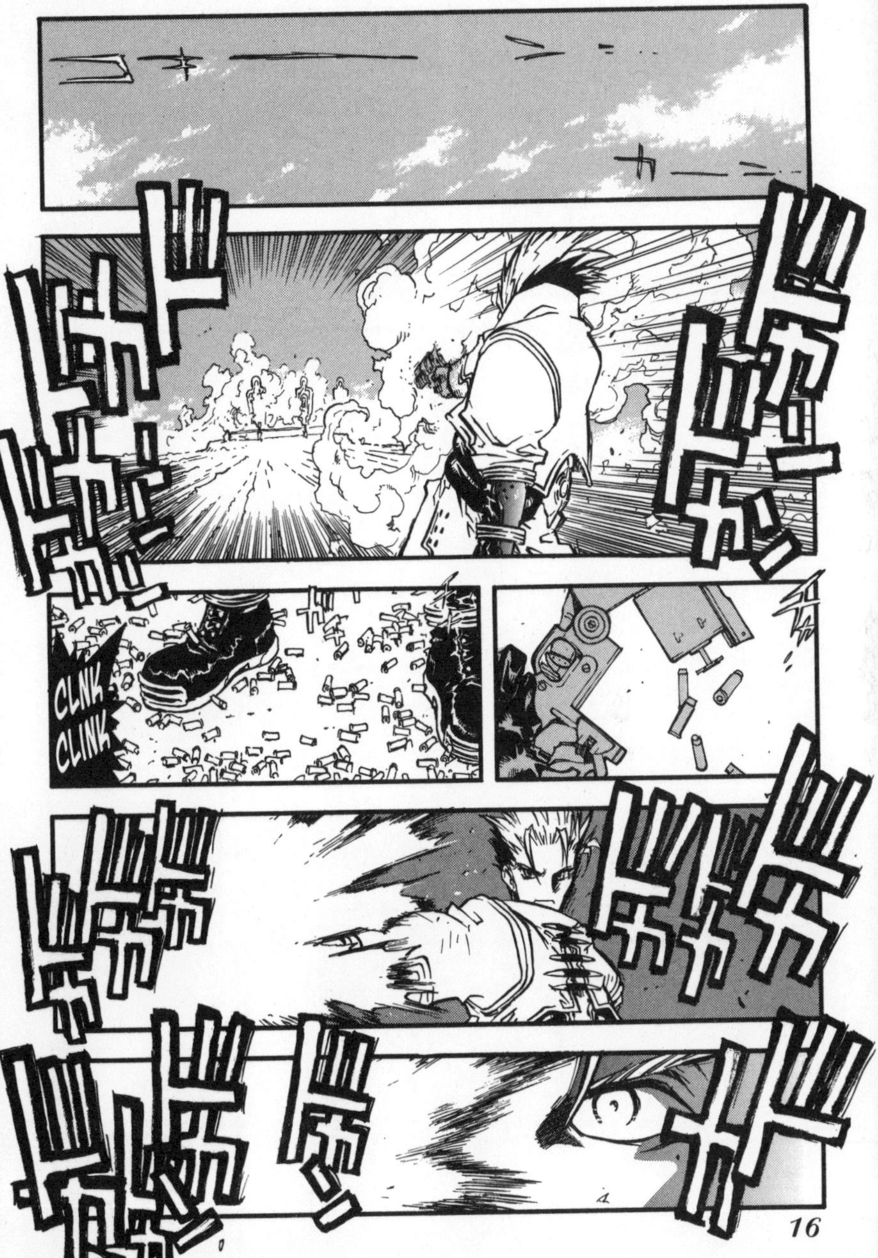
CLNK
CLINK

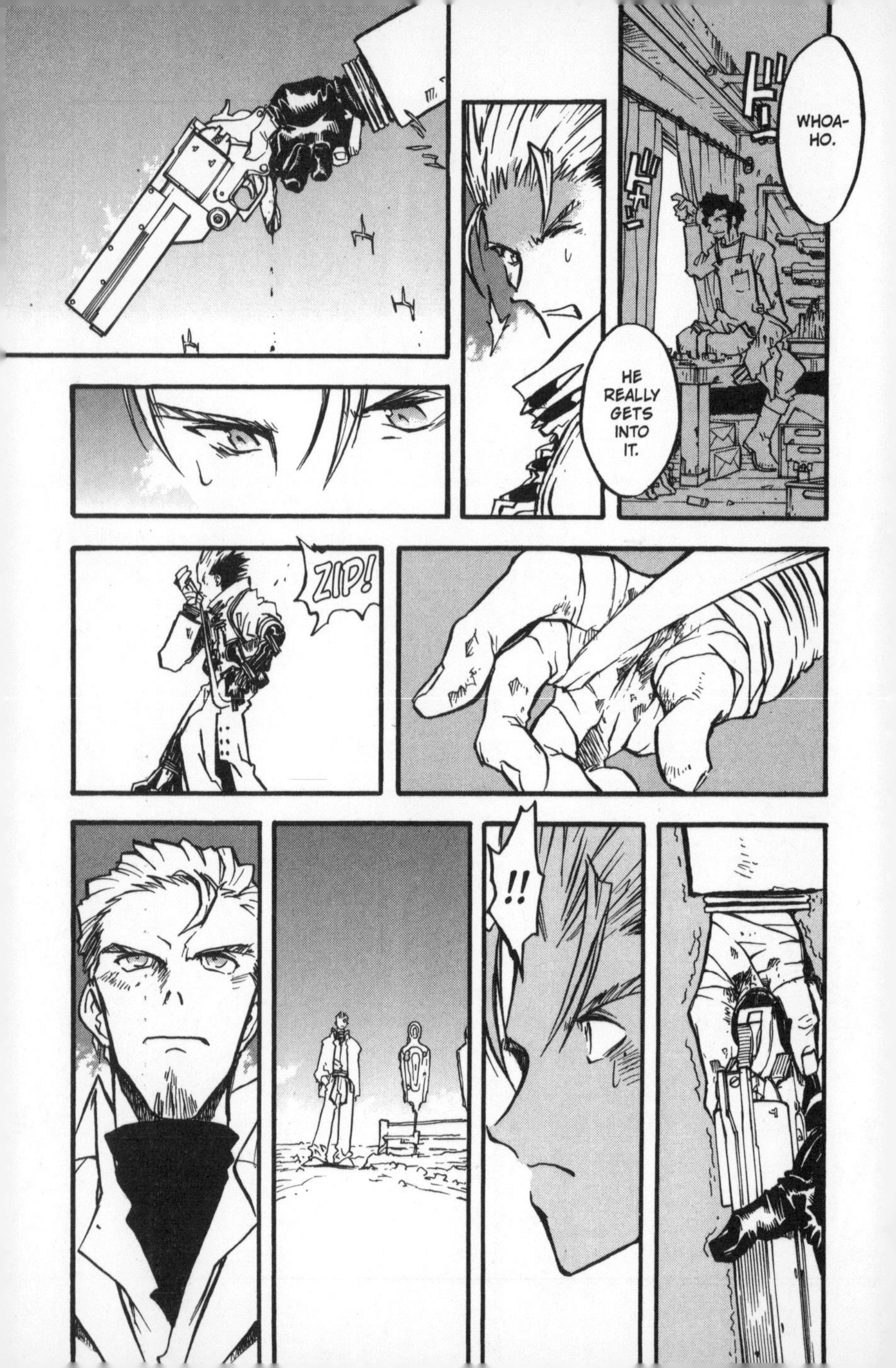
WHOA-HO.
HE REALLY GETS INTO IT.
ZIP!
!!

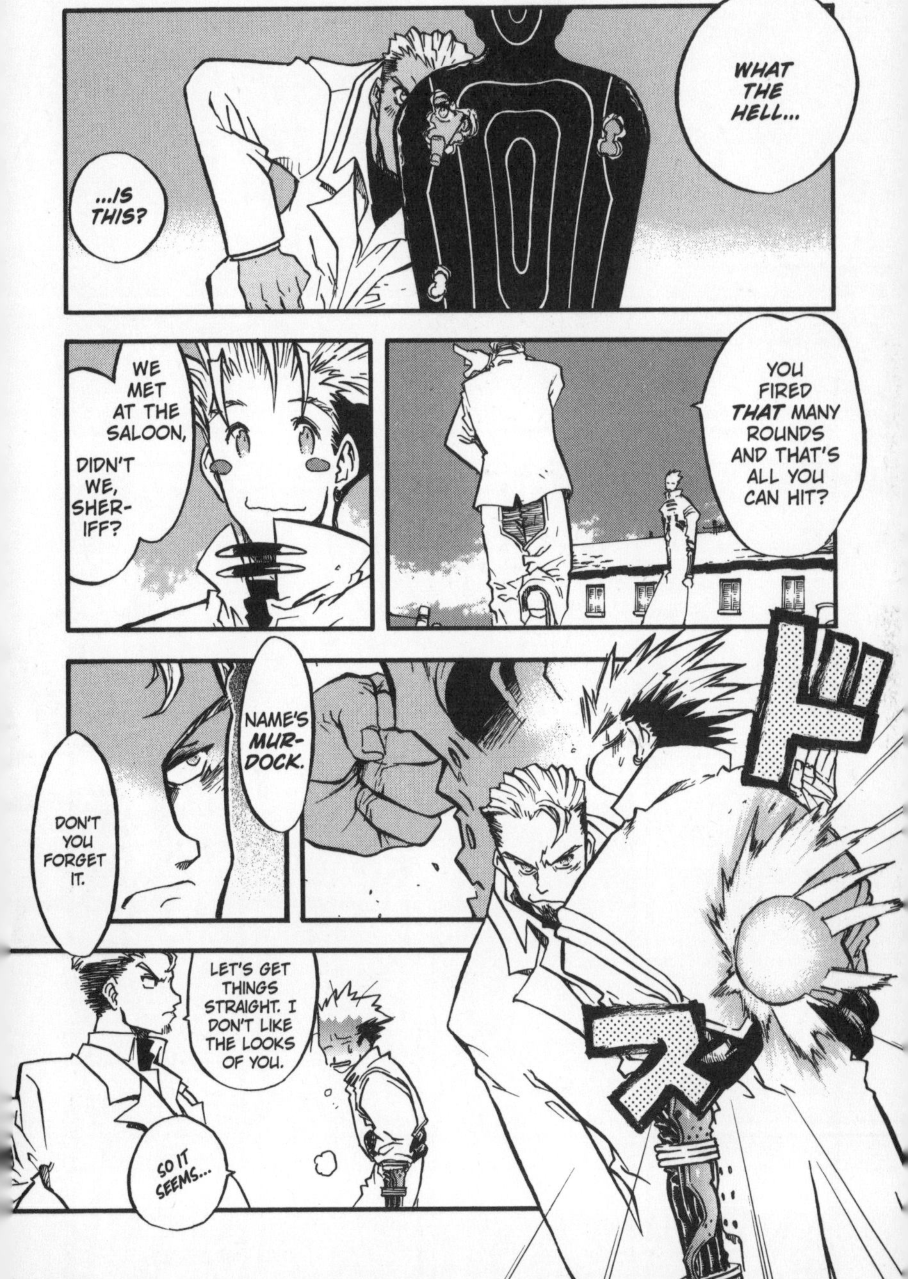
WHAT THE HELL...
...IS THIS?
YOU FIRED THAT MANY ROUNDS AND THAT'S ALL YOU CAN HIT?
WE MET AT THE SALOON,
DIDN'T WE, SHERIFF?
ド
ス
NAME'S MURDOCK.
DON'T YOU FORGET IT.
LET'S GET THINGS STRAIGHT. I DON'T LIKE THE LOOKS OF YOU.
SO IT SEEMS...

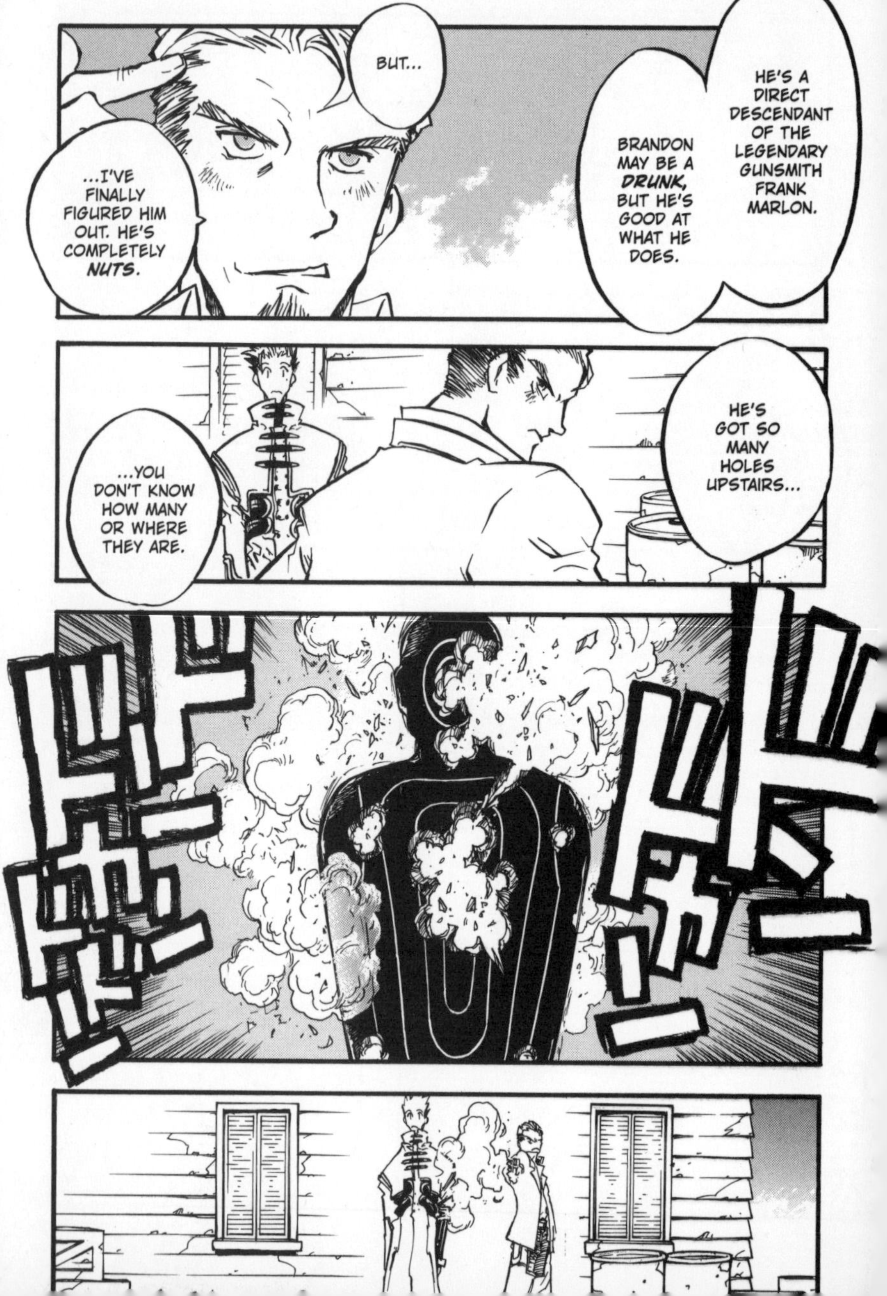
HE'S A DIRECT DESCENDANT OF THE LEGENDARY GUNSMITH FRANK MARLON.
BRANDON MAY BE A *DRUNK,* BUT HE'S GOOD AT WHAT HE DOES.
BUT...
...I'VE FINALLY FIGURED HIM OUT. HE'S COMPLETELY *NUTS.*
HE'S GOT SO MANY HOLES UPSTAIRS...
...YOU DON'T KNOW HOW MANY OR WHERE THEY ARE.

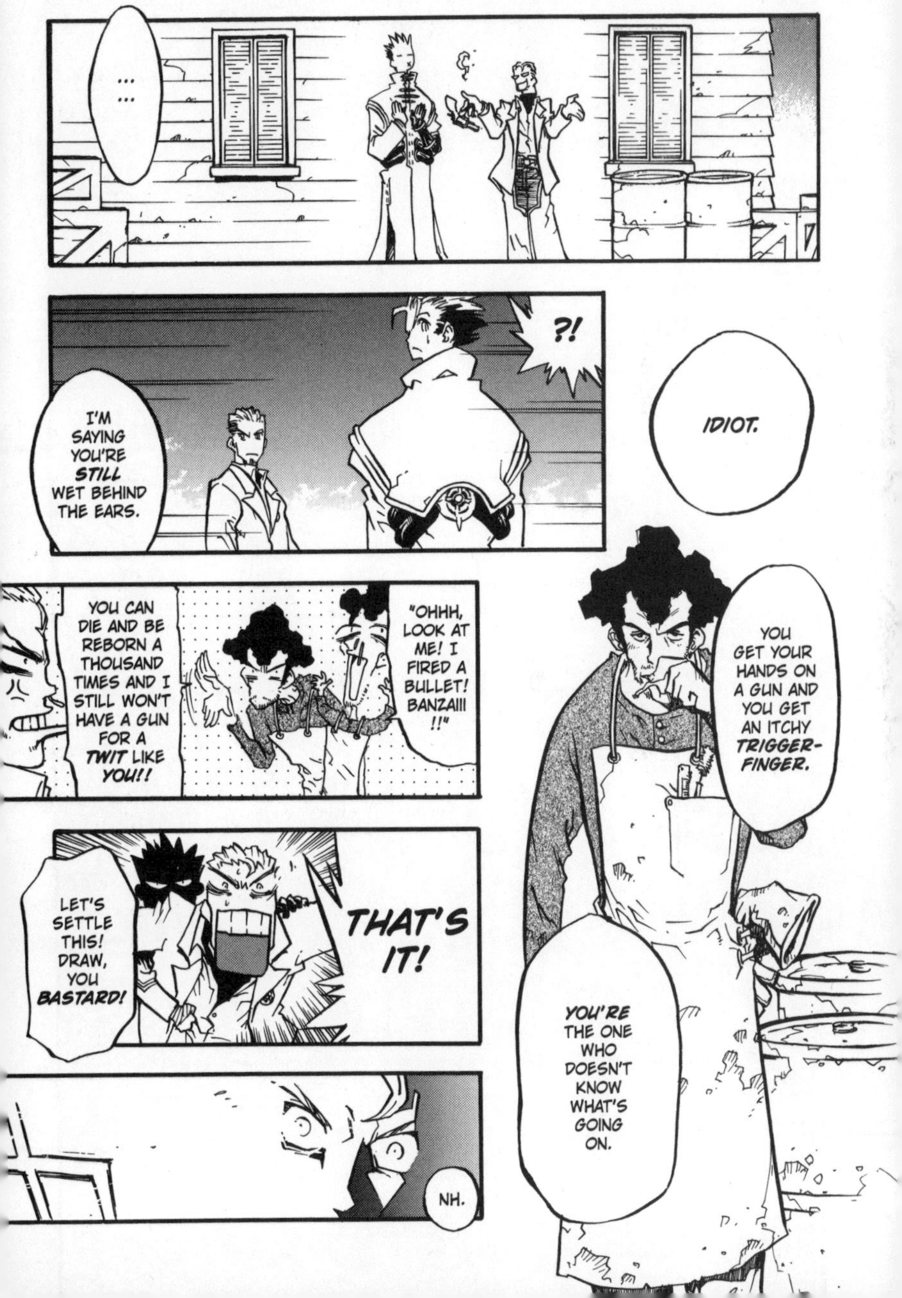
...
...
IDIOT.
?!
I'M SAYING YOU'RE *STILL* WET BEHIND THE EARS.
YOU GET YOUR HANDS ON A GUN AND YOU GET AN ITCHY *TRIGGER-FINGER.*
YOU'RE THE ONE WHO DOESN'T KNOW WHAT'S GOING ON.
"OHHH, LOOK AT ME! I FIRED A BULLET! BANZAIII !!"
YOU CAN DIE AND BE REBORN A THOUSAND TIMES AND I STILL WON'T HAVE A GUN FOR A *TWIT* LIKE *YOU!!*
THAT'S IT!
LET'S SETTLE THIS! DRAW, YOU *BASTARD!*
NH.

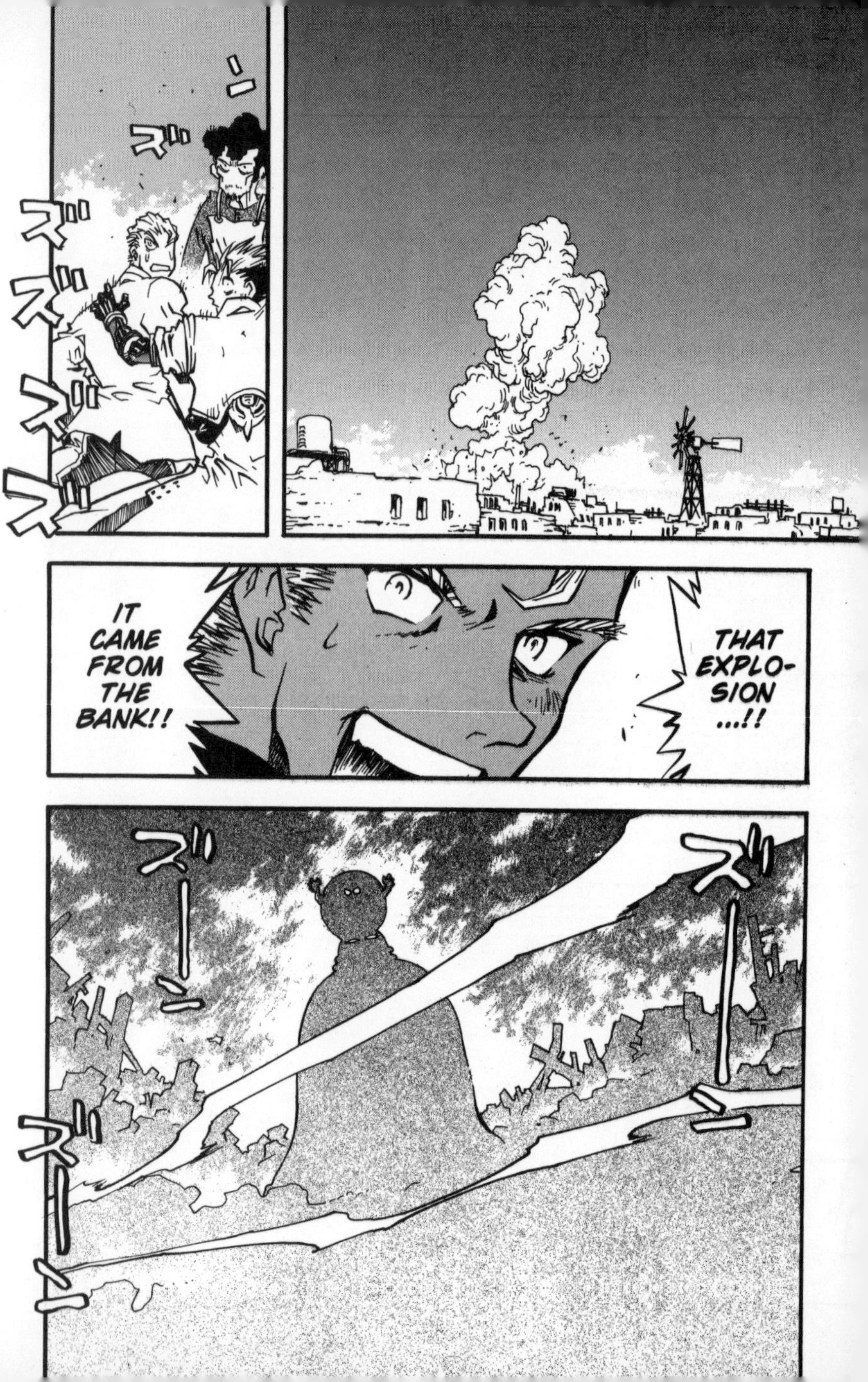
THAT EXPLOSION...!!
IT CAME FROM THE BANK!!

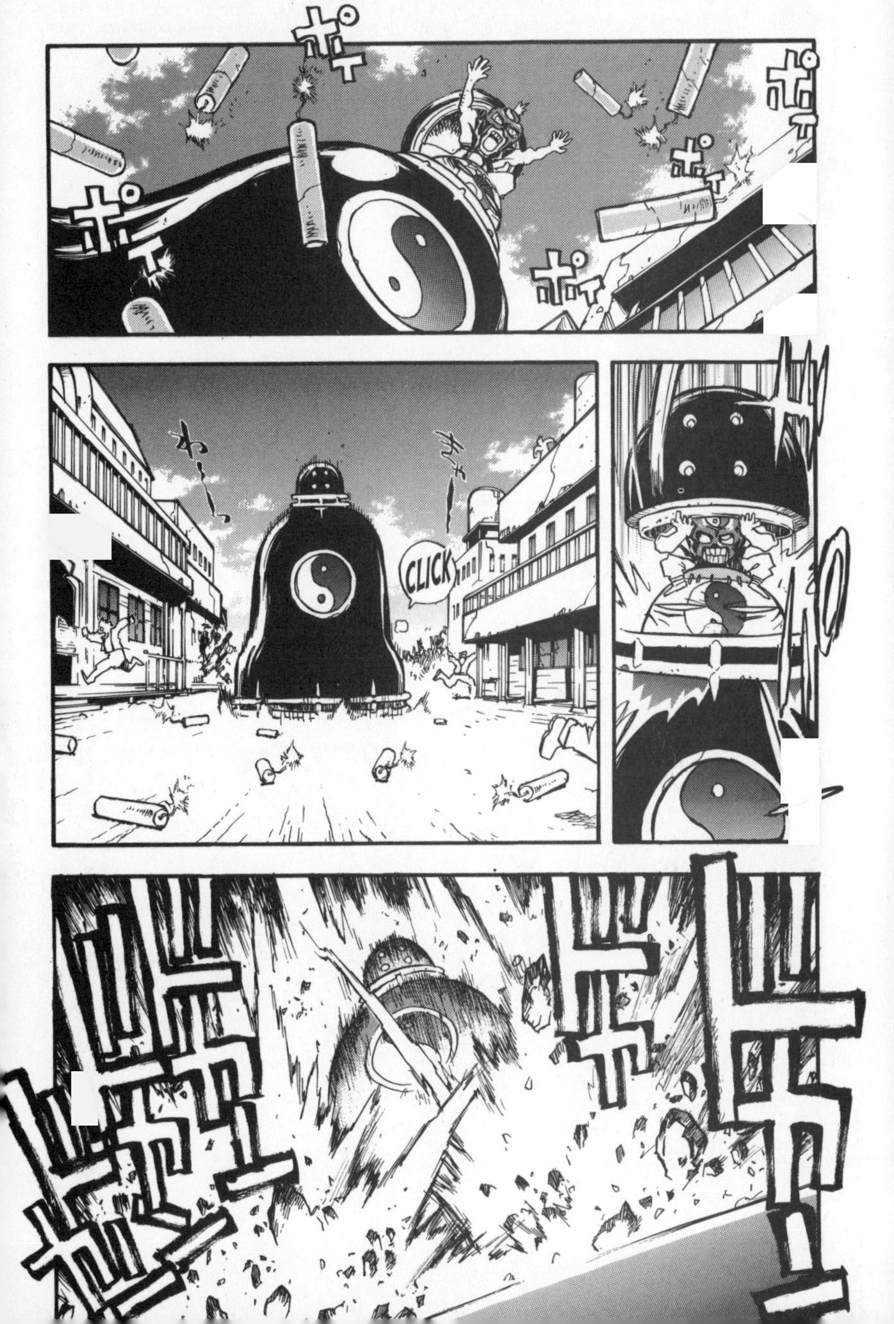
ポイ
ポイ
ポイ
ポイ
ポイ
CLICK

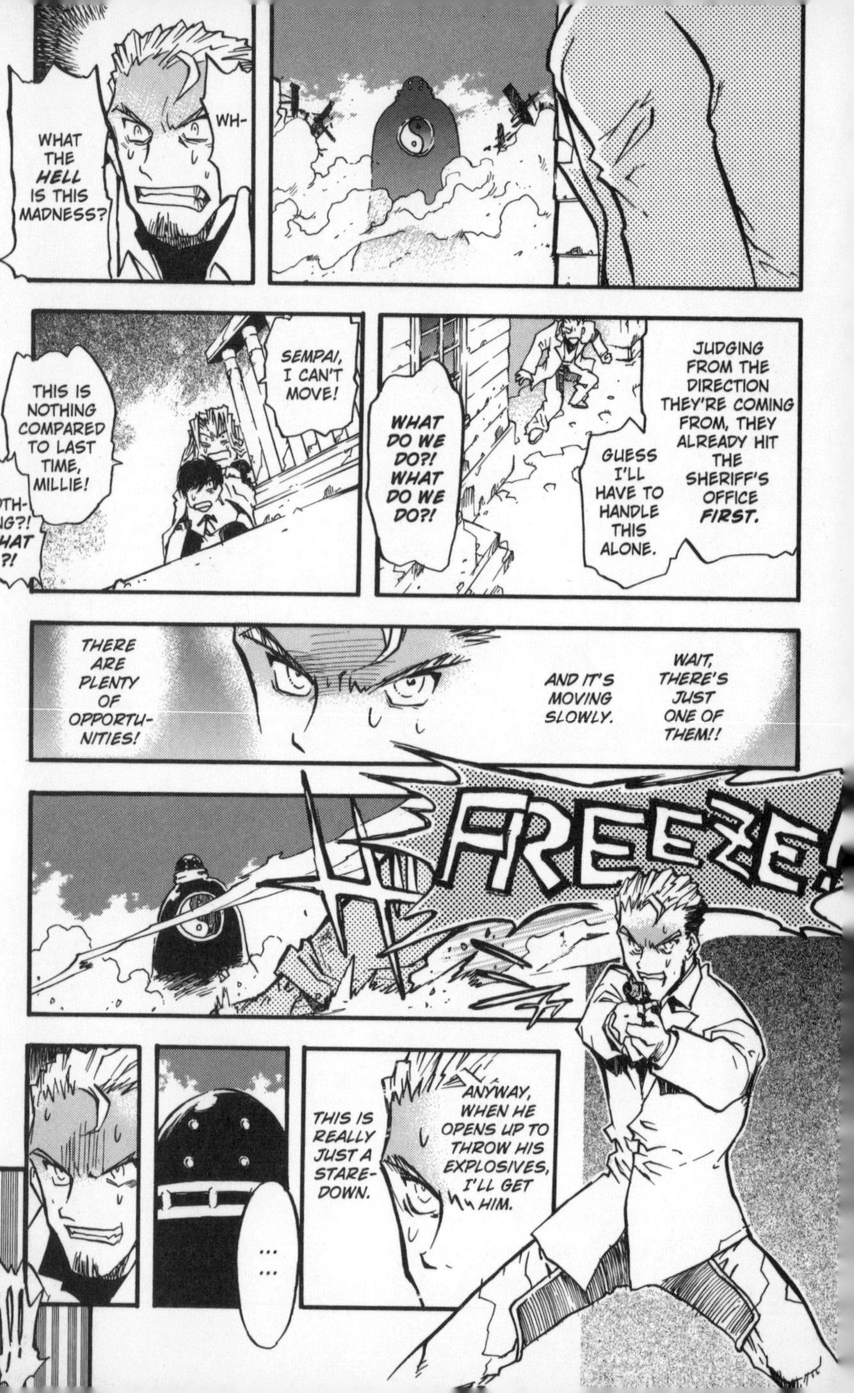
WH-
WHAT THE HELL IS THIS MADNESS?
JUDGING FROM THE DIRECTION THEY'RE COMING FROM, THEY ALREADY HIT THE SHERIFF'S OFFICE FIRST.
GUESS I'LL HAVE TO HANDLE THIS ALONE.
WHAT DO WE DO?! WHAT DO WE DO?!
SEMPAI, I CAN'T MOVE!
THIS IS NOTHING COMPARED TO LAST TIME, MILLIE!
NOTHING?! THAT?!
WAIT, THERE'S JUST ONE OF THEM!!
AND IT'S MOVING SLOWLY.
THERE ARE PLENTY OF OPPORTUNITIES!
FREEZE!
ANYWAY, WHEN HE OPENS UP TO THROW HIS EXPLOSIVES, I'LL GET HIM.
THIS IS REALLY JUST A STARE-DOWN.
......
!!

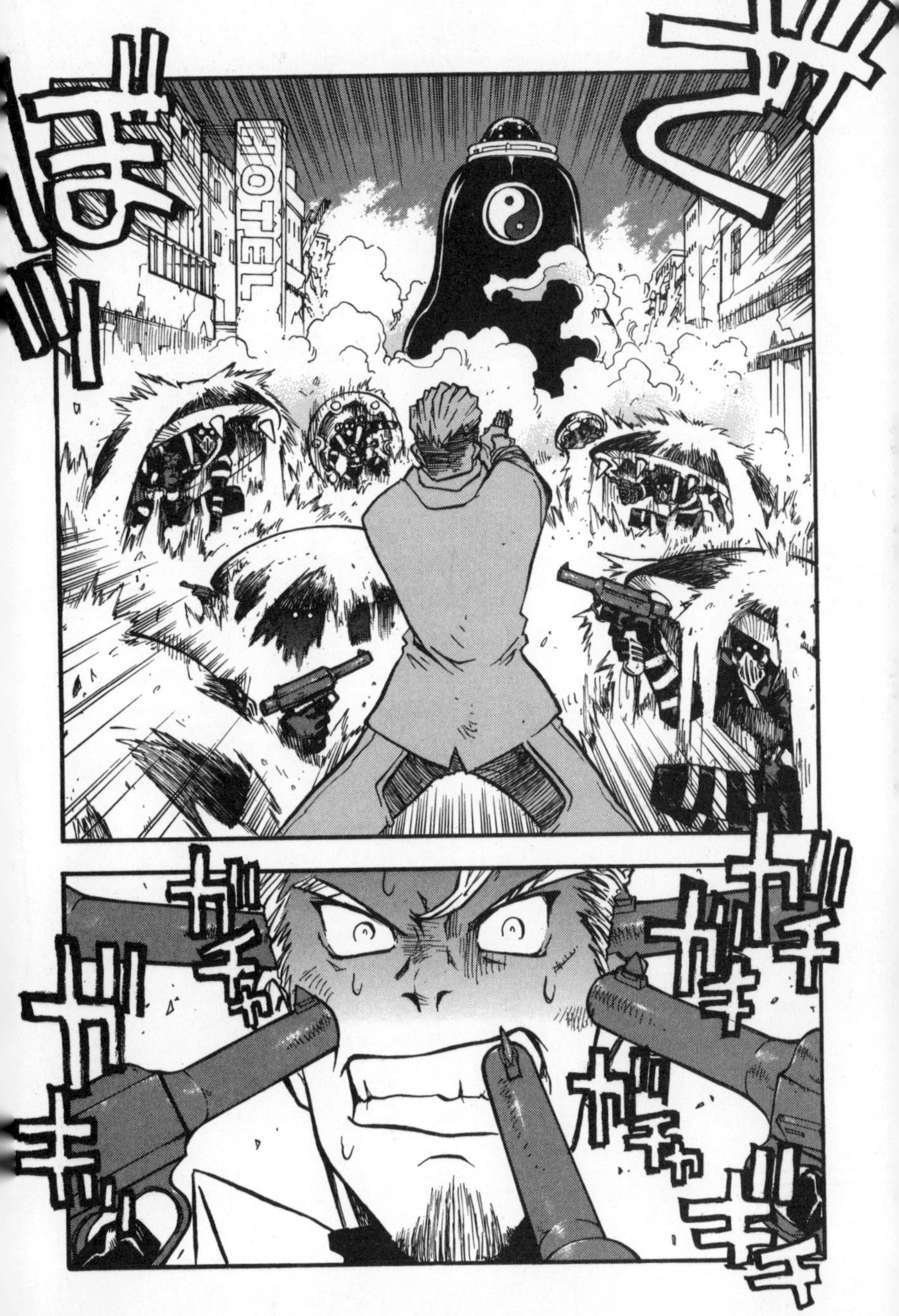
ざ
ぼ
ガチ
ガキ
ガチャ
ガチャ

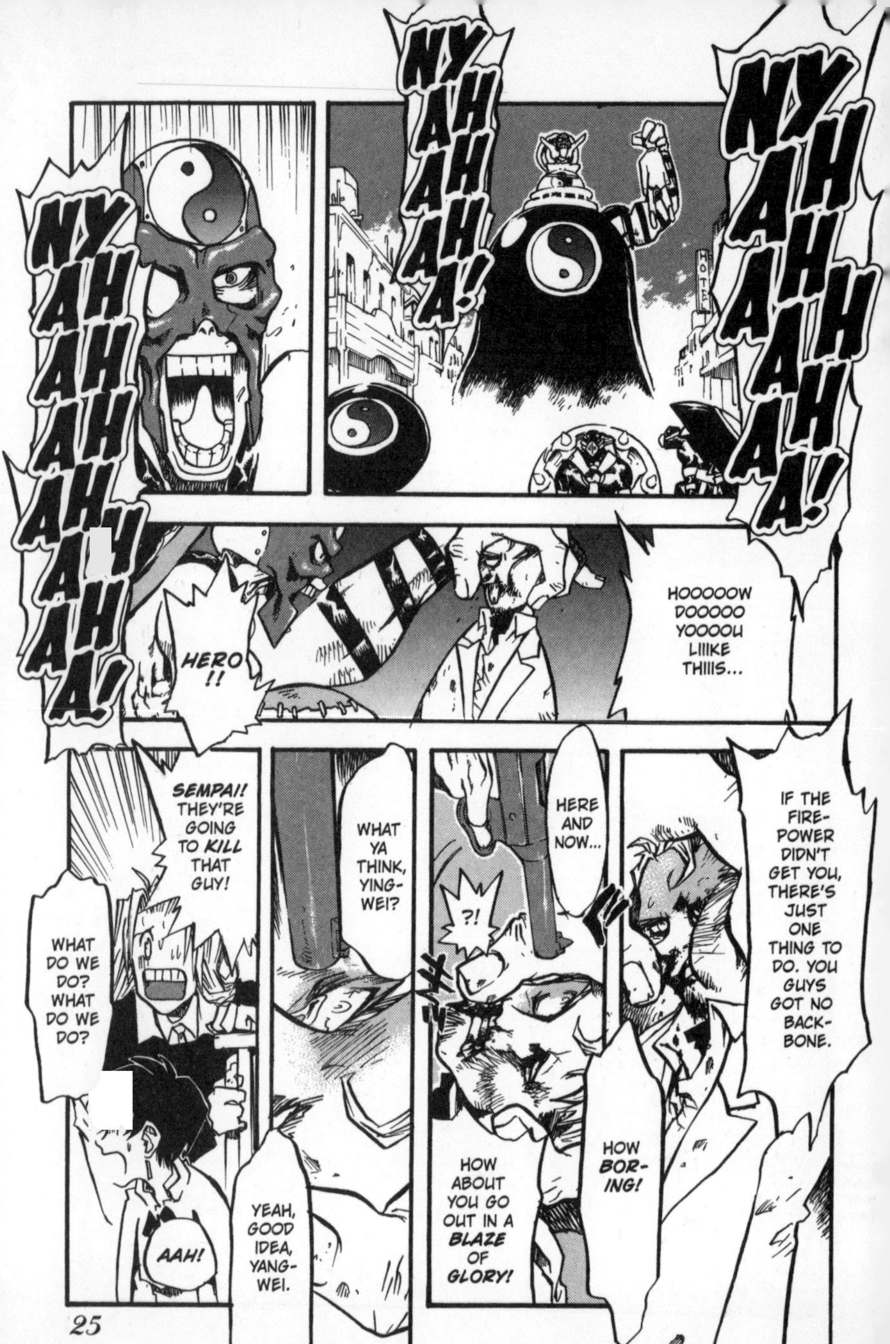
NYAHAHAHAHA!
NYAHAHAHA!
NYAHAHAHAHAHAHA!
HOOOOOW DOOOOO YOOOOU LIIIKE THIIIS...
HERO!!
IF THE FIRE-POWER DIDN'T GET YOU, THERE'S JUST ONE THING TO DO. YOU GUYS GOT NO BACK-BONE.
HOW *BORING!*
HERE AND NOW...
?!
HOW ABOUT YOU GO OUT IN A *BLAZE* OF *GLORY!*
WHAT YA THINK, YING-WEI?
YEAH, GOOD IDEA, YANG-WEI.
SEMPAI! THEY'RE GOING TO *KILL* THAT GUY!
WHAT DO WE DO? WHAT DO WE DO?
AAH!

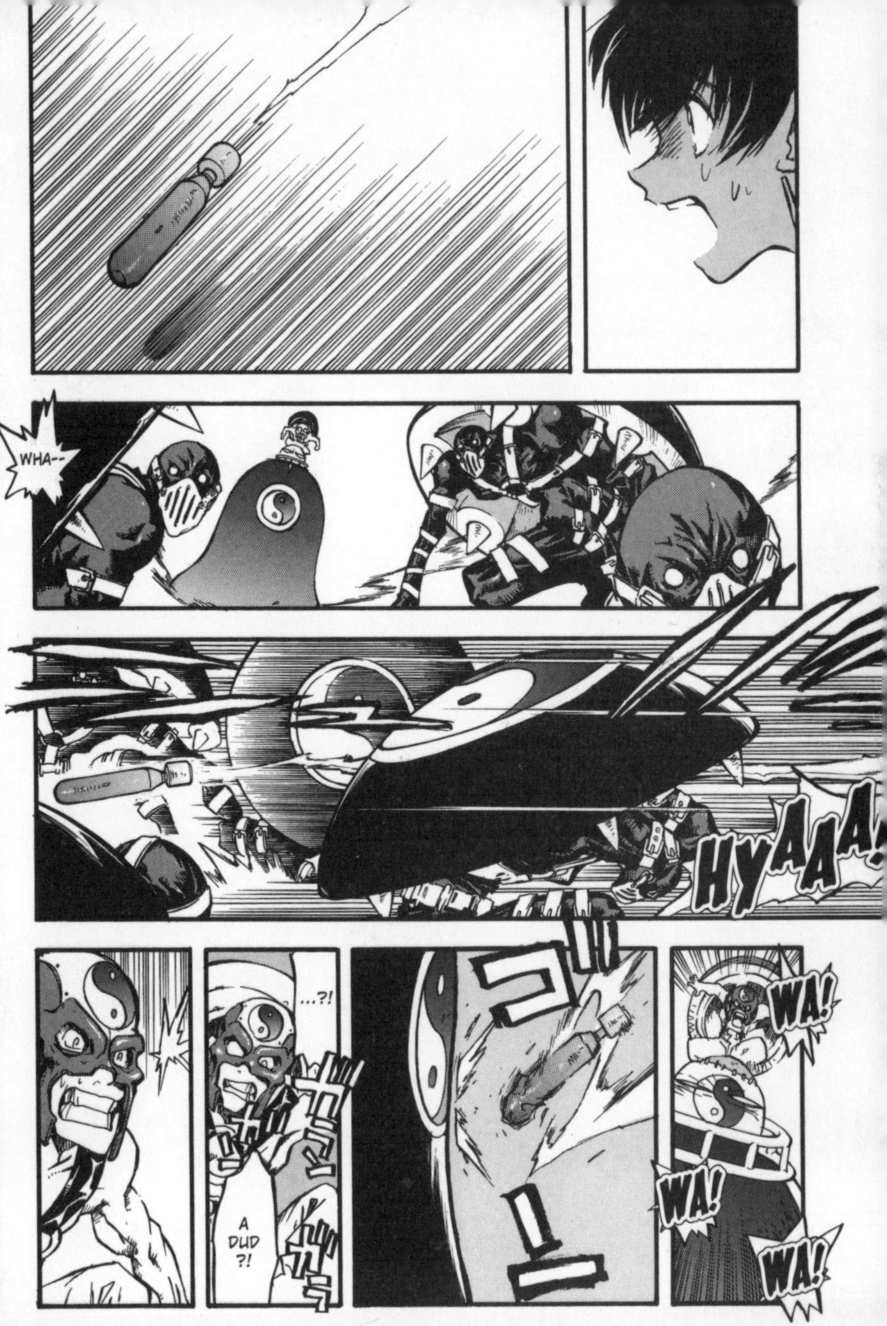
WHA--
HYAAA!
WA!
WA!
WA!
...?!
A DUD ?!

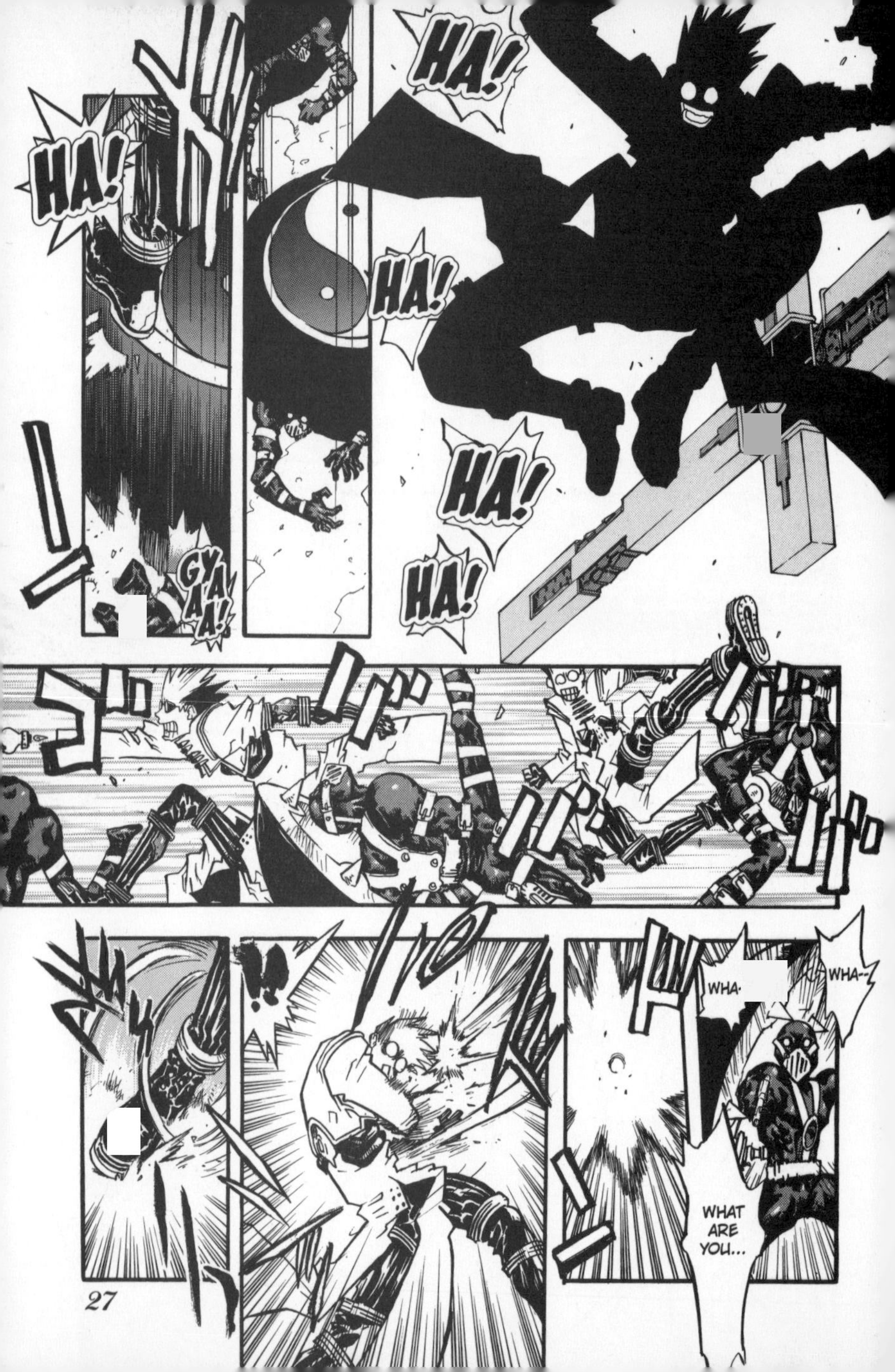
HA!
HA!
HA!
HA!
HA!
GYAAA!
WHA--
WHA-
WHAT ARE YOU...

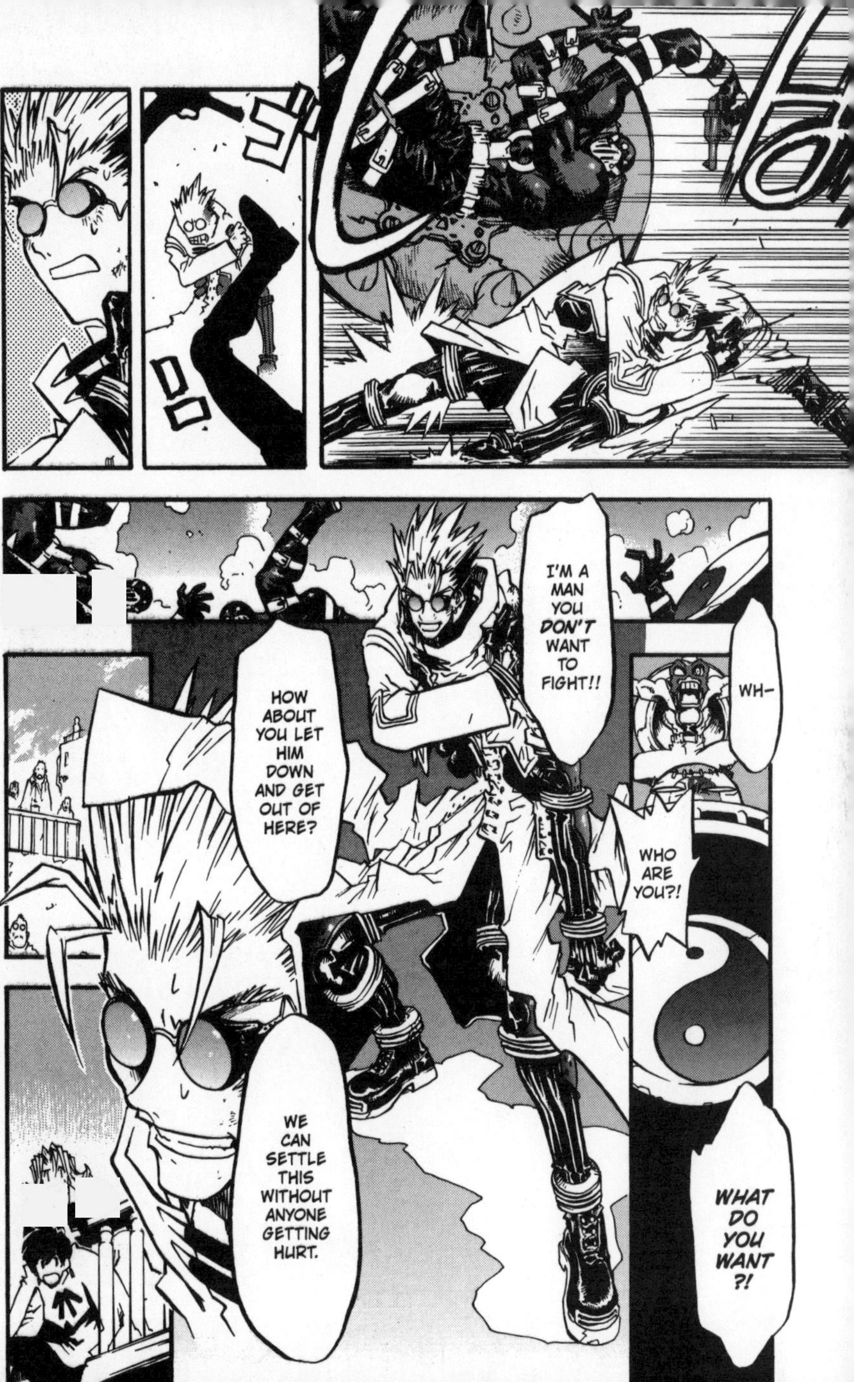
WH–
WHO ARE YOU?!
I'M A MAN YOU *DON'T* WANT TO FIGHT!!
HOW ABOUT YOU LET HIM DOWN AND GET OUT OF HERE?
WHAT DO YOU WANT?!
WE CAN SETTLE THIS WITHOUT ANYONE GETTING HURT.

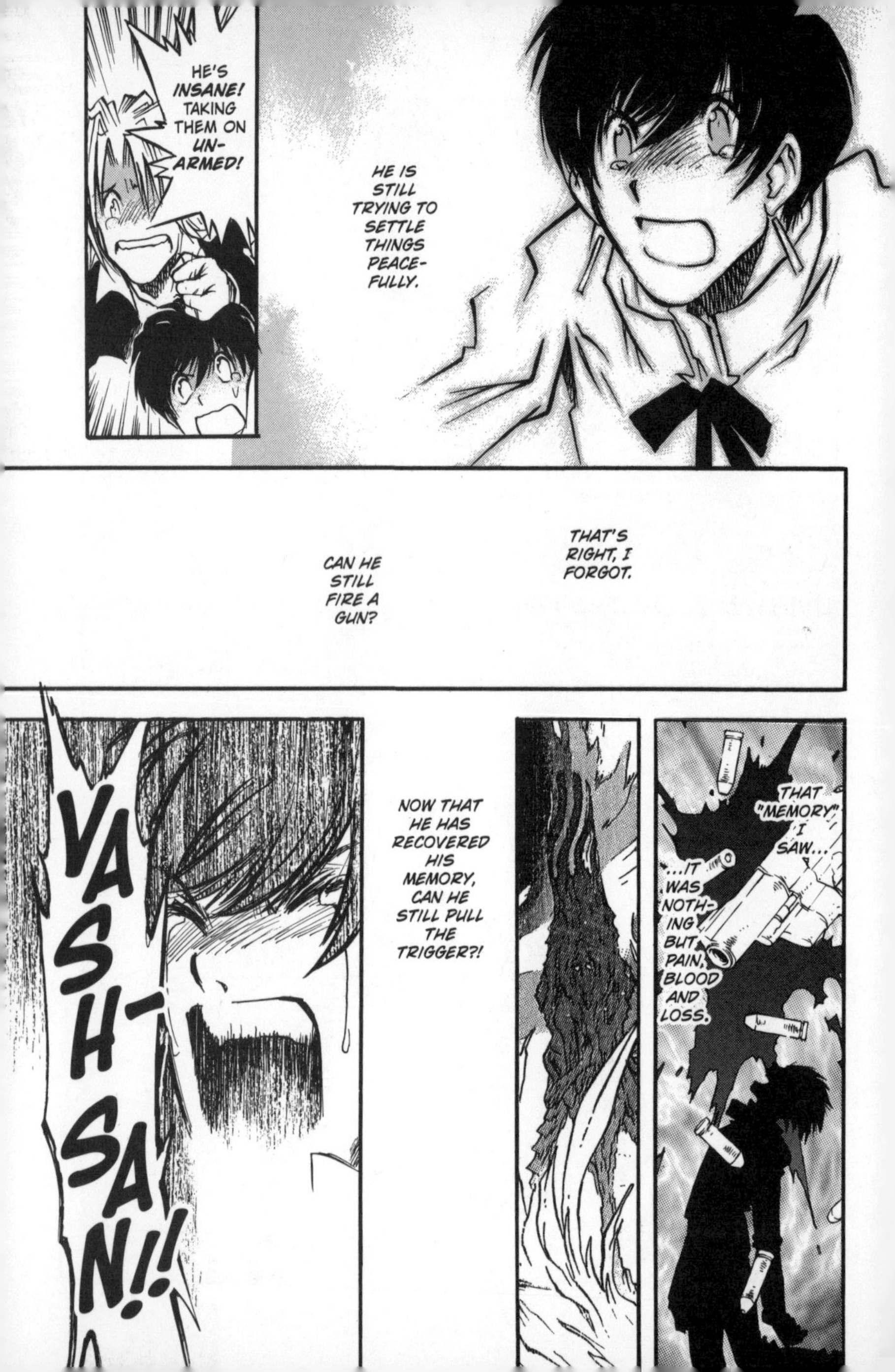
HE IS STILL TRYING TO SETTLE THINGS PEACE-FULLY.
HE'S INSANE! TAKING THEM ON UN-ARMED!
THAT'S RIGHT, I FORGOT.
CAN HE STILL FIRE A GUN?
THAT "MEMORY" I SAW...
...IT WAS NOTHING BUT PAIN, BLOOD AND LOSS.
NOW THAT HE HAS RECOVERED HIS MEMORY, CAN HE STILL PULL THE TRIGGER?!
VASH-SAN!!

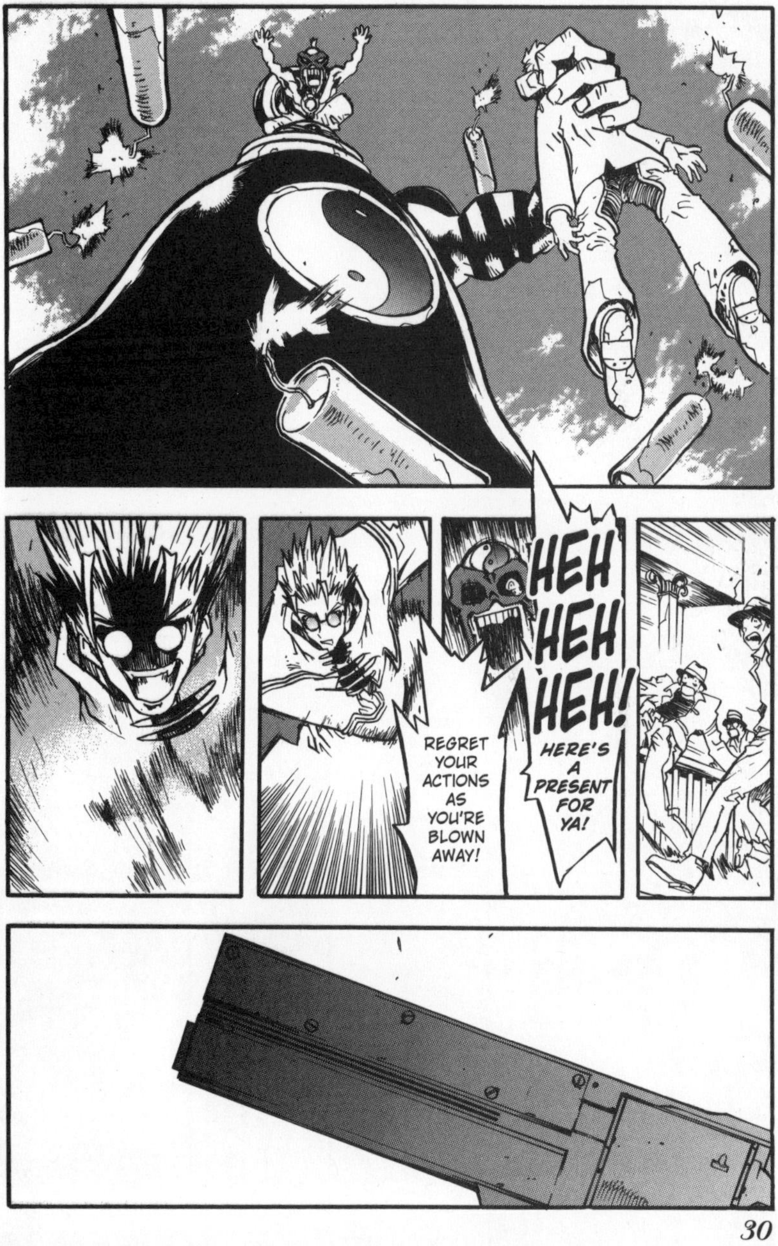
HEH HEH HEH!
HERE'S A PRESENT FOR YA!
REGRET YOUR ACTIONS AS YOU'RE BLOWN AWAY!

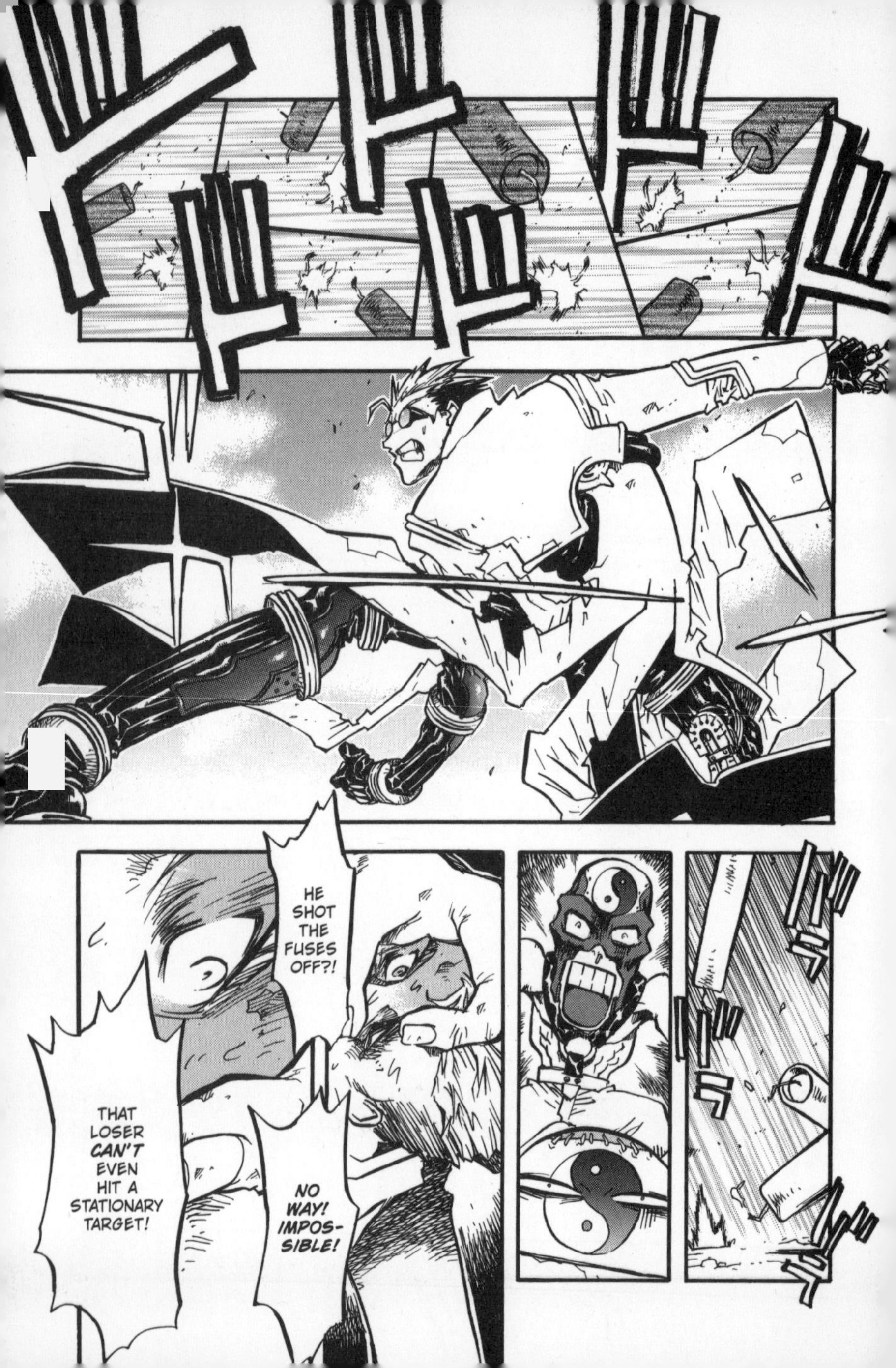
HE SHOT THE FUSES OFF?!
NO WAY! IMPOSSIBLE!
THAT LOSER CAN'T EVEN HIT A STATIONARY TARGET!

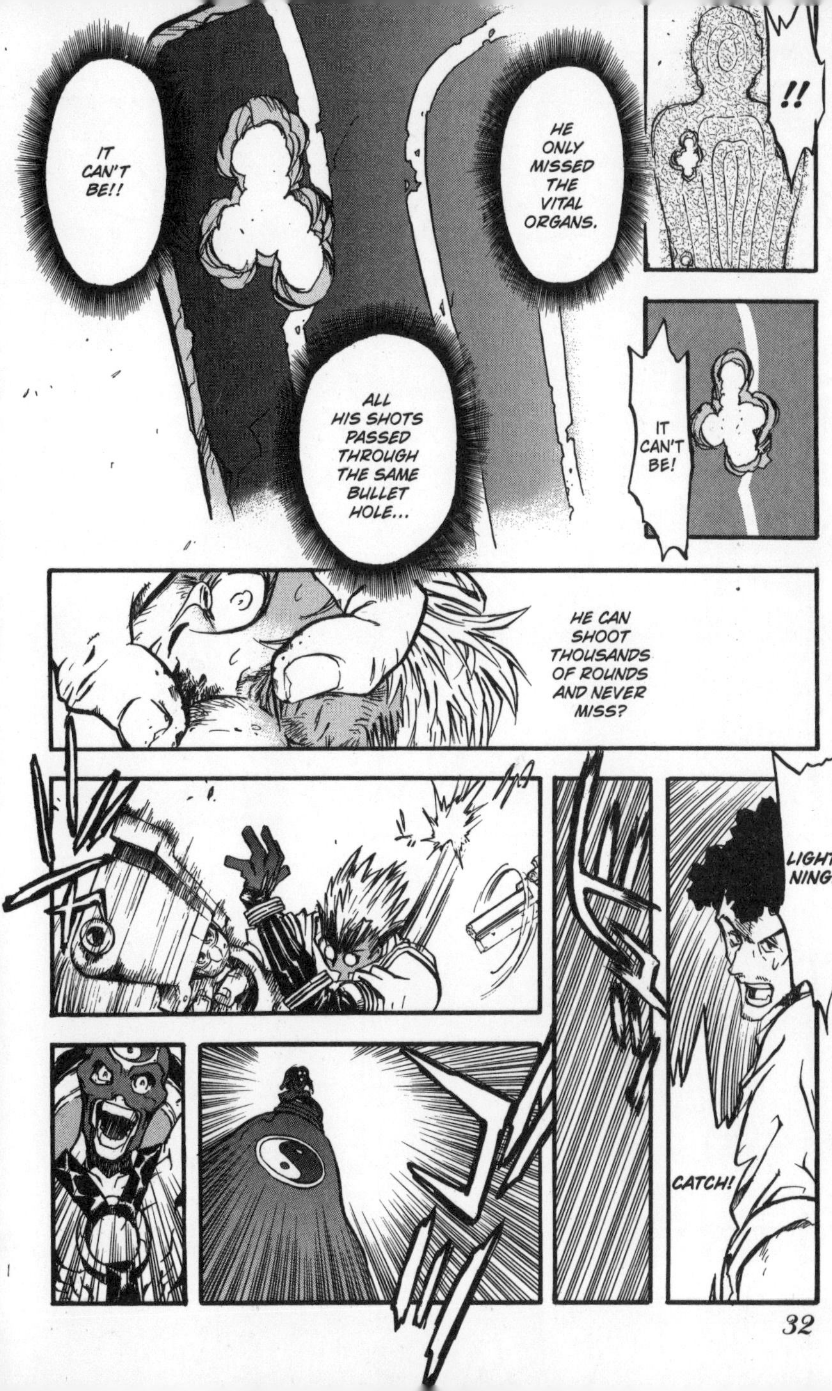
!!
IT CAN'T BE!
HE ONLY MISSED THE VITAL ORGANS.
IT CAN'T BE!!
ALL HIS SHOTS PASSED THROUGH THE SAME BULLET HOLE...
HE CAN SHOOT THOUSANDS OF ROUNDS AND NEVER MISS?
LIGHTNING!
CATCH!

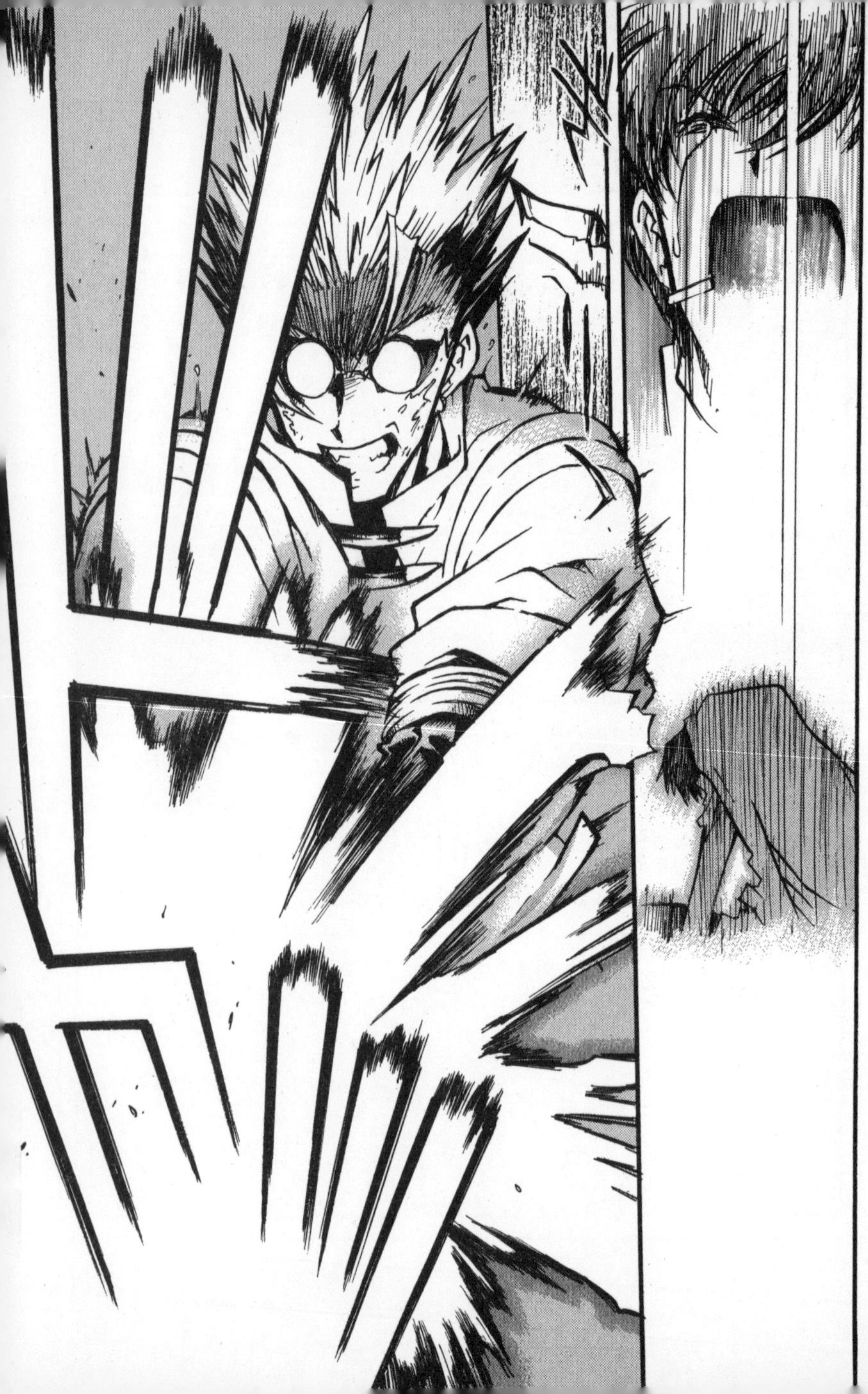

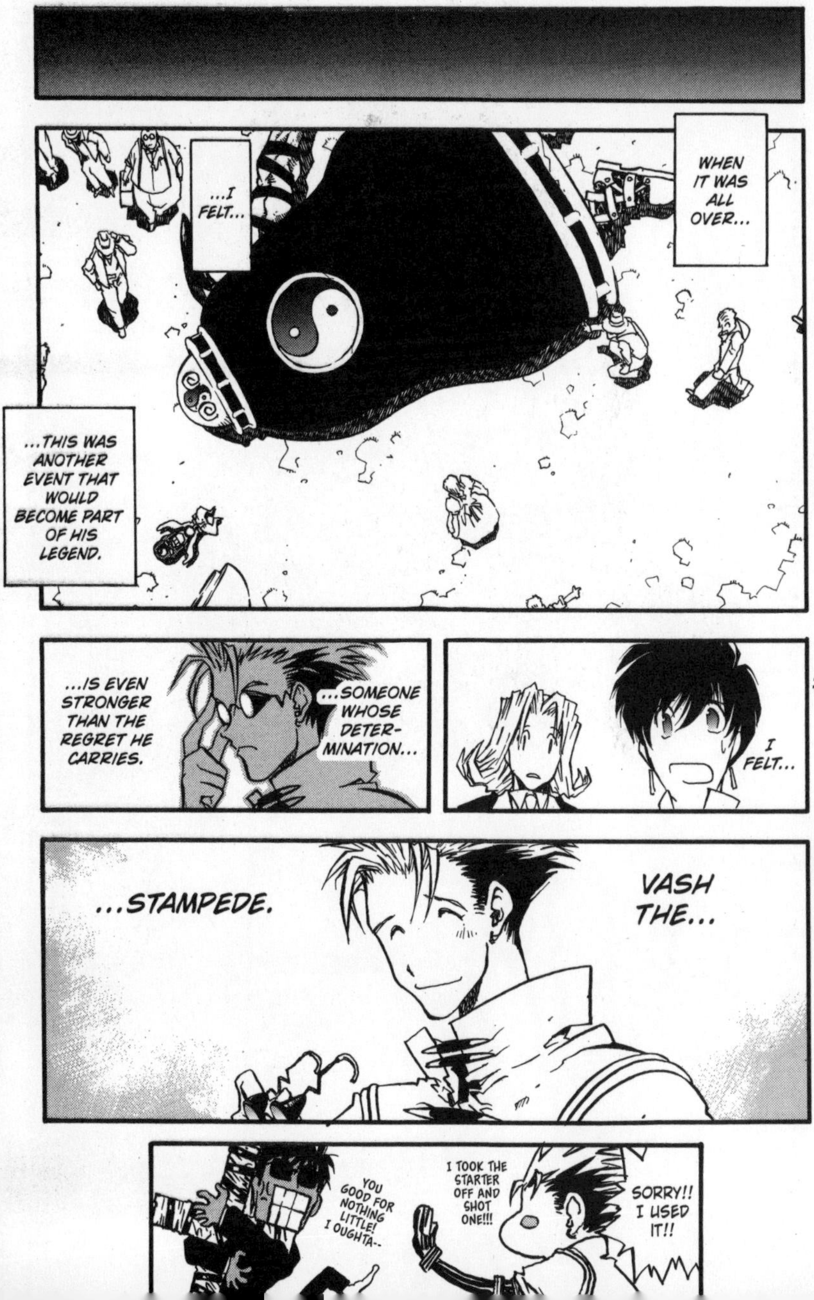
WHEN IT WAS ALL OVER...
...I FELT...
...THIS WAS ANOTHER EVENT THAT WOULD BECOME PART OF HIS LEGEND.
I FELT...
...SOMEONE WHOSE DETER-MINATION...
...IS EVEN STRONGER THAN THE REGRET HE CARRIES.
VASH THE...
...STAMPEDE.
SORRY!! I USED IT!!
I TOOK THE STARTER OFF AND SHOT ONE!!!
YOU GOOD FOR NOTHING LITTLE! I OUGHTA--

#1. THE GUNSLINGER/END

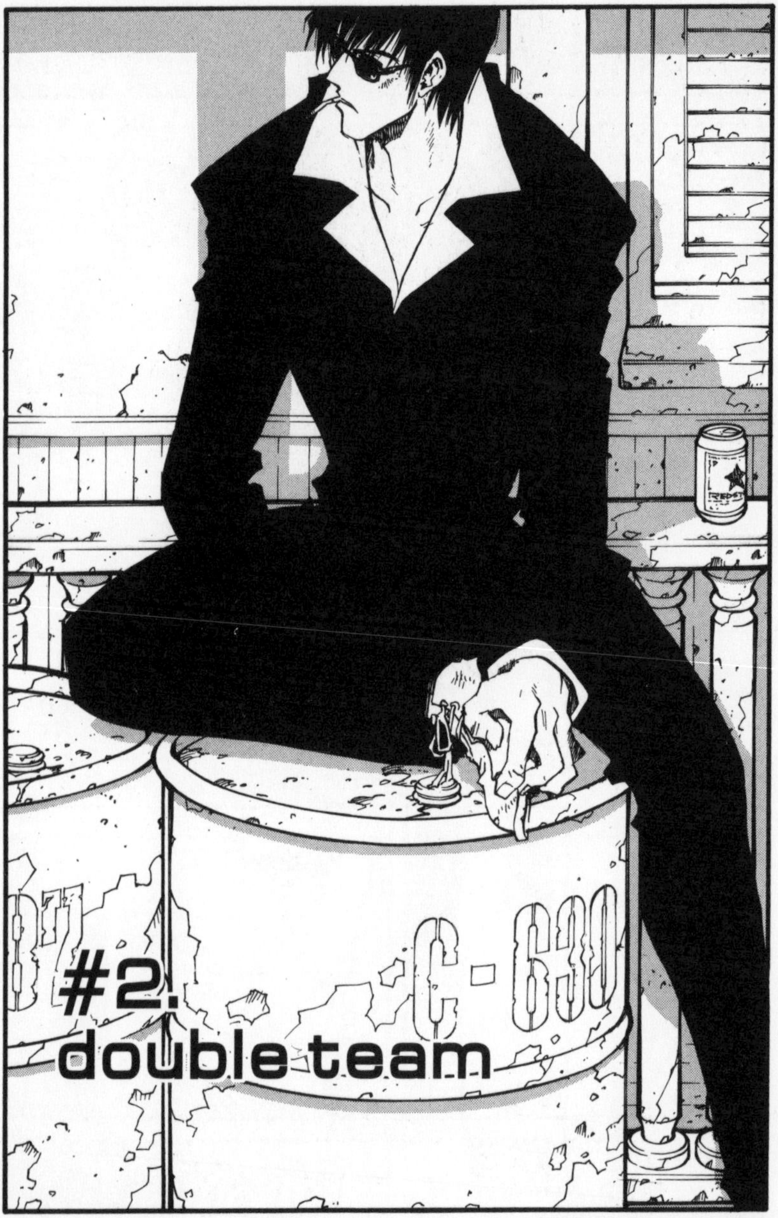
C-630
#2.
double team

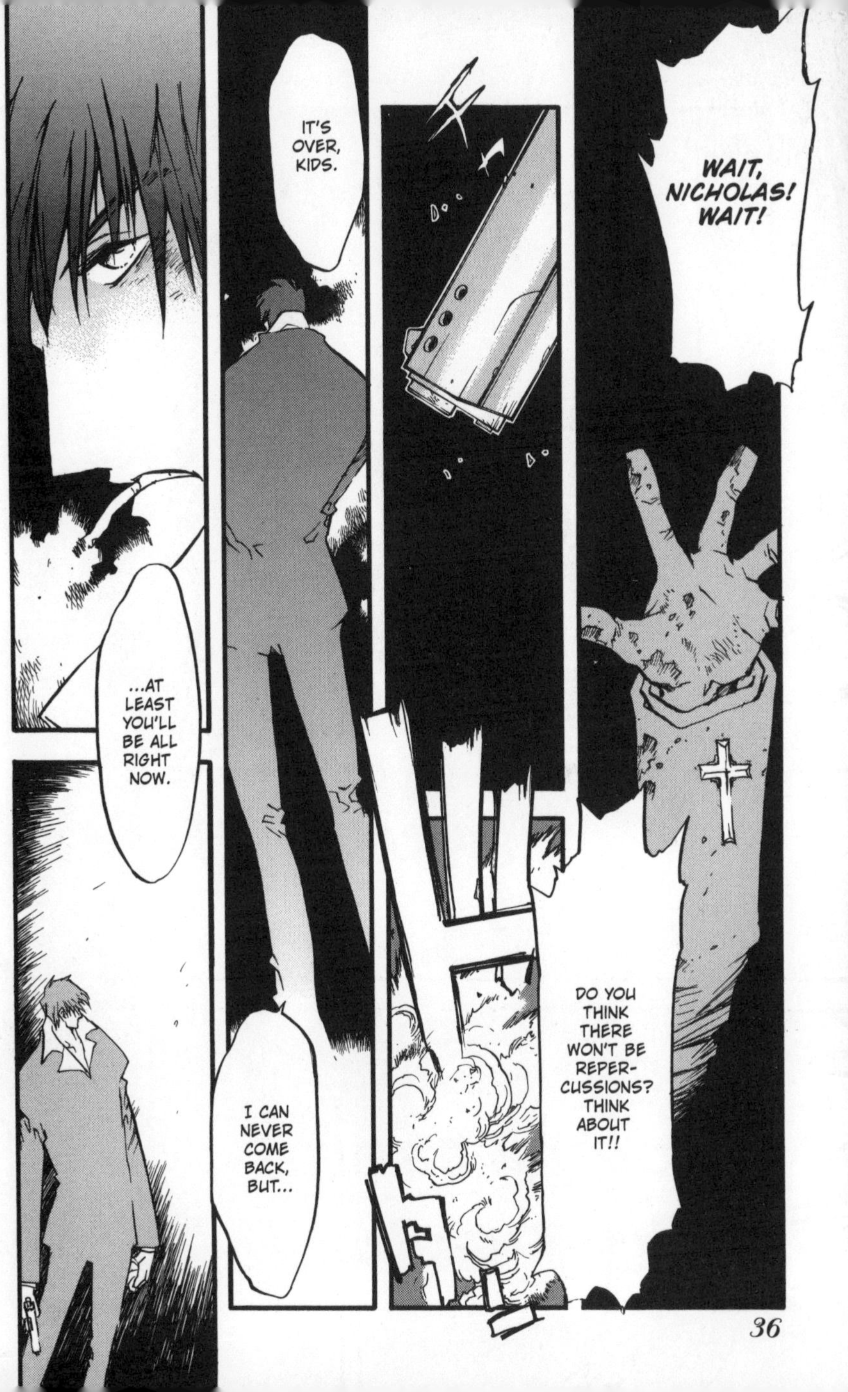
WAIT, NICHOLAS! WAIT!
DO YOU THINK THERE WON'T BE REPERCUSSIONS? THINK ABOUT IT!!
IT'S OVER, KIDS.
I CAN NEVER COME BACK, BUT...
...AT LEAST YOU'LL BE ALL RIGHT NOW.

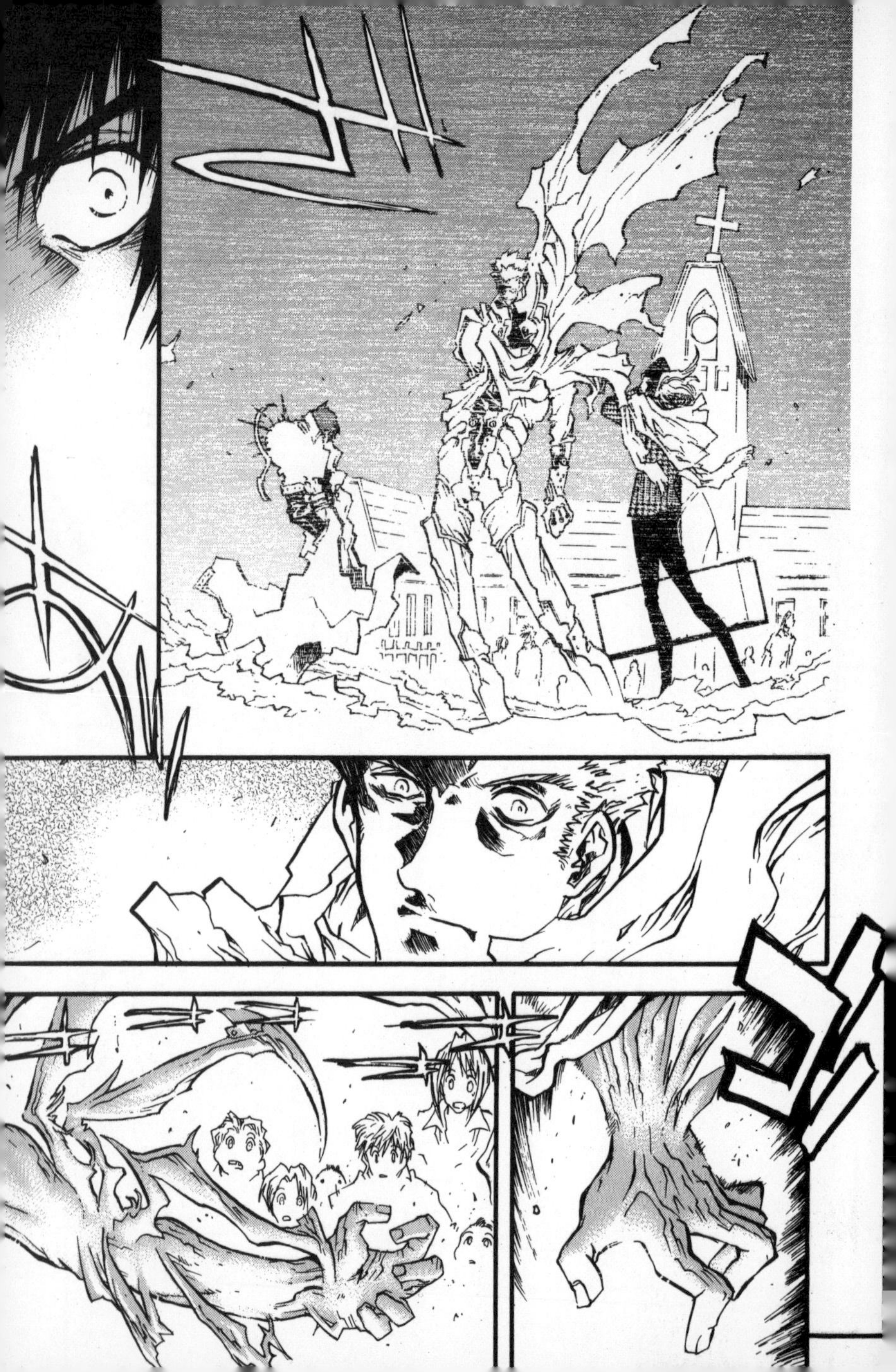

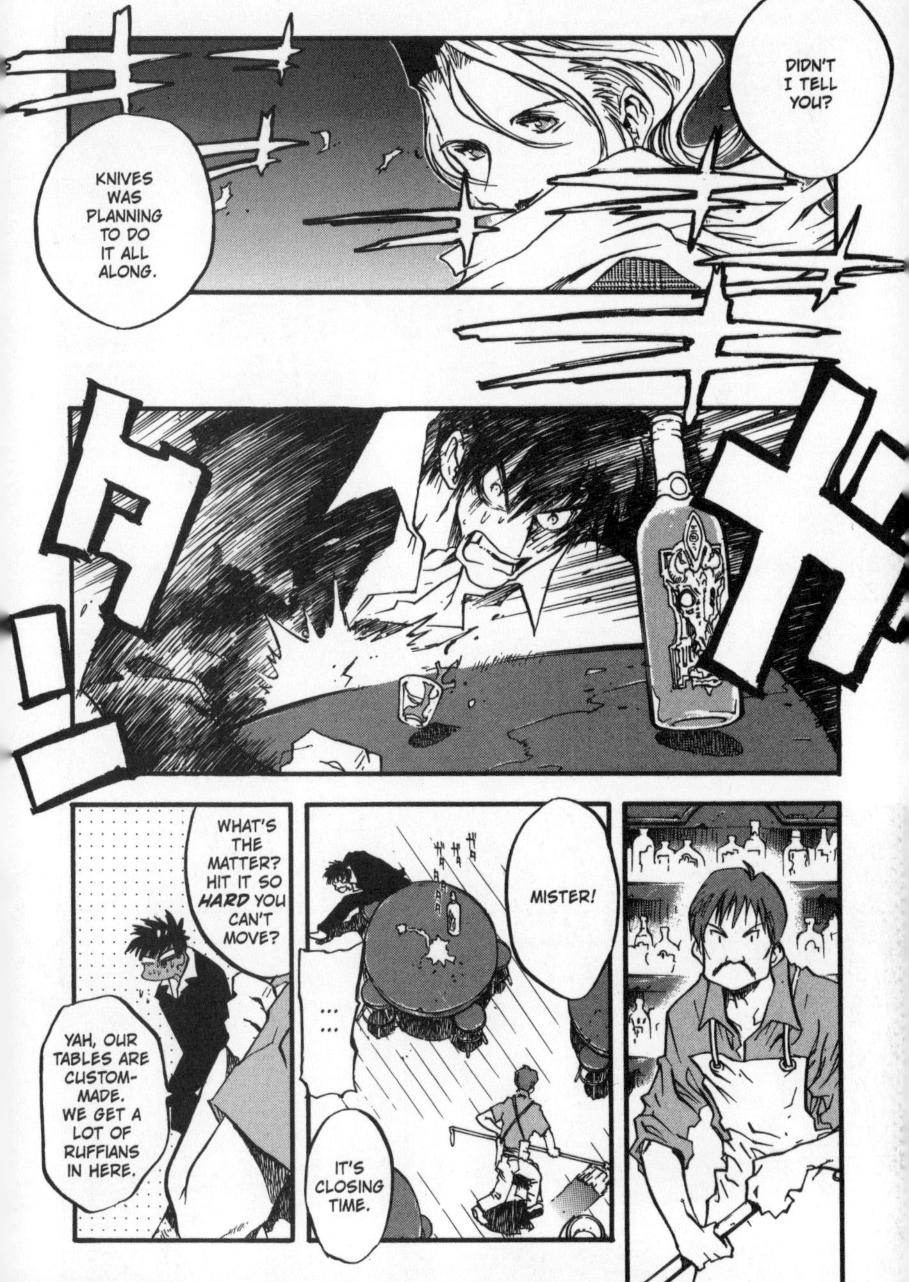
DIDN'T I TELL YOU?
KNIVES WAS PLANNING TO DO IT ALL ALONG.
MISTER!
... ...
IT'S CLOSING TIME.
WHAT'S THE MATTER? HIT IT SO *HARD* YOU CAN'T MOVE?
YAH, OUR TABLES ARE CUSTOM-MADE. WE GET A LOT OF RUFFIANS IN HERE.

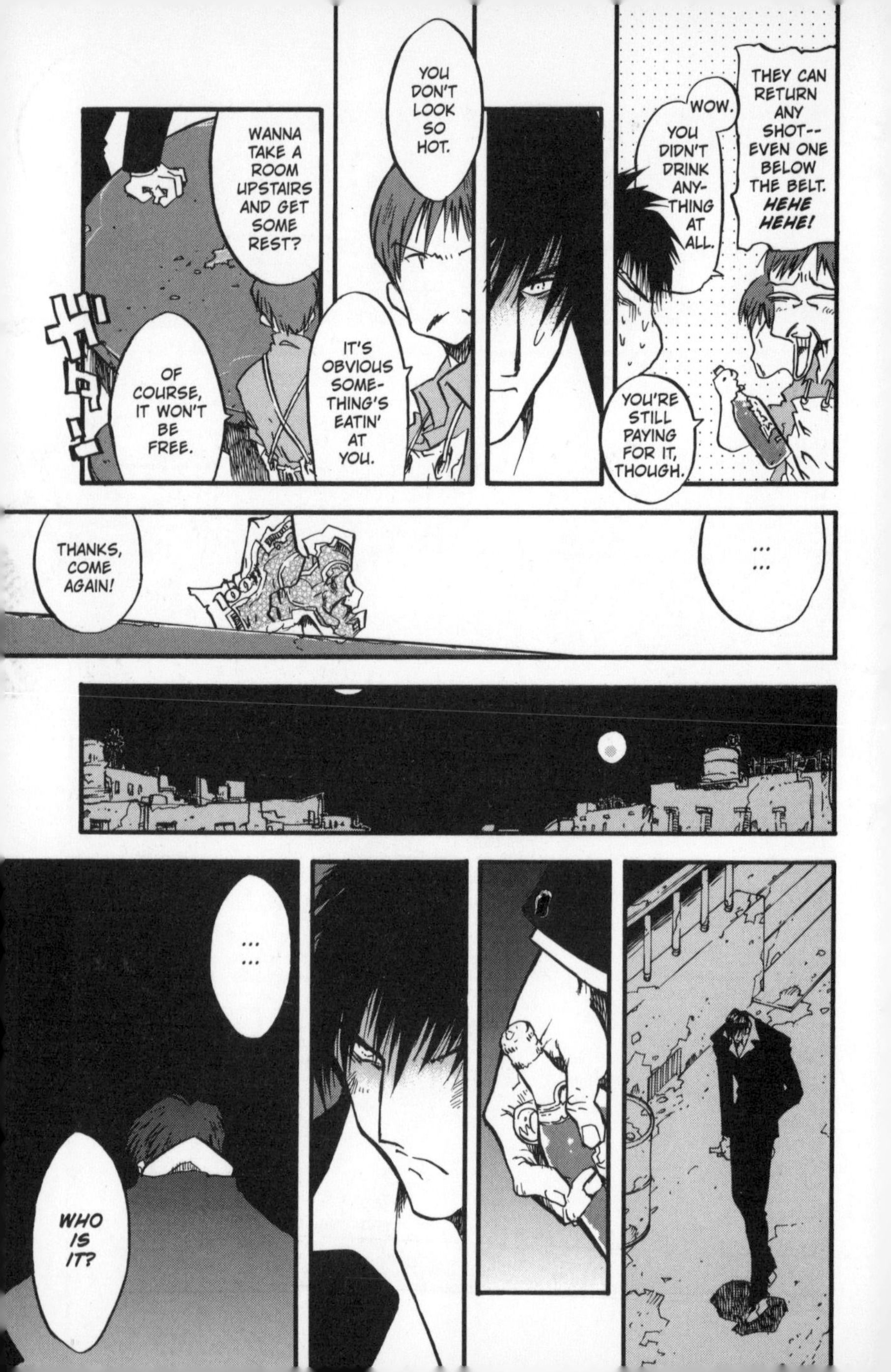
THEY CAN RETURN ANY SHOT-- EVEN ONE BELOW THE BELT. HEHE HEHE!
WOW. YOU DIDN'T DRINK ANY-THING AT ALL.
YOU'RE STILL PAYING FOR IT, THOUGH.
YOU DON'T LOOK SO HOT.
IT'S OBVIOUS SOME-THING'S EATIN' AT YOU.
WANNA TAKE A ROOM UPSTAIRS AND GET SOME REST?
OF COURSE, IT WON'T BE FREE.
... ...
THANKS, COME AGAIN!
... ...
WHO IS IT?

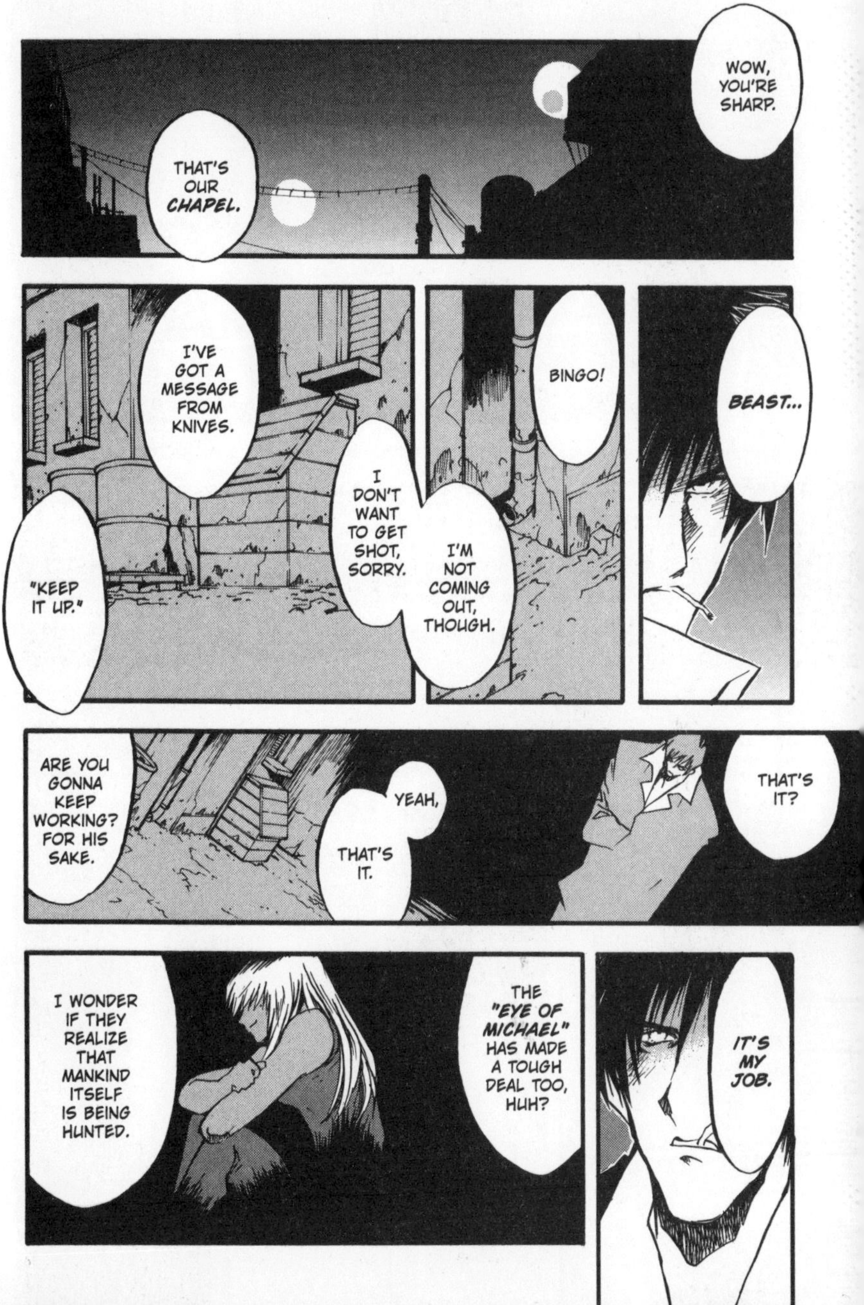
WOW, YOU'RE SHARP.
THAT'S OUR *CHAPEL.*
BEAST...
BINGO!
I'M NOT COMING OUT, THOUGH.
I DON'T WANT TO GET SHOT, SORRY.
I'VE GOT A MESSAGE FROM KNIVES.
"KEEP IT UP."
THAT'S IT?
YEAH,
THAT'S IT.
ARE YOU GONNA KEEP WORKING? FOR HIS SAKE.
IT'S MY JOB.
THE *"EYE OF MICHAEL"* HAS MADE A TOUGH DEAL TOO, HUH?
I WONDER IF THEY REALIZE THAT MANKIND ITSELF IS BEING HUNTED.

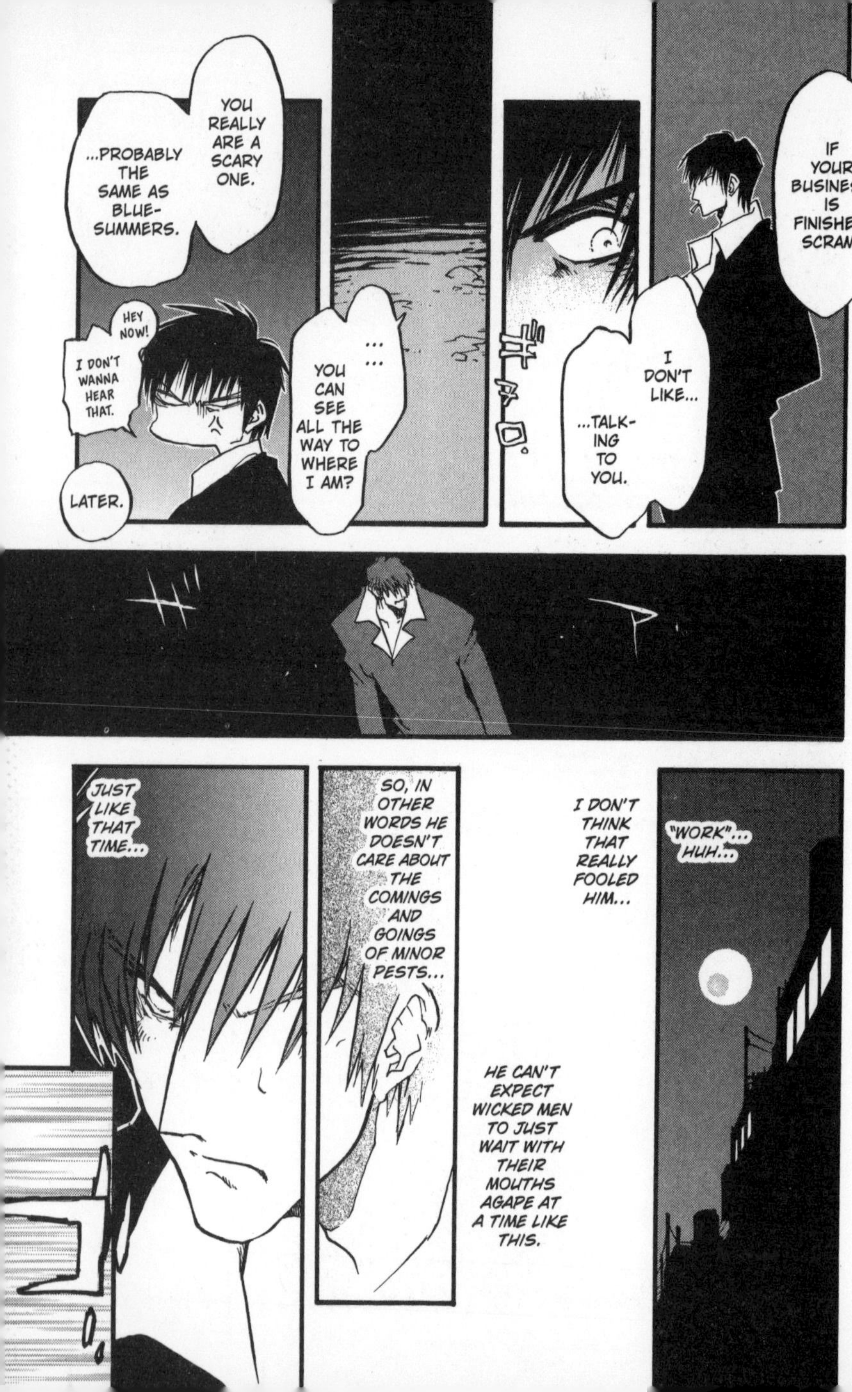

IF YOUR BUSINESS IS FINISHED, SCRAM.
I DON'T LIKE...
...TALKING TO YOU.
ギョロ。
......
YOU CAN SEE ALL THE WAY TO WHERE I AM?
YOU REALLY ARE A SCARY ONE.
...PROBABLY THE SAME AS BLUE-SUMMERS.
HEY NOW!
I DON'T WANNA HEAR THAT.
LATER.
"WORK"... HUH...
I DON'T THINK THAT REALLY FOOLED HIM...
SO, IN OTHER WORDS HE DOESN'T CARE ABOUT THE COMINGS AND GOINGS OF MINOR PESTS...
HE CAN'T EXPECT WICKED MEN TO JUST WAIT WITH THEIR MOUTHS AGAPE AT A TIME LIKE THIS.
JUST LIKE THAT TIME...

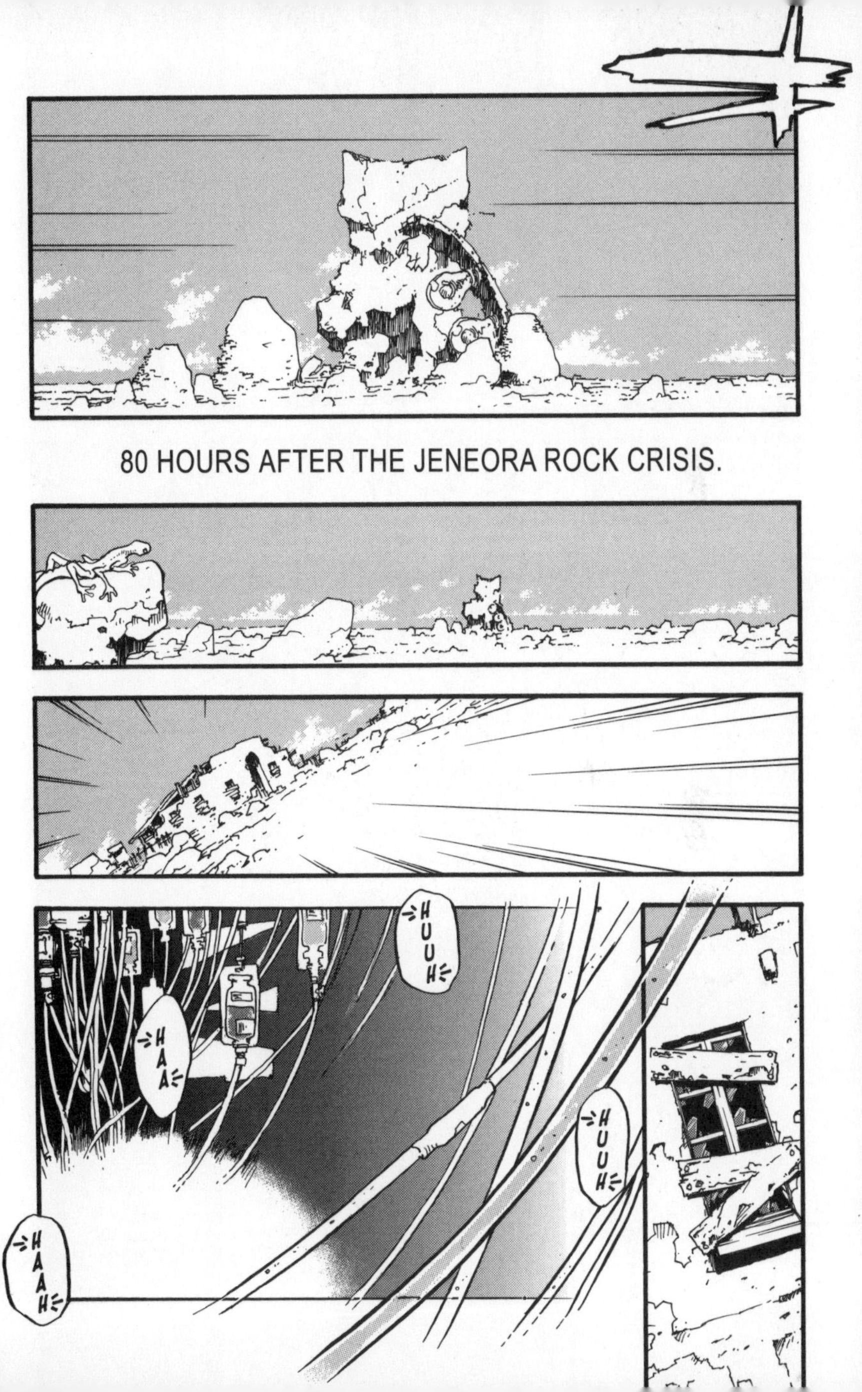
80 HOURS AFTER THE JENEORA ROCK CRISIS.
HUUH
HAA
HUUH
HAAH

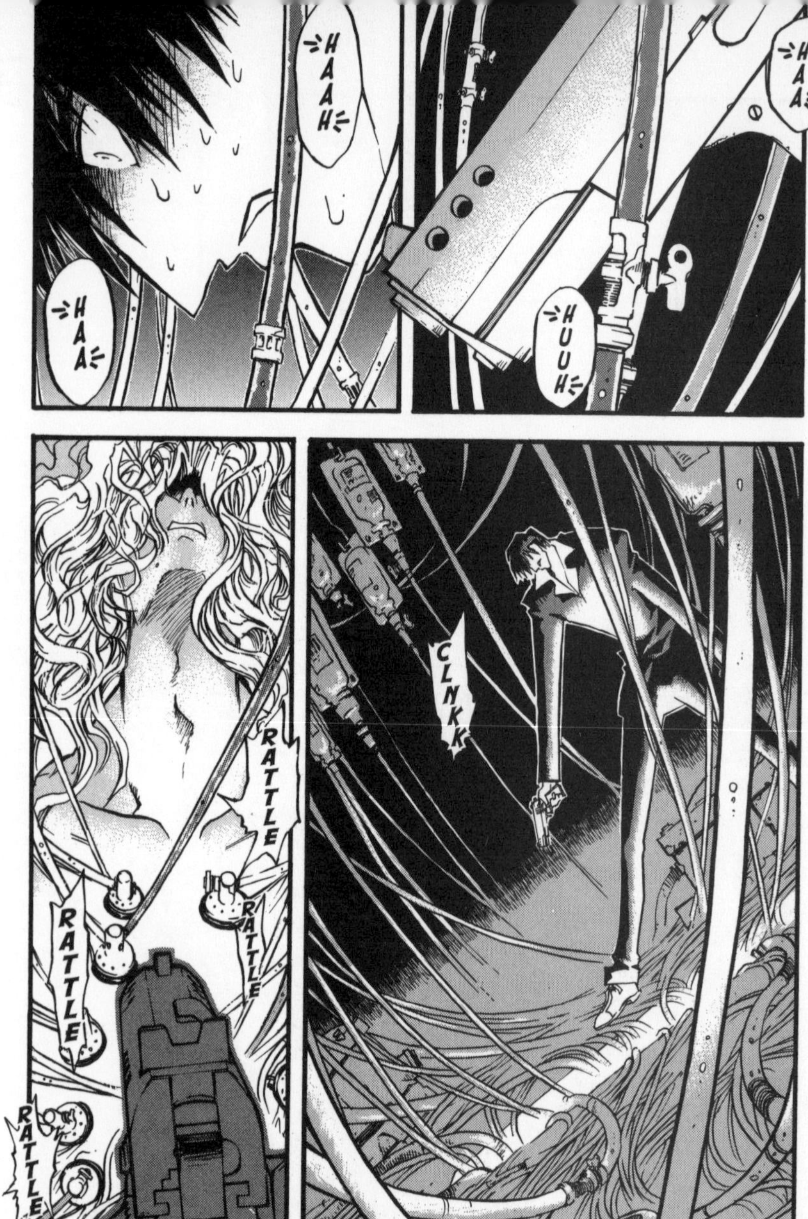
HAA
HUUH
HAAAH
HAA
CLNKK
RATTLE
RATTLE
RATTLE
RATTLE

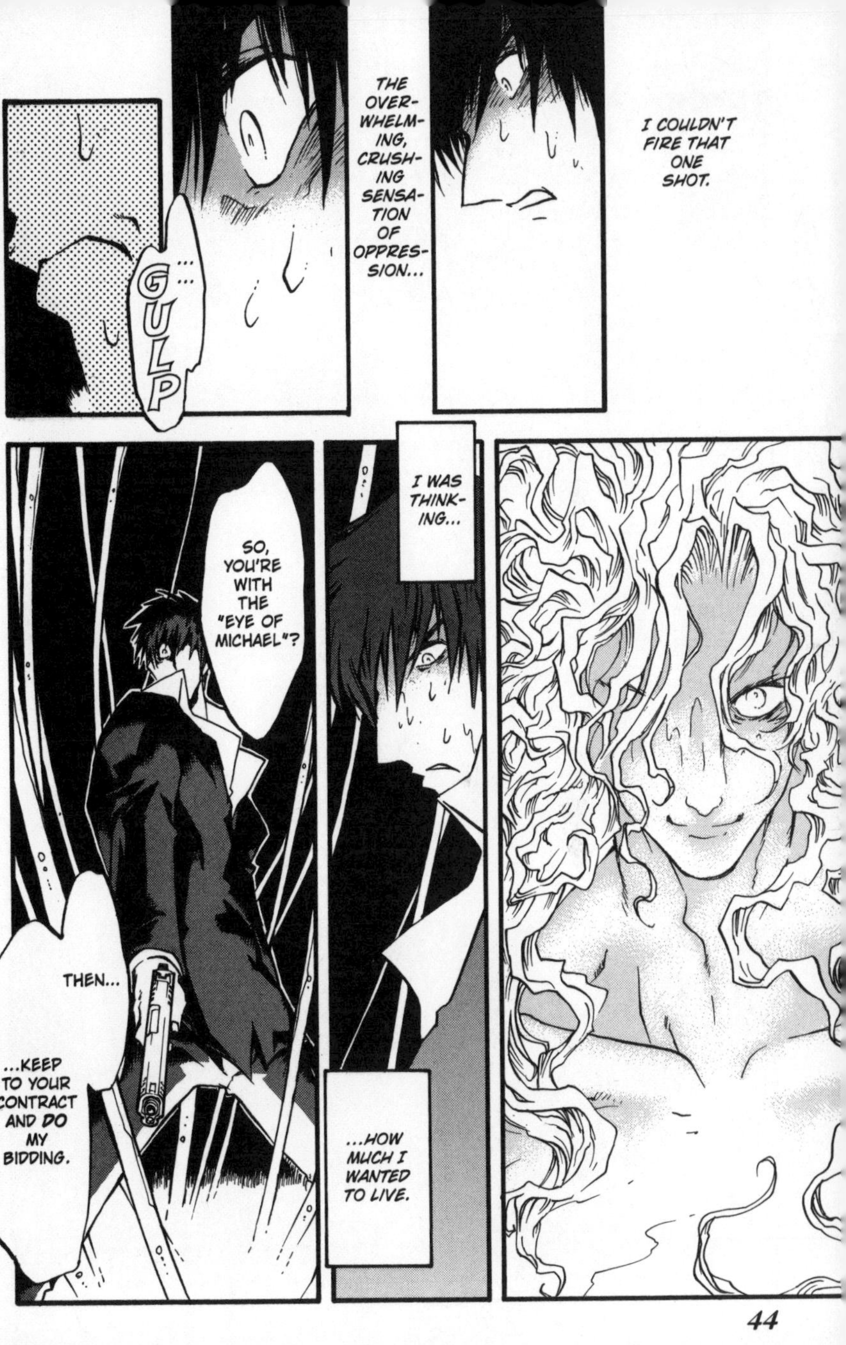
I COULDN'T FIRE THAT ONE SHOT.
THE OVERWHELMING, CRUSHING SENSATION OF OPPRESSION...
......
GULP
I WAS THINKING...
...HOW MUCH I WANTED TO LIVE.
SO, YOU'RE WITH THE "EYE OF MICHAEL"?
THEN...
...KEEP TO YOUR CONTRACT AND DO MY BIDDING.

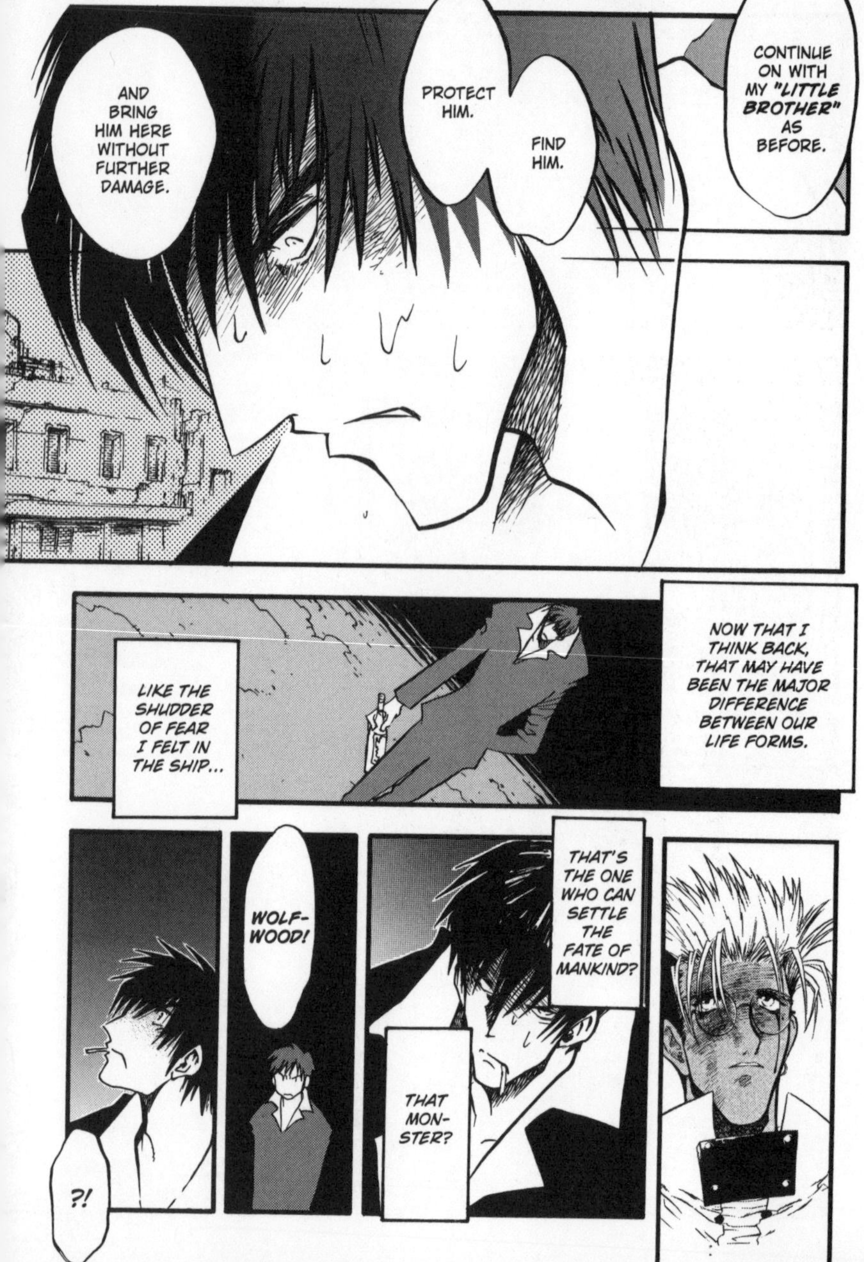
CONTINUE ON WITH MY "LITTLE BROTHER" AS BEFORE.
FIND HIM.
PROTECT HIM.
AND BRING HIM HERE WITHOUT FURTHER DAMAGE.
NOW THAT I THINK BACK, THAT MAY HAVE BEEN THE MAJOR DIFFERENCE BETWEEN OUR LIFE FORMS.
LIKE THE SHUDDER OF FEAR I FELT IN THE SHIP...
THAT'S THE ONE WHO CAN SETTLE THE FATE OF MANKIND?
THAT MON-STER?
WOLF-WOOD!
?!

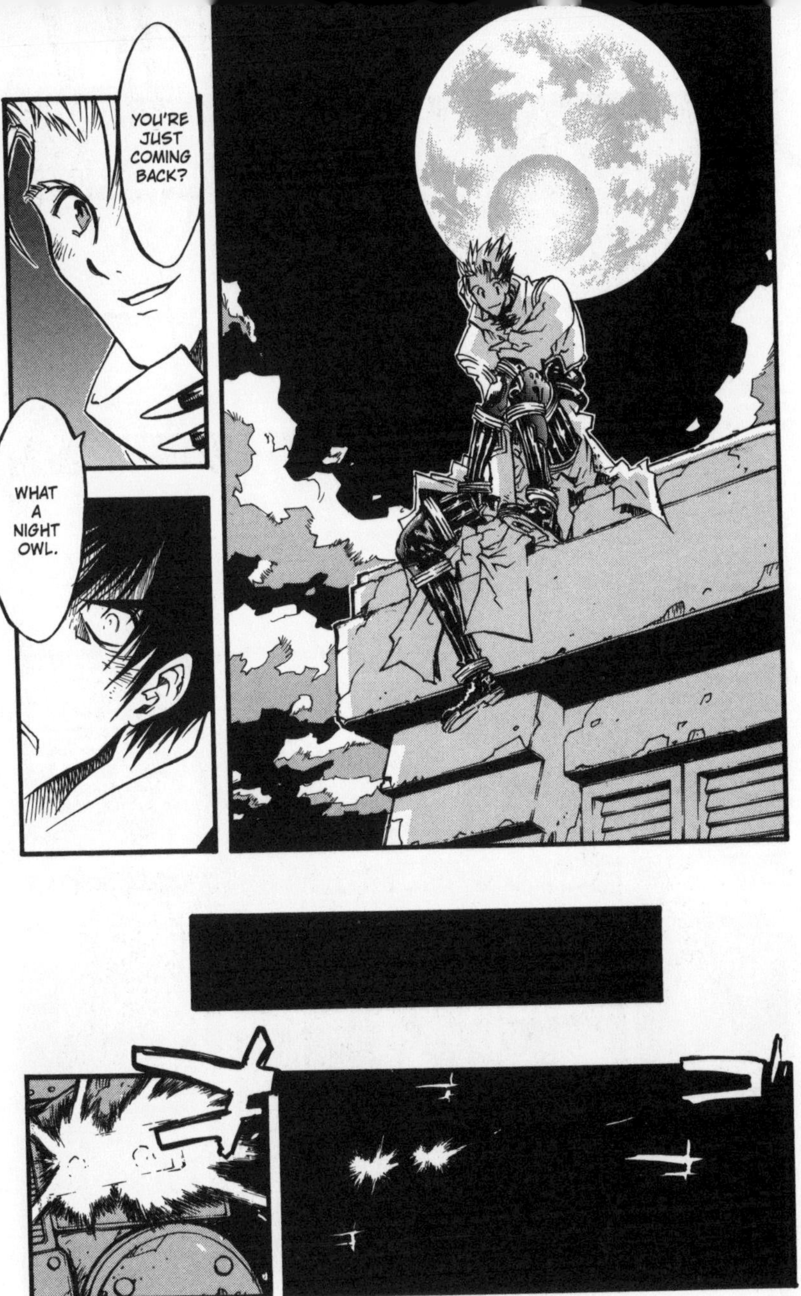
YOU'RE JUST COMING BACK?
WHAT A NIGHT OWL.

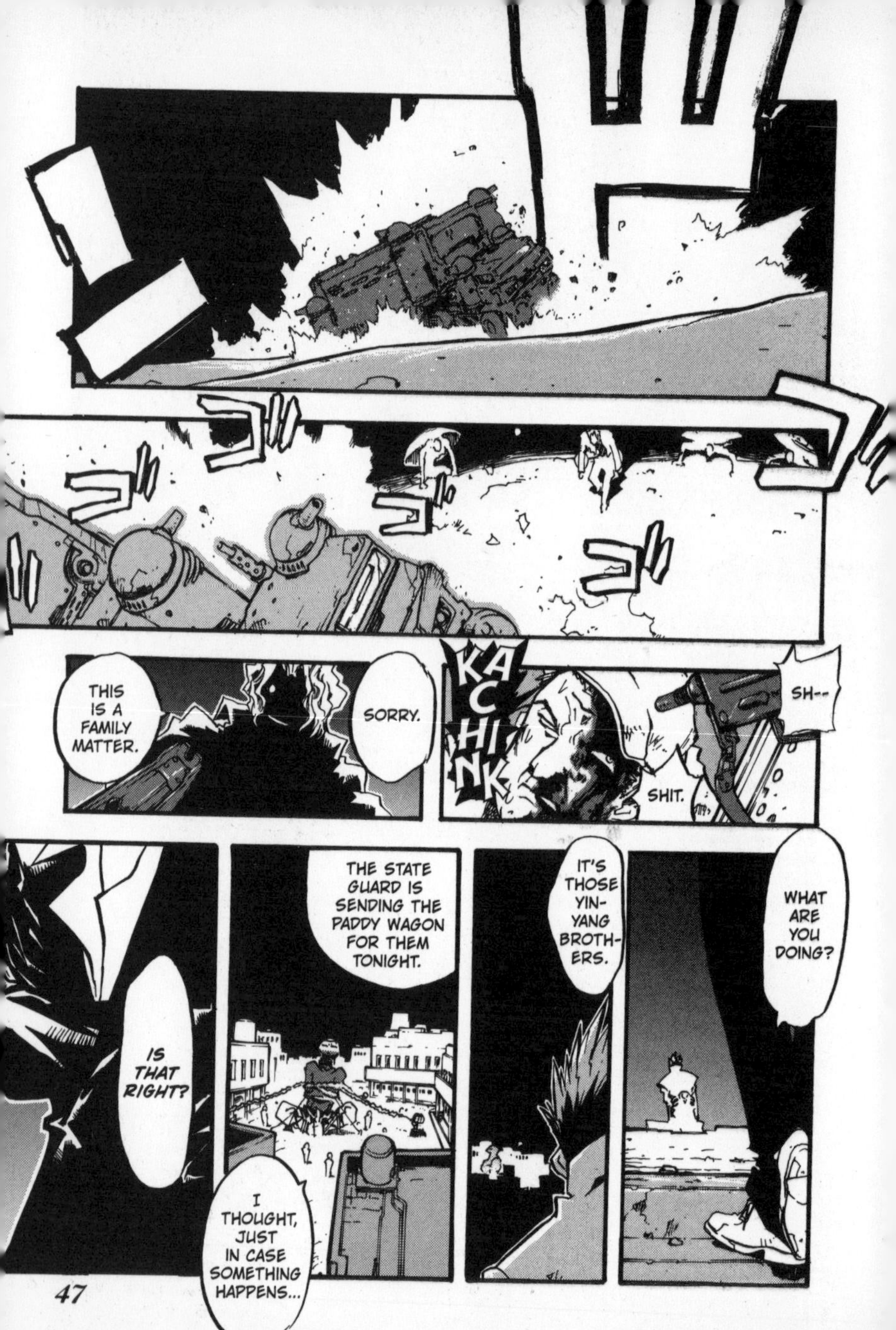
SH--
KACHINK
SHIT.
SORRY.
THIS IS A FAMILY MATTER.
WHAT ARE YOU DOING?
IT'S THOSE YIN-YANG BROTH-ERS.
THE STATE GUARD IS SENDING THE PADDY WAGON FOR THEM TONIGHT.
I THOUGHT, JUST IN CASE SOMETHING HAPPENS...
IS THAT RIGHT?

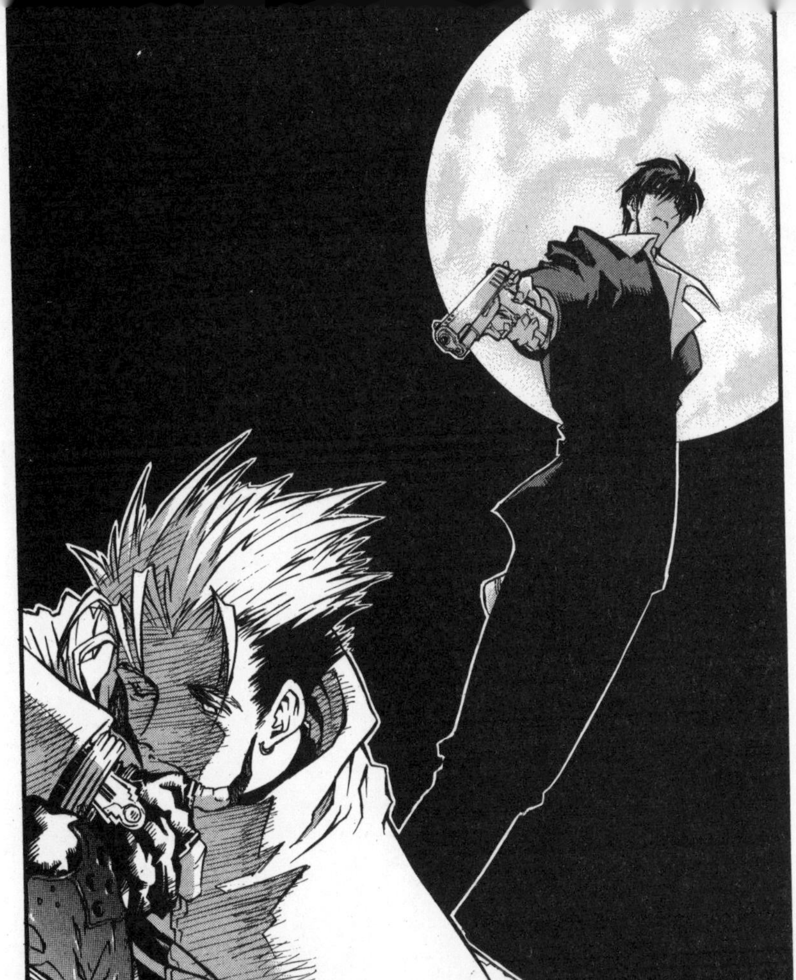
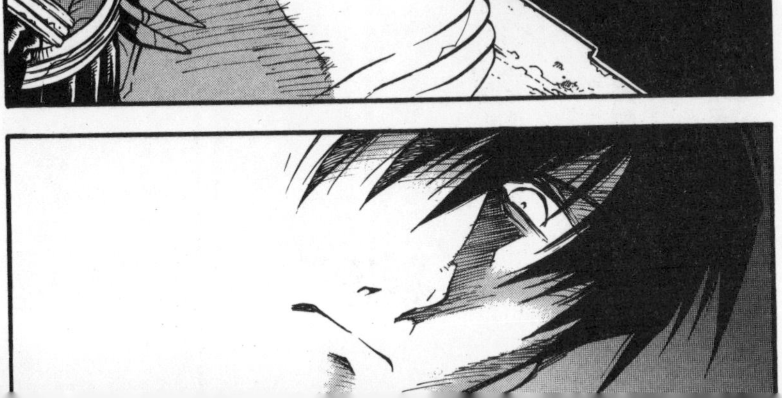

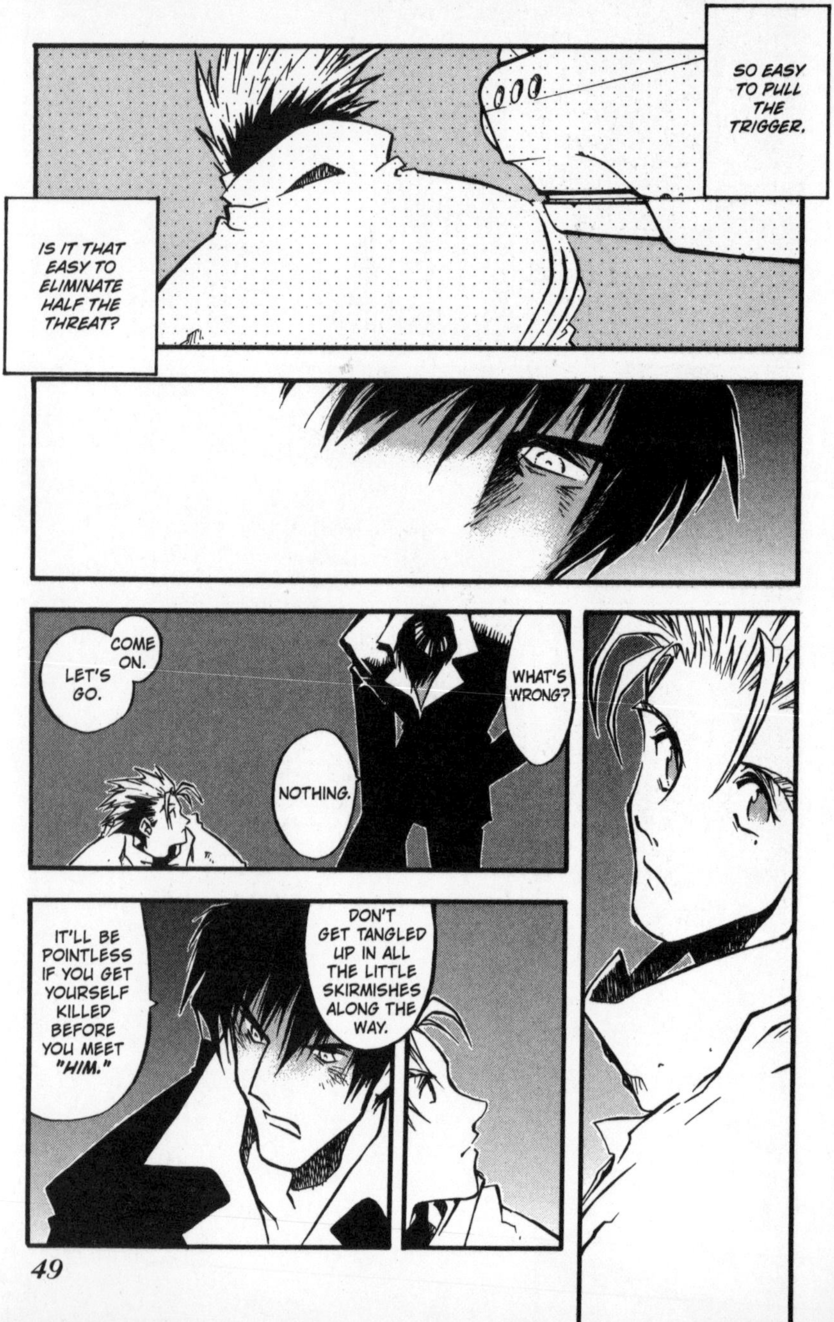
SO EASY TO PULL THE TRIGGER.
IS IT THAT EASY TO ELIMINATE HALF THE THREAT?
WHAT'S WRONG?
NOTHING.
COME ON. LET'S GO.
DON'T GET TANGLED UP IN ALL THE LITTLE SKIRMISHES ALONG THE WAY.
IT'LL BE POINTLESS IF YOU GET YOURSELF KILLED BEFORE YOU MEET "HIM."

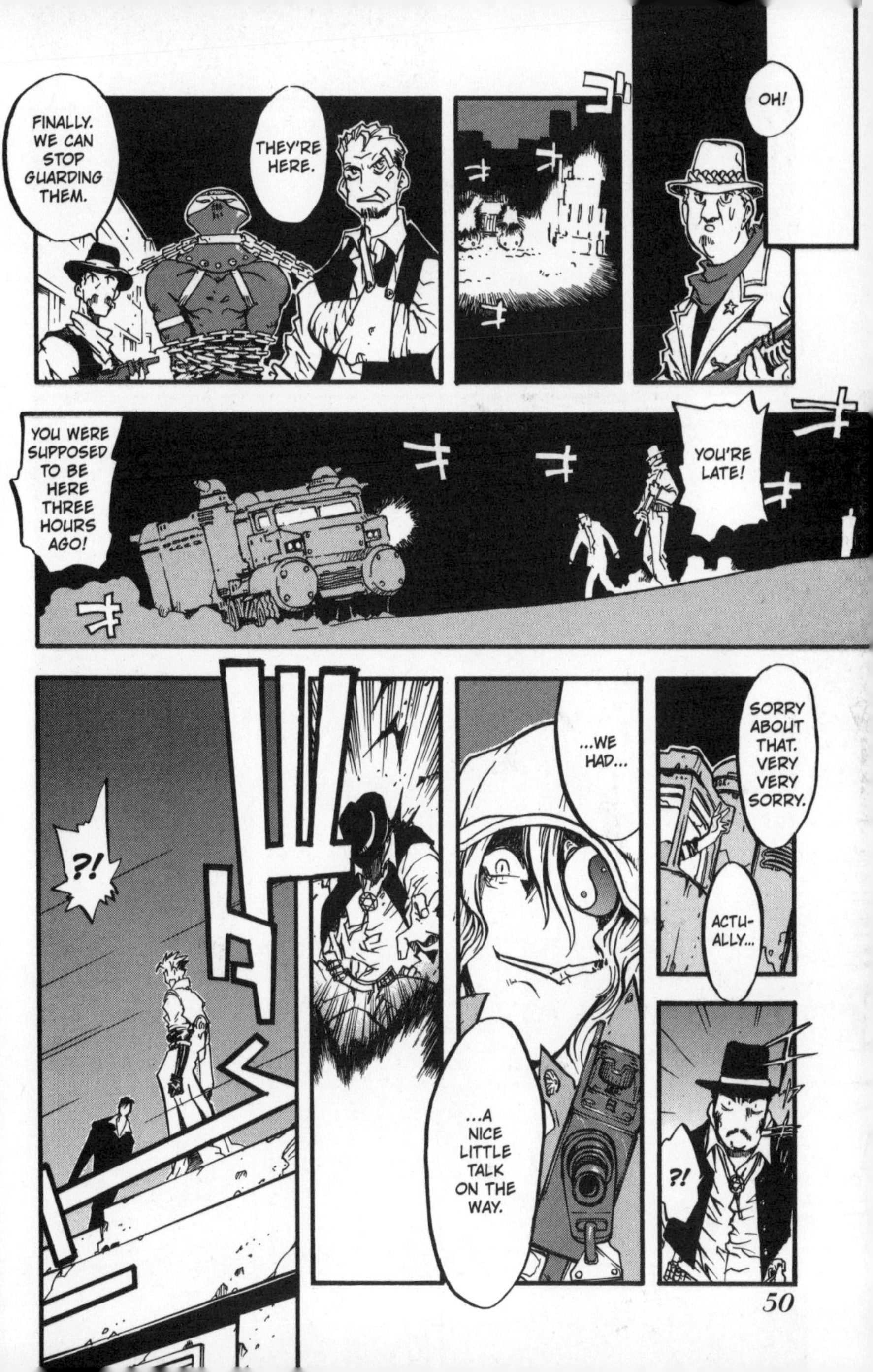
OH!
THEY'RE HERE.
FINALLY. WE CAN STOP GUARDING THEM.
YOU'RE LATE!
YOU WERE SUPPOSED TO BE HERE THREE HOURS AGO!
SORRY ABOUT THAT. VERY VERY SORRY.
ACTU-ALLY...
?!
...WE HAD...
...A NICE LITTLE TALK ON THE WAY.
?!

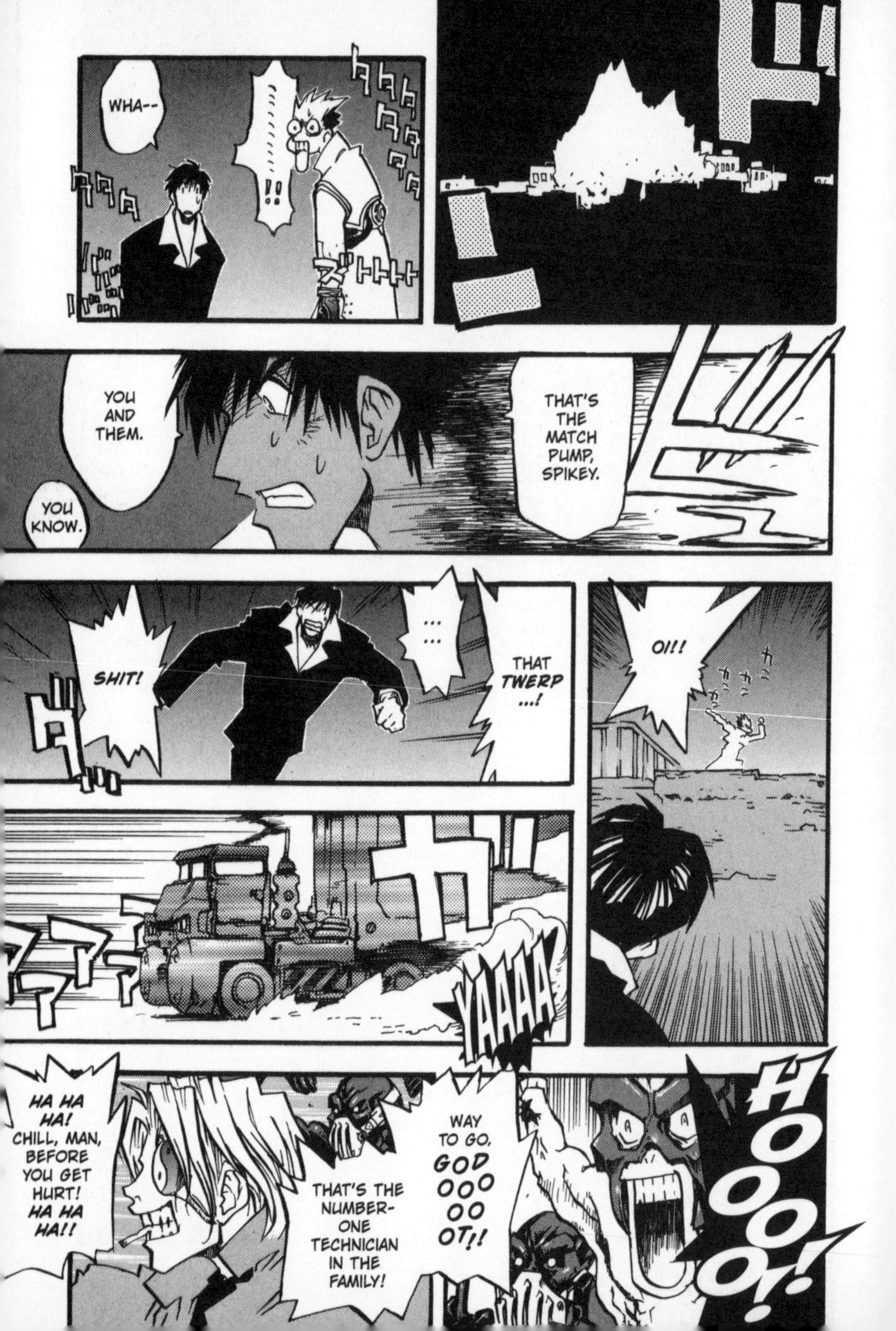

......!!
WHA--
THAT'S THE MATCH PUMP, SPIKEY.
YOU AND THEM.
YOU KNOW.
OI!!
......
THAT TWERP...!
SHIT!
YAAAA
HOOOOO!
WAY TO GO, GODOOOOOOOT!!
THAT'S THE NUMBER-ONE TECHNICIAN IN THE FAMILY!
HA HA HA! CHILL, MAN, BEFORE YOU GET HURT! HA HA HA!!

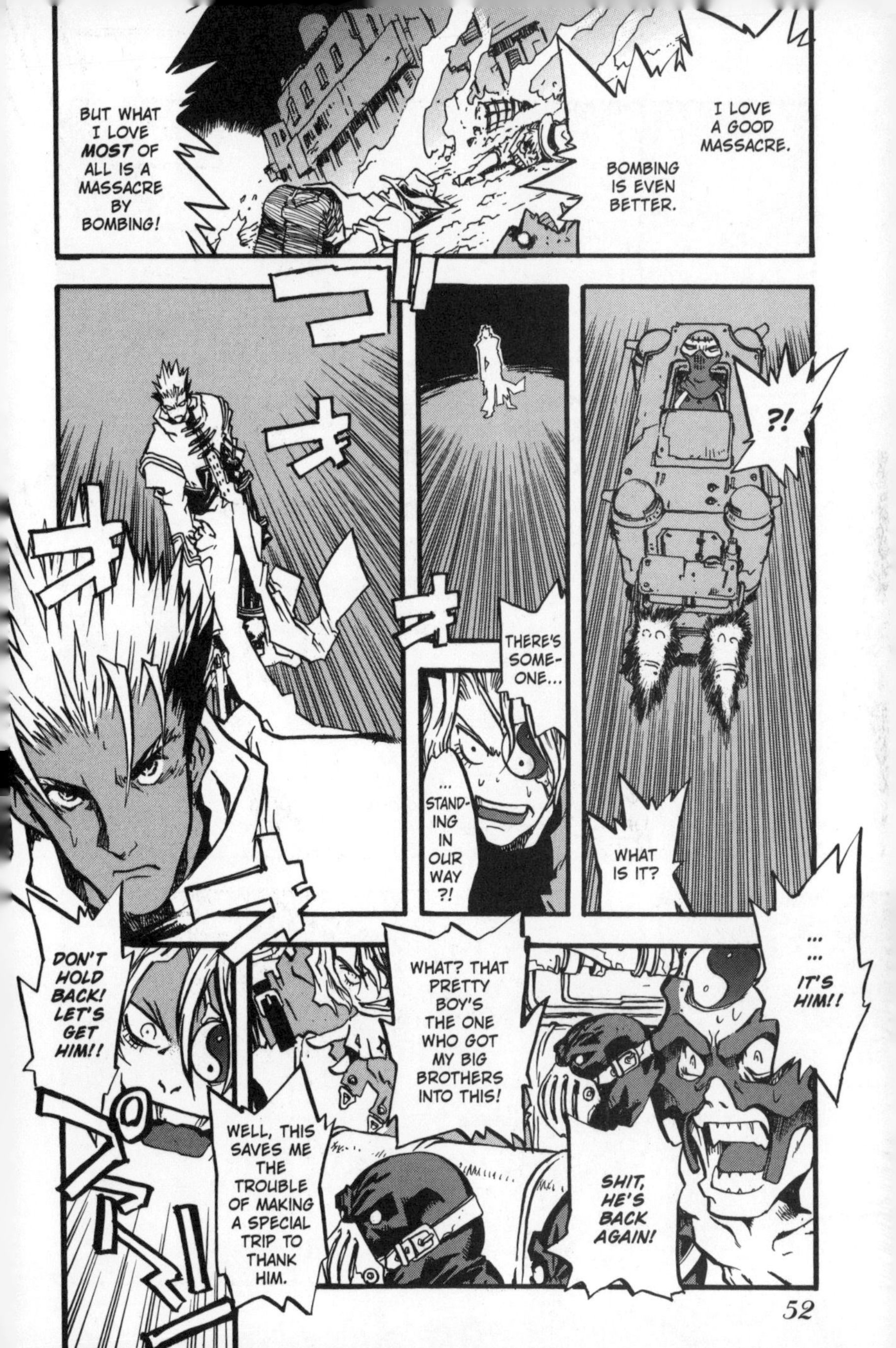
I LOVE A GOOD MASSACRE.
BOMBING IS EVEN BETTER.
BUT WHAT I LOVE MOST OF ALL IS A MASSACRE BY BOMBING!
?!
WHAT IS IT?
THERE'S SOME-ONE...
...STAND-ING IN OUR WAY?!
......IT'S HIM!!
SHIT, HE'S BACK AGAIN!
WHAT? THAT PRETTY BOY'S THE ONE WHO GOT MY BIG BROTHERS INTO THIS!
WELL, THIS SAVES ME THE TROUBLE OF MAKING A SPECIAL TRIP TO THANK HIM.
DON'T HOLD BACK! LET'S GET HIM!!

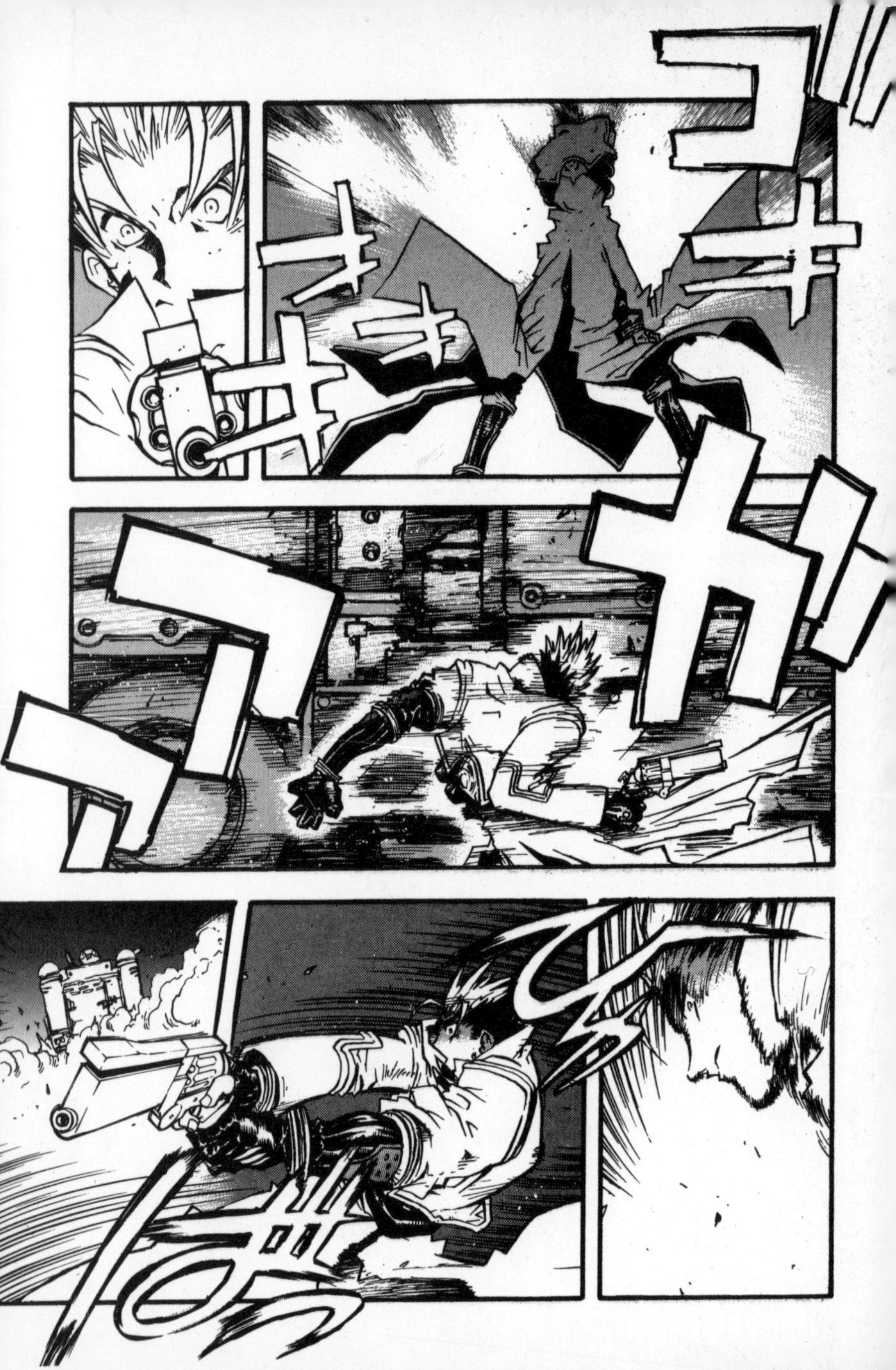

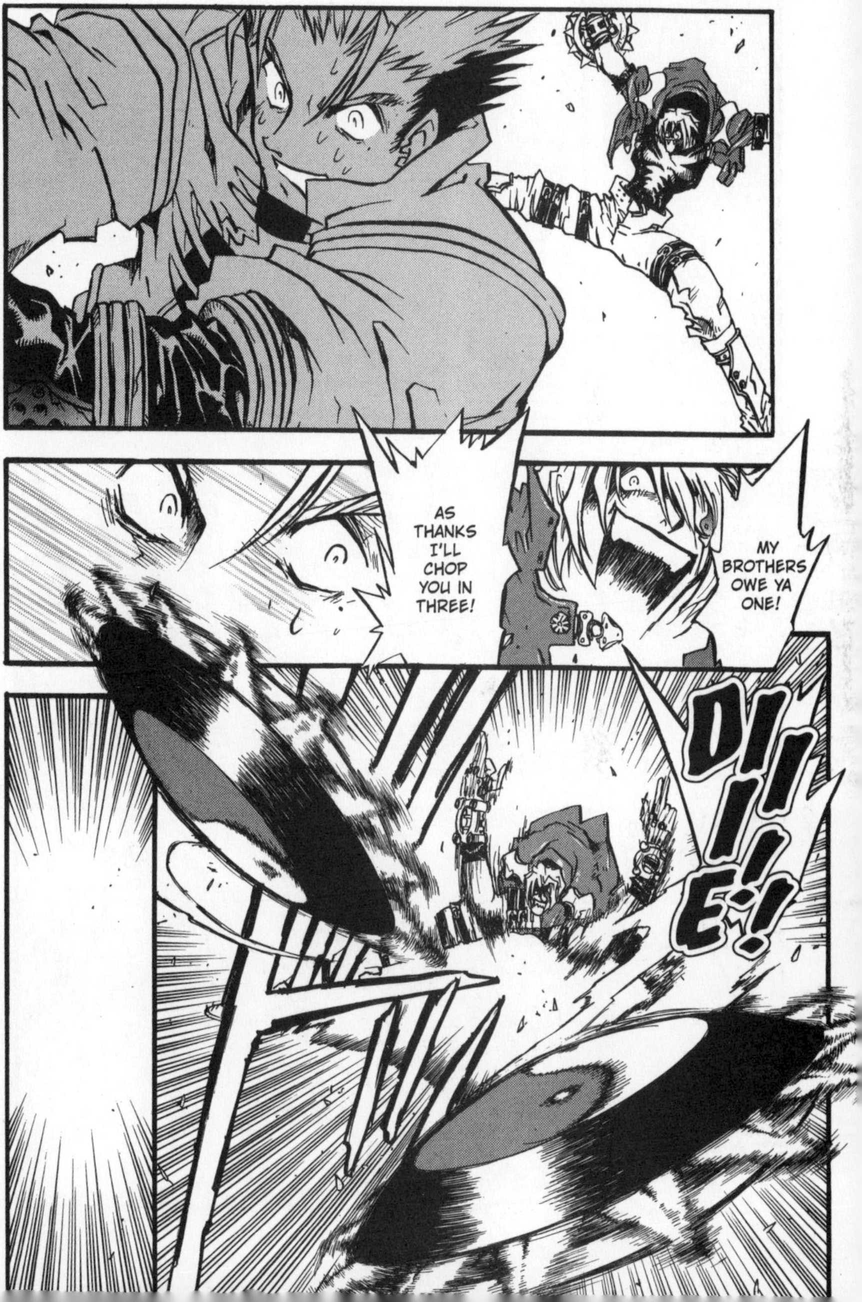
MY BROTHERS OWE YA ONE!
AS THANKS I'LL CHOP YOU IN THREE!
DIIIE-!!

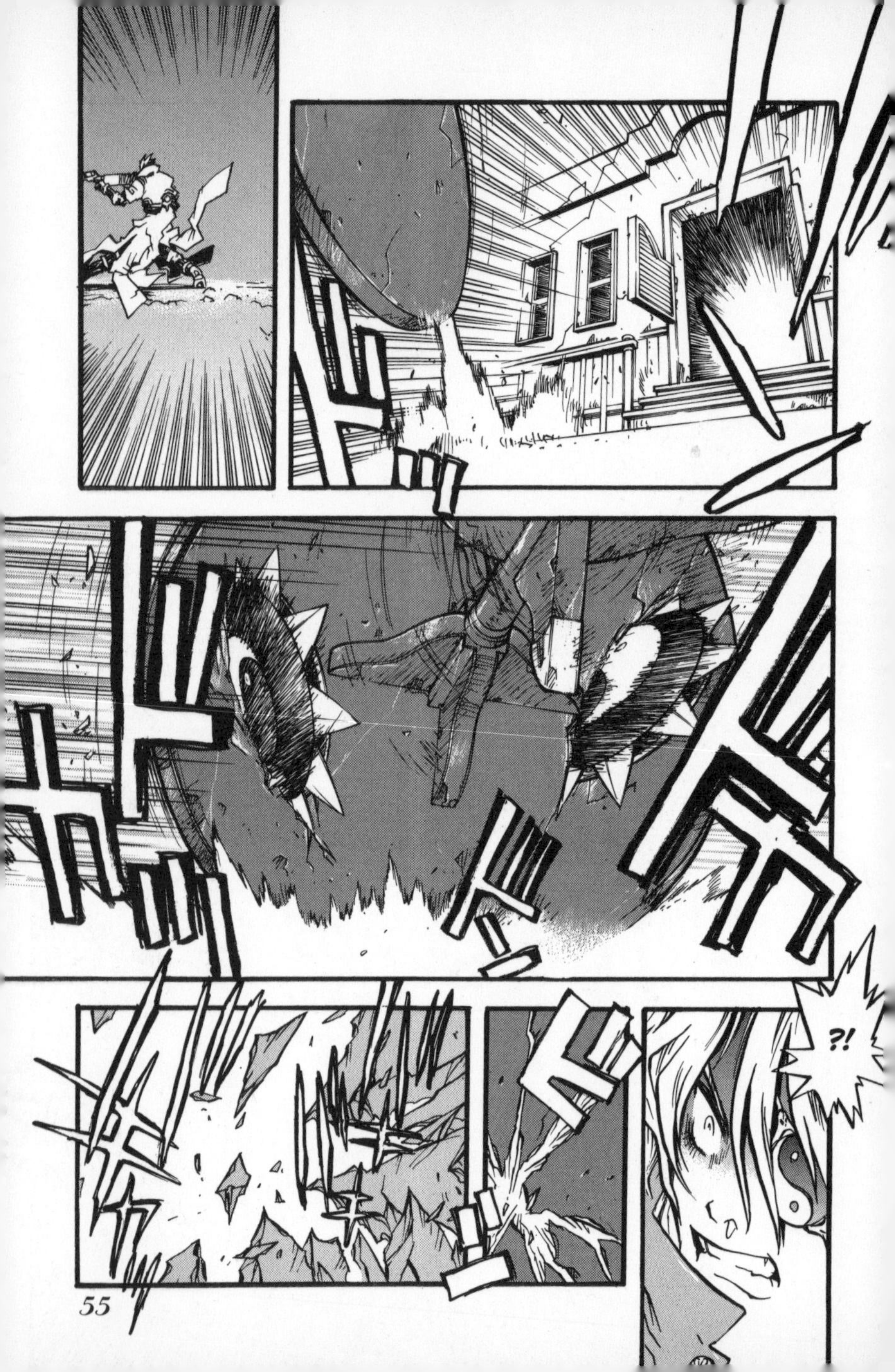
?!

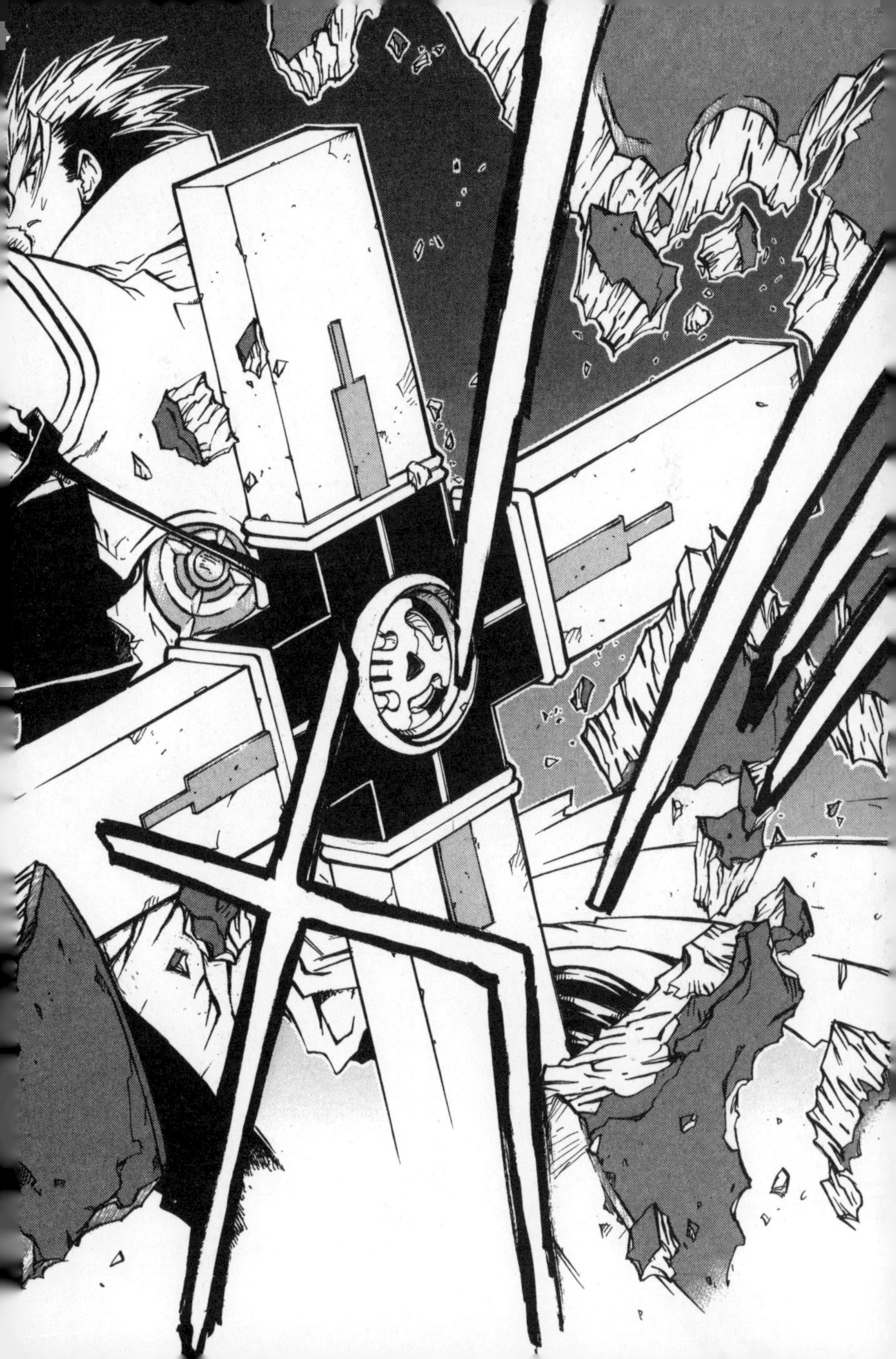

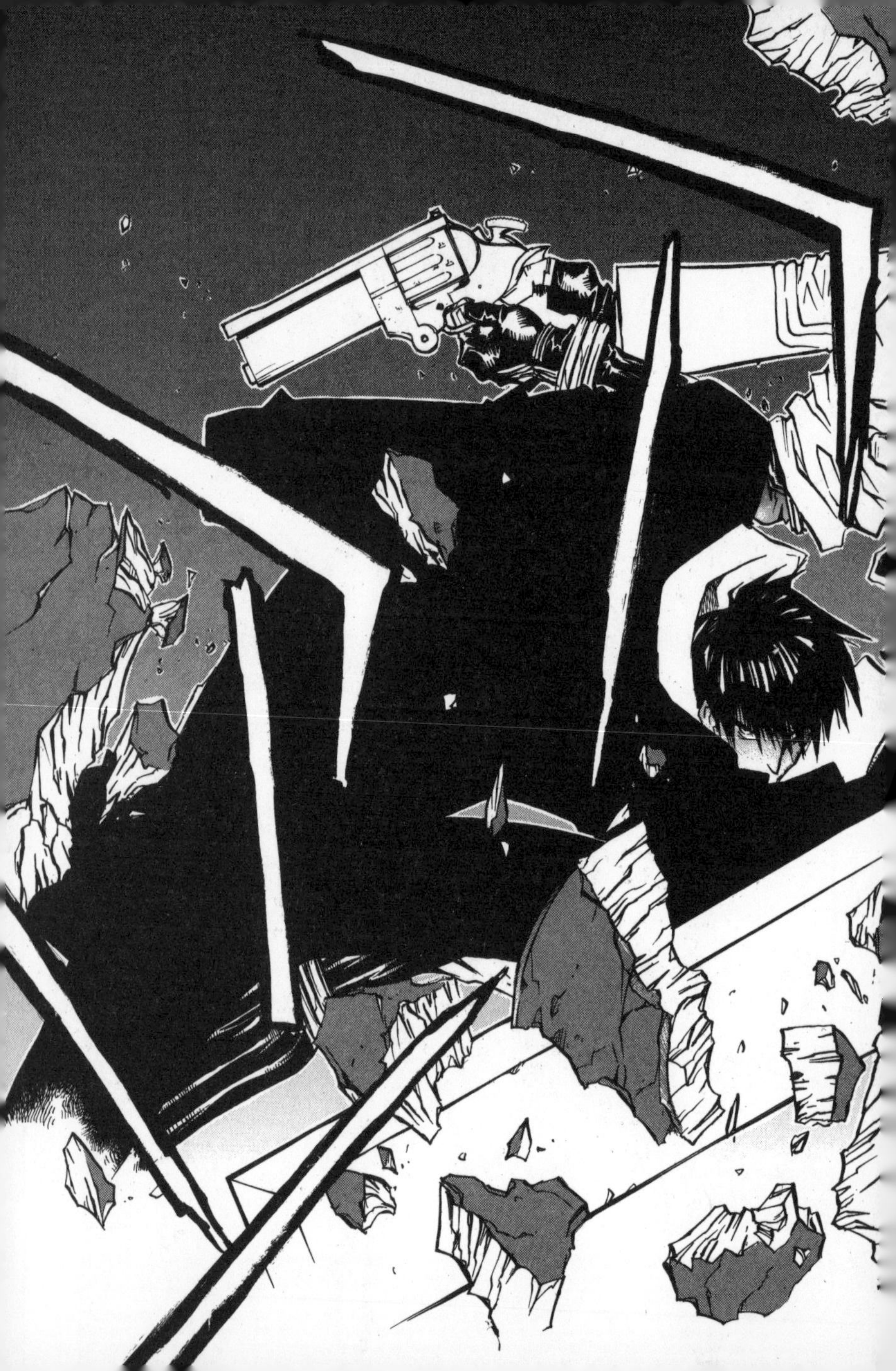

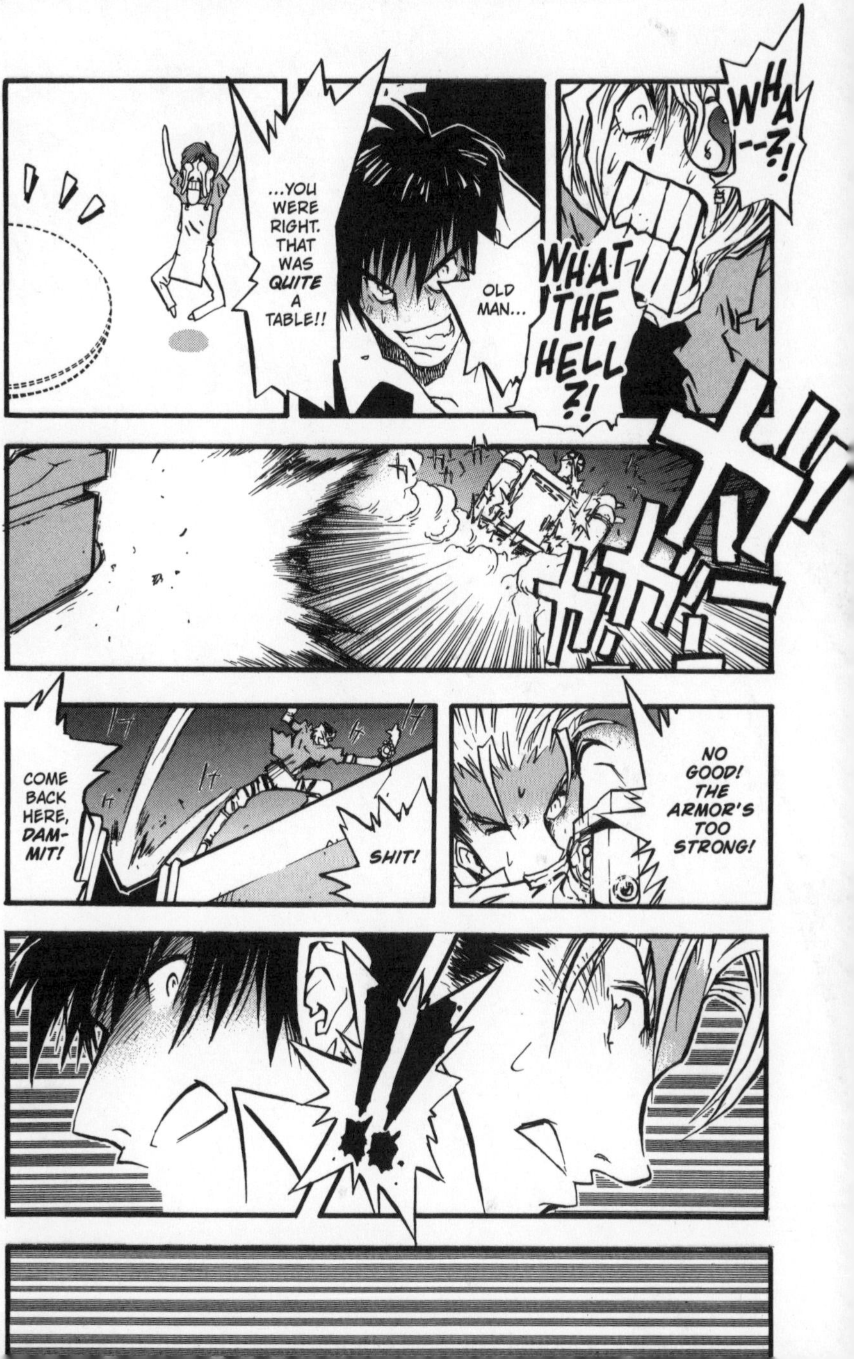
WHA--?!
WHAT THE HELL?!
OLD MAN...
...YOU WERE RIGHT. THAT WAS QUITE A TABLE!!
NO GOOD! THE ARMOR'S TOO STRONG!
SHIT!
COME BACK HERE, DAM-MIT!

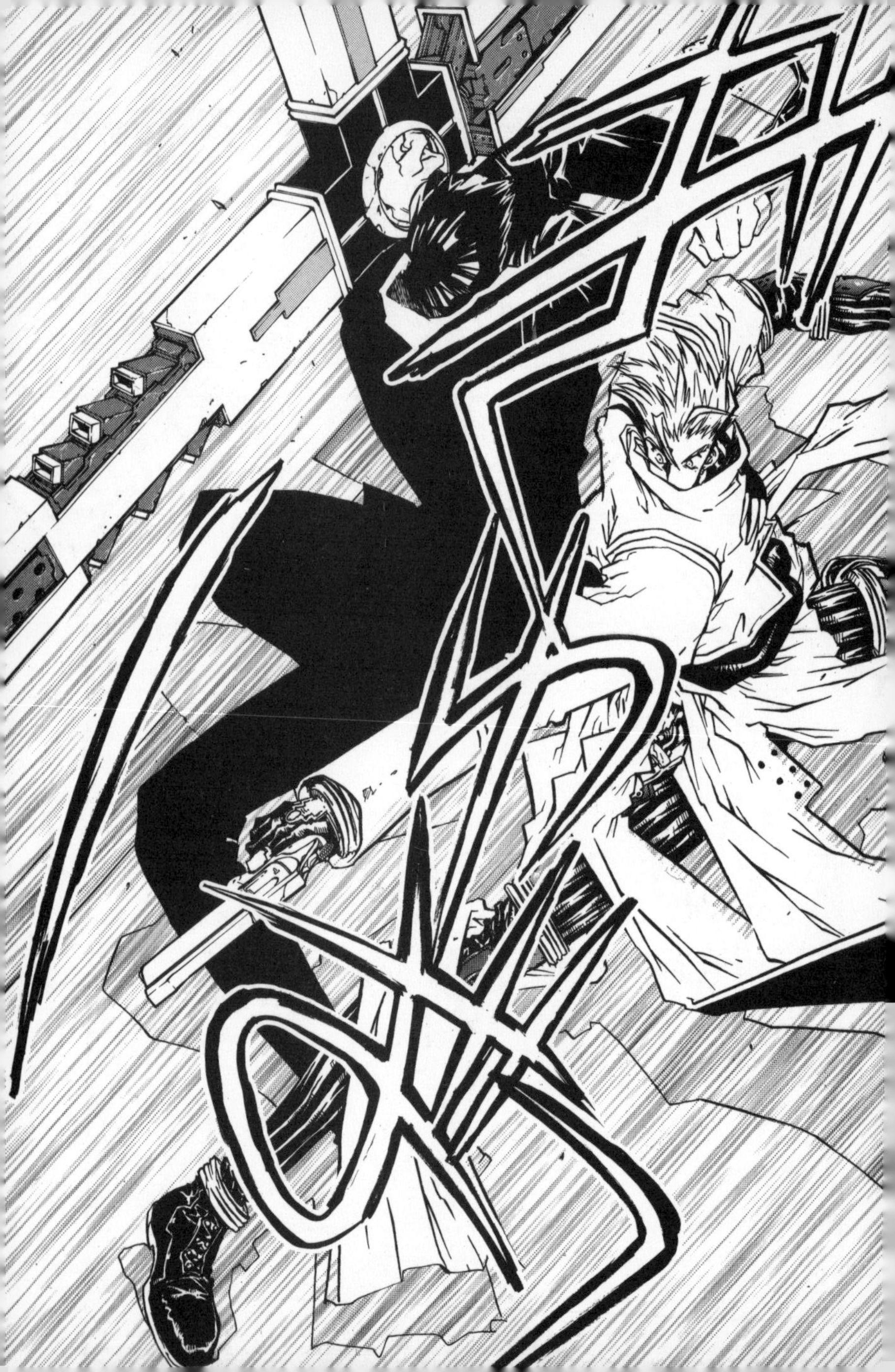

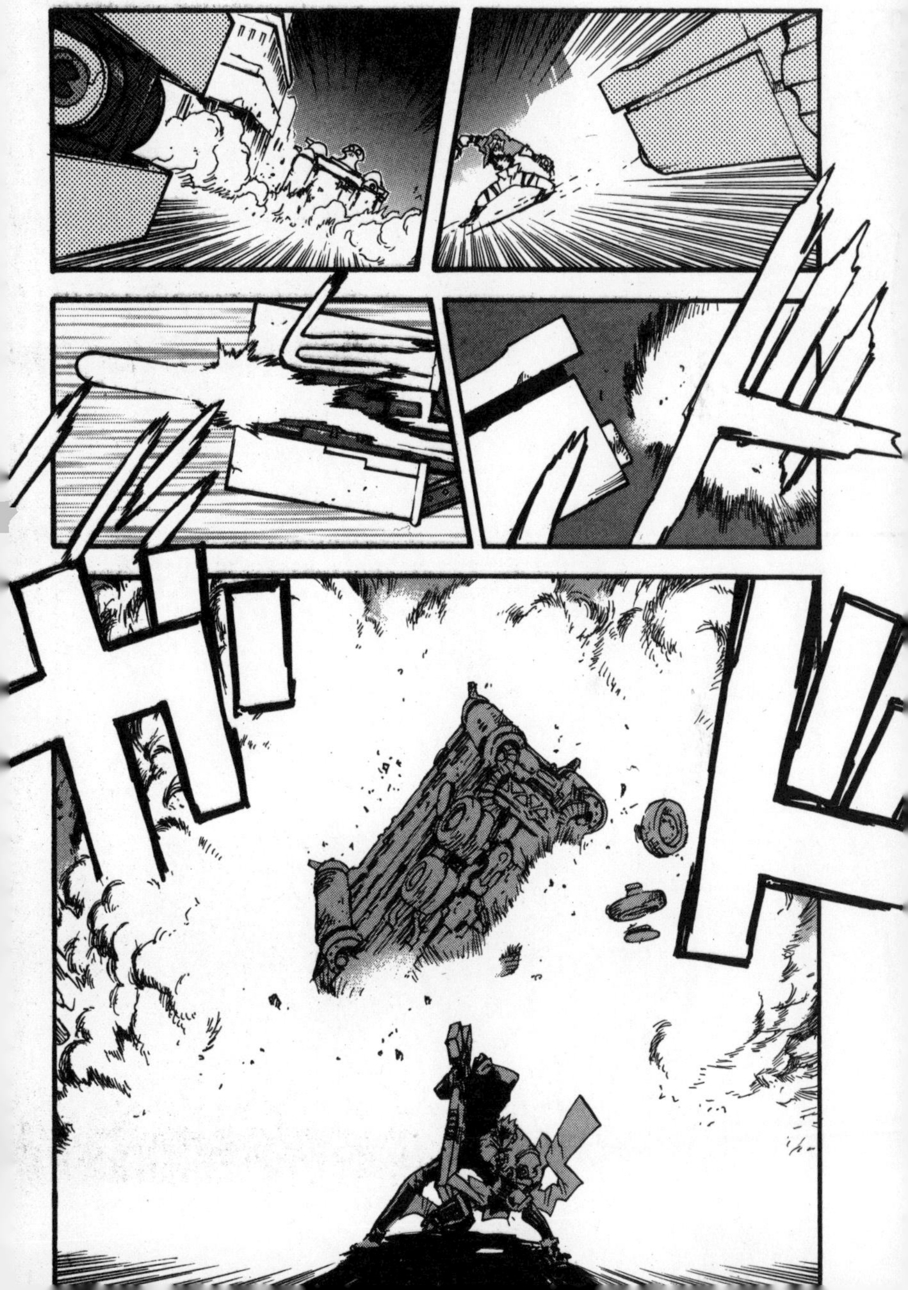

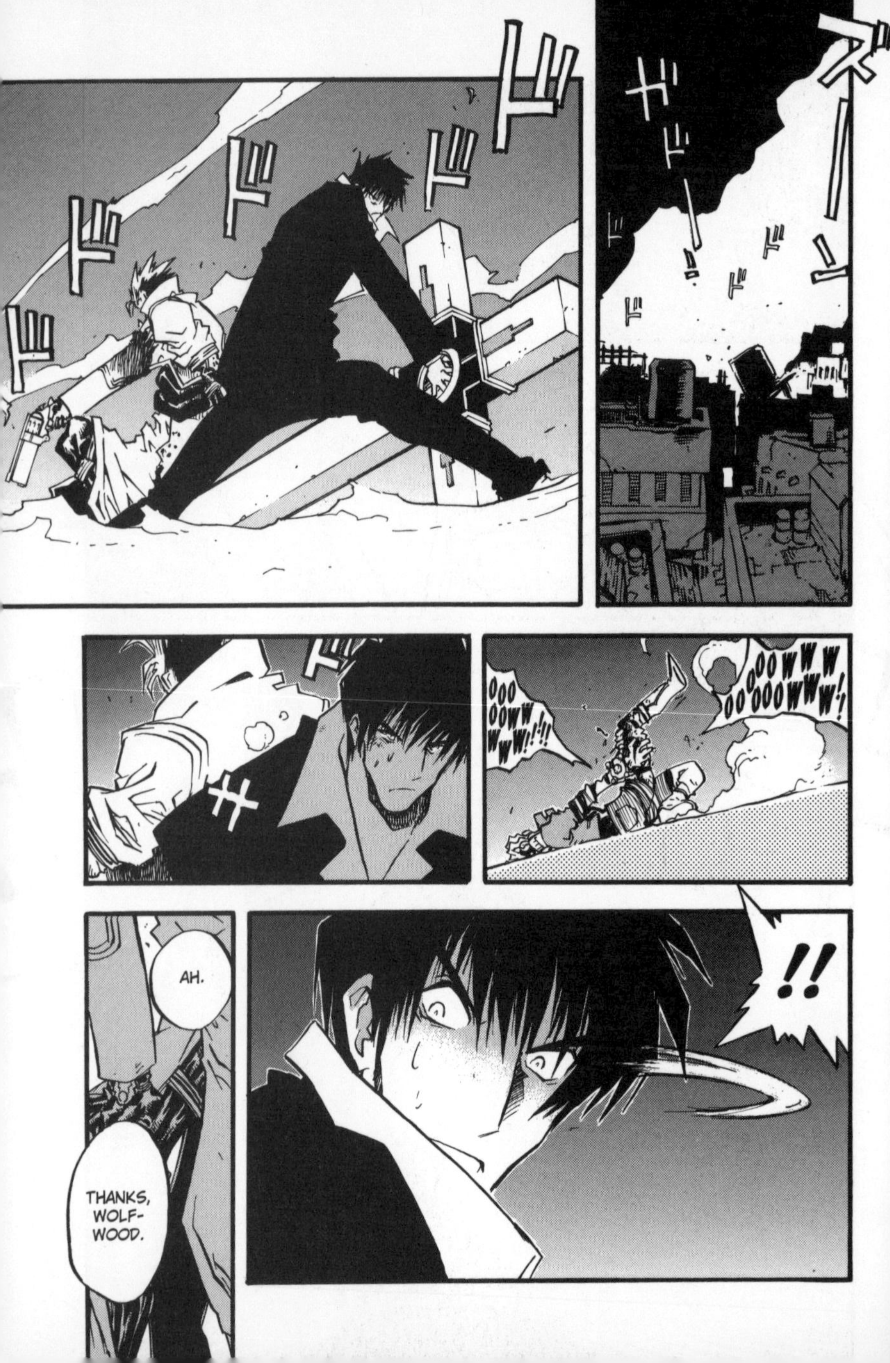
ズドーン
ガドー!!
ドドドド
ドドドドドド
OOOOWWW OOOOOWWW!!
OOOOWWWWW!!!!
!!
AH.
THANKS, WOLF-WOOD.

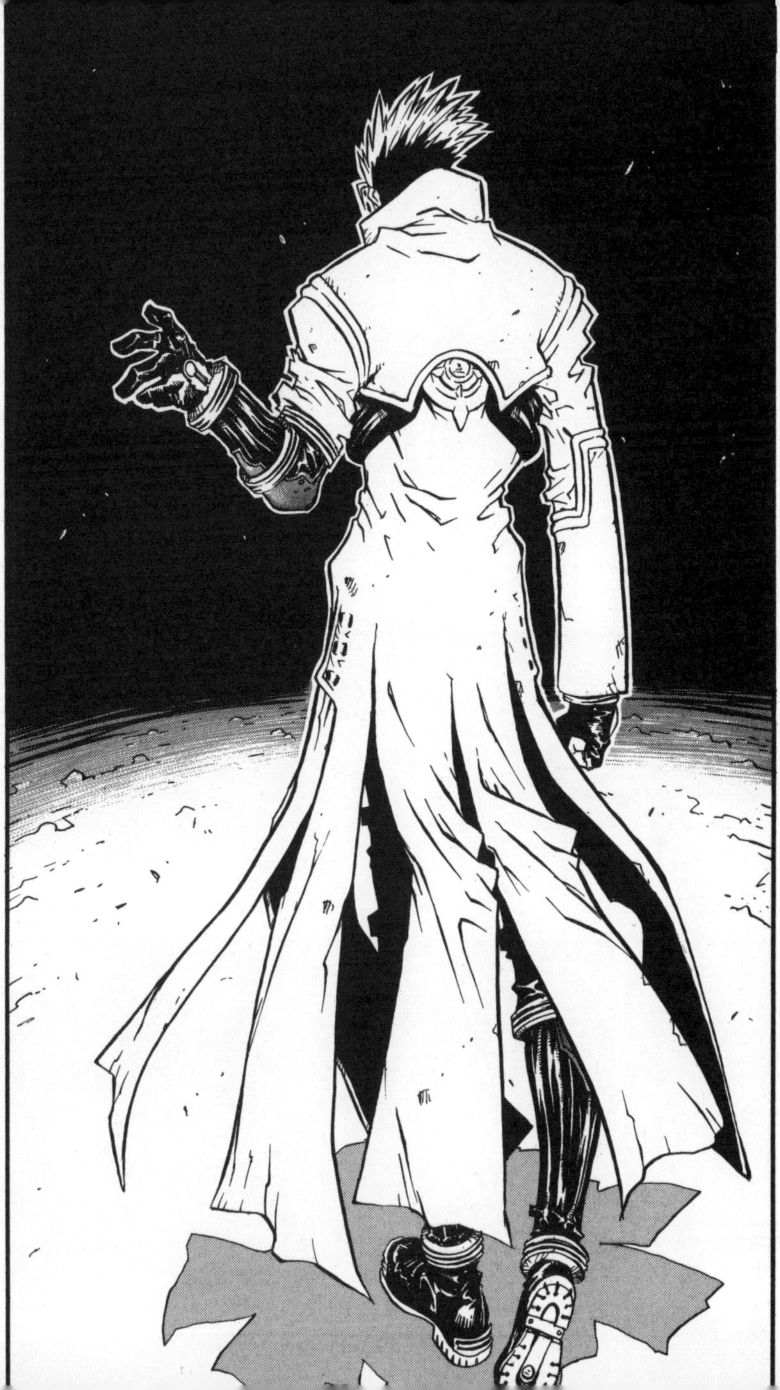

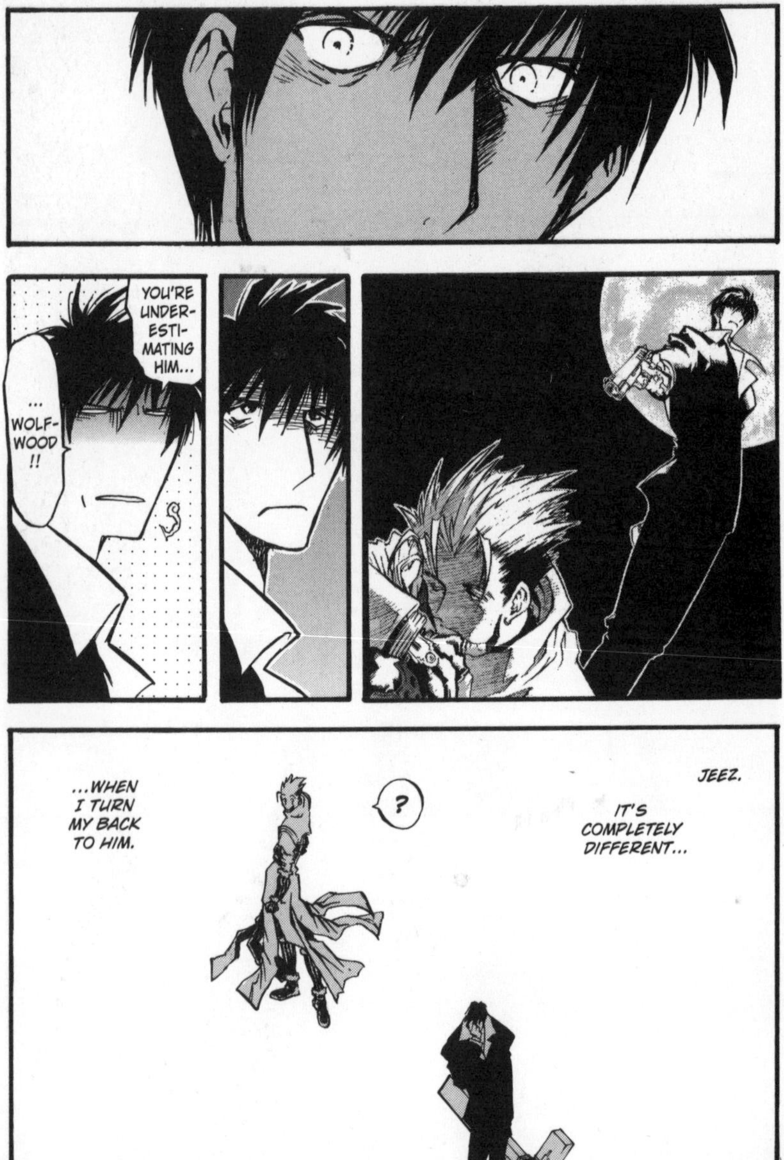
YOU'RE UNDER-ESTI-MATING HIM...
...WOLF-WOOD!!
JEEZ.
IT'S COMPLETELY DIFFERENT...
?
...WHEN I TURN MY BACK TO HIM.

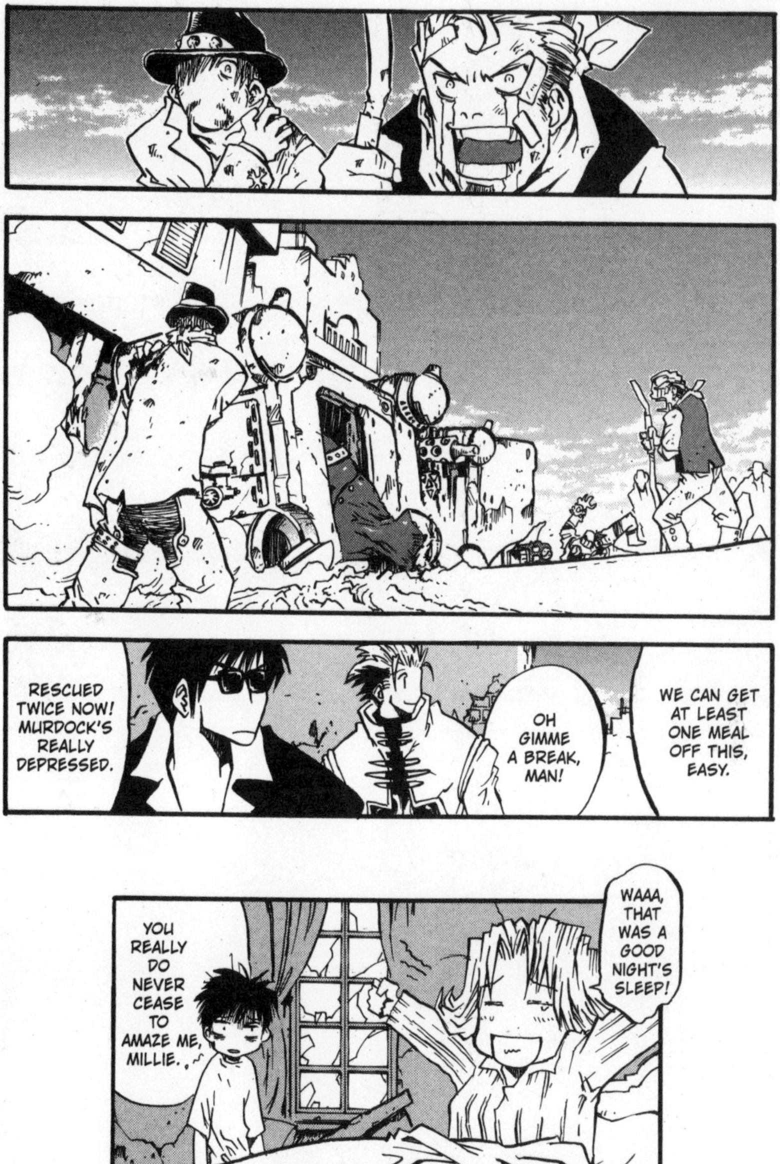
WE CAN GET AT LEAST ONE MEAL OFF THIS, EASY.
OH GIMME A BREAK, MAN!
RESCUED TWICE NOW! MURDOCK'S REALLY DEPRESSED.
WAAA, THAT WAS A GOOD NIGHT'S SLEEP!
YOU REALLY DO NEVER CEASE TO AMAZE ME, MILLIE.

#2. double team / END

TRIGUN MAXIMUM

YASUHIRO NIGHTOW

DEEP SPACE PLANET FUTURE GUN ACTION!!

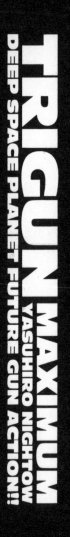

#3. CROSS X ASSASSINS

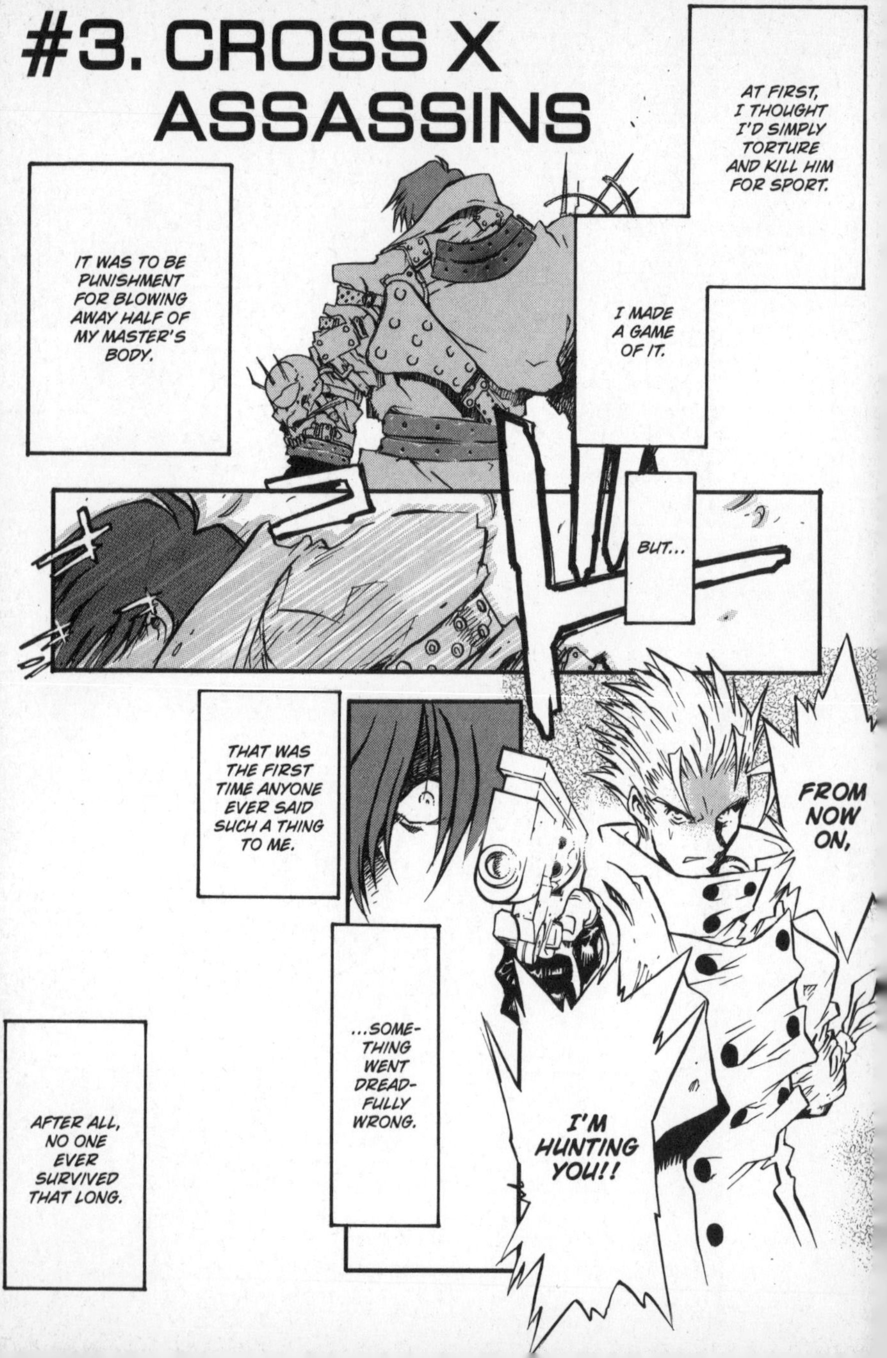
AT FIRST, I THOUGHT I'D SIMPLY TORTURE AND KILL HIM FOR SPORT.
I MADE A GAME OF IT.
IT WAS TO BE PUNISHMENT FOR BLOWING AWAY HALF OF MY MASTER'S BODY.
BUT...
FROM NOW ON,
I'M HUNTING YOU!!
THAT WAS THE FIRST TIME ANYONE EVER SAID SUCH A THING TO ME.
...SOME-THING WENT DREAD-FULLY WRONG.
AFTER ALL, NO ONE EVER SURVIVED THAT LONG.

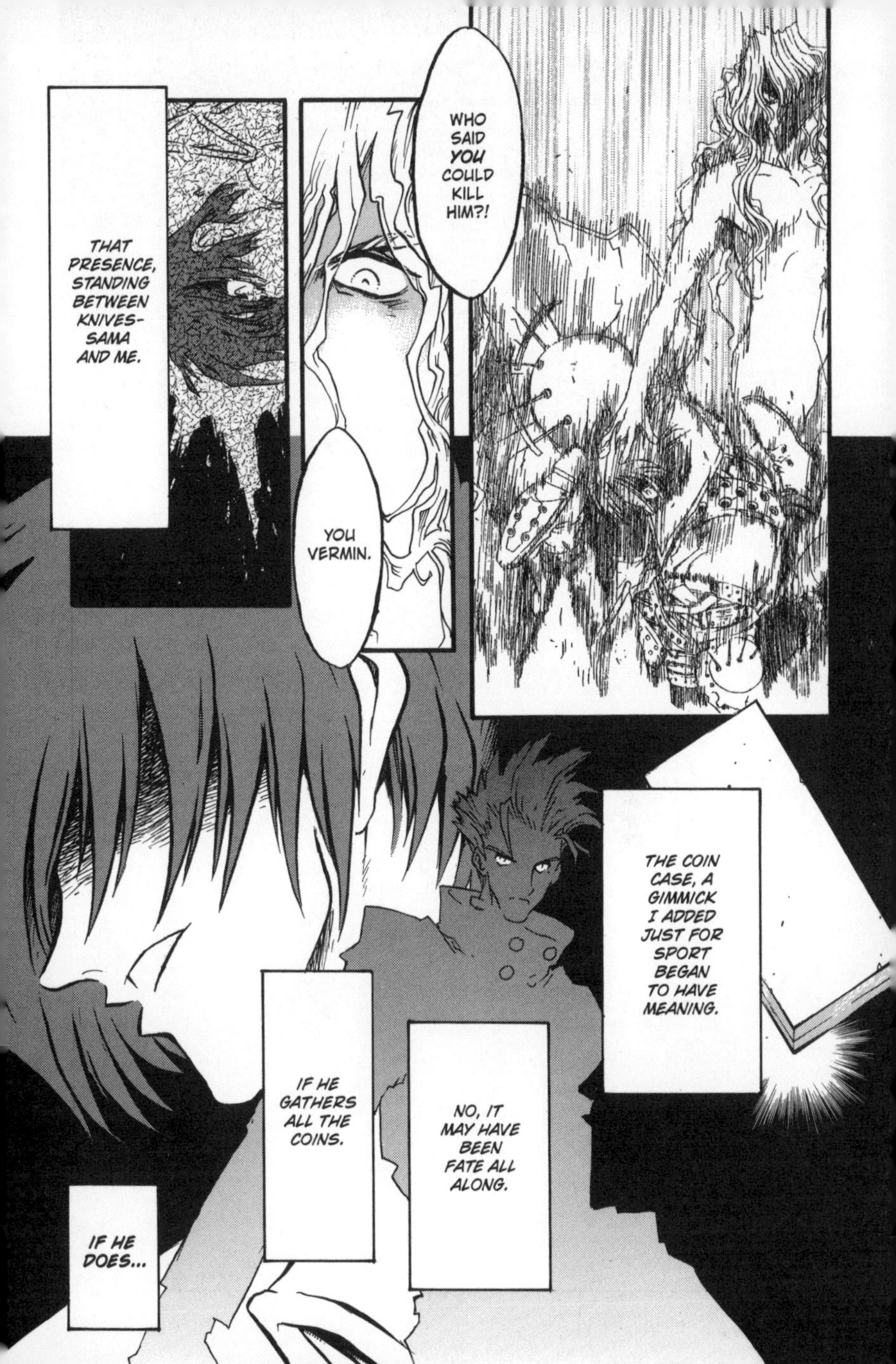
WHO SAID *YOU* COULD KILL HIM?!
YOU VERMIN.
THAT PRESENCE, STANDING BETWEEN KNIVES-SAMA AND ME.
THE COIN CASE, A GIMMICK I ADDED JUST FOR SPORT BEGAN TO HAVE MEANING.
NO, IT MAY HAVE BEEN FATE ALL ALONG.
IF HE GATHERS ALL THE COINS.
IF HE DOES...

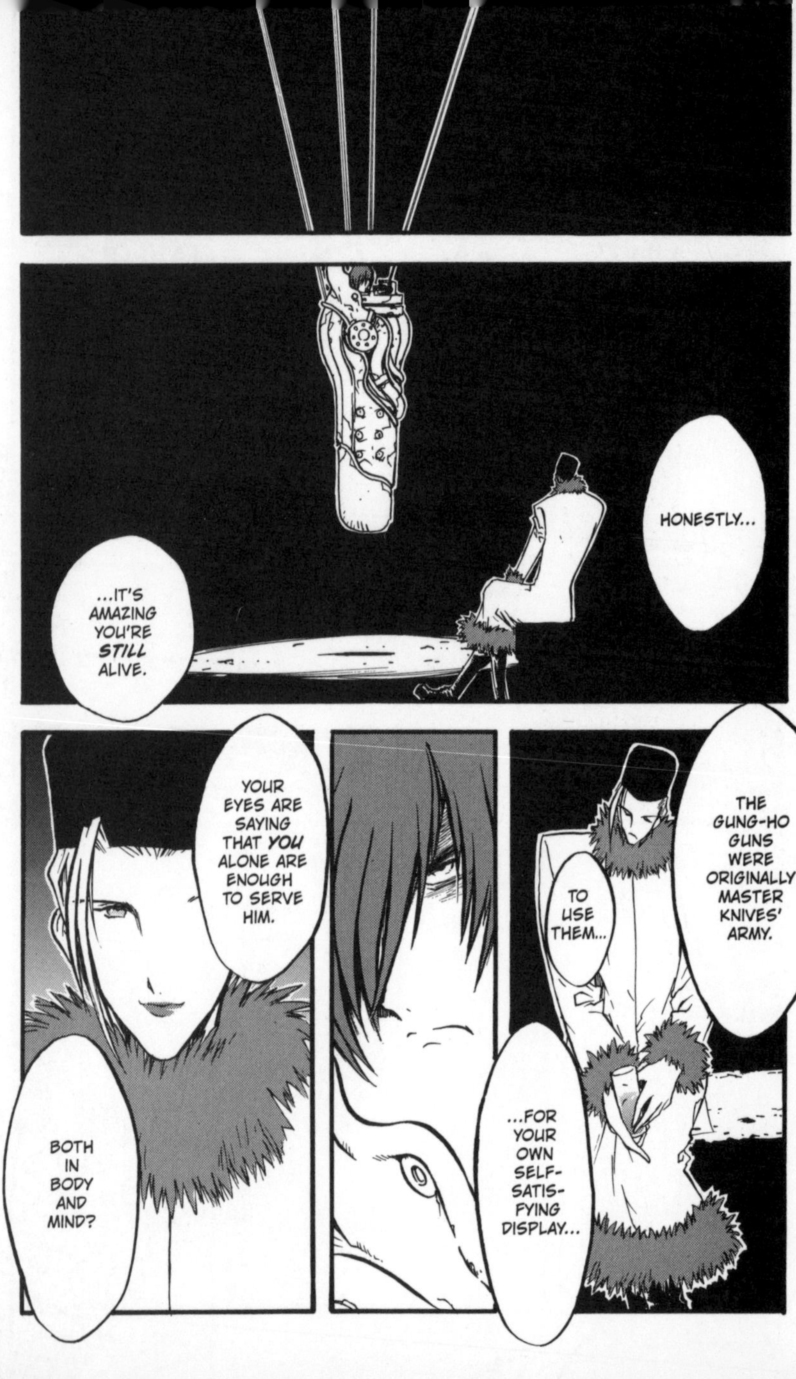
HONESTLY...
...IT'S AMAZING YOU'RE *STILL* ALIVE.
THE GUNG-HO GUNS WERE ORIGINALLY MASTER KNIVES' ARMY.
TO USE THEM...
...FOR YOUR OWN SELF-SATISFYING DISPLAY...
YOUR EYES ARE SAYING THAT *YOU* ALONE ARE ENOUGH TO SERVE HIM.
BOTH IN BODY AND MIND?

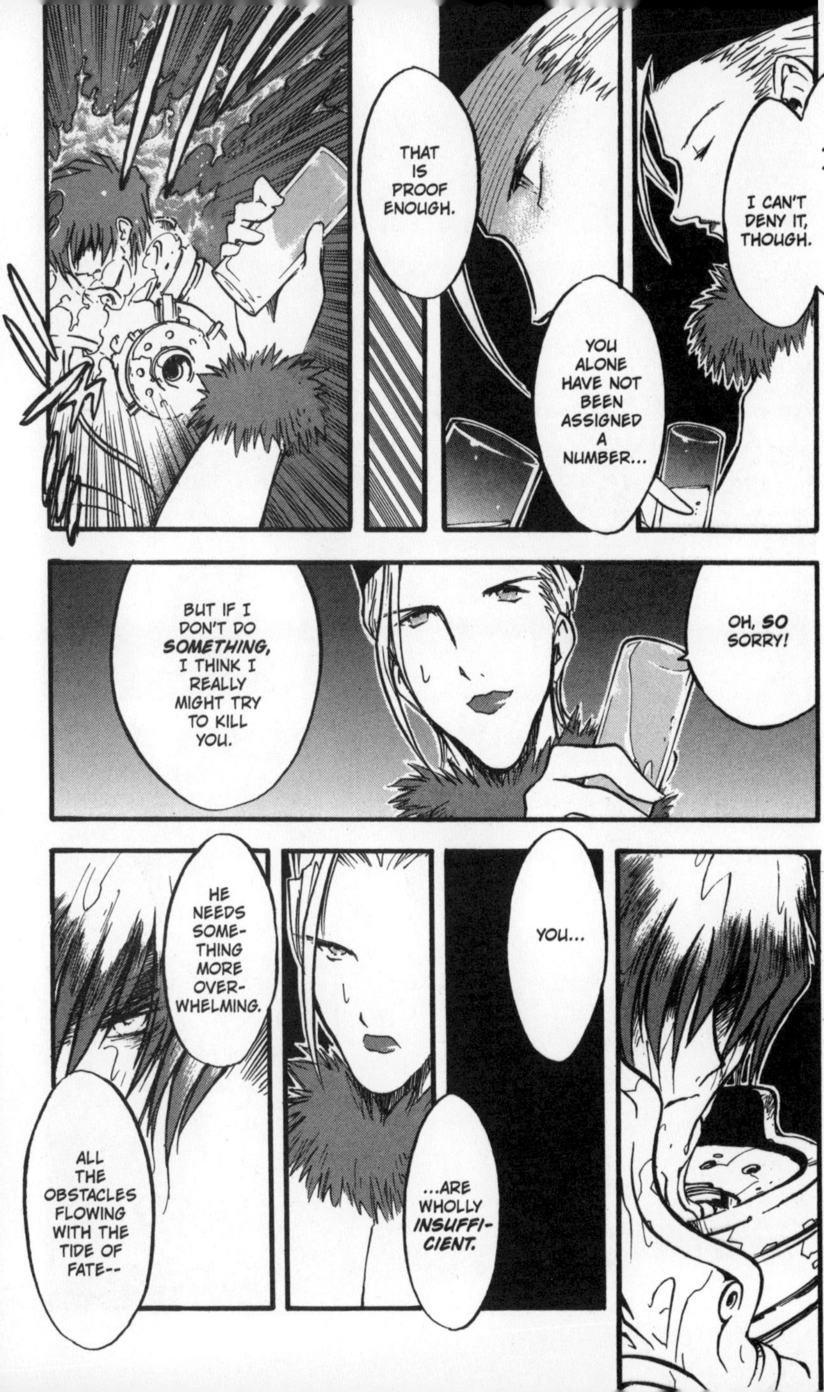

... ...
I CAN'T DENY IT, THOUGH.
THAT IS PROOF ENOUGH.
YOU ALONE HAVE NOT BEEN ASSIGNED A NUMBER...
OH, SO SORRY!
BUT IF I DON'T DO *SOMETHING,* I THINK I REALLY MIGHT TRY TO KILL YOU.
YOU...
...ARE WHOLLY *INSUFFICIENT.*
HE NEEDS SOME-THING MORE OVER-WHELMING.
ALL THE OBSTACLES FLOWING WITH THE TIDE OF FATE--

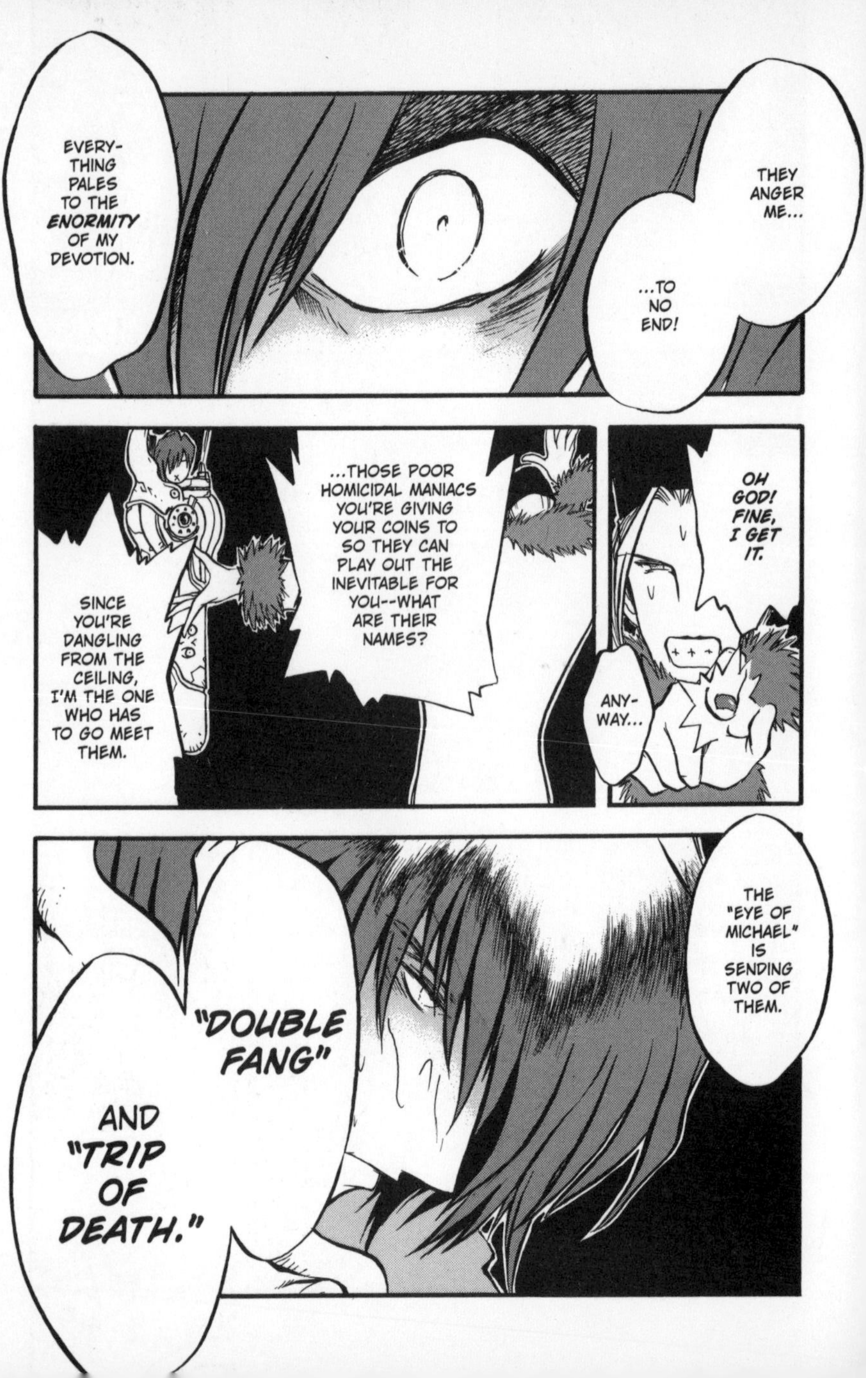
THEY ANGER ME...
...TO NO END!
EVERYTHING PALES TO THE *ENORMITY* OF MY DEVOTION.
OH GOD! FINE, I GET IT.
ANYWAY...
...THOSE POOR HOMICIDAL MANIACS YOU'RE GIVING YOUR COINS TO SO THEY CAN PLAY OUT THE INEVITABLE FOR YOU--WHAT ARE THEIR NAMES?
SINCE YOU'RE DANGLING FROM THE CEILING, I'M THE ONE WHO HAS TO GO MEET THEM.
THE "EYE OF MICHAEL" IS SENDING TWO OF THEM.
"*DOUBLE FANG*" AND "*TRIP OF DEATH*."

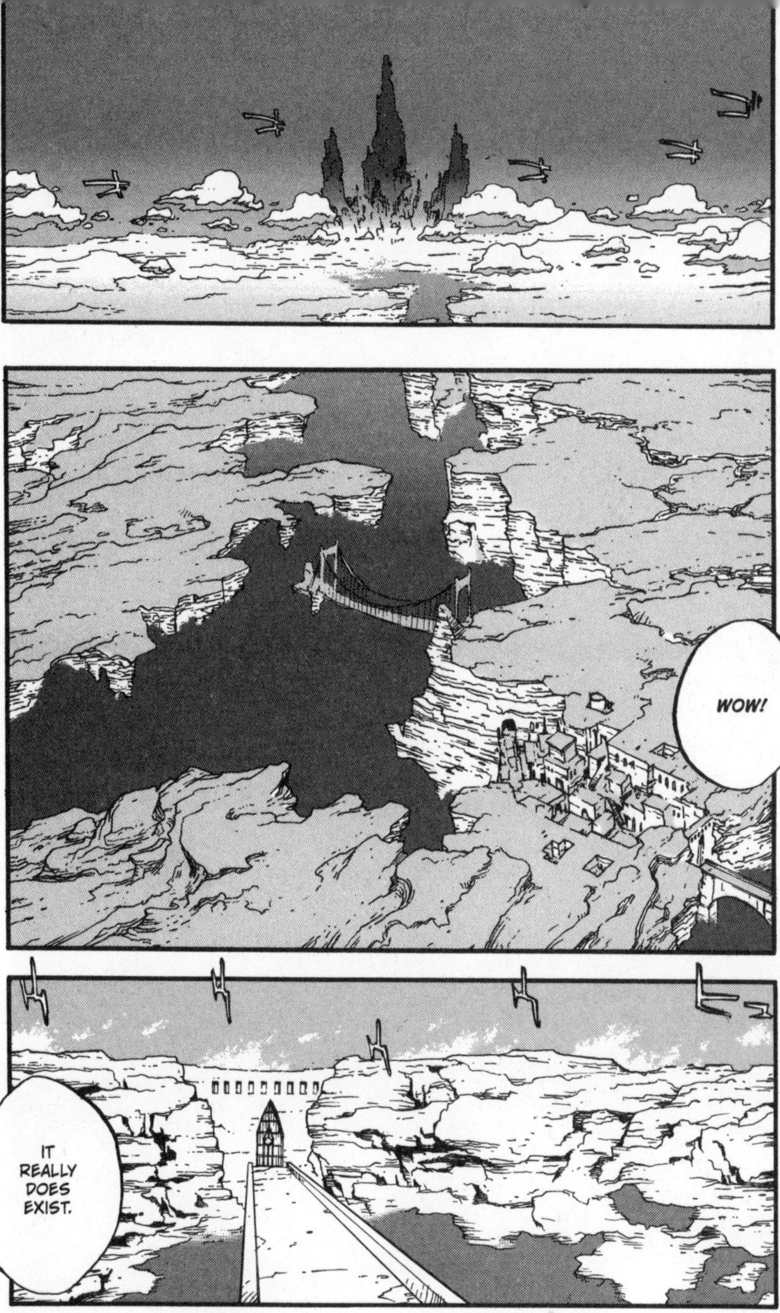
WOW!
IT REALLY DOES EXIST.

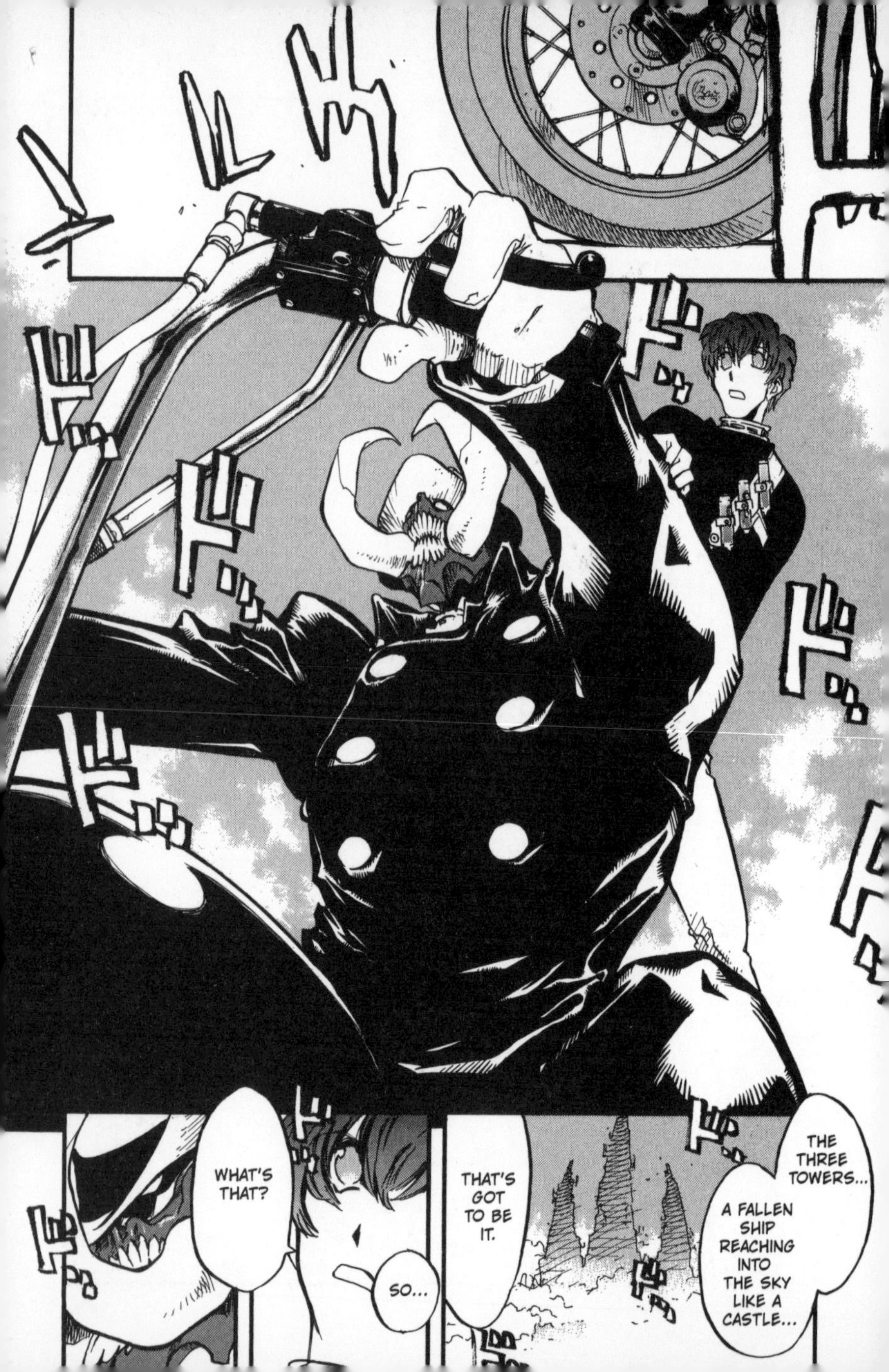
THE THREE TOWERS...
A FALLEN SHIP REACHING INTO THE SKY LIKE A CASTLE...
THAT'S GOT TO BE IT.
WHAT'S THAT?
SO...

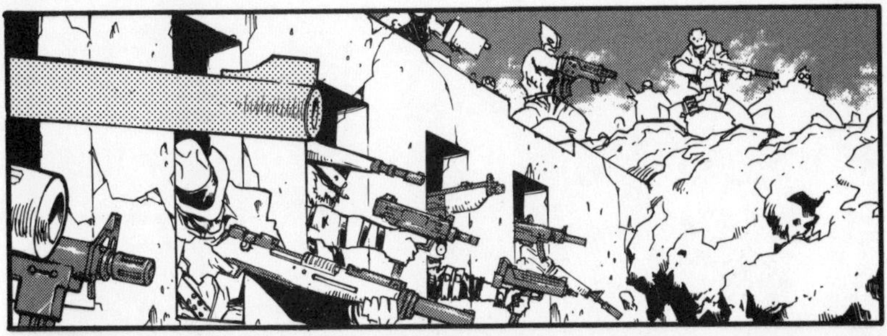

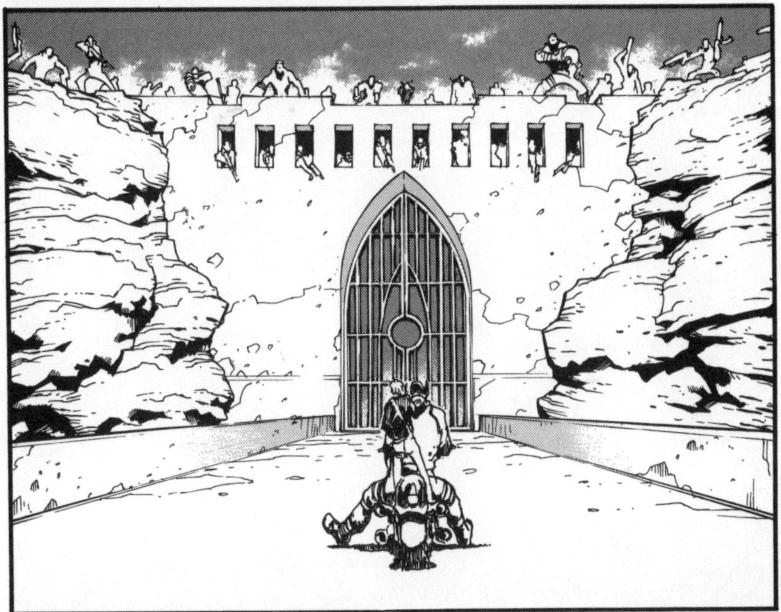

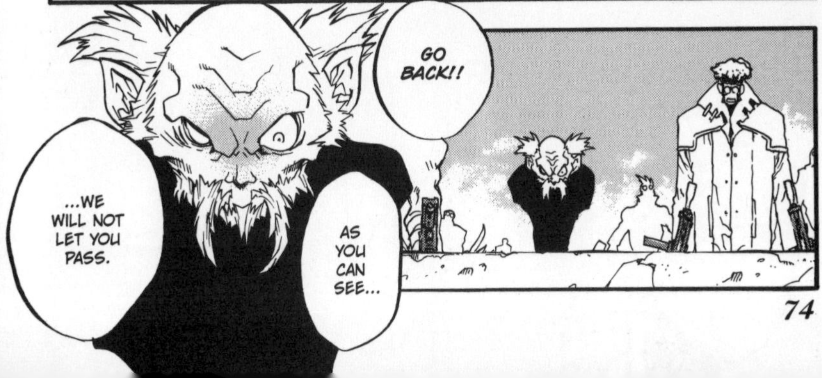
GO BACK!!
AS YOU CAN SEE...
...WE WILL NOT LET YOU PASS.

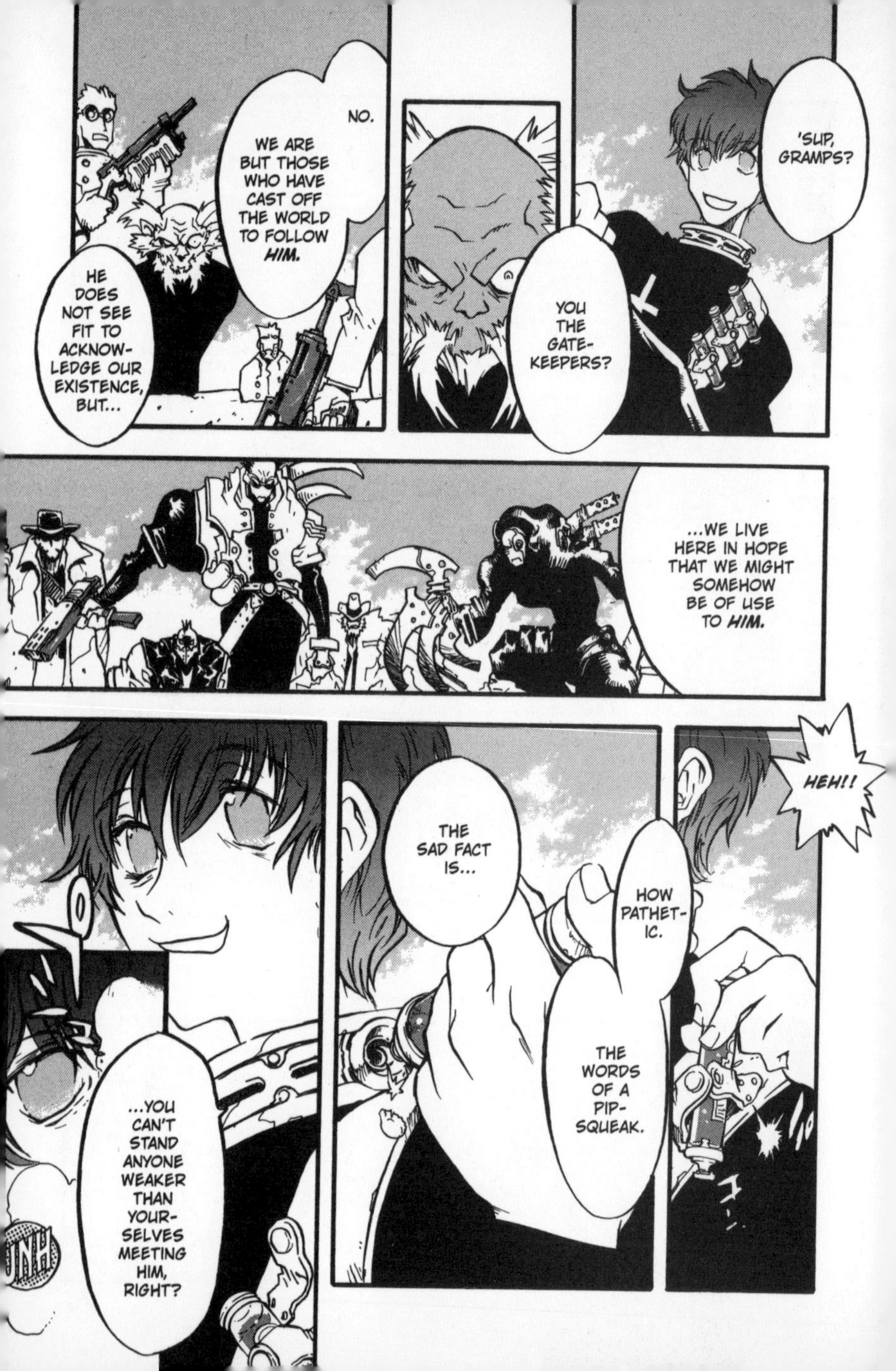

'SUP, GRAMPS?
YOU THE GATE-KEEPERS?
NO.
WE ARE BUT THOSE WHO HAVE CAST OFF THE WORLD TO FOLLOW *HIM.*
HE DOES NOT SEE FIT TO ACKNOWLEDGE OUR EXISTENCE, BUT...
...WE LIVE HERE IN HOPE THAT WE MIGHT SOMEHOW BE OF USE TO *HIM.*
HEH!!
HOW PATHETIC.
THE WORDS OF A PIPSQUEAK.
THE SAD FACT IS...
...YOU CAN'T STAND ANYONE WEAKER THAN YOURSELVES MEETING HIM, RIGHT?
UNH

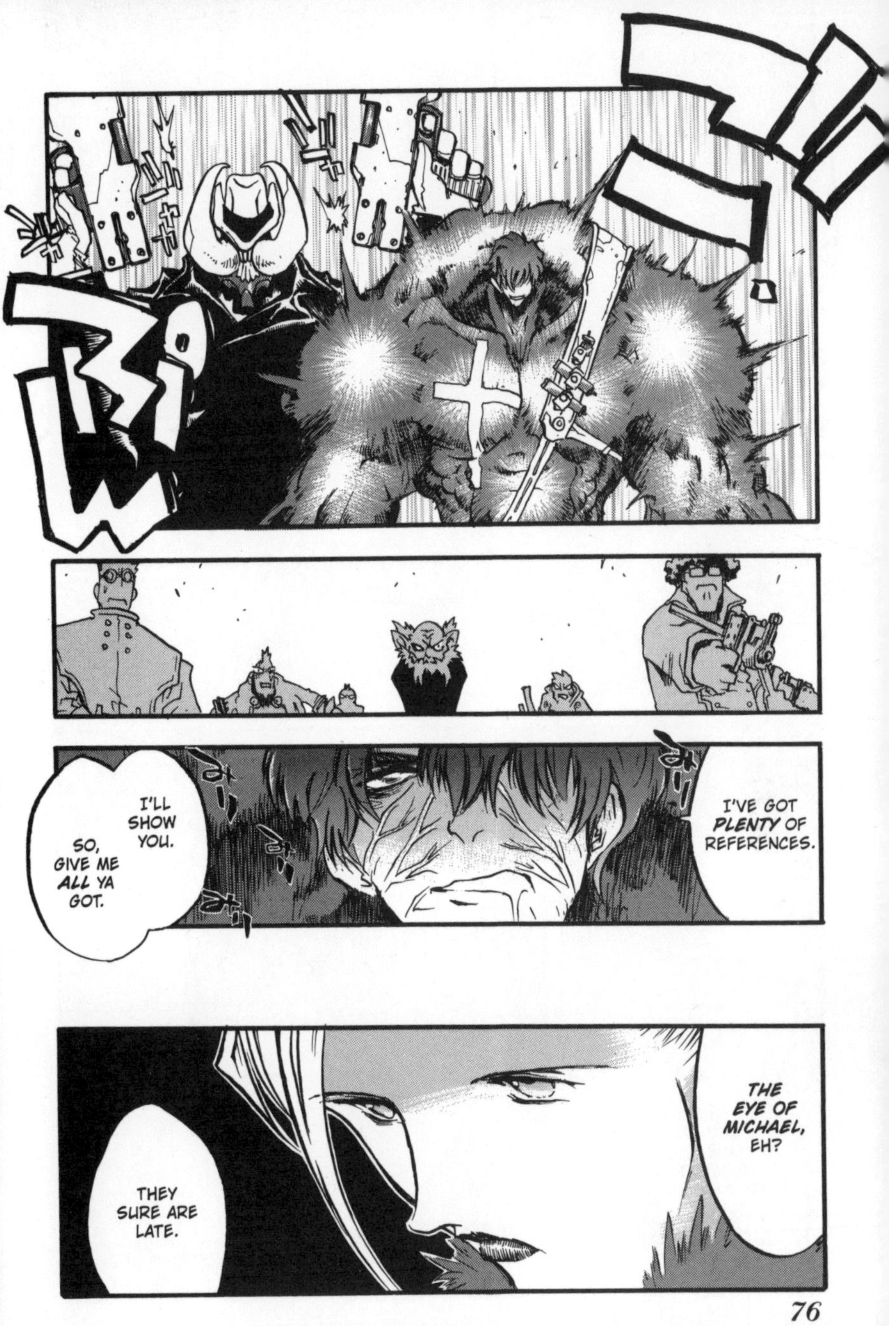
I'VE GOT PLENTY OF REFERENCES.
I'LL SHOW YOU.
SO, GIVE ME ALL YA GOT.
THE EYE OF MICHAEL, EH?
THEY SURE ARE LATE.

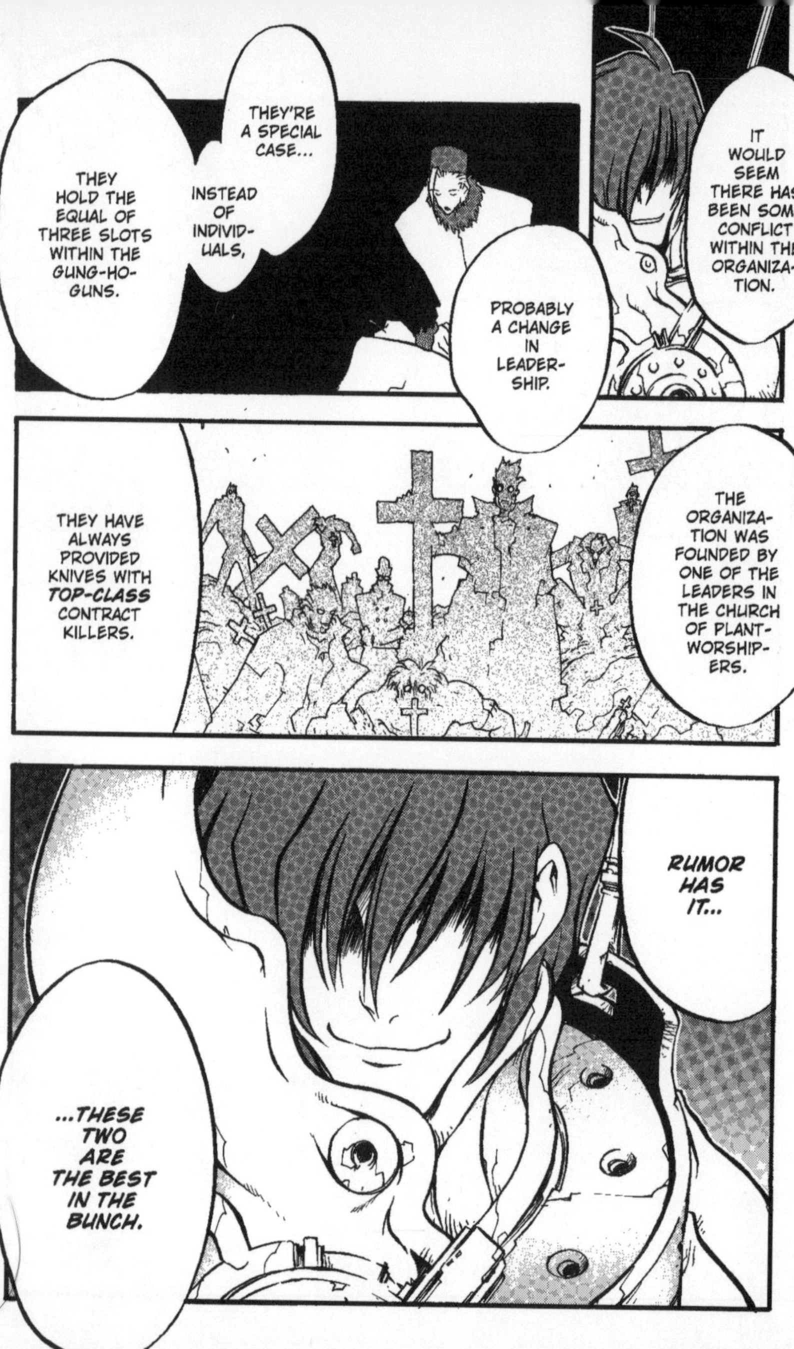
IT WOULD SEEM THERE HAS BEEN SOME CONFLICT WITHIN THE ORGANIZATION.
PROBABLY A CHANGE IN LEADERSHIP.
THEY'RE A SPECIAL CASE...
INSTEAD OF INDIVIDUALS,
THEY HOLD THE EQUAL OF THREE SLOTS WITHIN THE GUNG-HO-GUNS.
THE ORGANIZATION WAS FOUNDED BY ONE OF THE LEADERS IN THE CHURCH OF PLANT-WORSHIPERS.
THEY HAVE ALWAYS PROVIDED KNIVES WITH *TOP-CLASS* CONTRACT KILLERS.
RUMOR HAS IT...
...THESE TWO ARE THE BEST IN THE BUNCH.

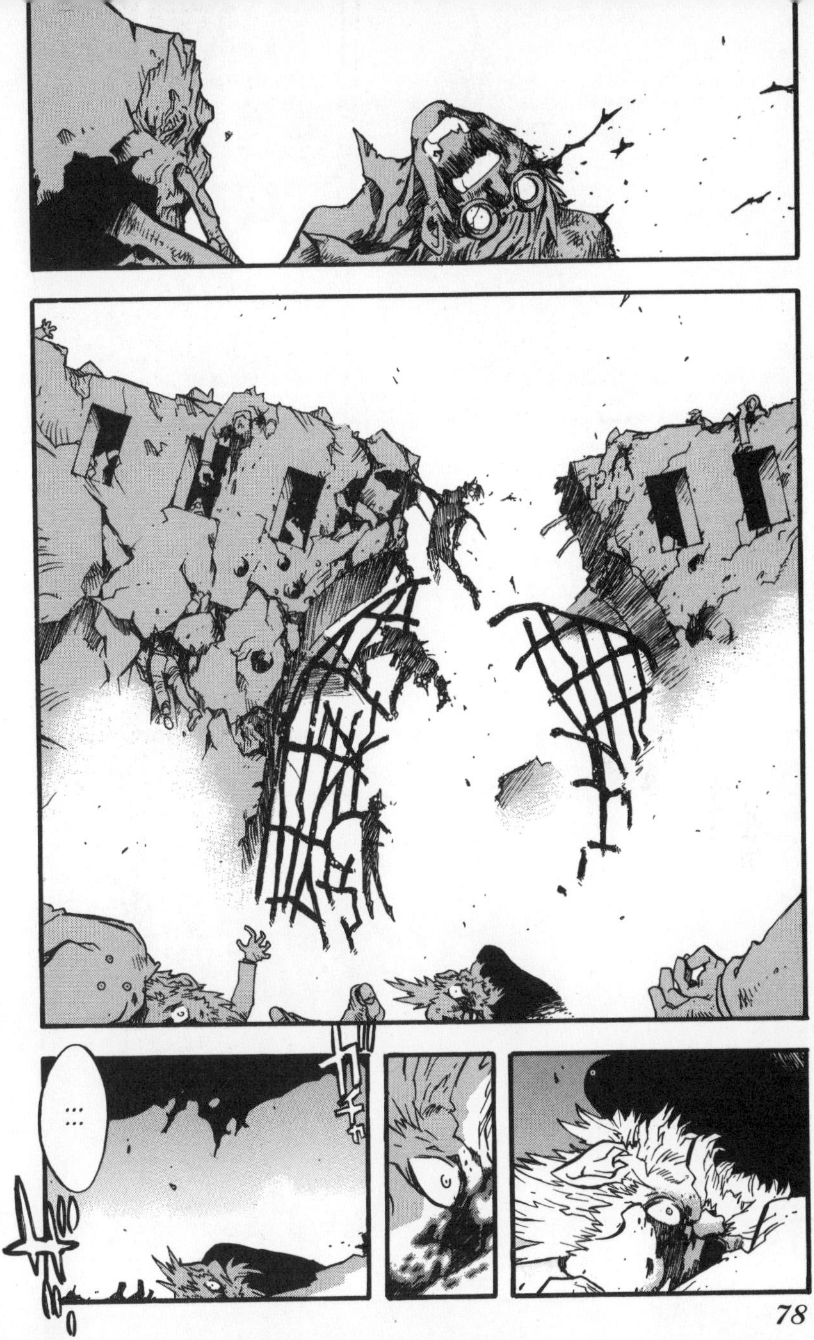
……

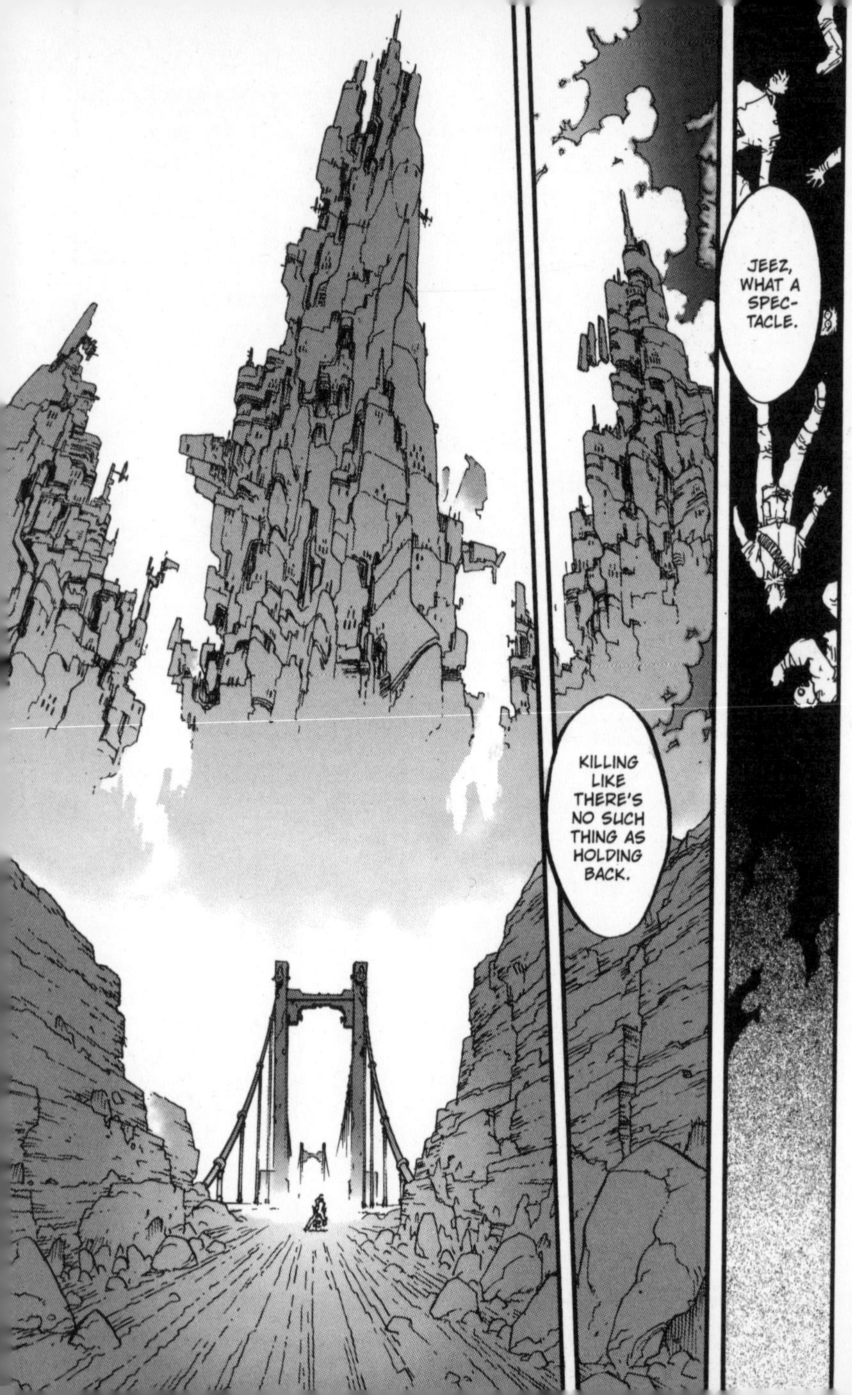
JEEZ, WHAT A SPEC- TACLE.
KILLING LIKE THERE'S NO SUCH THING AS HOLDING BACK.

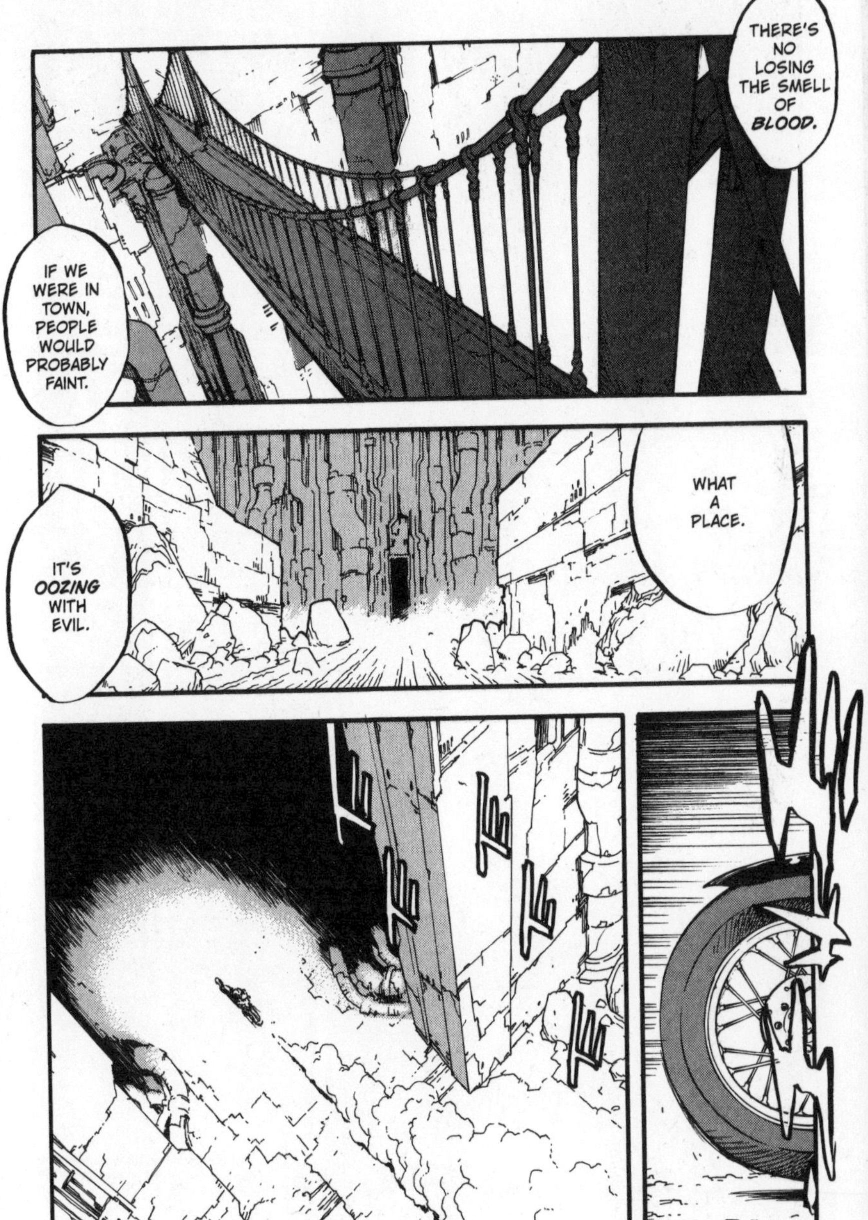
THERE'S NO LOSING THE SMELL OF *BLOOD.*
IF WE WERE IN TOWN, PEOPLE WOULD PROBABLY FAINT.
WHAT A PLACE.
IT'S *OOZING* WITH EVIL.

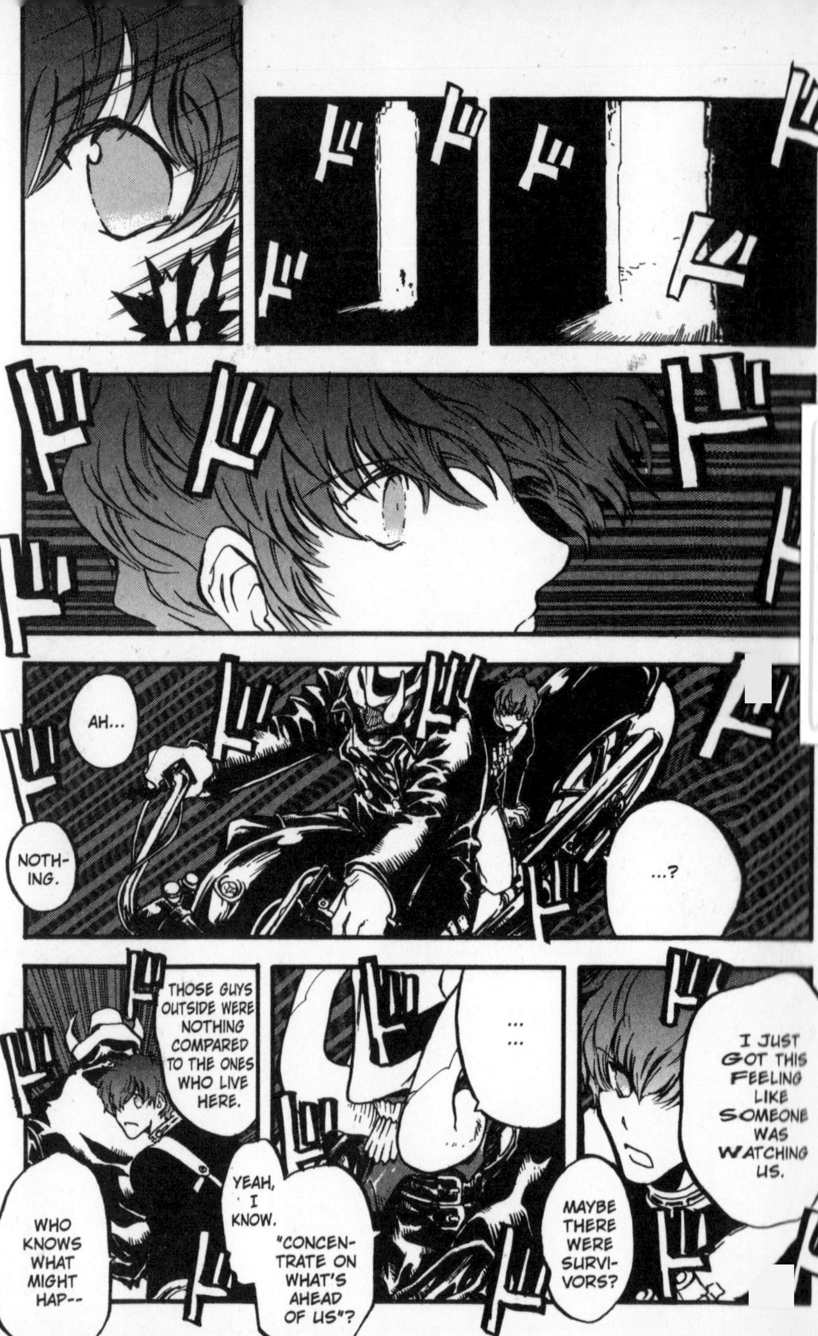
...?
AH...
NOTHING.
I JUST GOT THIS FEELING LIKE SOMEONE WAS WATCHING US.
MAYBE THERE WERE SURVIVORS?
... ...
YEAH, I KNOW.
"CONCENTRATE ON WHAT'S AHEAD OF US"?
THOSE GUYS OUTSIDE WERE NOTHING COMPARED TO THE ONES WHO LIVE HERE.
WHO KNOWS WHAT MIGHT HAP--

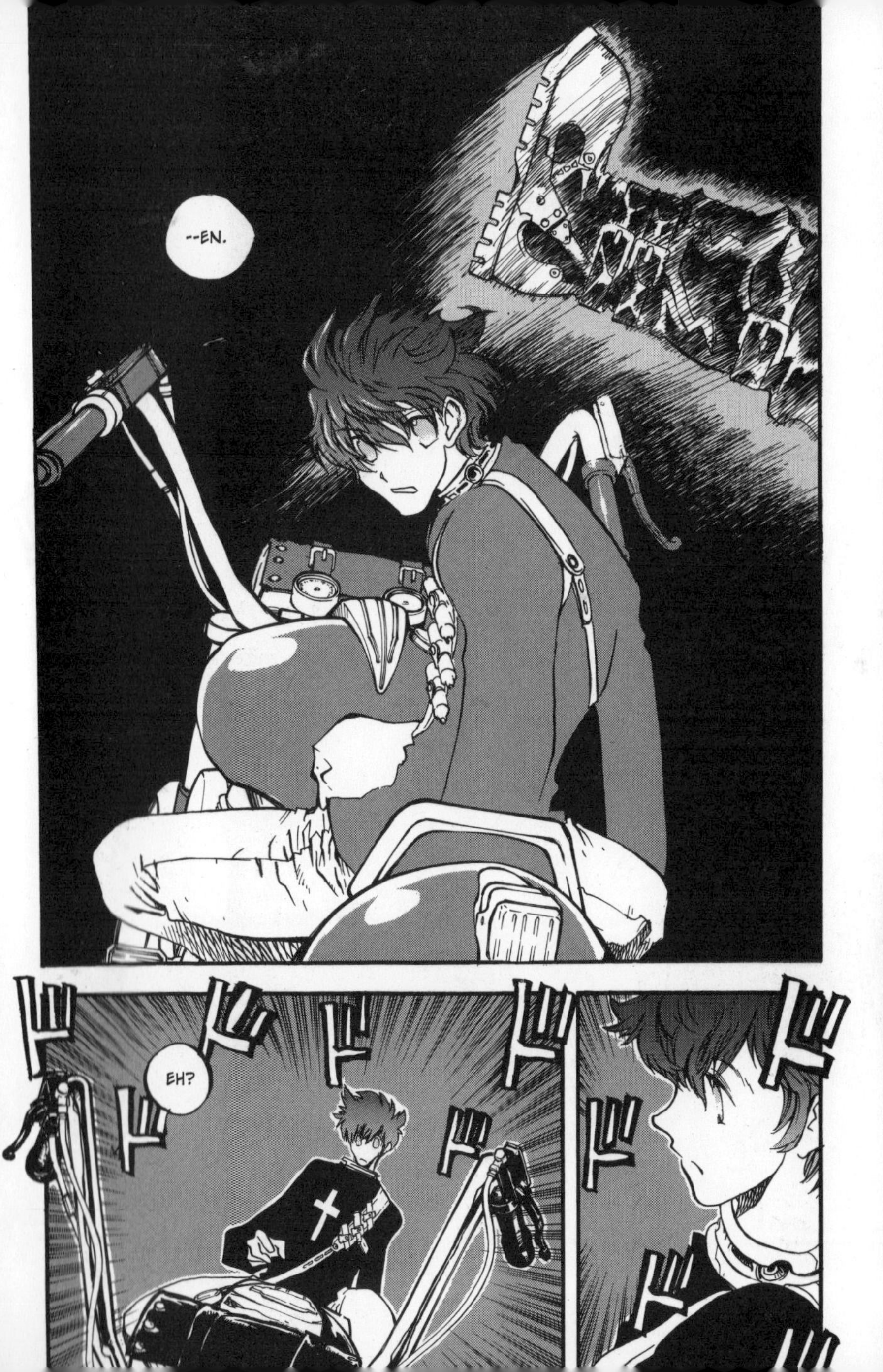
--EN.
EH?

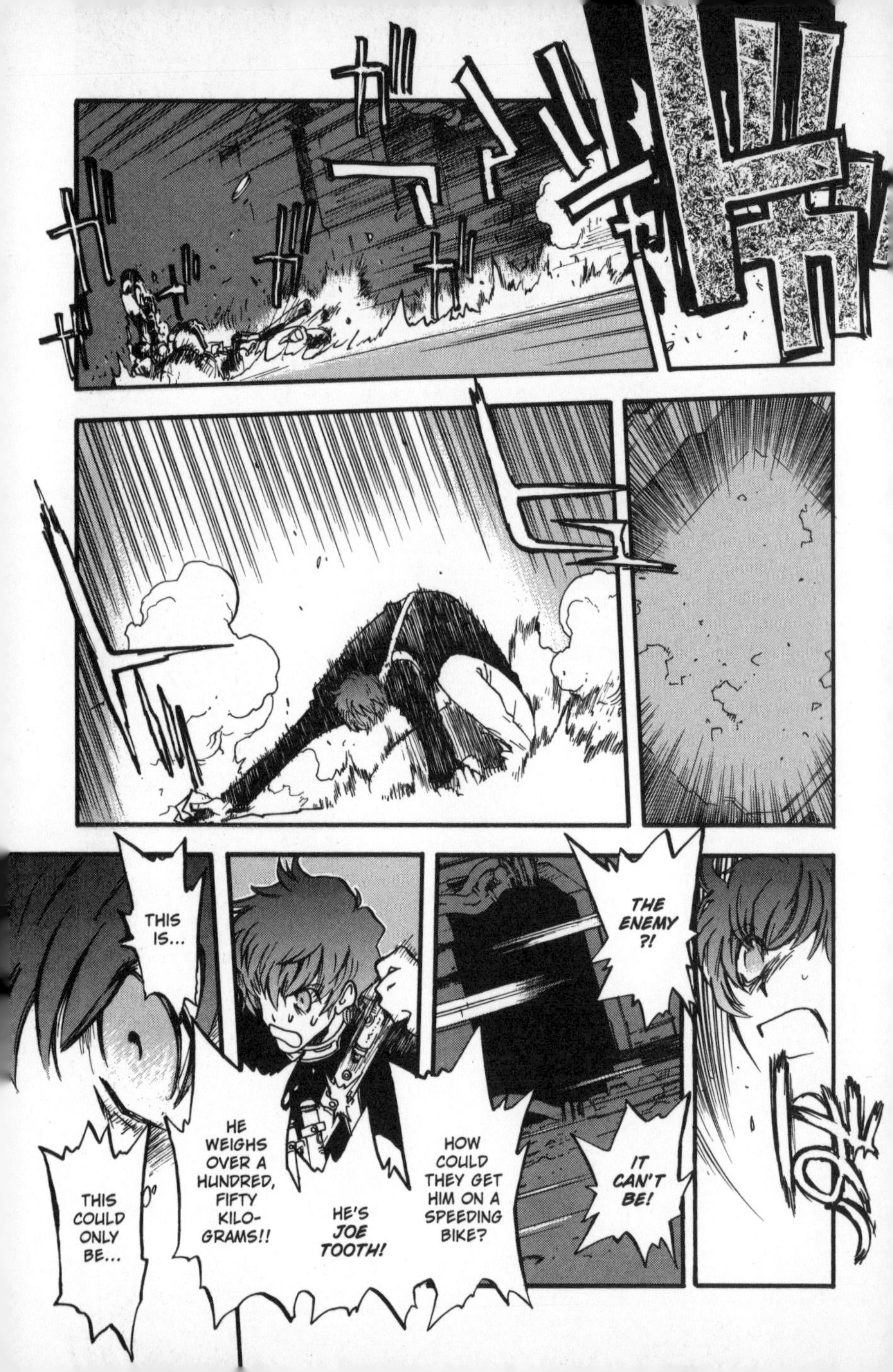
THE ENEMY ?!
IT CAN'T BE!
HOW COULD THEY GET HIM ON A SPEEDING BIKE?
HE'S JOE TOOTH!
HE WEIGHS OVER A HUNDRED, FIFTY KILO-GRAMS!!
THIS IS...
THIS COULD ONLY BE...

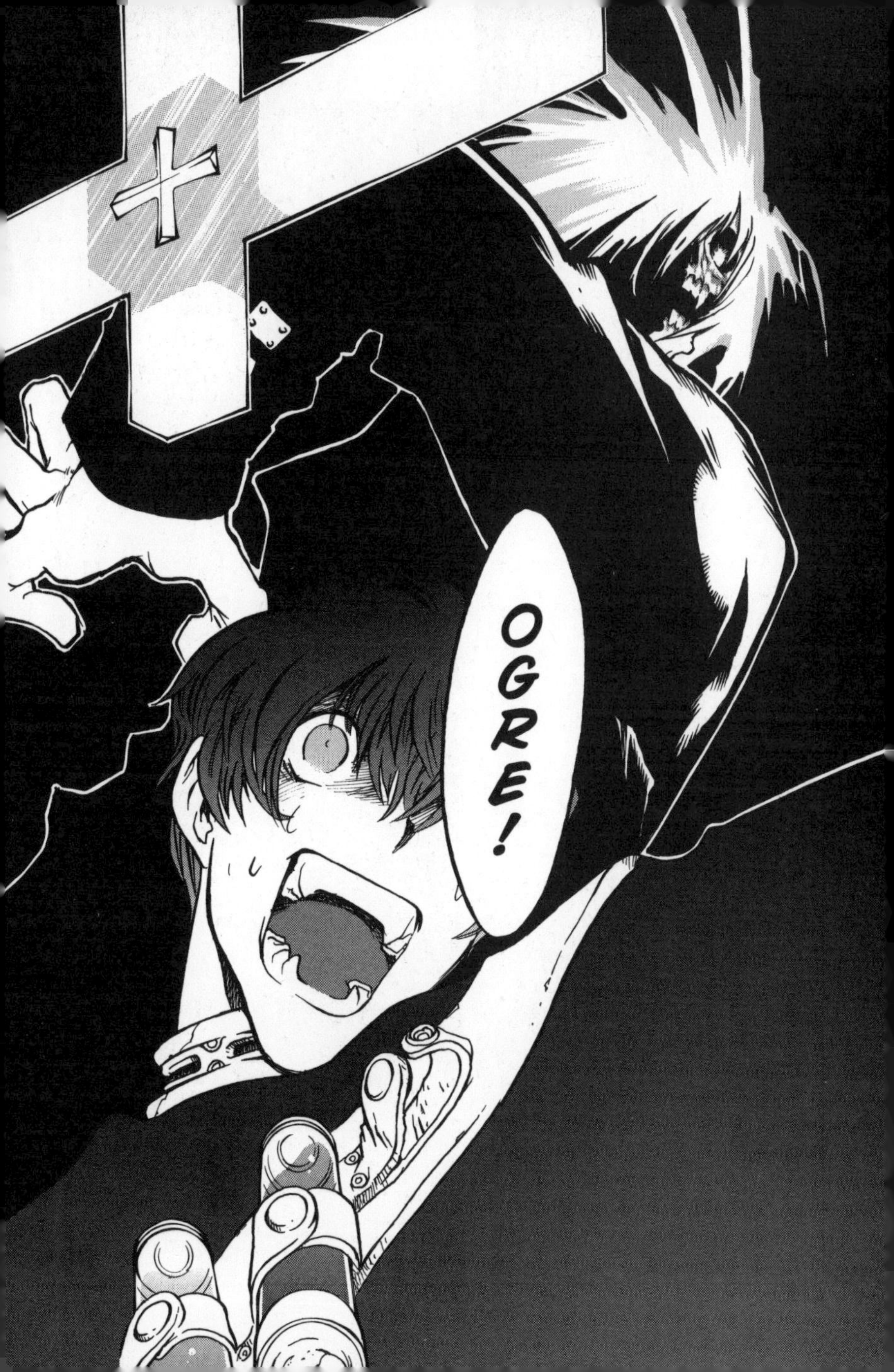
OGRE!

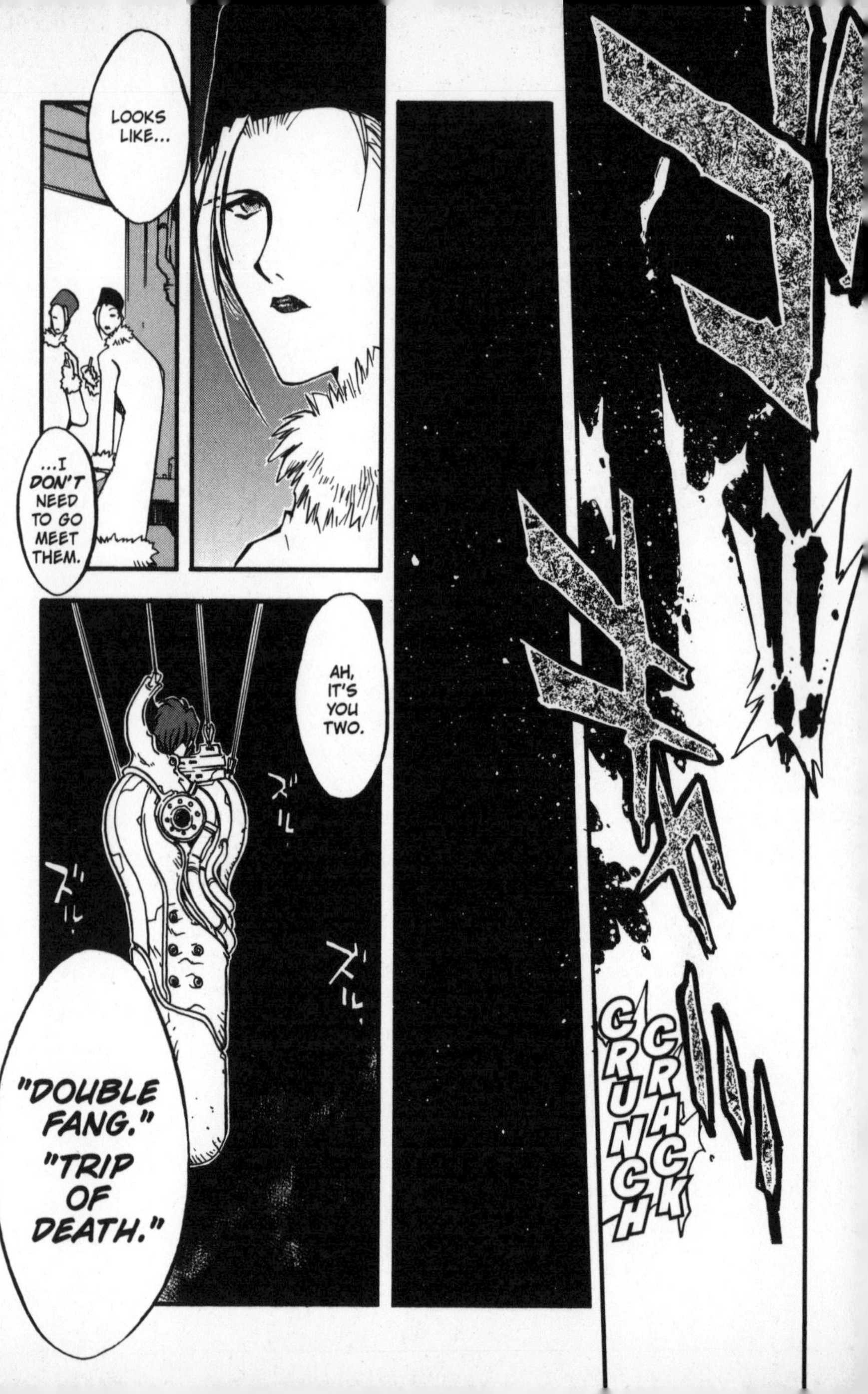
CRACK
CRUNCH
LOOKS LIKE...
...I DON'T NEED TO GO MEET THEM.
AH, IT'S YOU TWO.
ズル
ズル
ズル
"DOUBLE FANG." "TRIP OF DEATH."

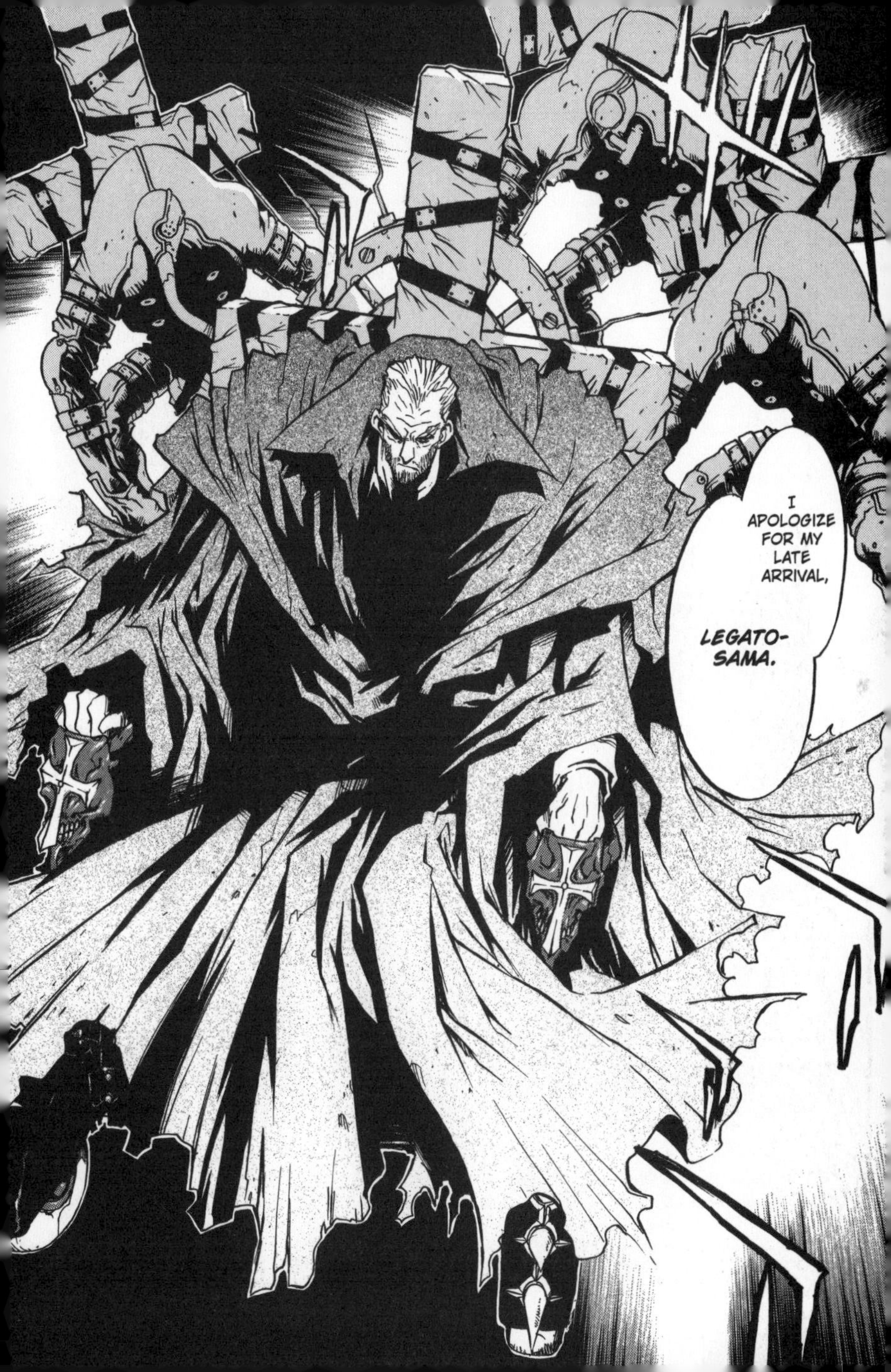
I APOLOGIZE FOR MY LATE ARRIVAL,
LEGATO-SAMA.

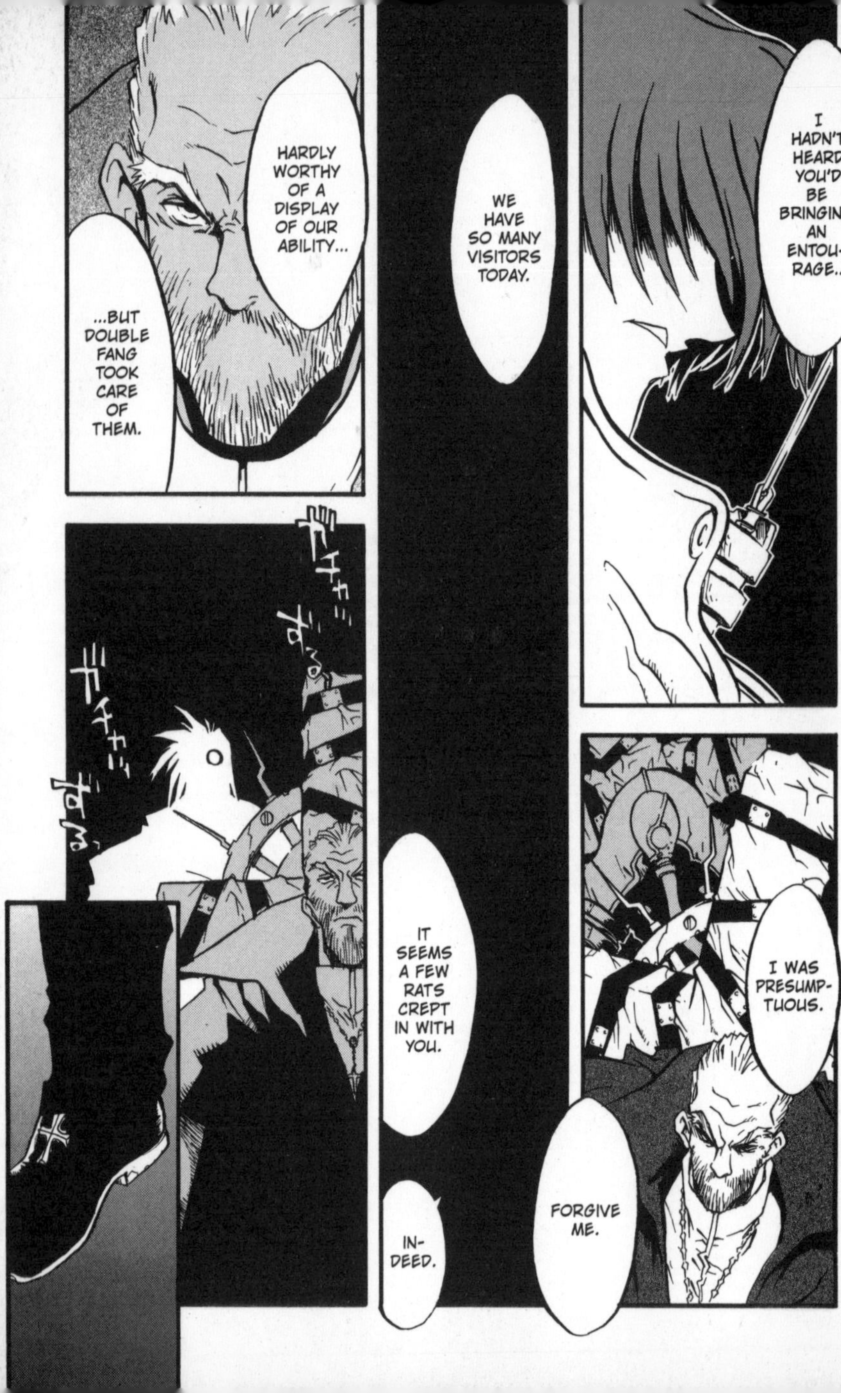
I HADN'T HEARD YOU'D BE BRINGING AN ENTOU-RAGE...
I WAS PRESUMP-TUOUS.
FORGIVE ME.
WE HAVE SO MANY VISITORS TODAY.
IT SEEMS A FEW RATS CREPT IN WITH YOU.
IN-DEED.
HARDLY WORTHY OF A DISPLAY OF OUR ABILITY...
...BUT DOUBLE FANG TOOK CARE OF THEM.

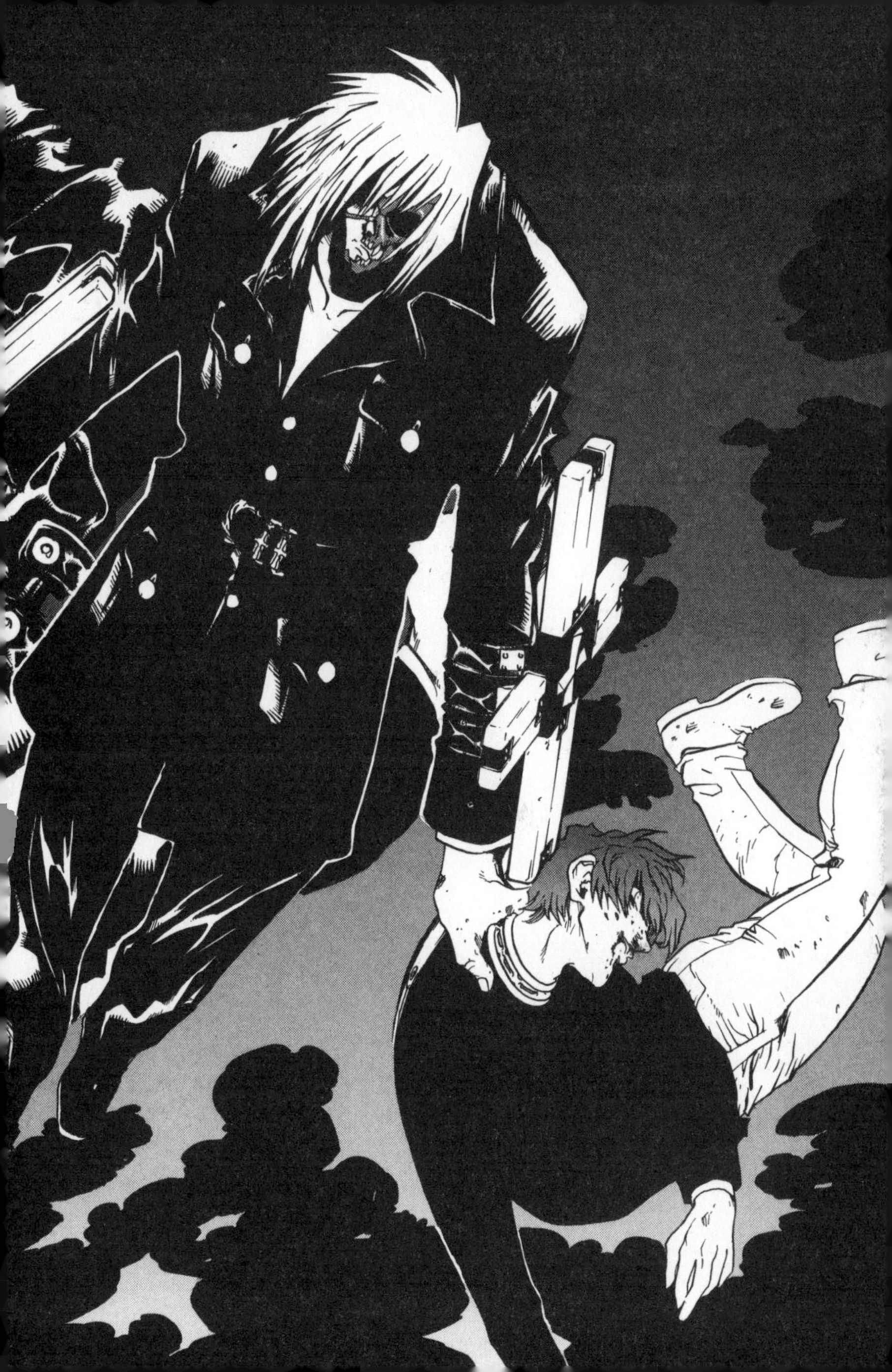

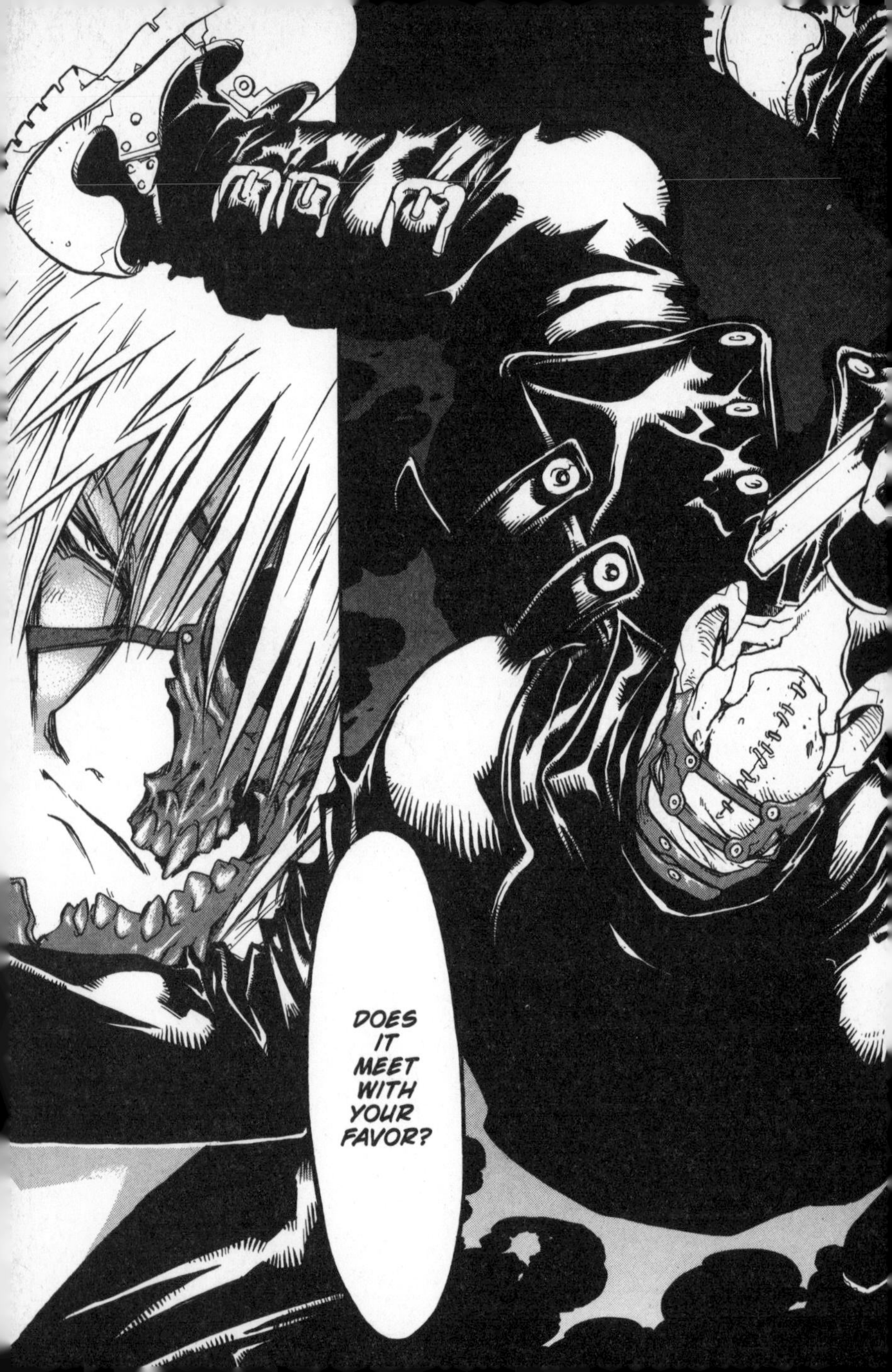
DOES IT MEET WITH YOUR FAVOR?

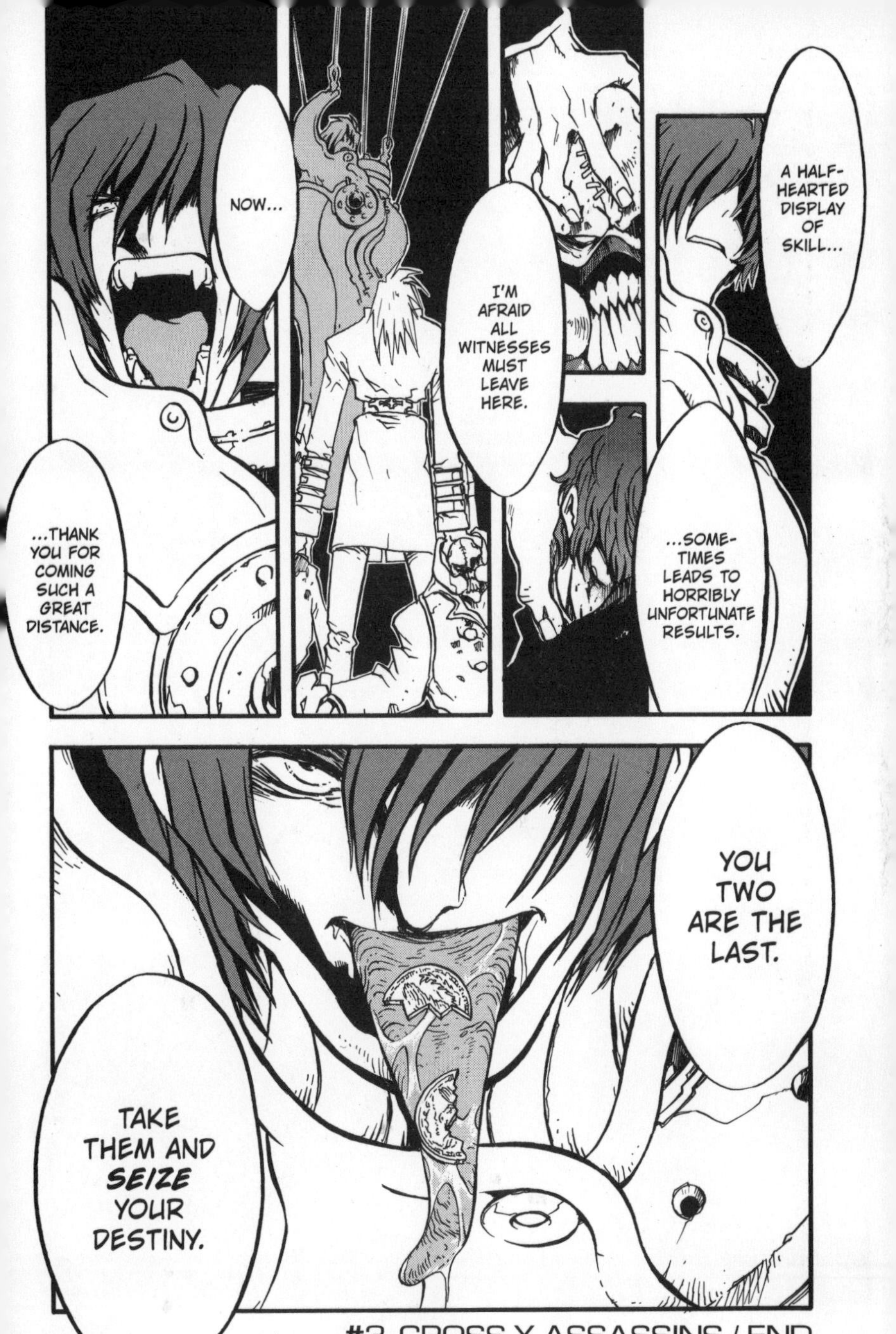
A HALF-HEARTED DISPLAY OF SKILL...
...SOMETIMES LEADS TO HORRIBLY UNFORTUNATE RESULTS.
I'M AFRAID ALL WITNESSES MUST LEAVE HERE.
NOW...
...THANK YOU FOR COMING SUCH A GREAT DISTANCE.
YOU TWO ARE THE LAST.
TAKE THEM AND *SEIZE* YOUR DESTINY.

#3. CROSS X ASSASSINS / END

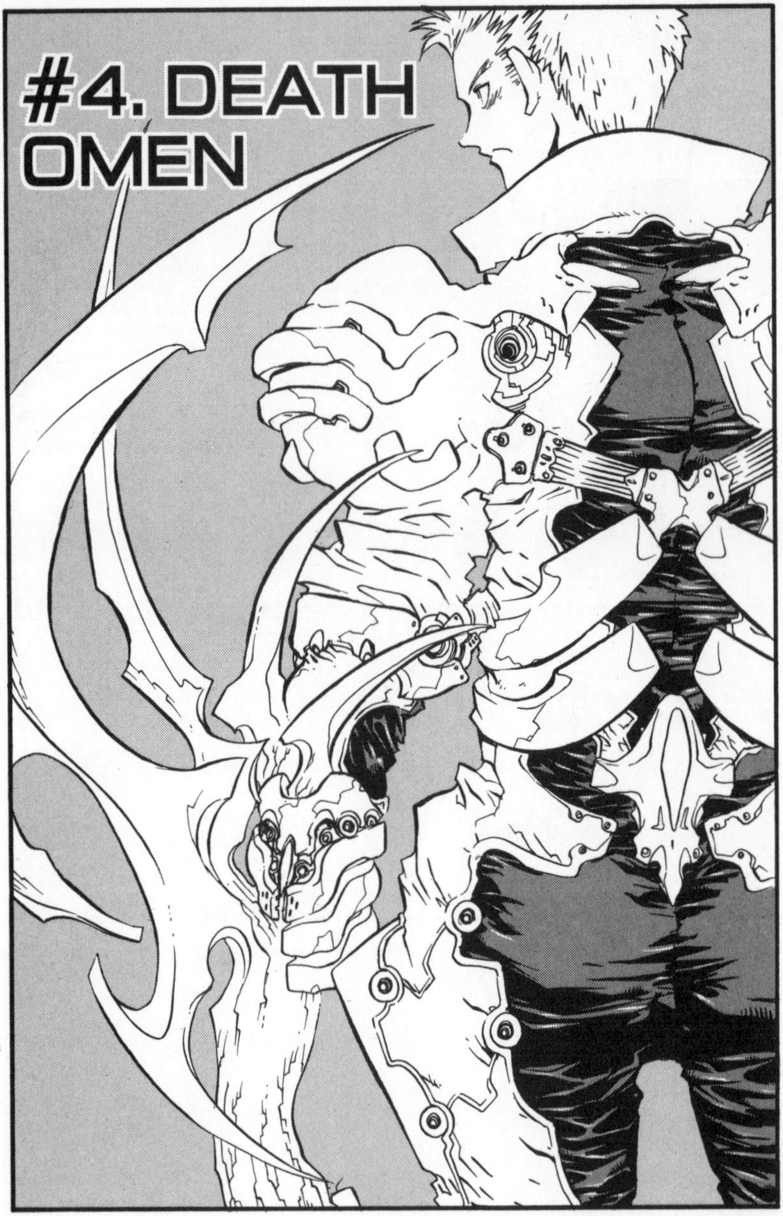
#4. DEATH
OMEN

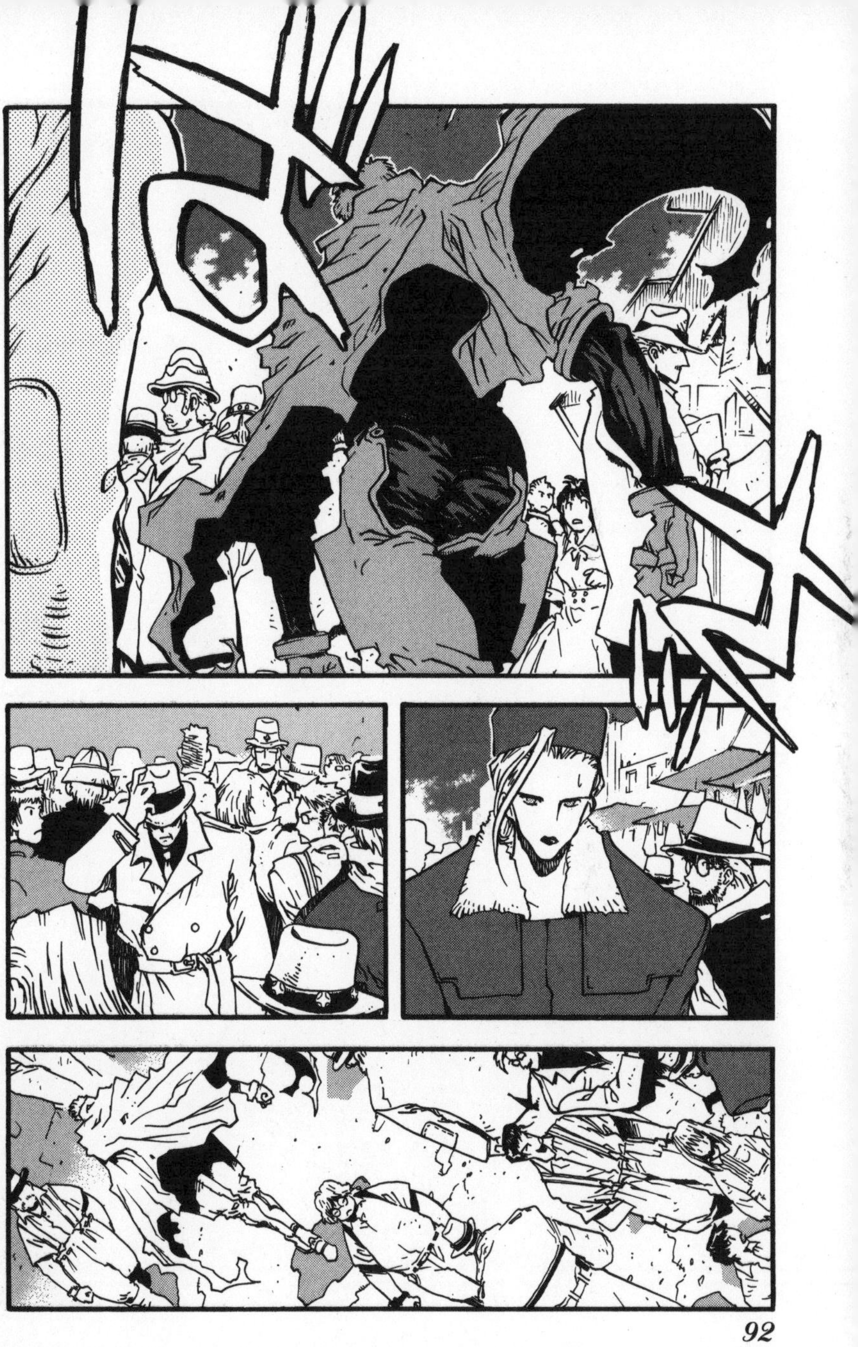

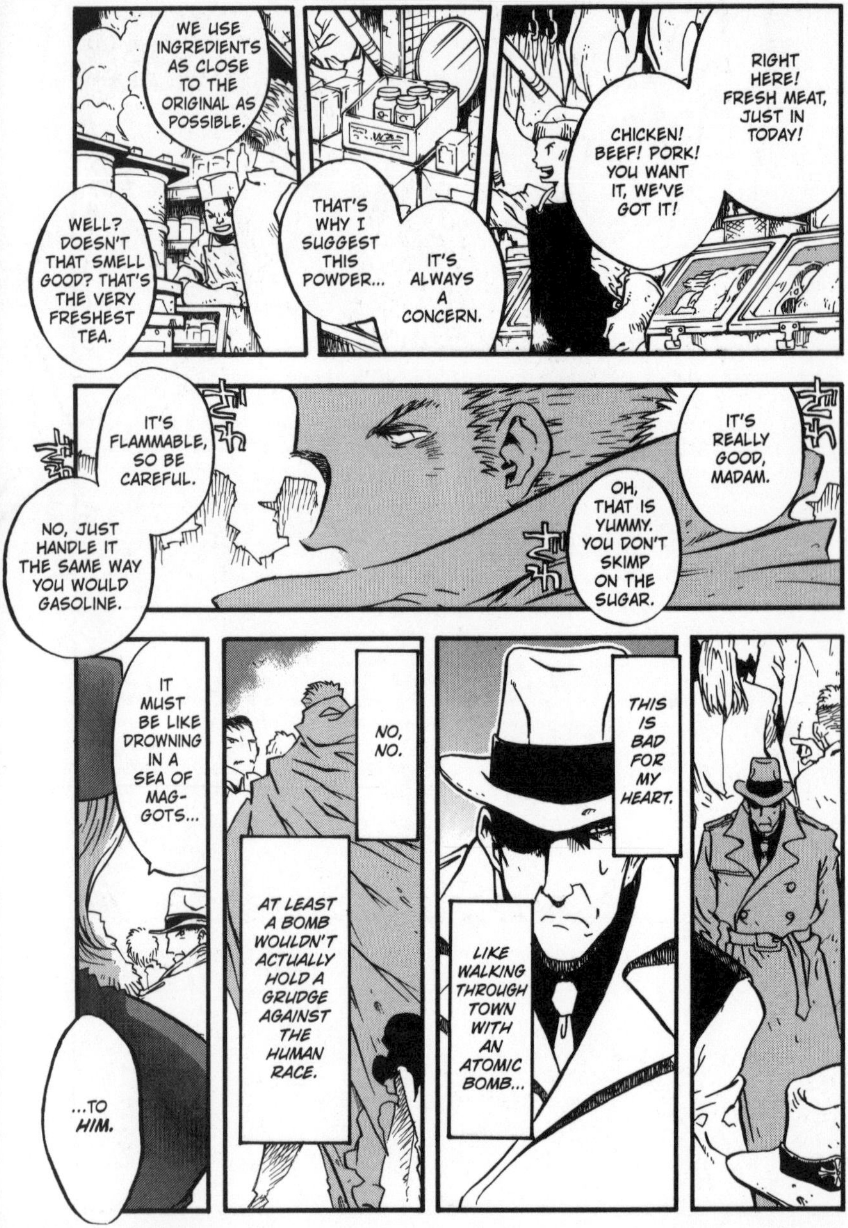
RIGHT HERE! FRESH MEAT, JUST IN TODAY!
CHICKEN! BEEF! PORK! YOU WANT IT, WE'VE GOT IT!
IT'S ALWAYS A CONCERN.
THAT'S WHY I SUGGEST THIS POWDER...
WE USE INGREDIENTS AS CLOSE TO THE ORIGINAL AS POSSIBLE.
WELL? DOESN'T THAT SMELL GOOD? THAT'S THE VERY FRESHEST TEA.
IT'S REALLY GOOD, MADAM.
OH, THAT IS YUMMY. YOU DON'T SKIMP ON THE SUGAR.
IT'S FLAMMABLE, SO BE CAREFUL.
NO, JUST HANDLE IT THE SAME WAY YOU WOULD GASOLINE.
THIS IS BAD FOR MY HEART.
LIKE WALKING THROUGH TOWN WITH AN ATOMIC BOMB...
NO, NO.
AT LEAST A BOMB WOULDN'T ACTUALLY HOLD A GRUDGE AGAINST THE HUMAN RACE.
IT MUST BE LIKE DROWNING IN A SEA OF MAG-GOTS...
...TO ***HIM.***

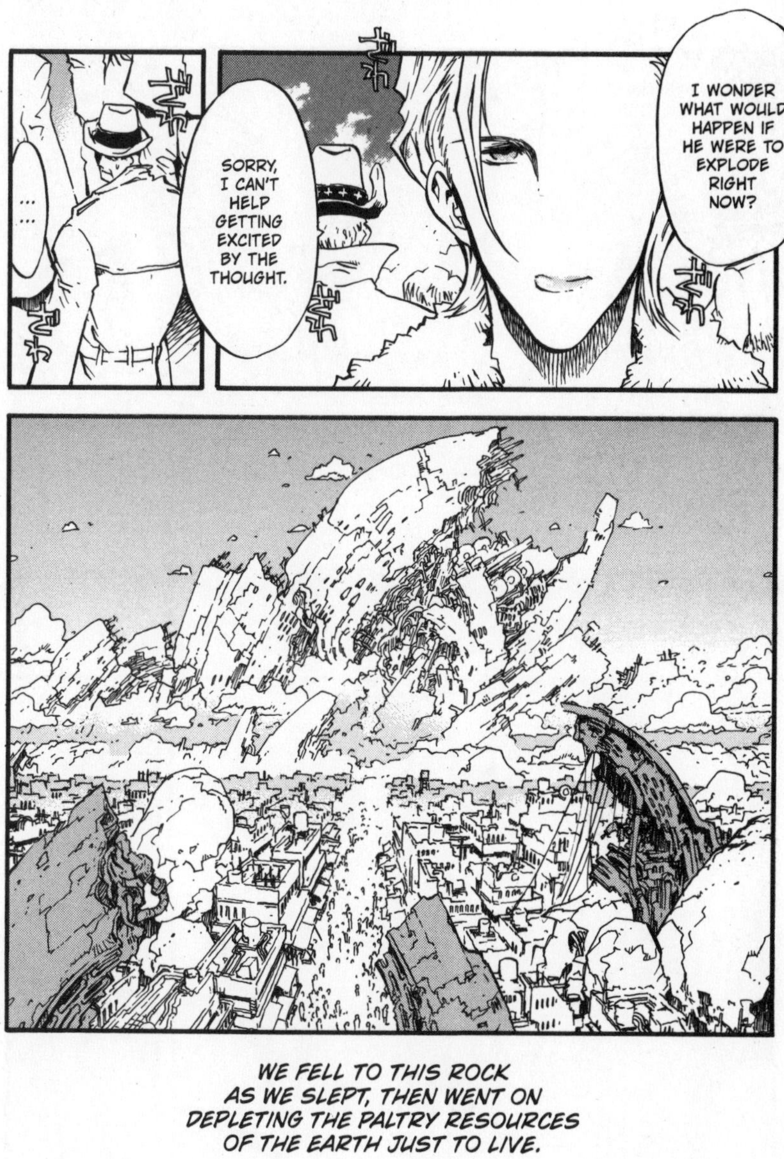
I WONDER WHAT WOULD HAPPEN IF HE WERE TO EXPLODE RIGHT NOW?
SORRY, I CAN'T HELP GETTING EXCITED BY THE THOUGHT.
...
...

WE FELL TO THIS ROCK AS WE SLEPT, THEN WENT ON DEPLETING THE PALTRY RESOURCES OF THE EARTH JUST TO LIVE.

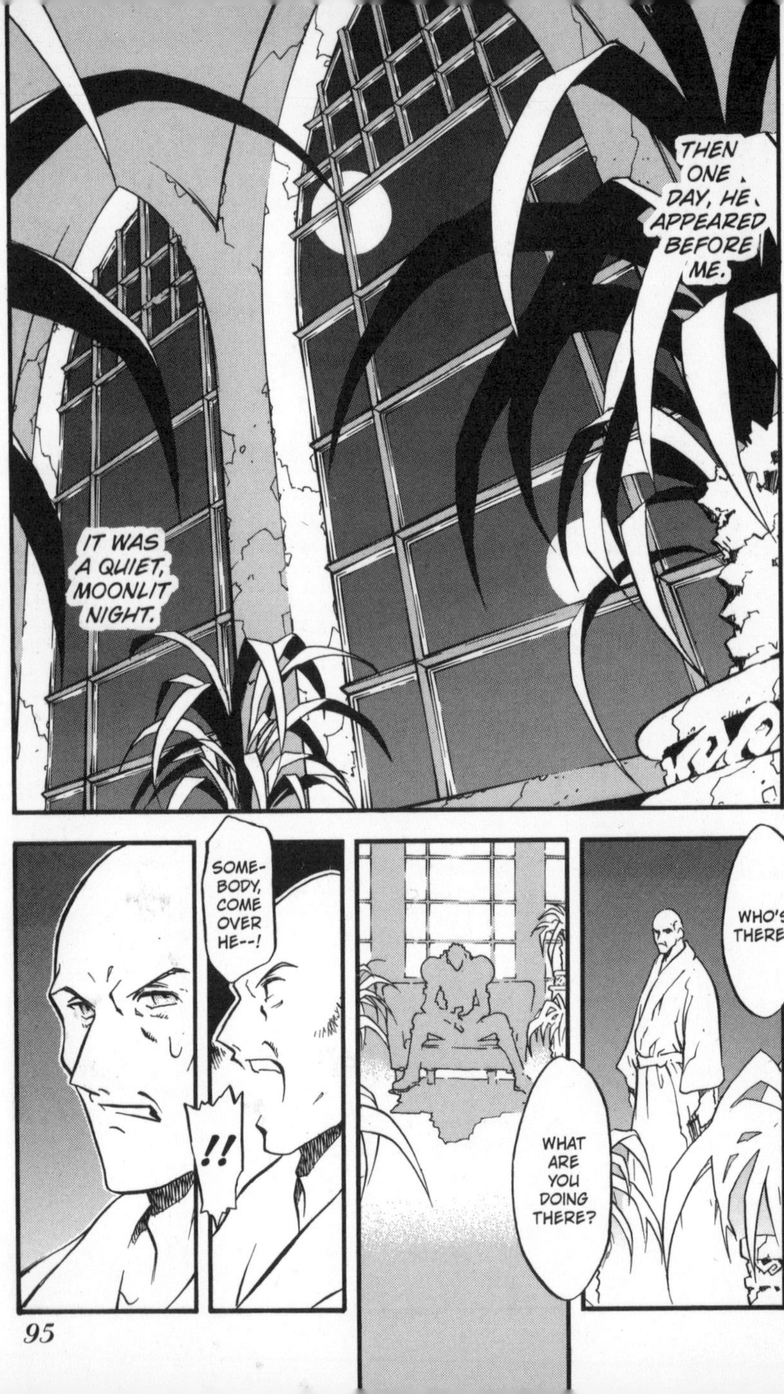
THEN ONE DAY, HE APPEARED BEFORE ME.
IT WAS A QUIET, MOONLIT NIGHT.
WHO'S THERE?
WHAT ARE YOU DOING THERE?
SOME-BODY, COME OVER HE--!
!!

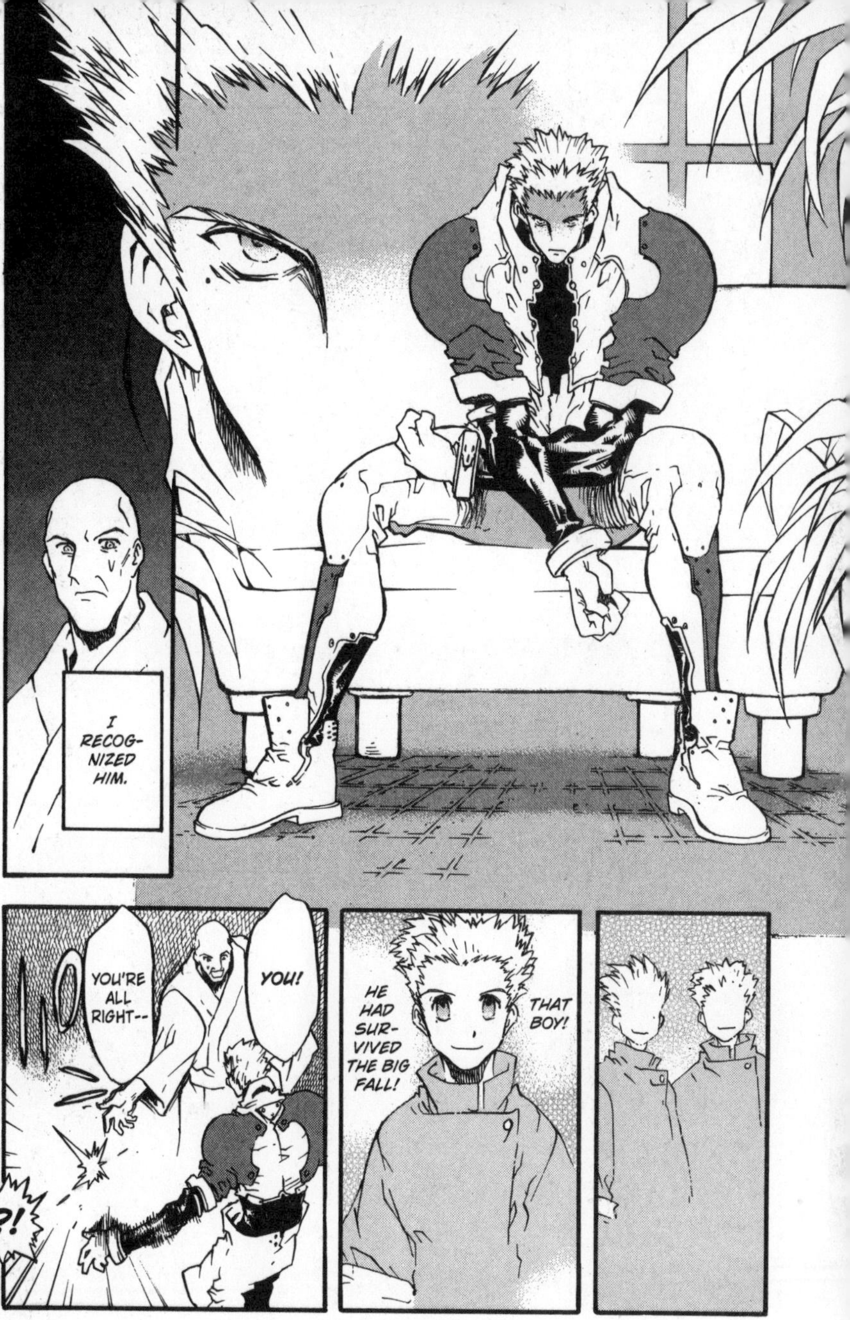
I RECOG-NIZED HIM.
THAT BOY!
HE HAD SUR-VIVED THE BIG FALL!
YOU!
YOU'RE ALL RIGHT--
?!

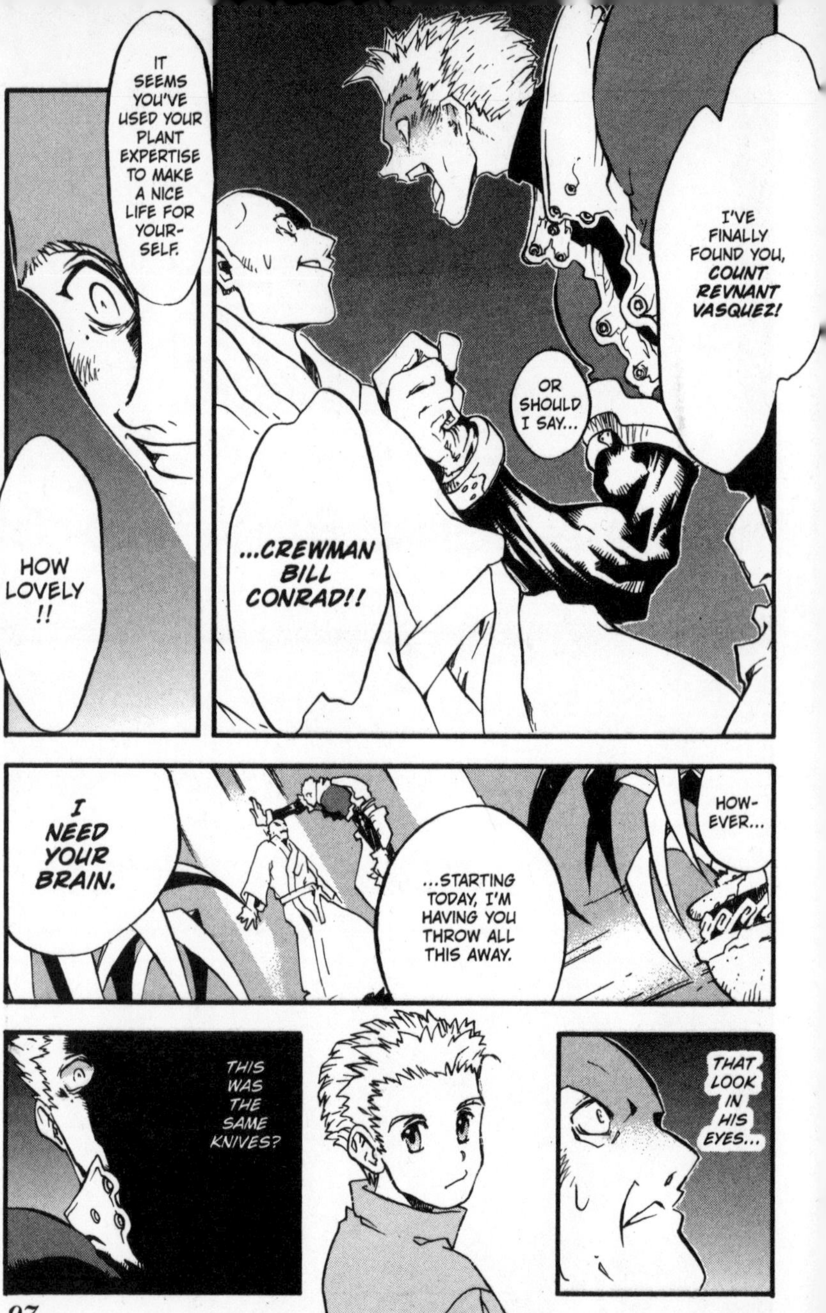
I'VE FINALLY FOUND YOU, COUNT REVNANT VASQUEZ!
OR SHOULD I SAY...
...CREWMAN BILL CONRAD!!
IT SEEMS YOU'VE USED YOUR PLANT EXPERTISE TO MAKE A NICE LIFE FOR YOURSELF.
HOW LOVELY !!
HOW-EVER...
...STARTING TODAY, I'M HAVING YOU THROW ALL THIS AWAY.
I NEED YOUR BRAIN.
THAT LOOK IN HIS EYES...
THIS WAS THE SAME KNIVES?

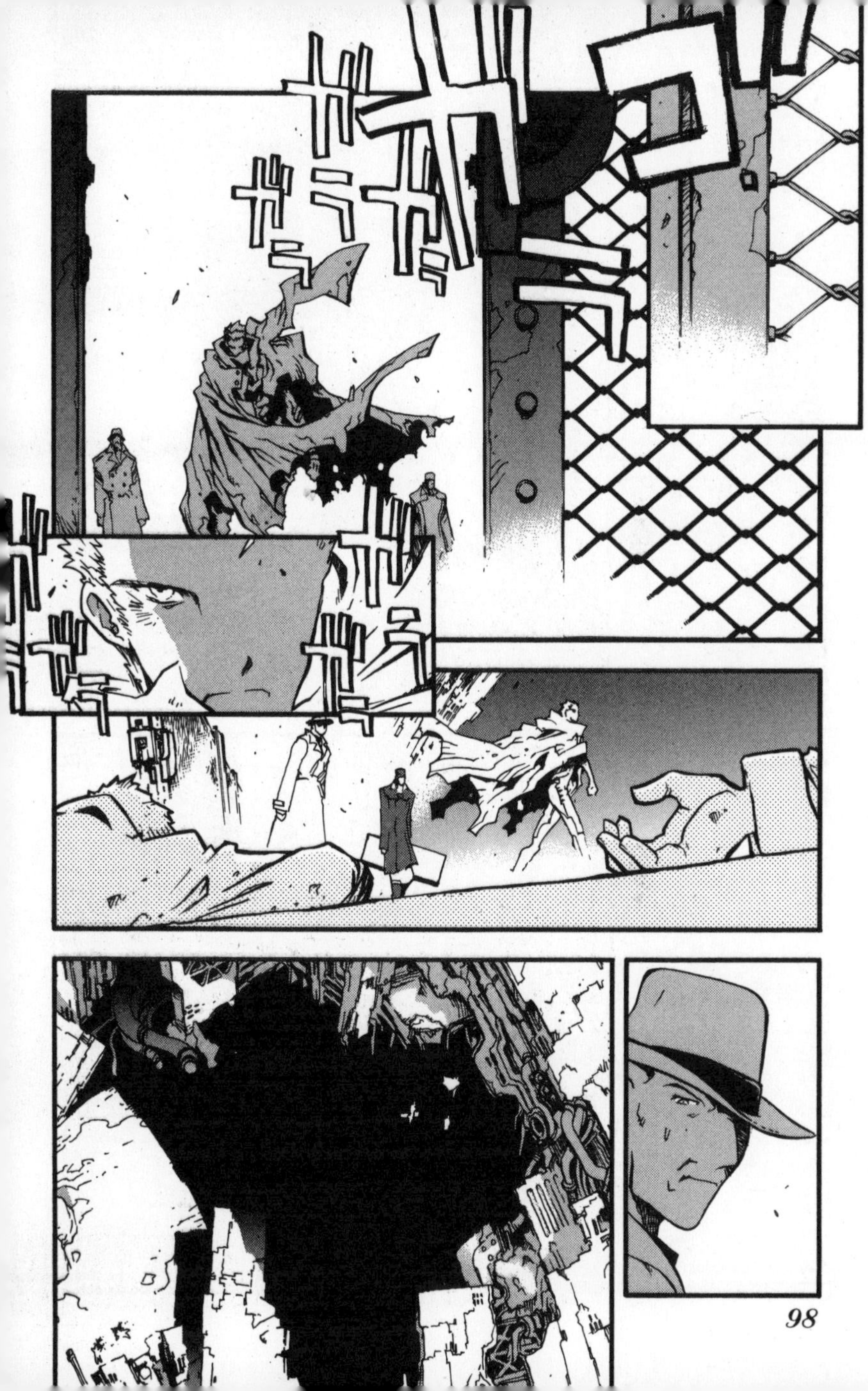
ガラガラ
ガラガラ

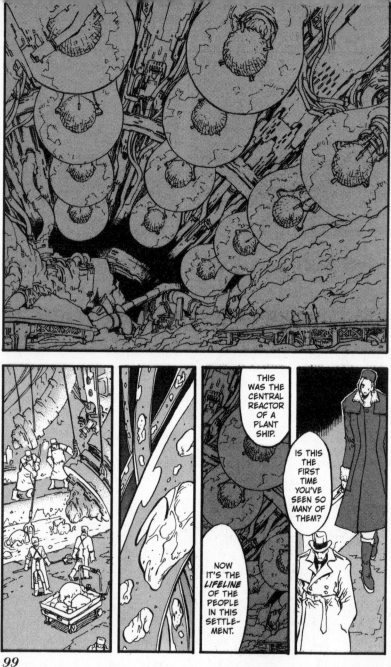

THIS WAS THE CENTRAL REACTOR OF A PLANT SHIP.

IS THIS THE FIRST TIME YOU'VE SEEN SO MANY OF THEM?

NOW IT'S THE *LIFELINE* OF THE PEOPLE IN THIS SETTLEMENT.

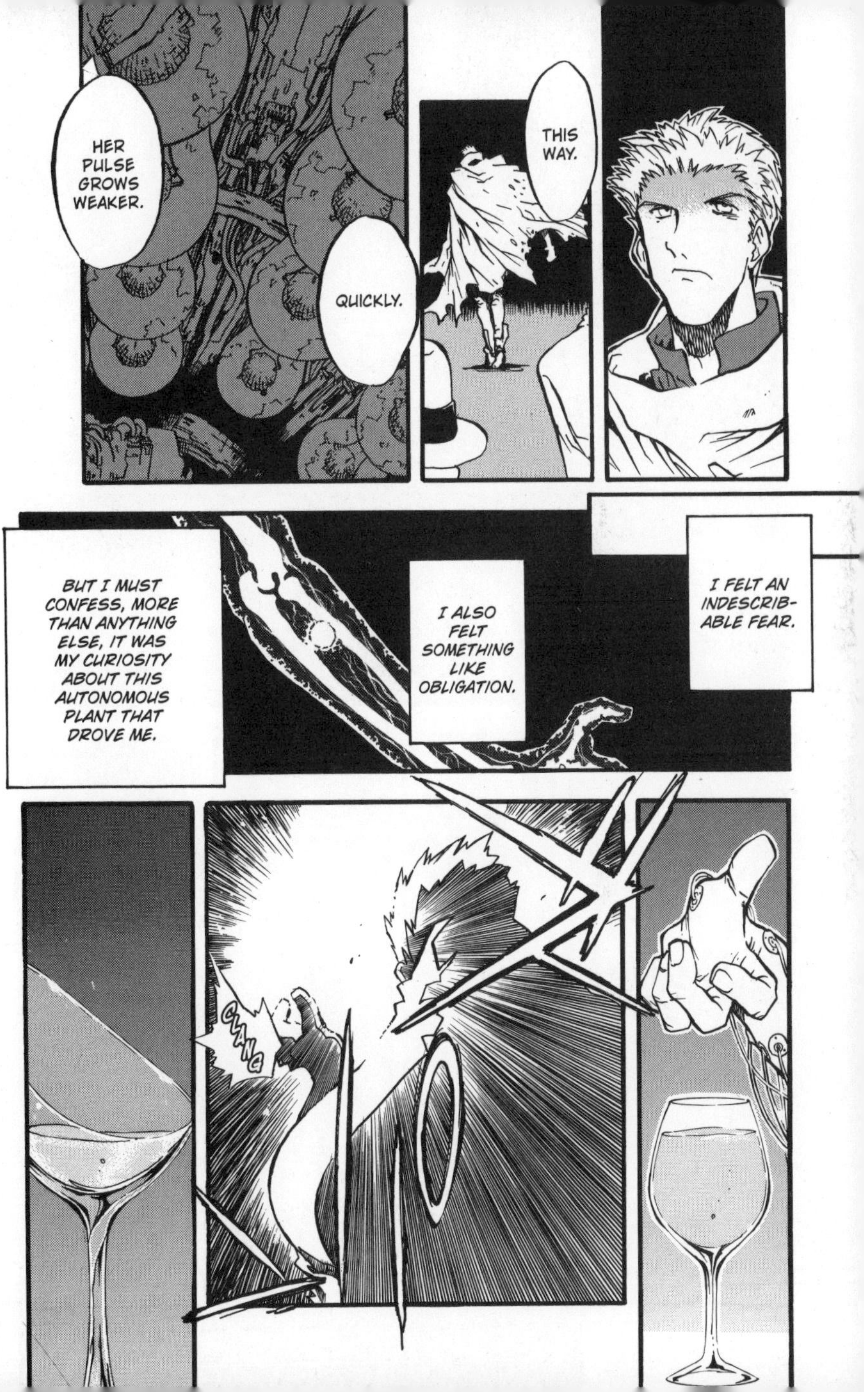
THIS WAY.
HER PULSE GROWS WEAKER.
QUICKLY.
I FELT AN INDESCRIB-ABLE FEAR.
I ALSO FELT SOMETHING LIKE OBLIGATION.
BUT I MUST CONFESS, MORE THAN ANYTHING ELSE, IT WAS MY CURIOSITY ABOUT THIS AUTONOMOUS PLANT THAT DROVE ME.
CLANG

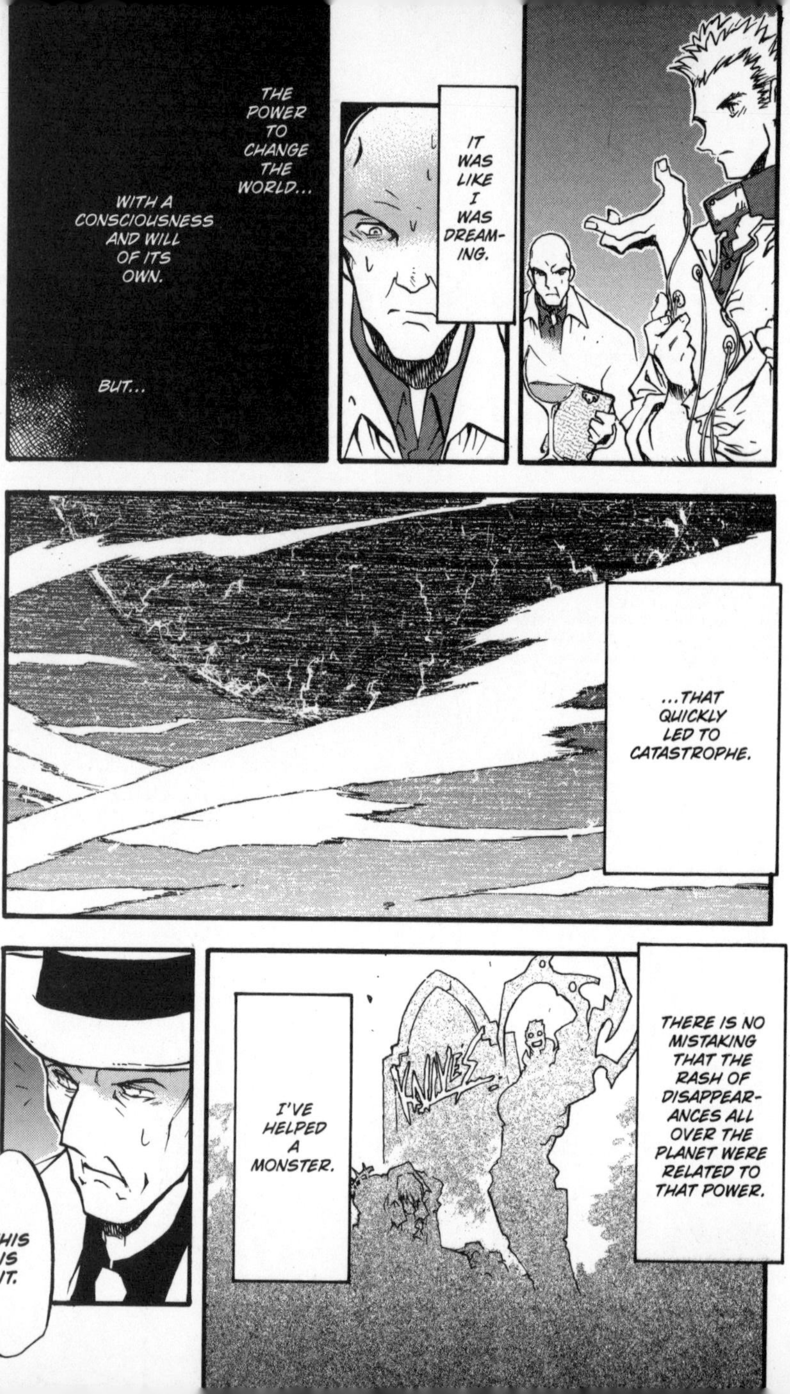
IT WAS LIKE I WAS DREAMING.
THE POWER TO CHANGE THE WORLD...
WITH A CONSCIOUSNESS AND WILL OF ITS OWN.
BUT...
...THAT QUICKLY LED TO CATASTROPHE.
THERE IS NO MISTAKING THAT THE RASH OF DISAPPEARANCES ALL OVER THE PLANET WERE RELATED TO THAT POWER.
I'VE HELPED A MONSTER.
THIS IS IT.

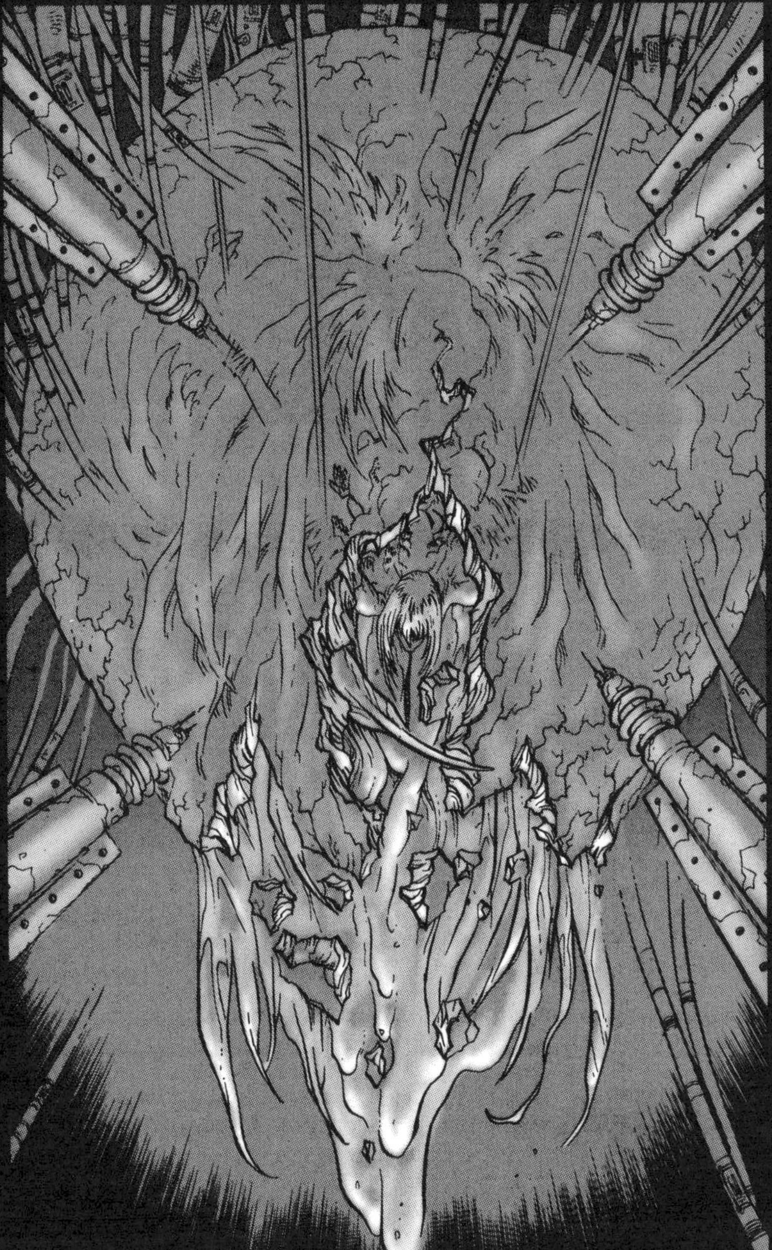

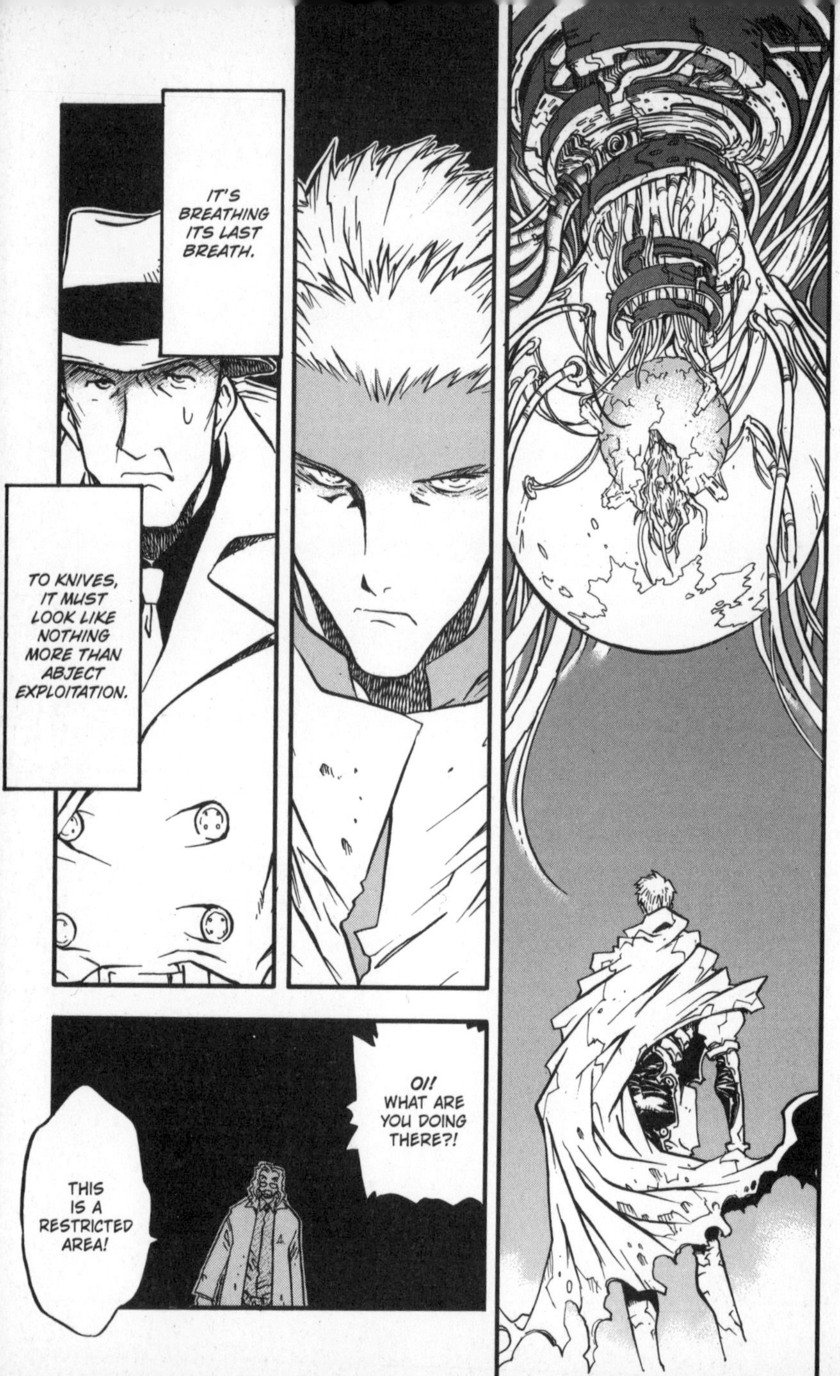
IT'S BREATHING ITS LAST BREATH.
TO KNIVES, IT MUST LOOK LIKE NOTHING MORE THAN ABJECT EXPLOITATION.
OI! WHAT ARE YOU DOING THERE?!
THIS IS A RESTRICTED AREA!

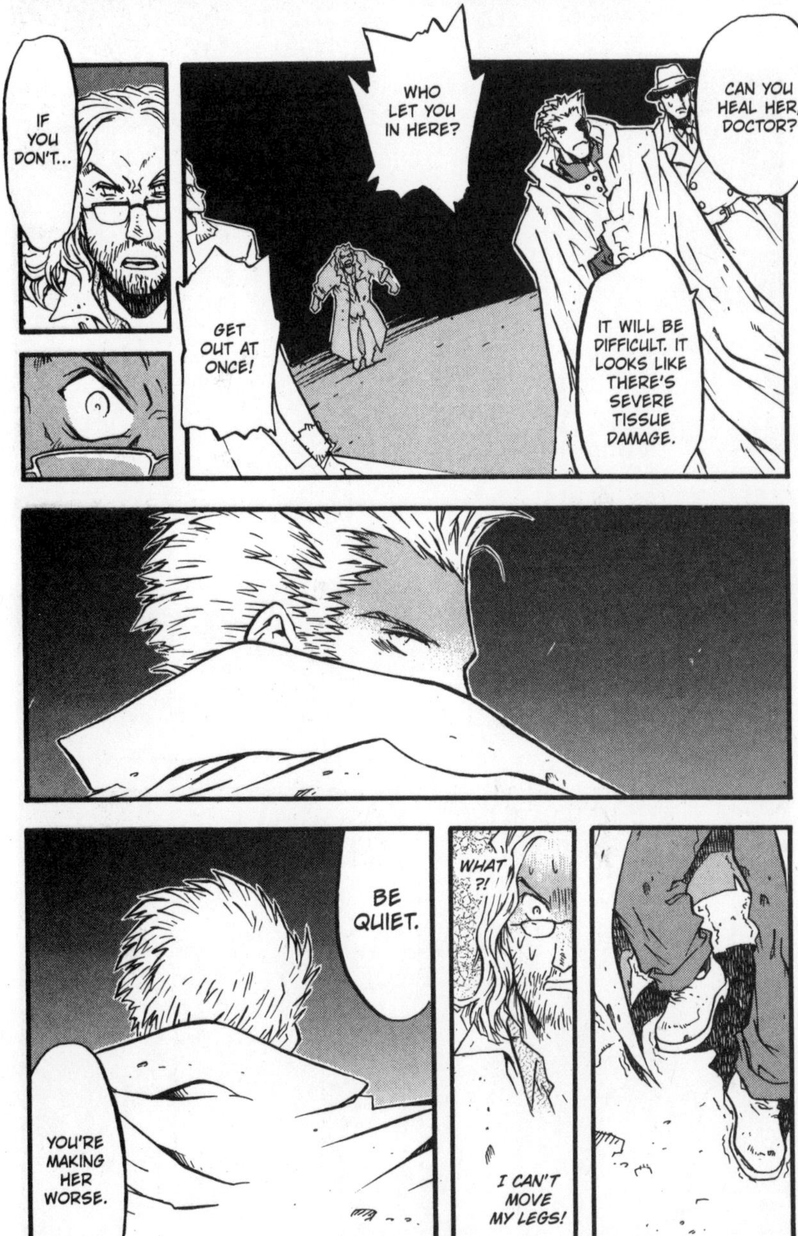
CAN YOU HEAL HER, DOCTOR?
IT WILL BE DIFFICULT. IT LOOKS LIKE THERE'S SEVERE TISSUE DAMAGE.
WHO LET YOU IN HERE?
GET OUT AT ONCE!
IF YOU DON'T...
BE QUIET.
YOU'RE MAKING HER WORSE.
WHAT?!
I CAN'T MOVE MY LEGS!

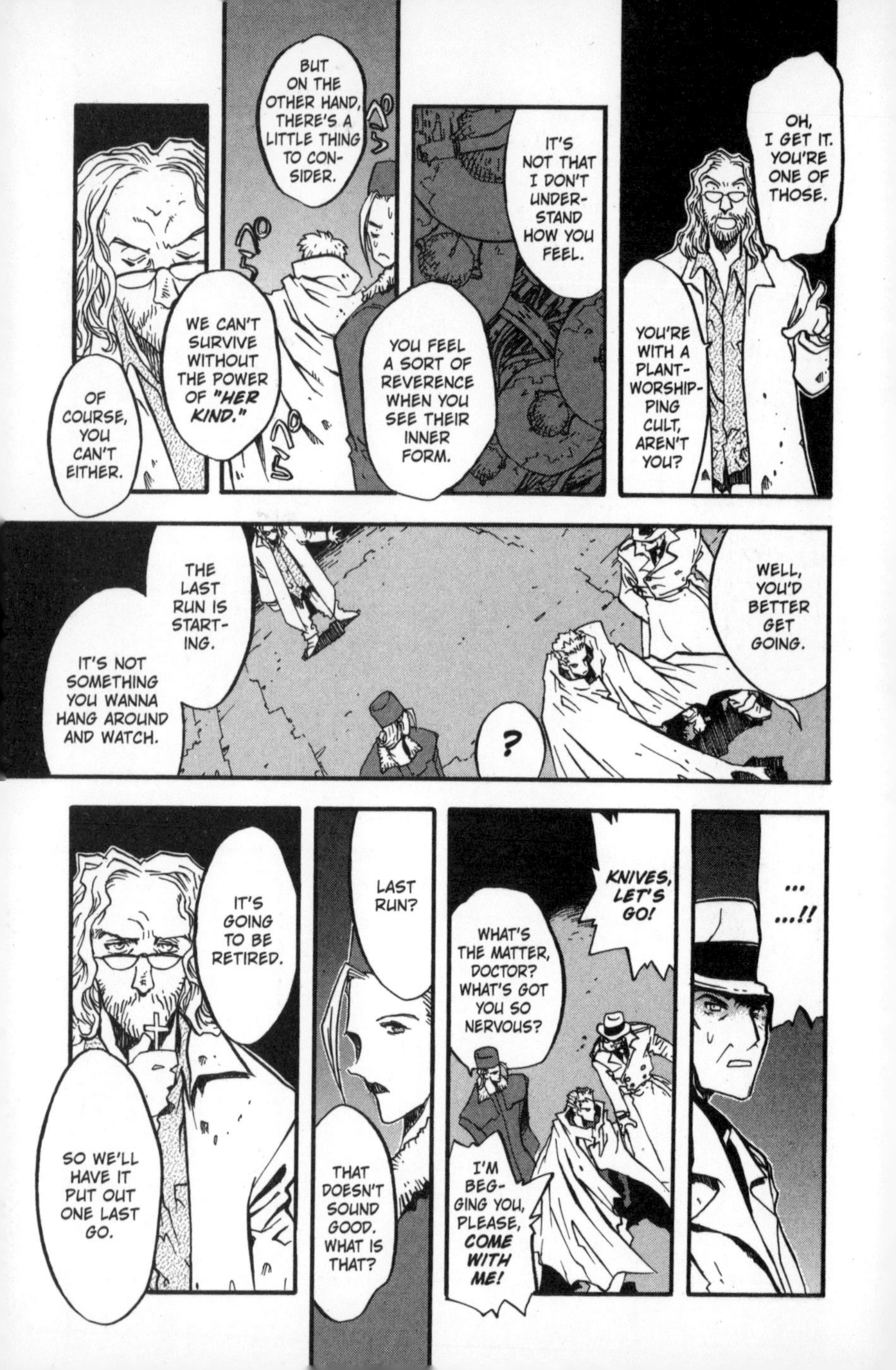
OH, I GET IT. YOU'RE ONE OF THOSE.
YOU'RE WITH A PLANT-WORSHIPPING CULT, AREN'T YOU?
IT'S NOT THAT I DON'T UNDERSTAND HOW YOU FEEL.
YOU FEEL A SORT OF REVERENCE WHEN YOU SEE THEIR INNER FORM.
BUT ON THE OTHER HAND, THERE'S A LITTLE THING TO CONSIDER.
WE CAN'T SURVIVE WITHOUT THE POWER OF ***"HER KIND."***
OF COURSE, YOU CAN'T EITHER.
WELL, YOU'D BETTER GET GOING.
?
THE LAST RUN IS STARTING.
IT'S NOT SOMETHING YOU WANNA HANG AROUND AND WATCH.
... ...!!
KNIVES, LET'S GO!
WHAT'S THE MATTER, DOCTOR? WHAT'S GOT YOU SO NERVOUS?
I'M BEGGING YOU, PLEASE, ***COME WITH ME!***
LAST RUN?
THAT DOESN'T SOUND GOOD. WHAT IS THAT?
IT'S GOING TO BE RETIRED.
SO WE'LL HAVE IT PUT OUT ONE LAST GO.

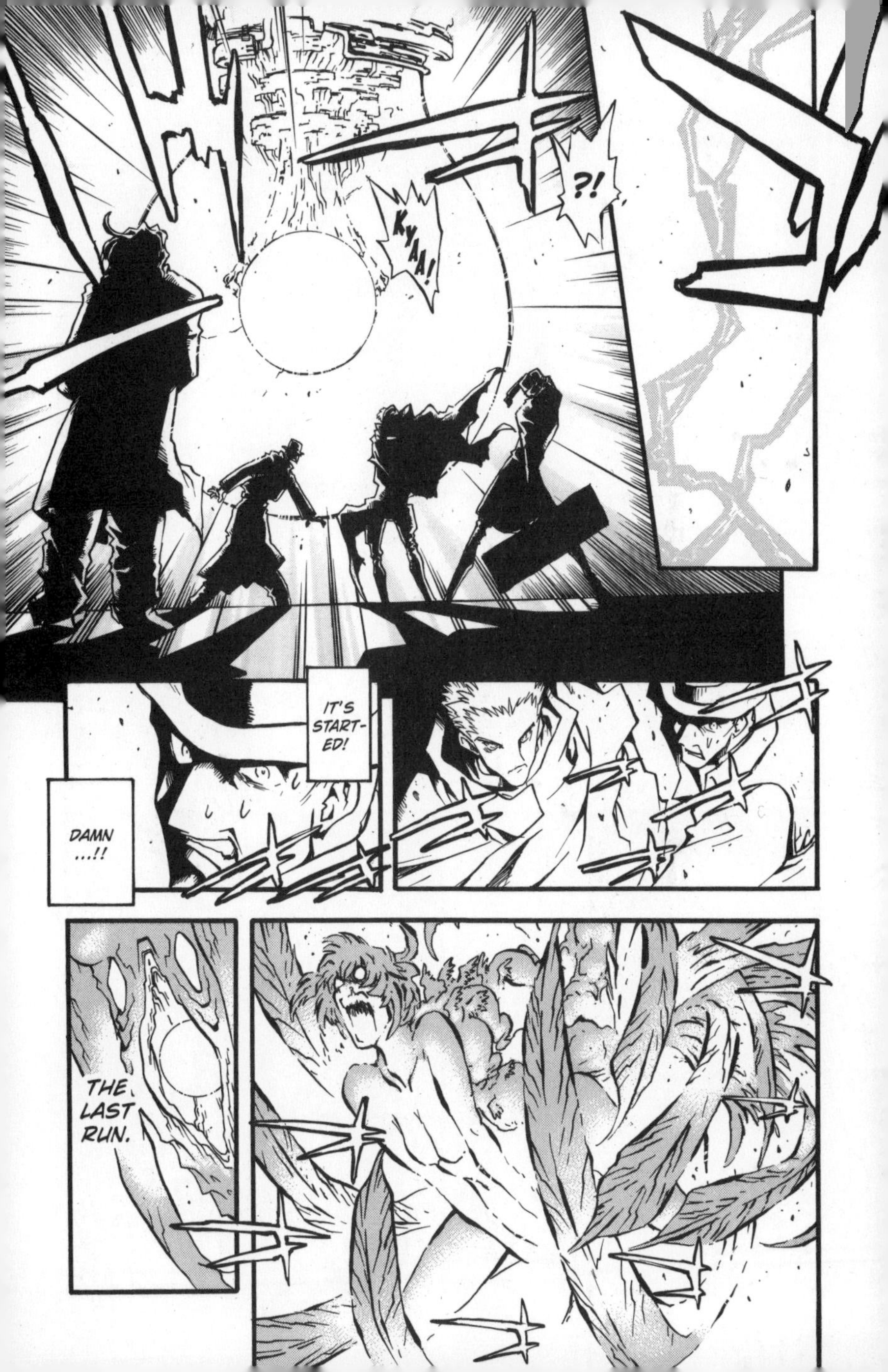
?!
KYAAA!
IT'S STARTED!
DAMN ...!!
THE LAST RUN.

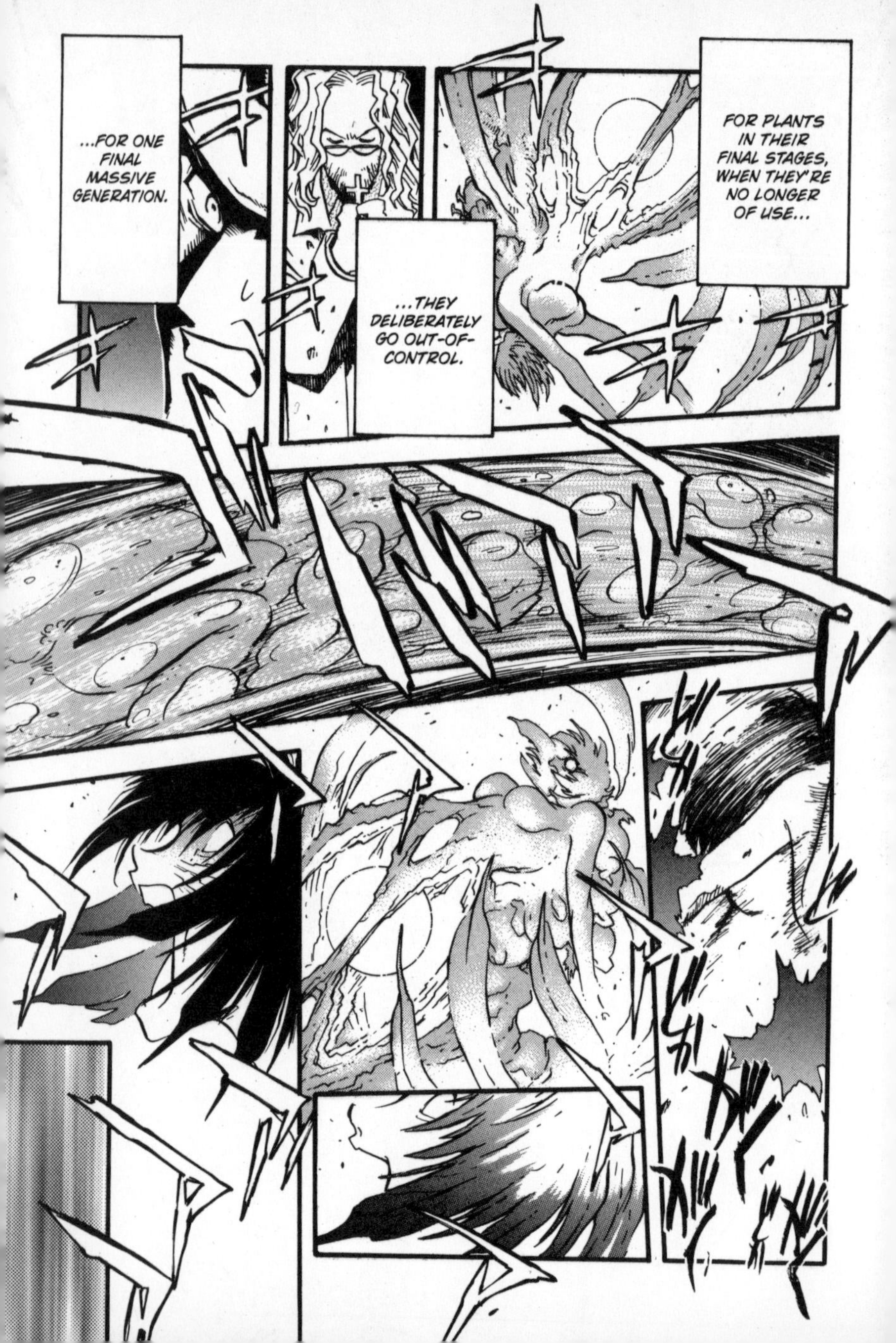
FOR PLANTS IN THEIR FINAL STAGES, WHEN THEY'RE NO LONGER OF USE...
...THEY DELIBERATELY GO OUT-OF-CONTROL.
...FOR ONE FINAL MASSIVE GENERATION.

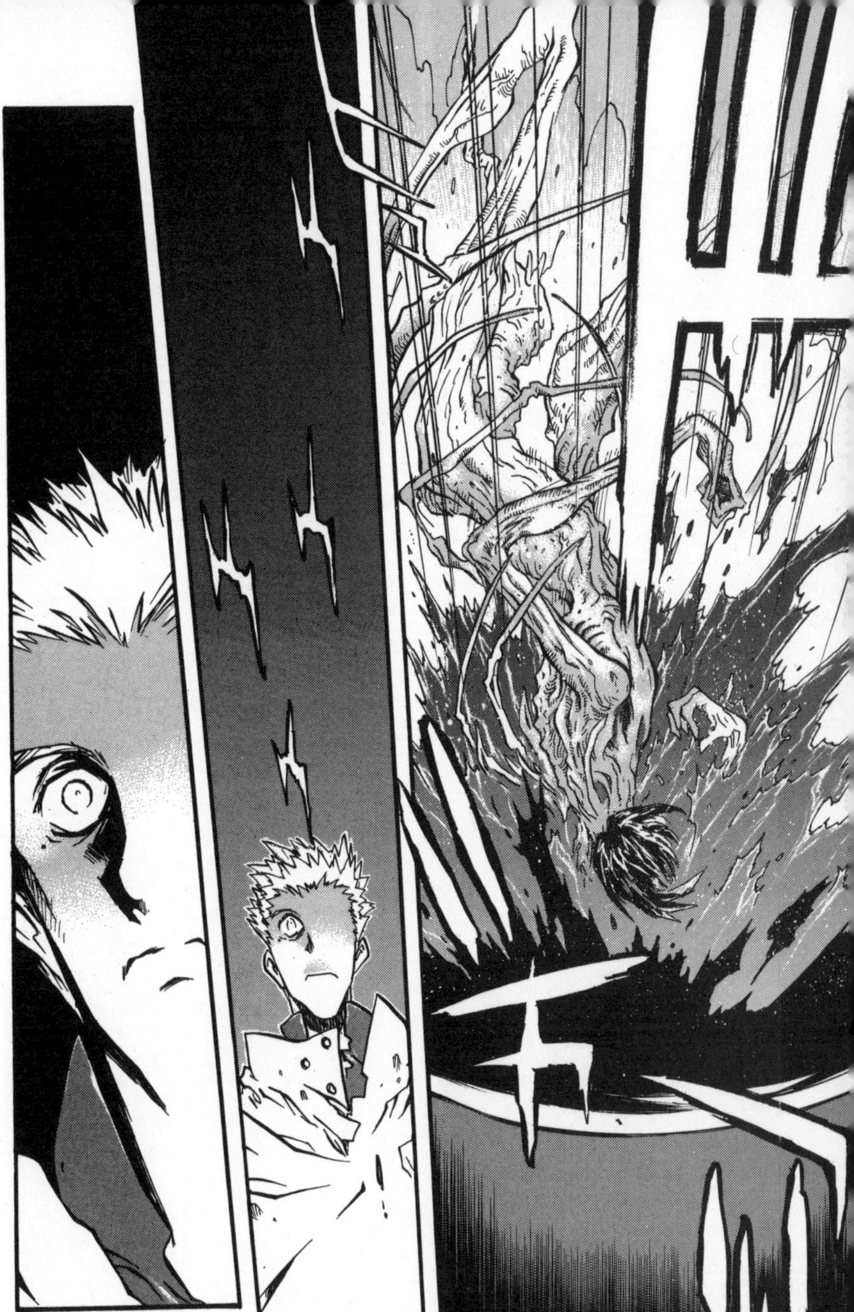

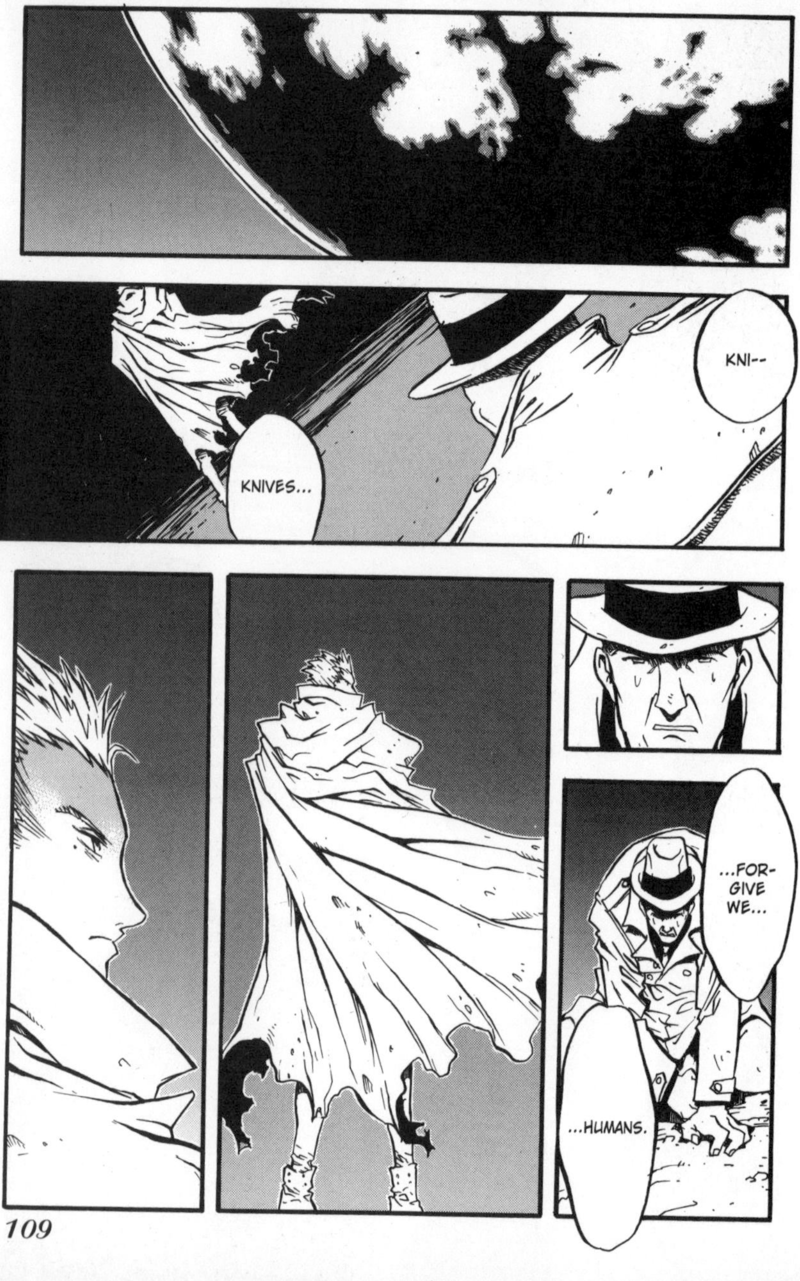
KNI--
KNIVES...
...FORGIVE WE...
...HUMANS.

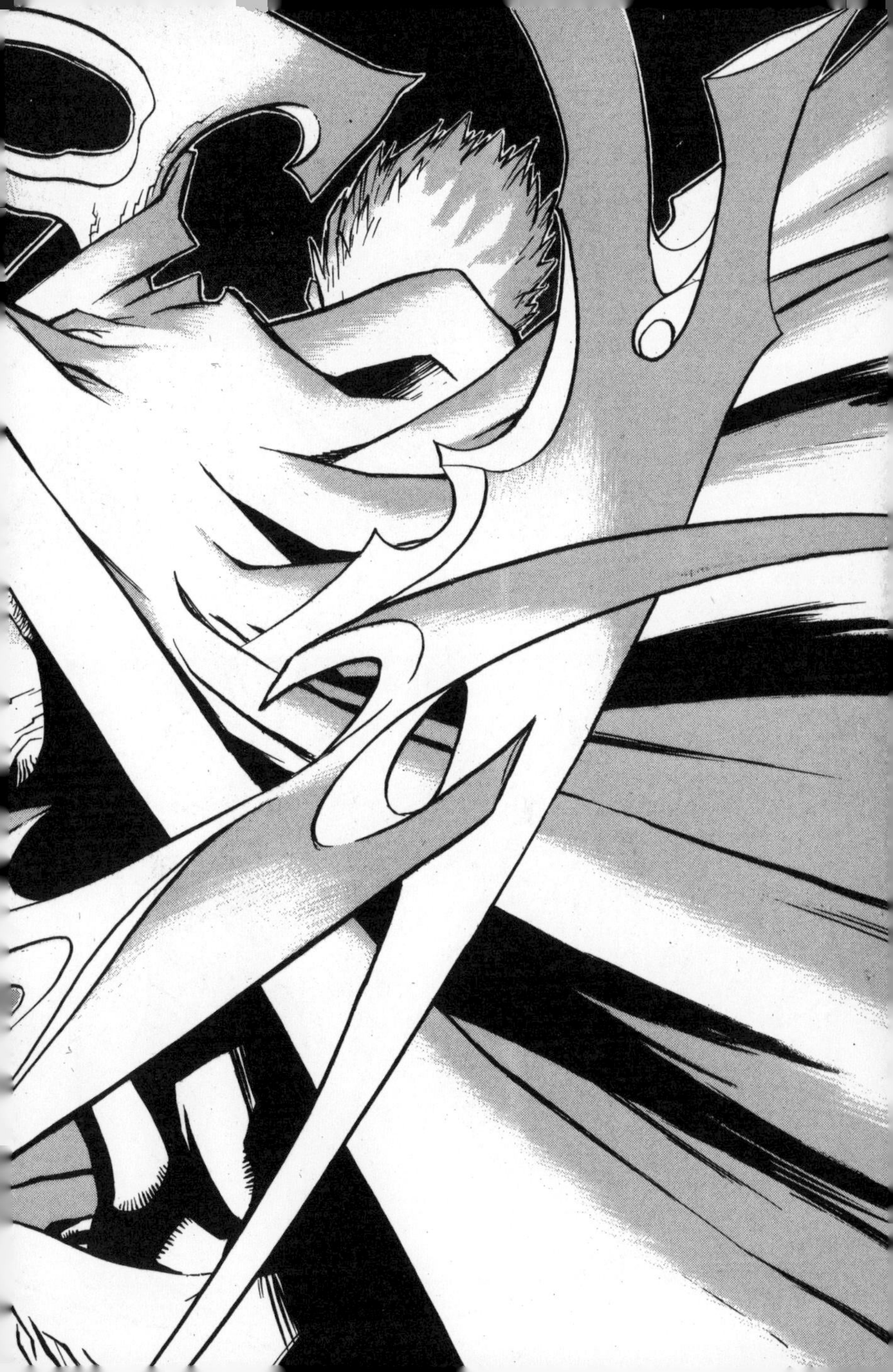

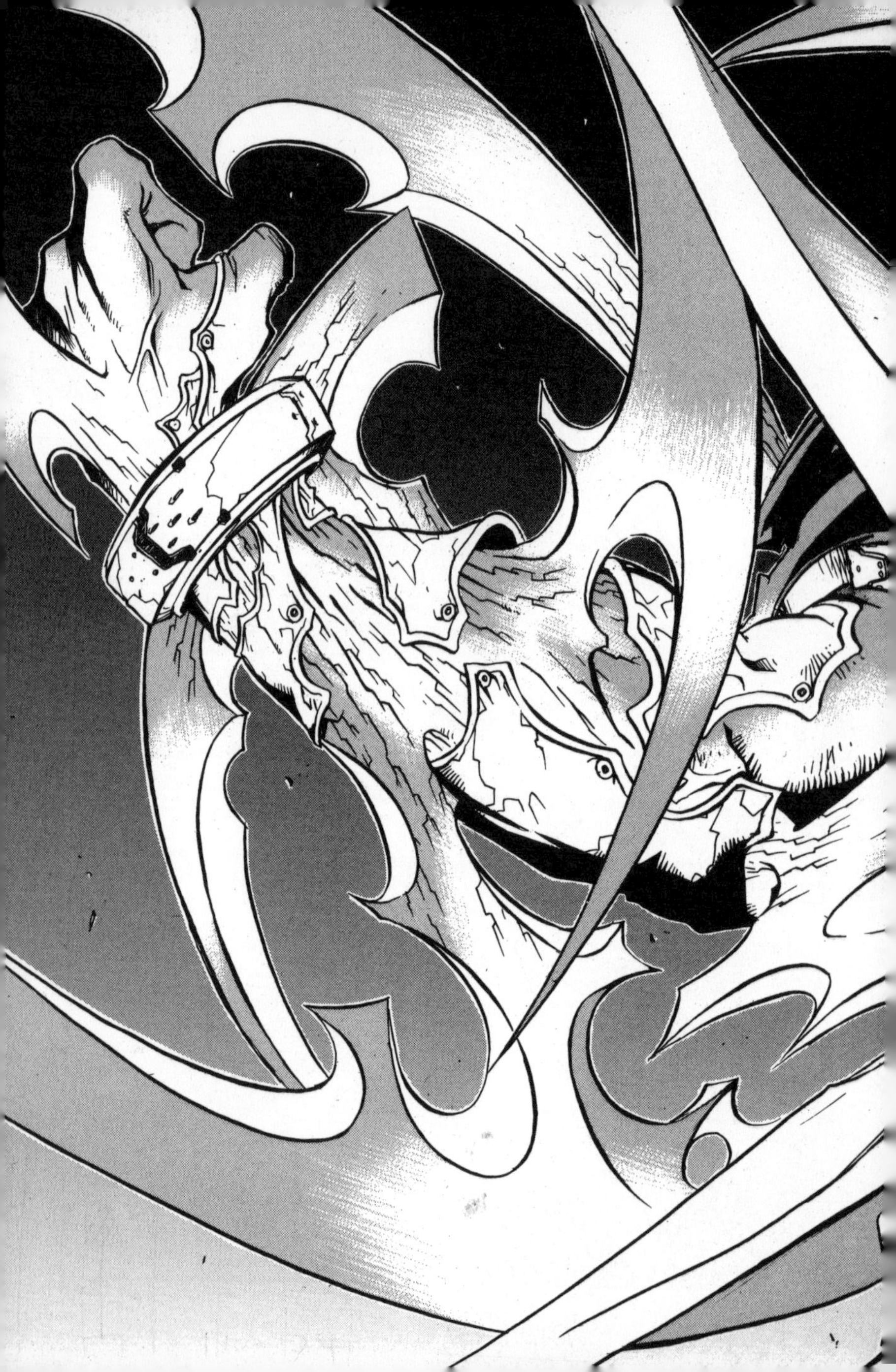

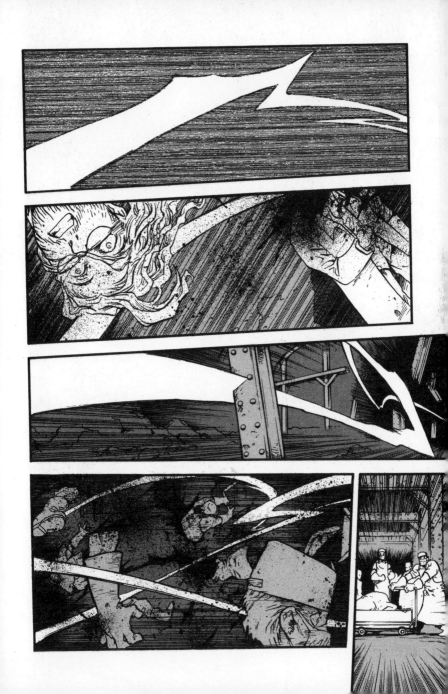

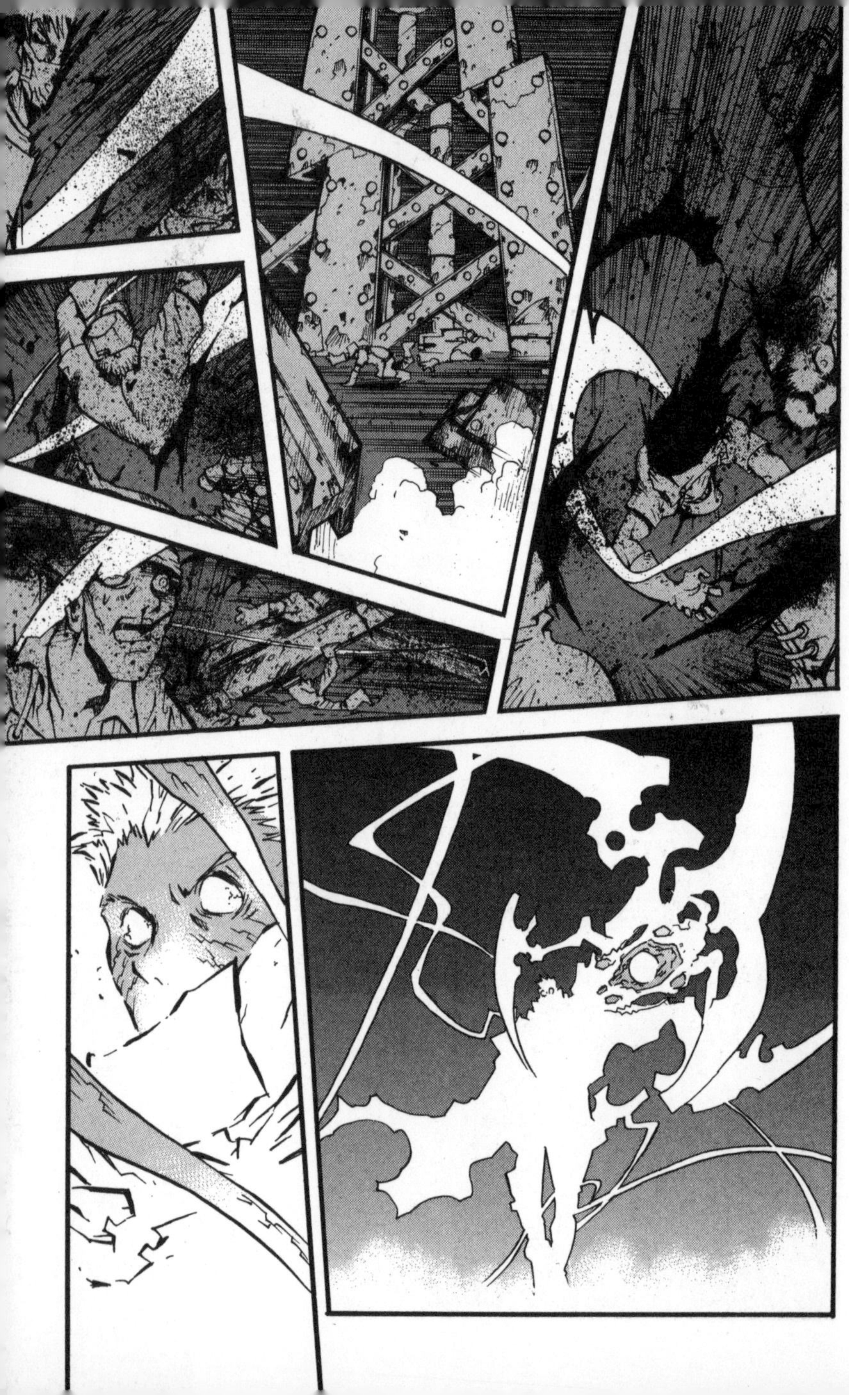

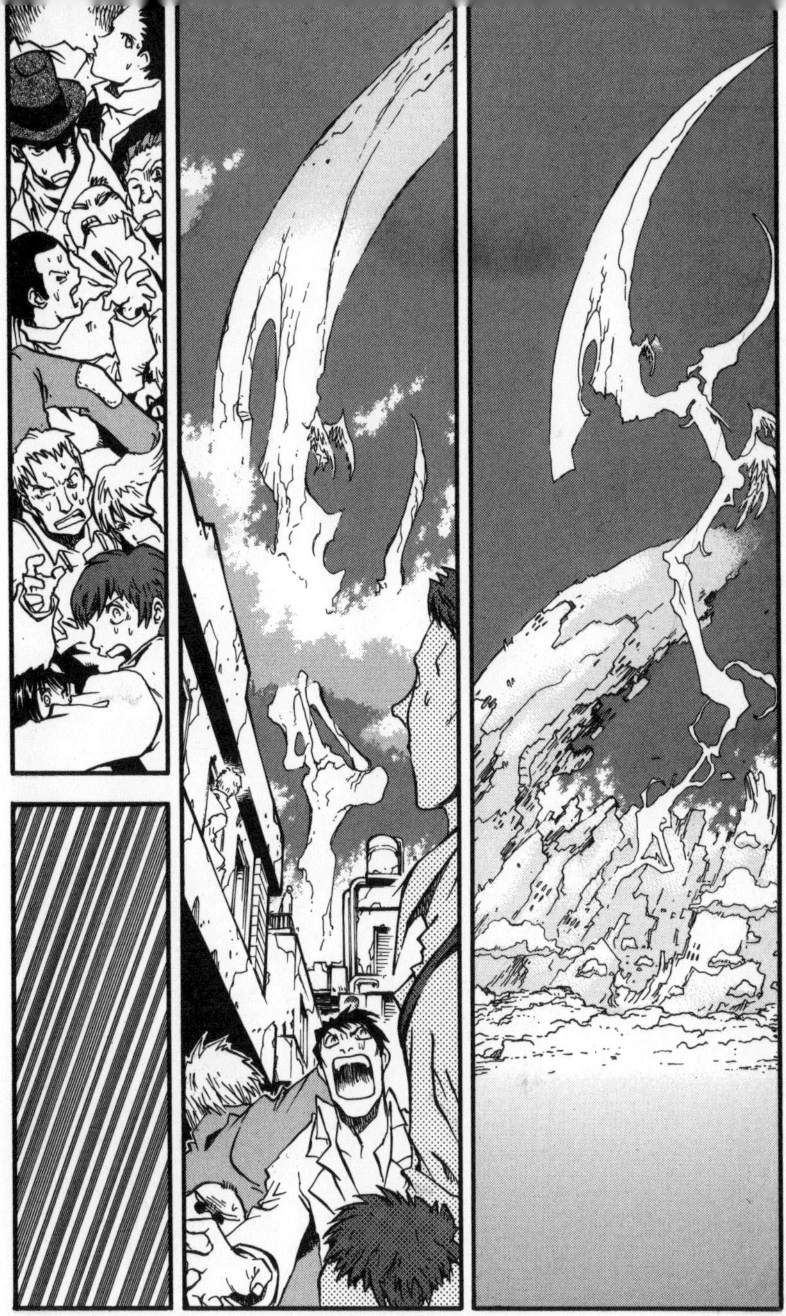

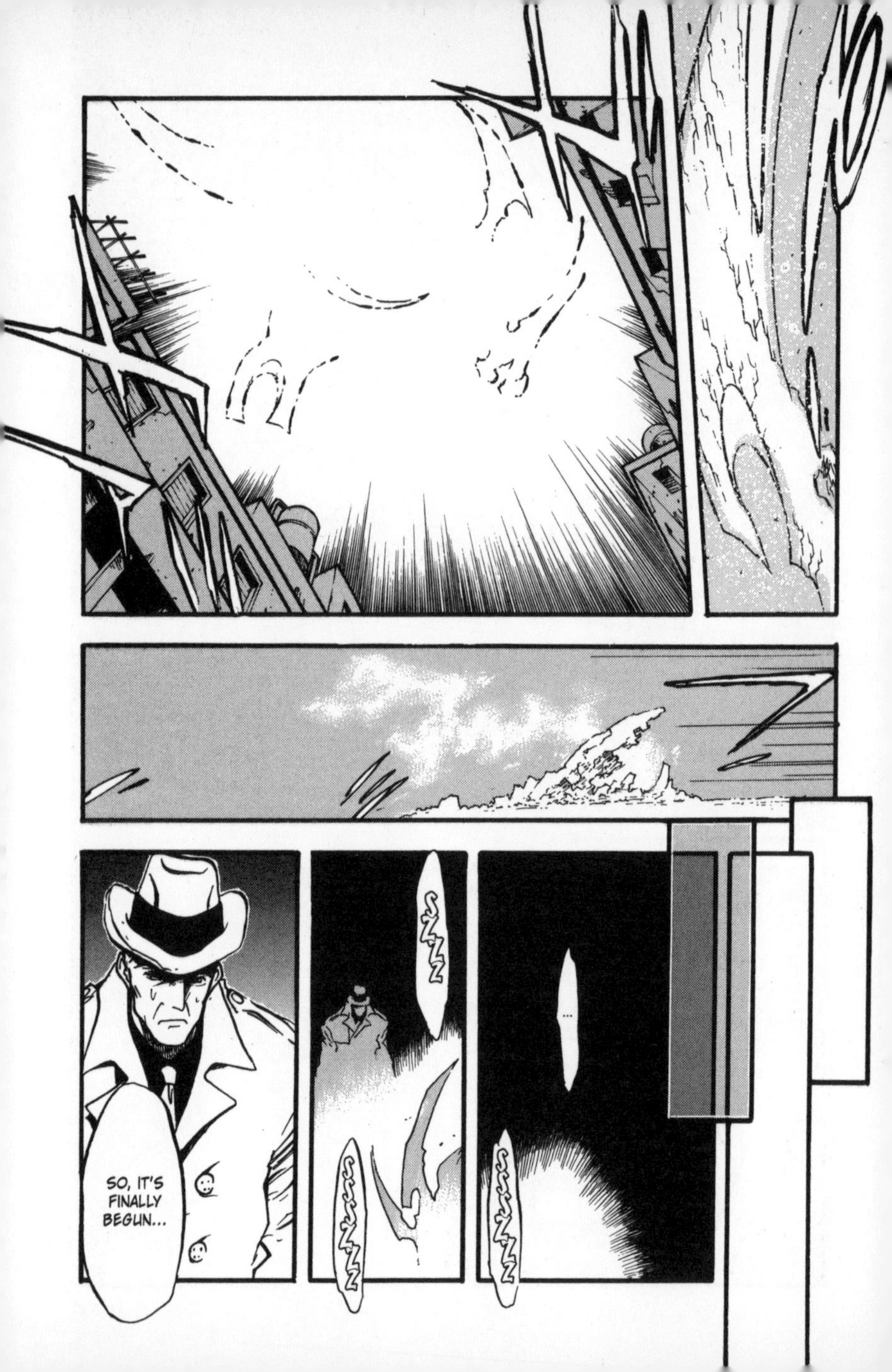
...
SSSZZZZ
SZZZ
SSSZZZZ
SO, IT'S FINALLY BEGUN...

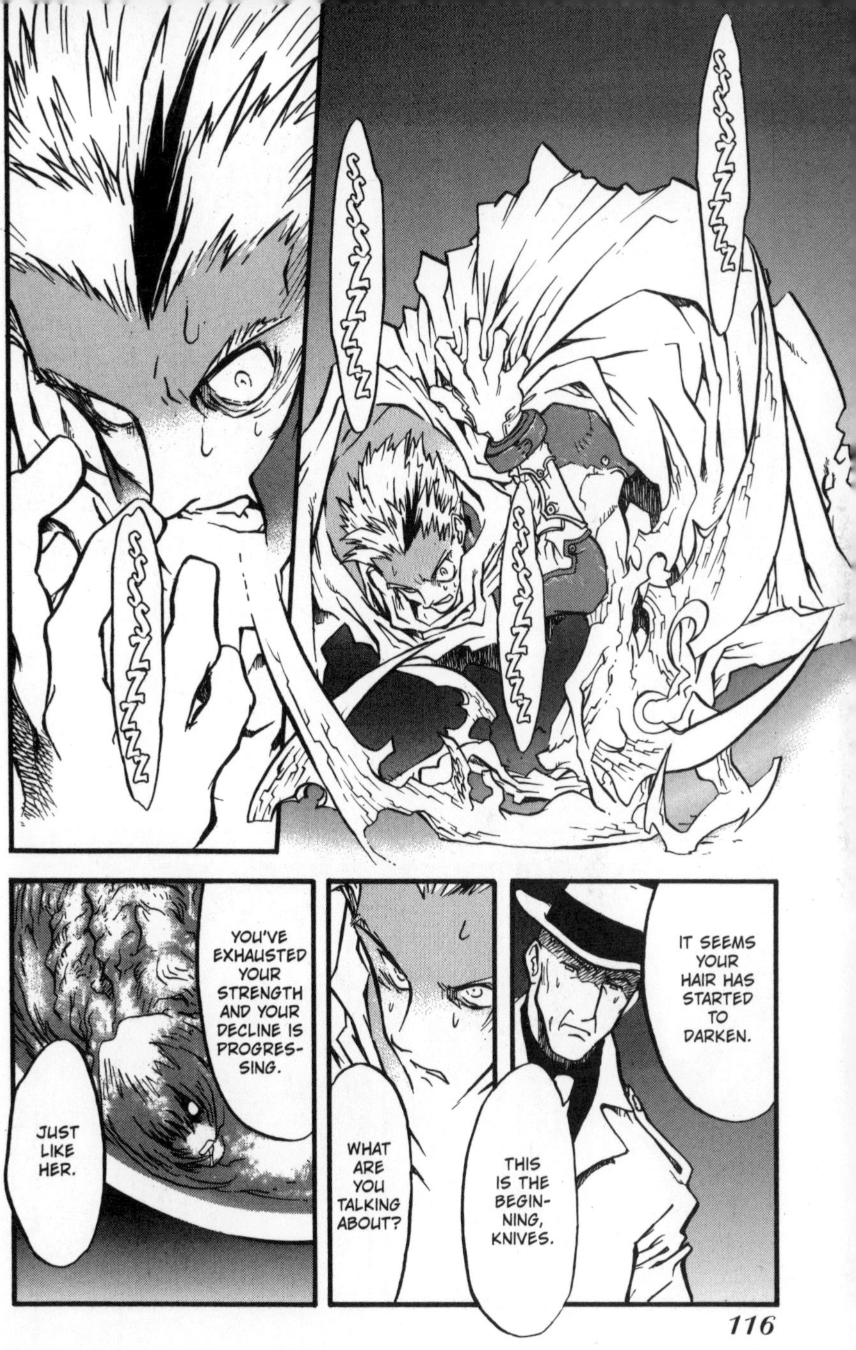
SSSSZZZZZZ
SSSSZZZZZZ
SSSSZZZZZZ
SSSSZZZZZZ
IT SEEMS YOUR HAIR HAS STARTED TO DARKEN.
WHAT ARE YOU TALKING ABOUT?
THIS IS THE BEGIN-NING, KNIVES.
YOU'VE EXHAUSTED YOUR STRENGTH AND YOUR DECLINE IS PROGRES-SING.
JUST LIKE HER.

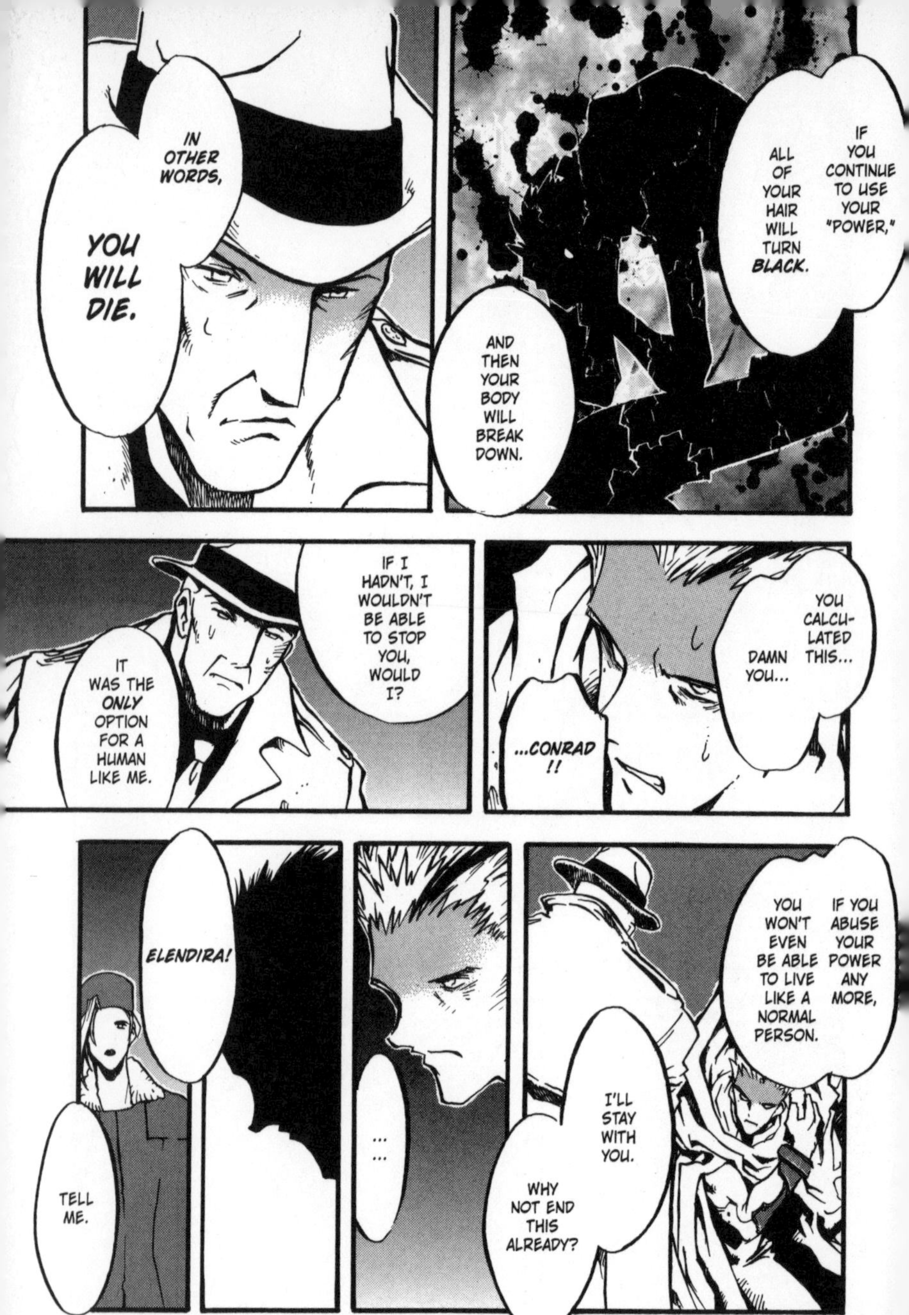
IF YOU CONTINUE TO USE YOUR "POWER,"
ALL OF YOUR HAIR WILL TURN *BLACK.*
AND THEN YOUR BODY WILL BREAK DOWN.
IN OTHER WORDS,
YOU WILL DIE.
YOU CALCULATED THIS...
DAMN YOU...
...CONRAD !!
IF I HADN'T, I WOULDN'T BE ABLE TO STOP YOU, WOULD I?
IT WAS THE *ONLY* OPTION FOR A HUMAN LIKE ME.
IF YOU ABUSE YOUR POWER ANY MORE,
YOU WON'T EVEN BE ABLE TO LIVE LIKE A NORMAL PERSON.
I'LL STAY WITH YOU.
WHY NOT END THIS ALREADY?
... ...
ELENDIRA!
TELL ME.

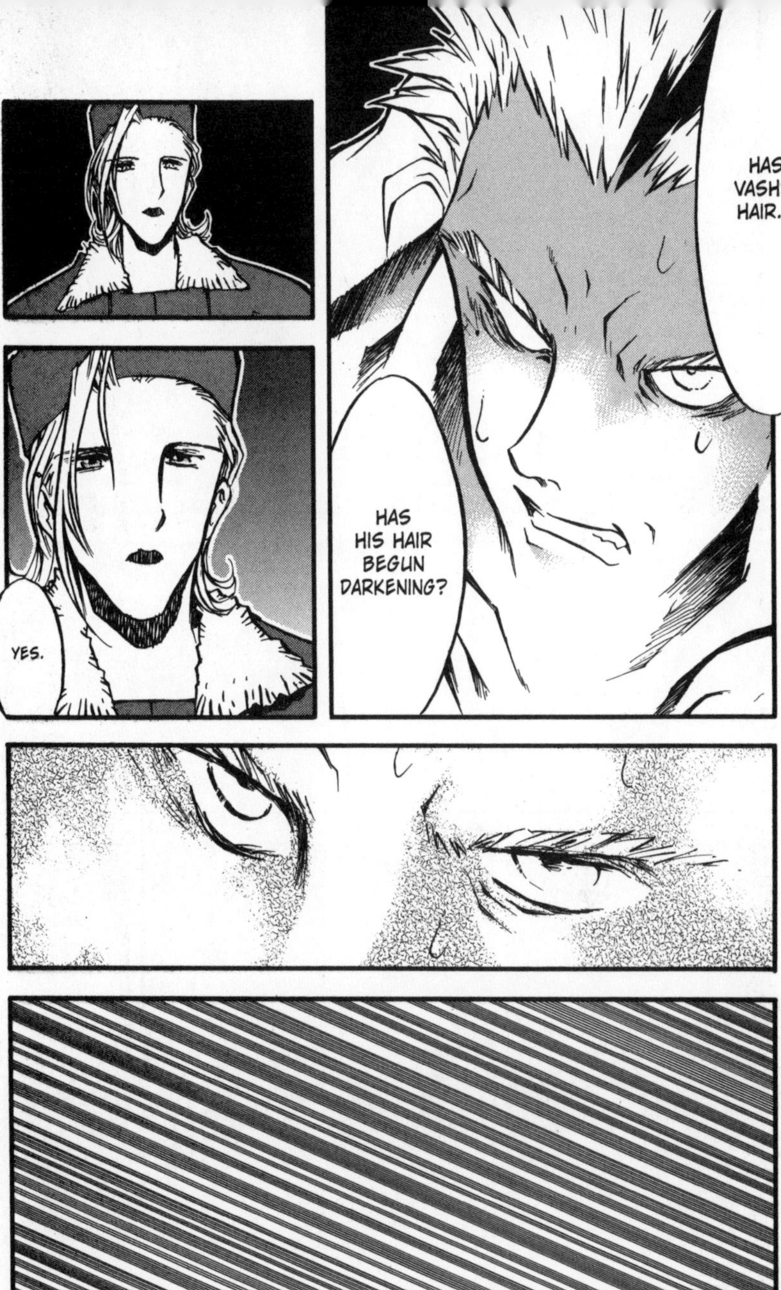
HAS VASH'S HAIR...
HAS HIS HAIR BEGUN DARKENING?
YES.

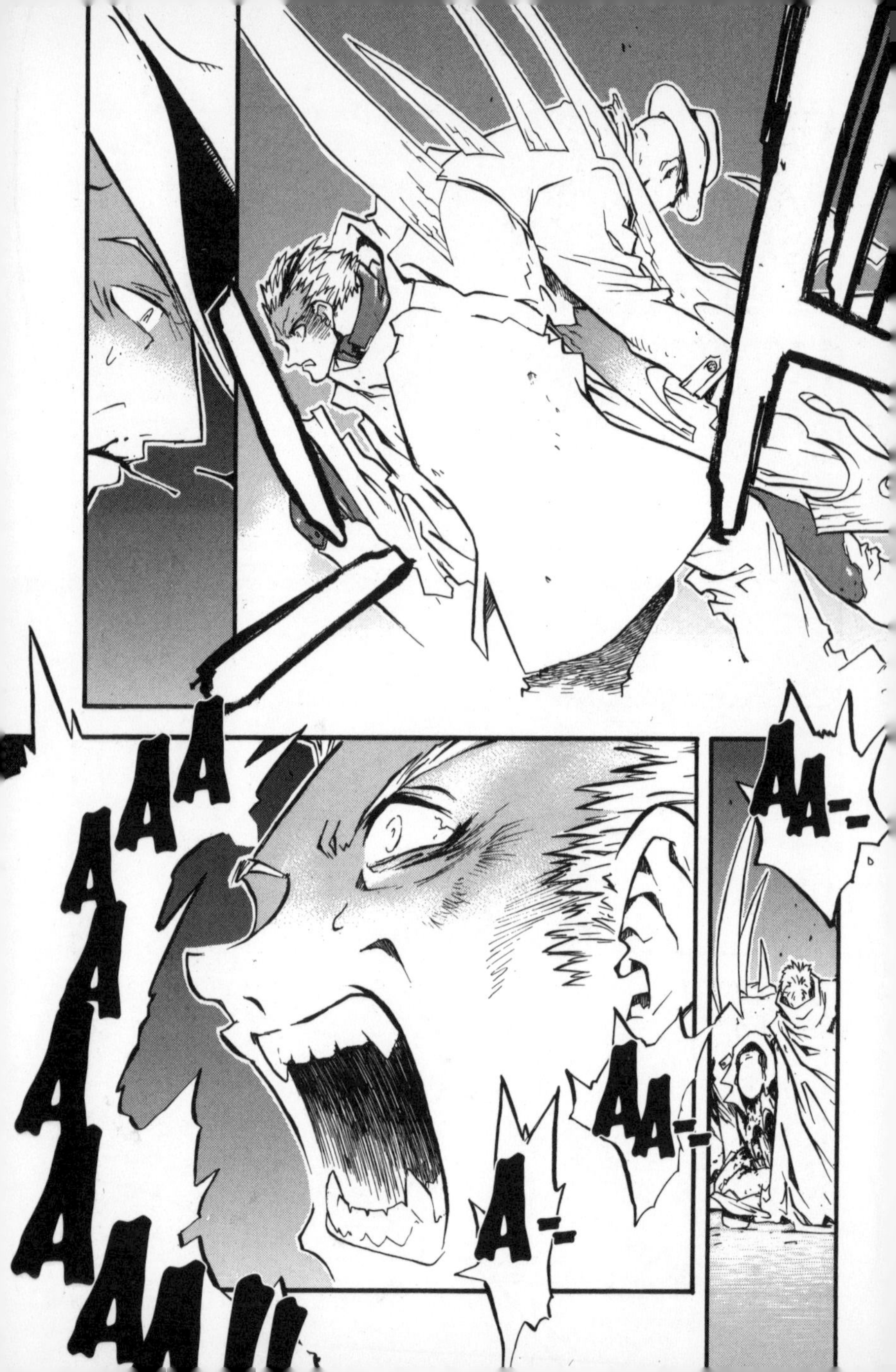
AA--
AA--
A--
AAAAAAAAAAA!!

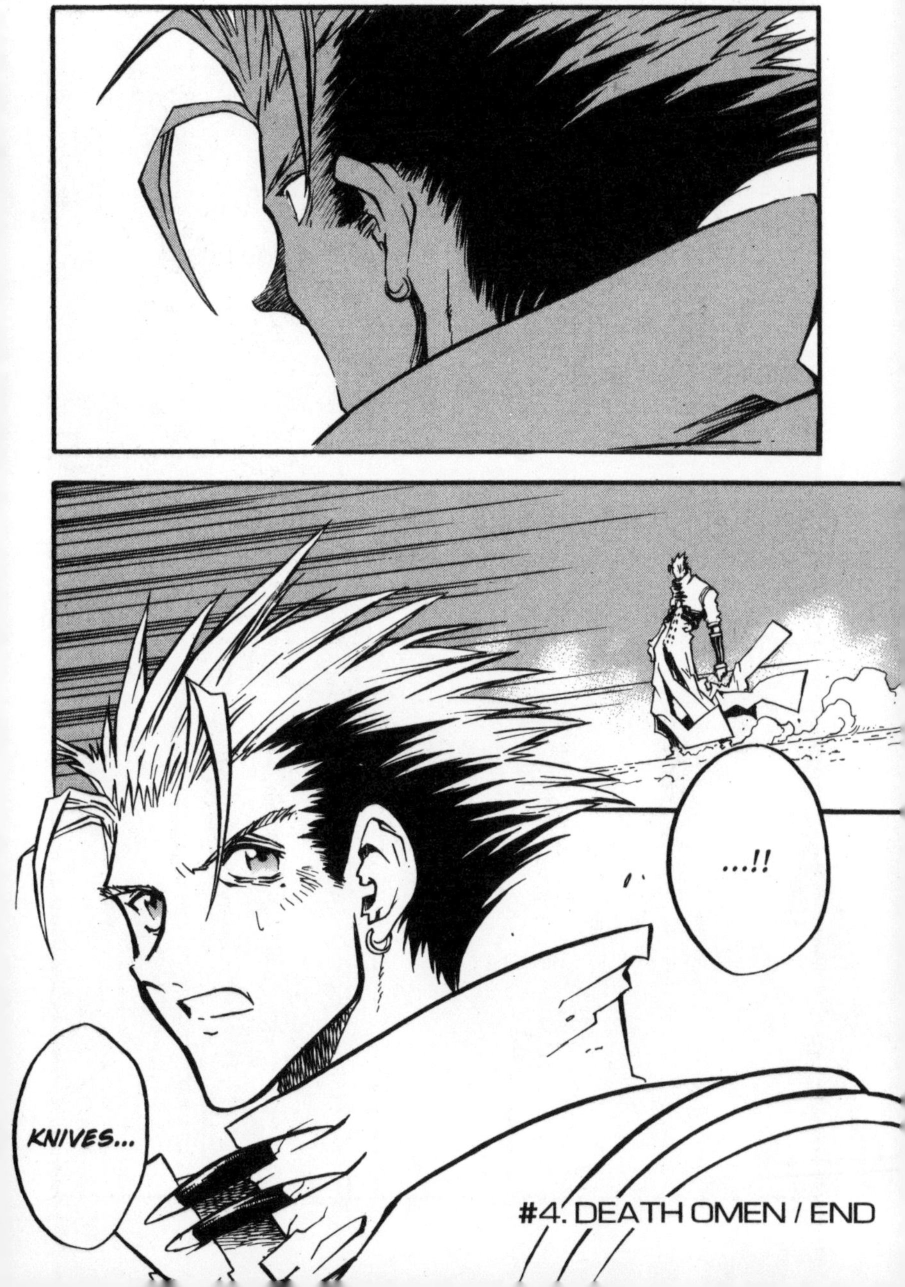
...!!
KNIVES...
#4. DEATH OMEN / END

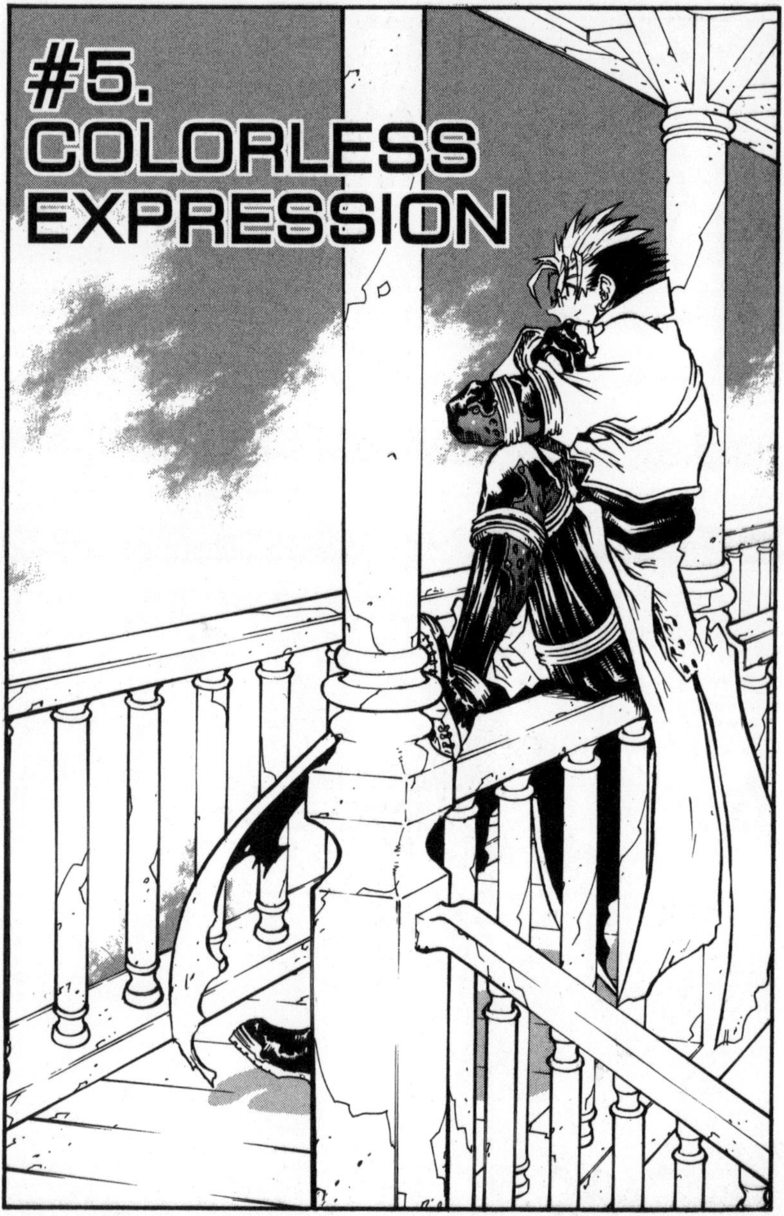
#5.
COLORLESS
EXPRESSION

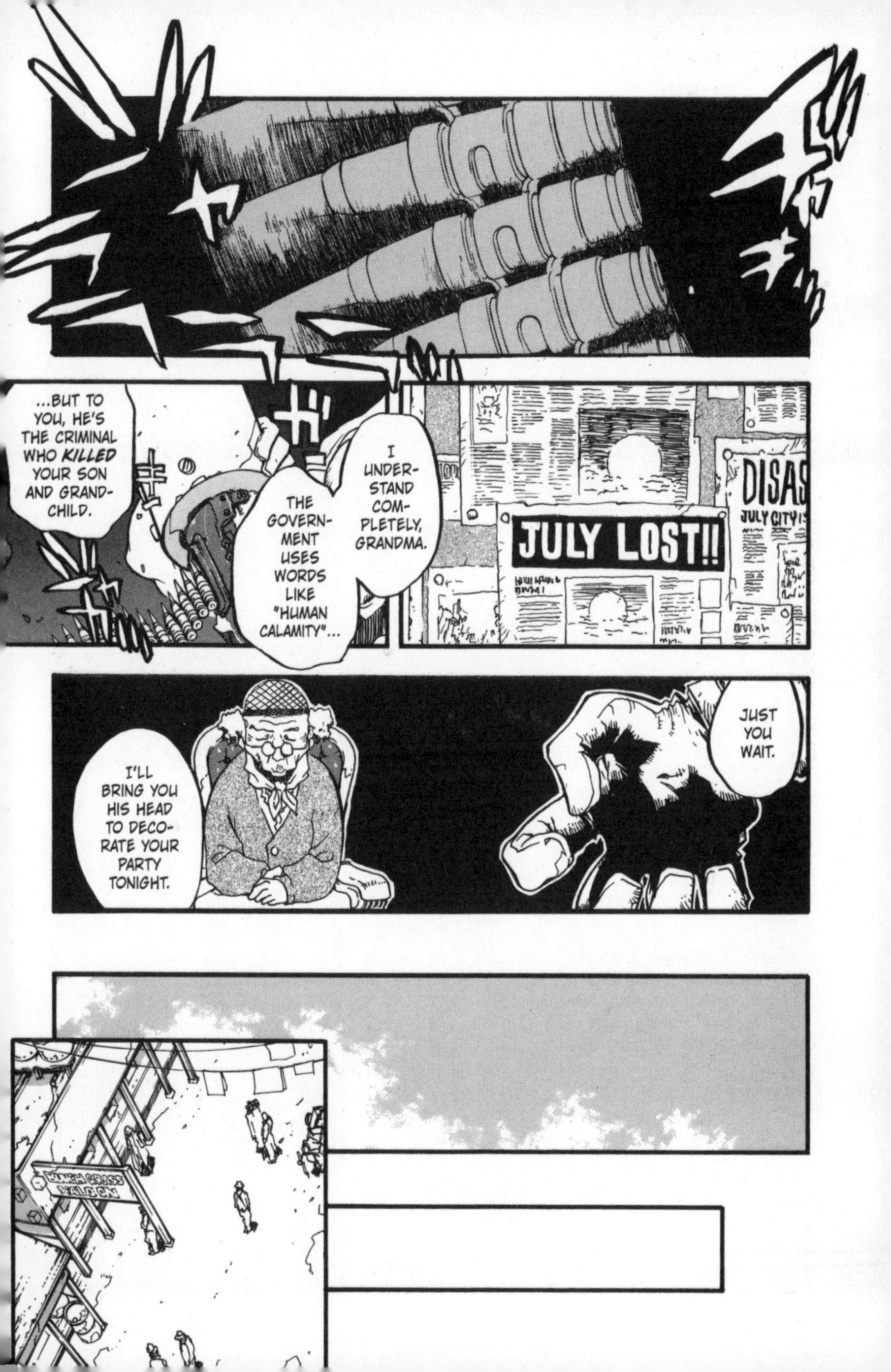
JULY LOST!!
DISAS
JULY CITY IS
I UNDER-STAND COM-PLETELY, GRANDMA.
THE GOVERN-MENT USES WORDS LIKE "HUMAN CALAMITY"...
...BUT TO YOU, HE'S THE CRIMINAL WHO *KILLED* YOUR SON AND GRAND-CHILD.
JUST YOU WAIT.
I'LL BRING YOU HIS HEAD TO DECO-RATE YOUR PARTY TONIGHT.
BUNCH GRASS SALOON

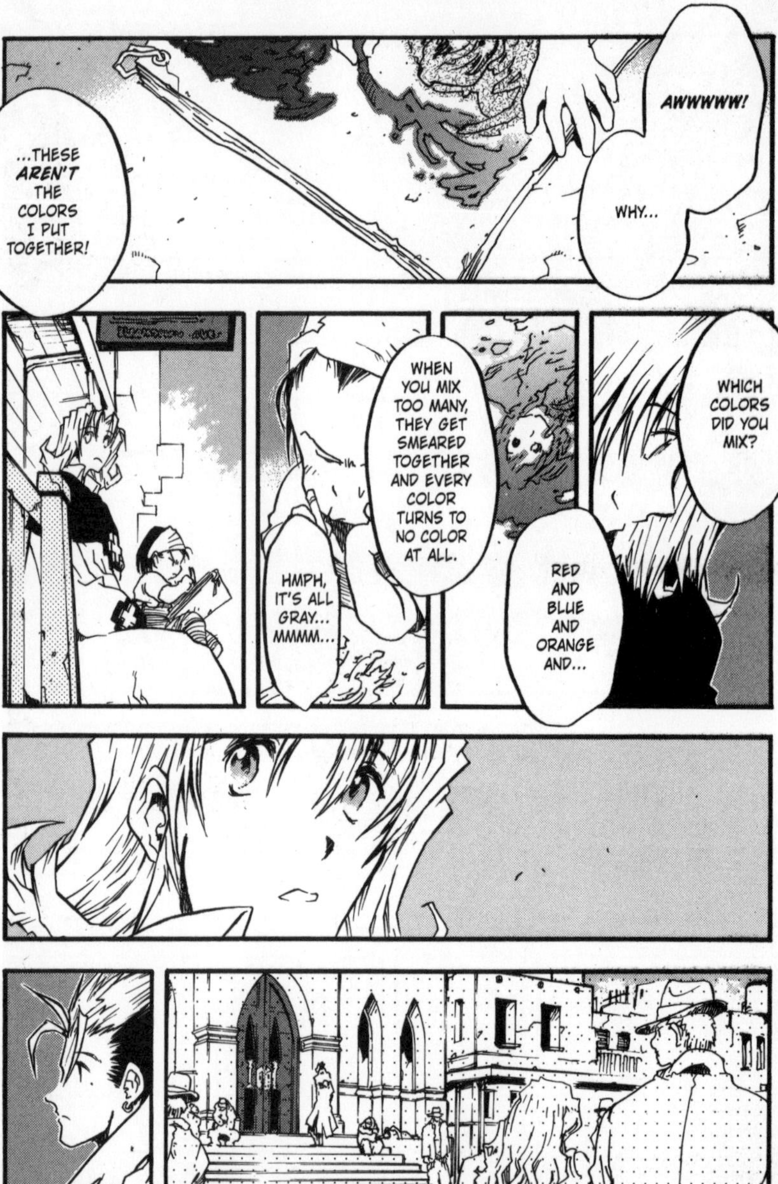
AWWWWW!
WHY...
...THESE AREN'T THE COLORS I PUT TOGETHER!
WHICH COLORS DID YOU MIX?
RED AND BLUE AND ORANGE AND...
WHEN YOU MIX TOO MANY, THEY GET SMEARED TOGETHER AND EVERY COLOR TURNS TO NO COLOR AT ALL.
HMPH, IT'S ALL GRAY... MMMM...

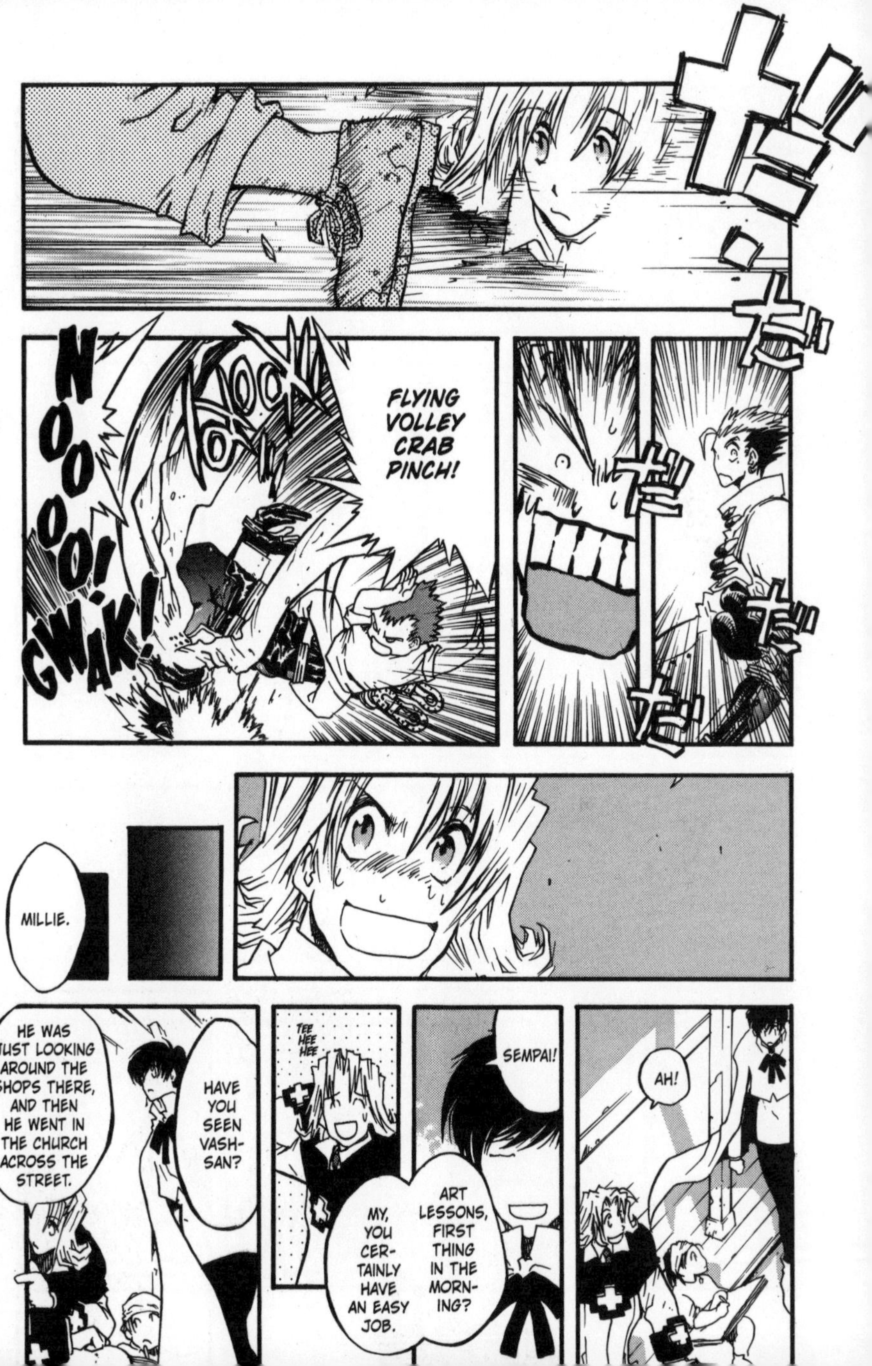
FLYING VOLLEY CRAB PINCH!
KOOOK
NOOOOO!
GWAK!
MILLIE.
AH!
SEMPAI!
ART LESSONS, FIRST THING IN THE MORNING?
TEE HEE HEE
MY, YOU CERTAINLY HAVE AN EASY JOB.
HAVE YOU SEEN VASH-SAN?
HE WAS JUST LOOKING AROUND THE SHOPS THERE, AND THEN HE WENT IN THE CHURCH ACROSS THE STREET.

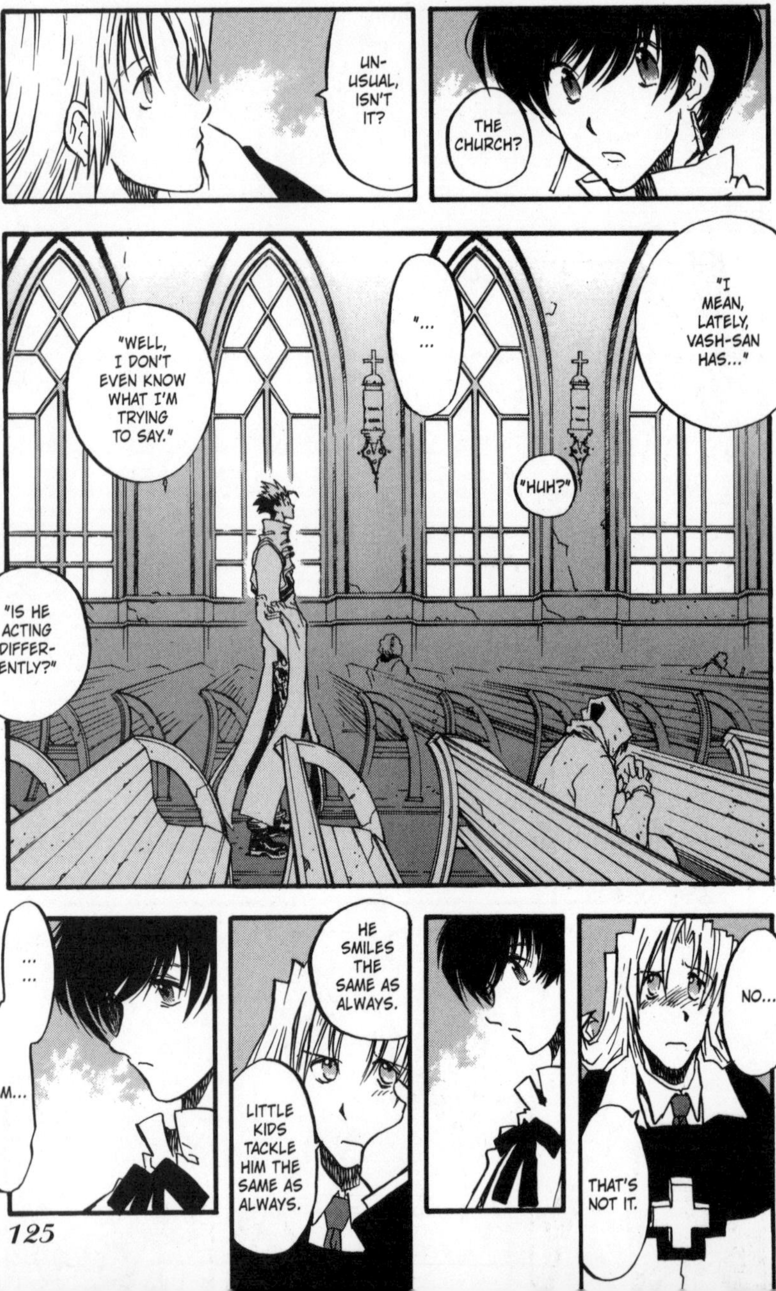
THE CHURCH?
UN-USUAL, ISN'T IT?
"I MEAN, LATELY, VASH-SAN HAS..."
"HUH?"
"... ..."
"WELL, I DON'T EVEN KNOW WHAT I'M TRYING TO SAY."
"IS HE ACTING DIFFER-ENTLY?"
NO...
THAT'S NOT IT.
HE SMILES THE SAME AS ALWAYS.
LITTLE KIDS TACKLE HIM THE SAME AS ALWAYS.
... ...
HMM...

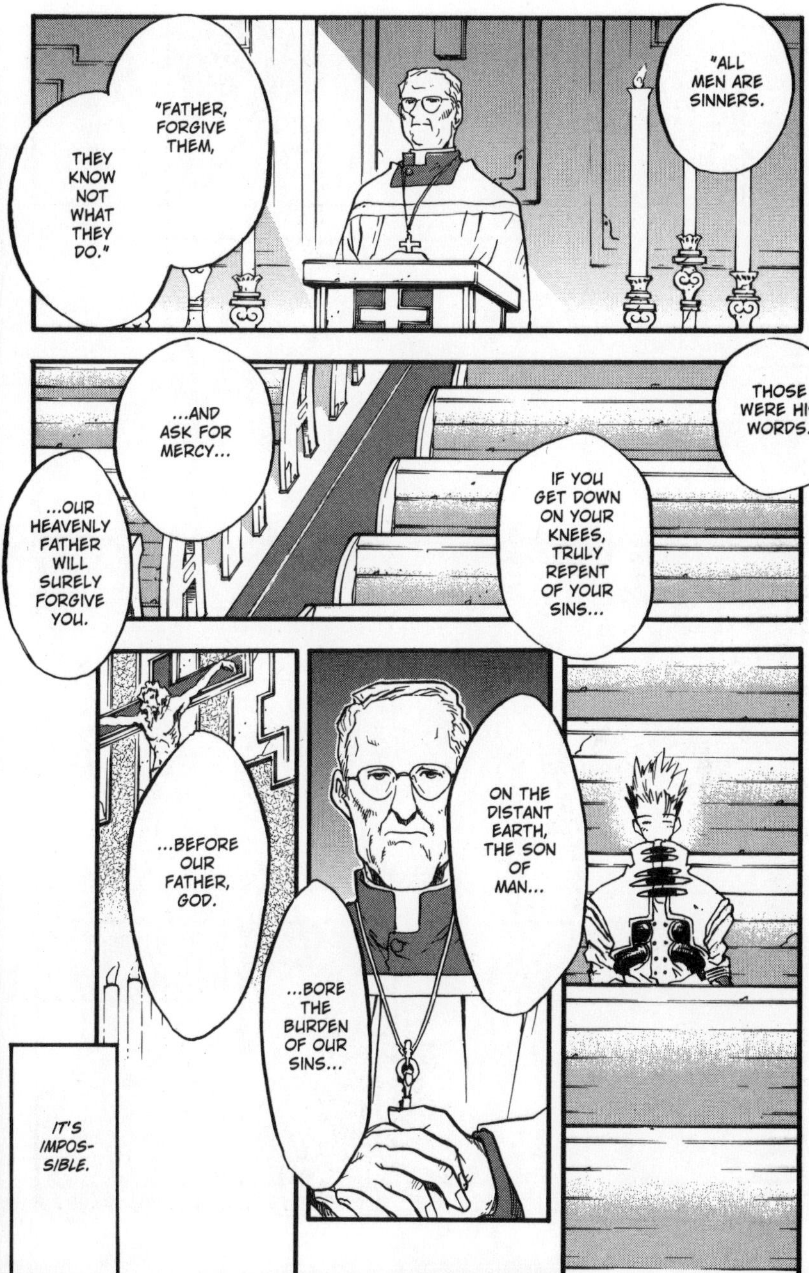
"ALL MEN ARE SINNERS.
"FATHER, FORGIVE THEM,
THEY KNOW NOT WHAT THEY DO."
THOSE WERE HIS WORDS.
IF YOU GET DOWN ON YOUR KNEES, TRULY REPENT OF YOUR SINS...
...AND ASK FOR MERCY...
...OUR HEAVENLY FATHER WILL SURELY FORGIVE YOU.
ON THE DISTANT EARTH, THE SON OF MAN...
...BORE THE BURDEN OF OUR SINS...
...BEFORE OUR FATHER, GOD.
IT'S IMPOS-SIBLE.

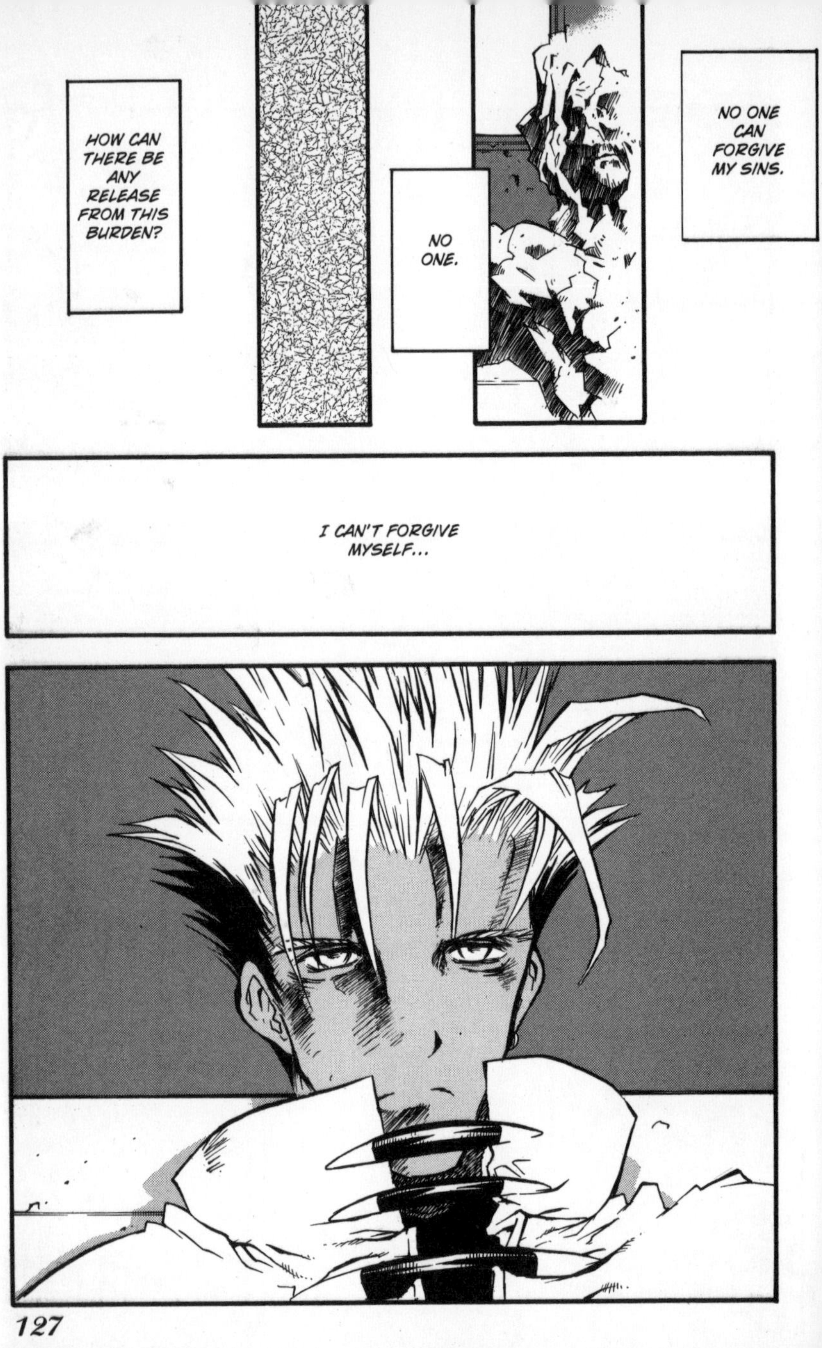
NO ONE CAN FORGIVE MY SINS.
NO ONE.
HOW CAN THERE BE ANY RELEASE FROM THIS BURDEN?
I CAN'T FORGIVE MYSELF...

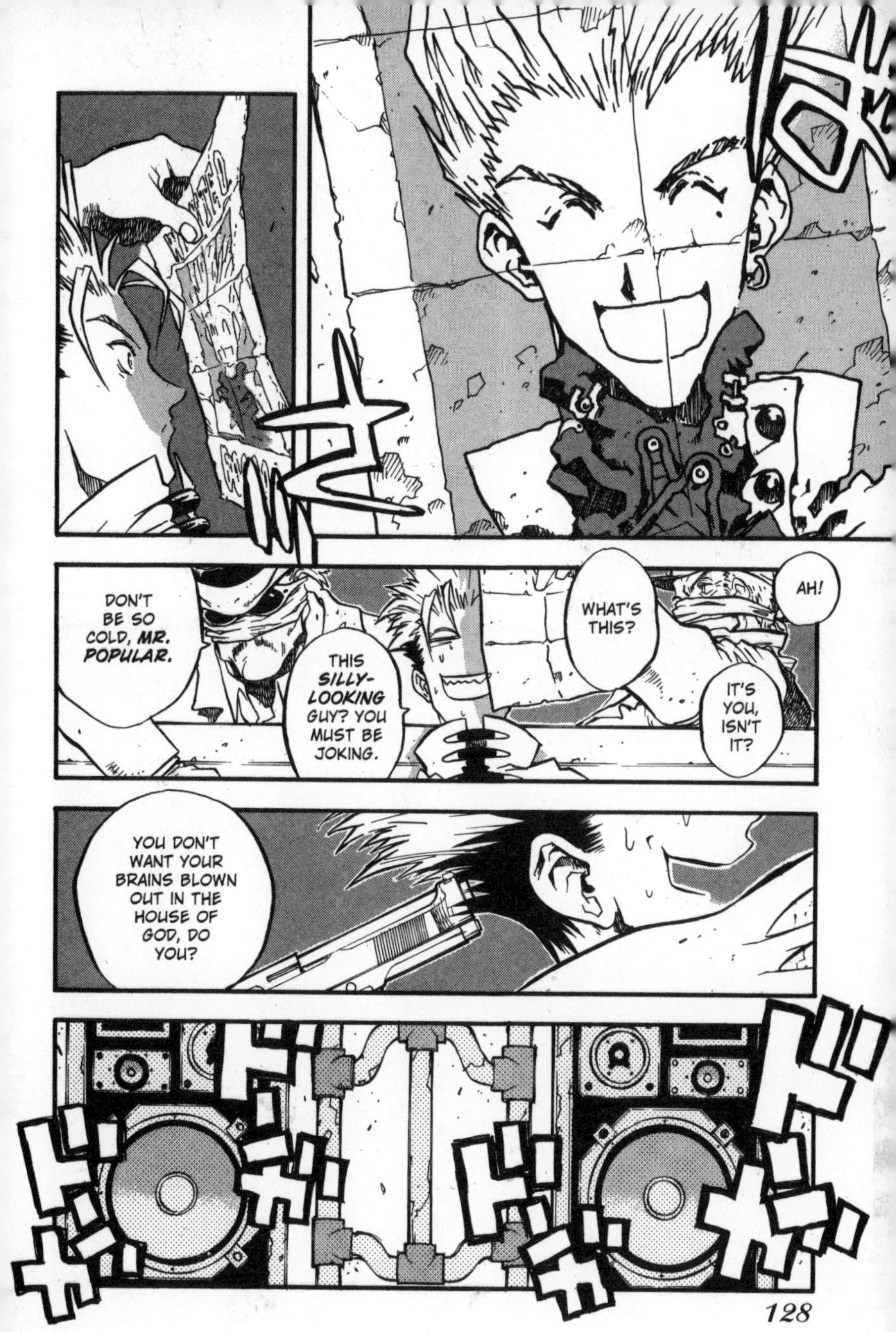
AH!
WHAT'S THIS?
IT'S YOU, ISN'T IT?
THIS SILLY-LOOKING GUY? YOU MUST BE JOKING.
DON'T BE SO COLD, MR. POPULAR.
YOU DON'T WANT YOUR BRAINS BLOWN OUT IN THE HOUSE OF GOD, DO YOU?

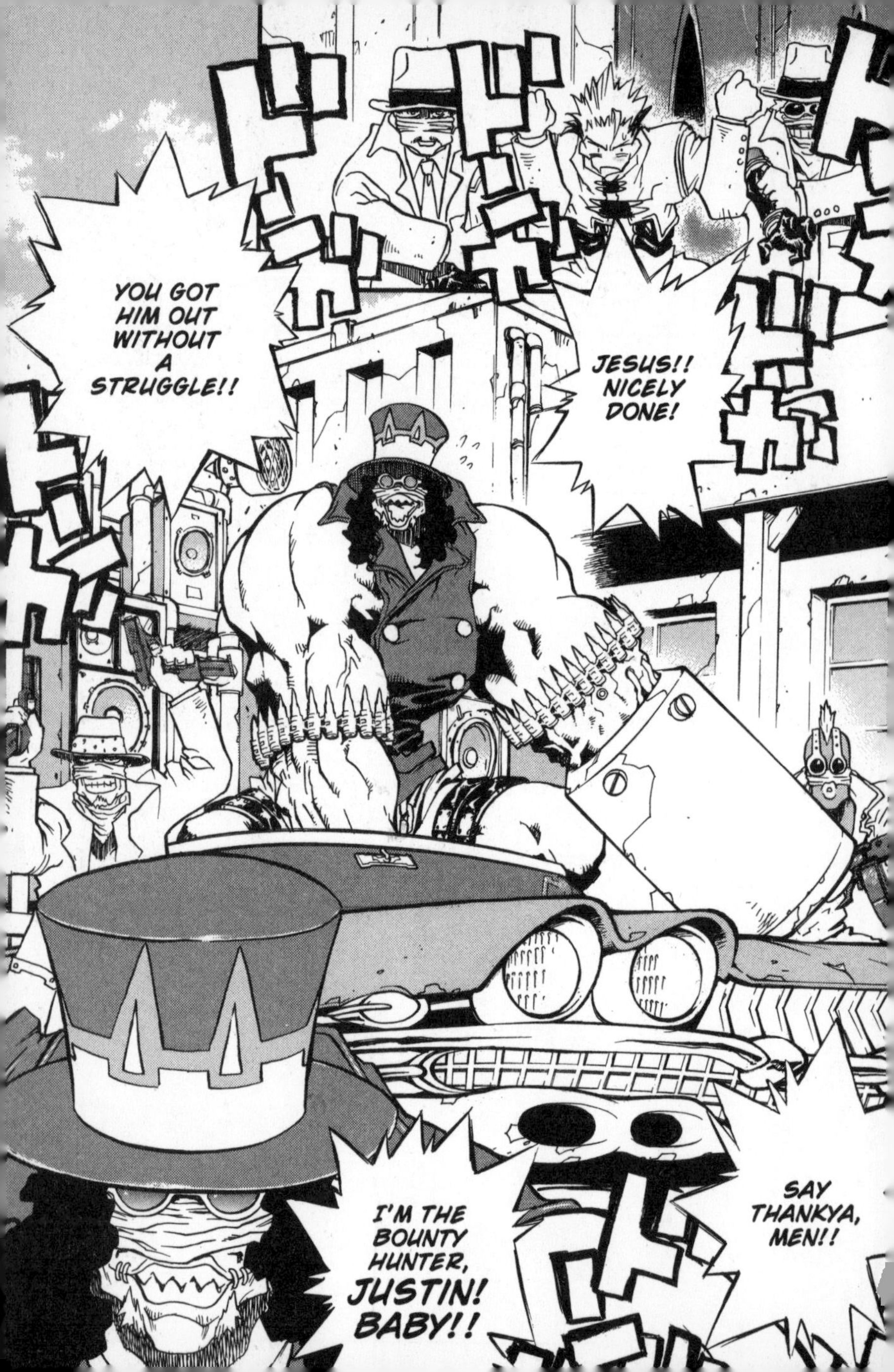
JESUS!! NICELY DONE!
YOU GOT HIM OUT WITHOUT A STRUGGLE!!
SAY THANKYA, MEN!!
I'M THE BOUNTY HUNTER, JUSTIN! BABY!!

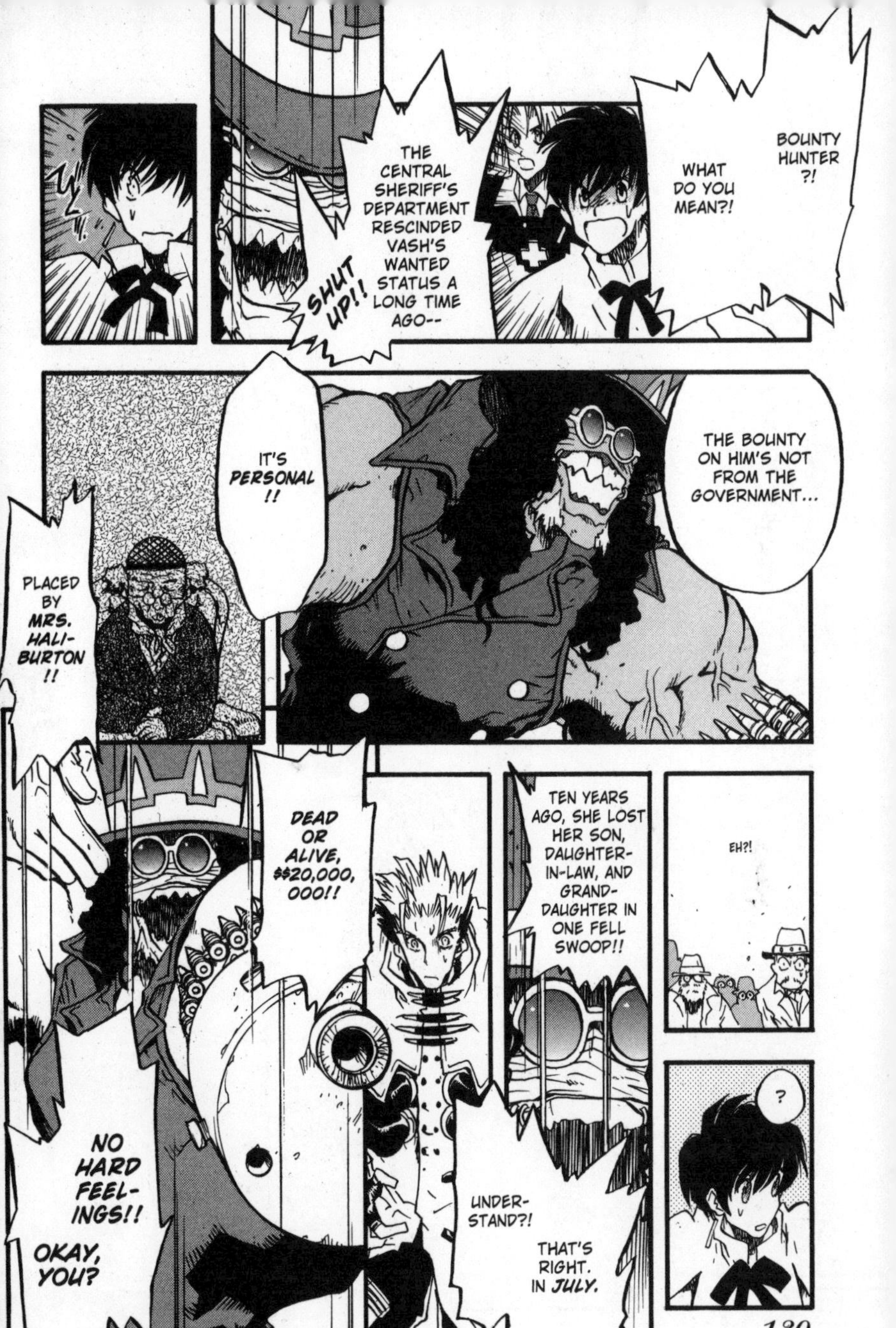
BOUNTY HUNTER?!
WHAT DO YOU MEAN?!
THE CENTRAL SHERIFF'S DEPARTMENT RESCINDED VASH'S WANTED STATUS A LONG TIME AGO--
SHUT UP!!
THE BOUNTY ON HIM'S NOT FROM THE GOVERNMENT...
IT'S PERSONAL!!
PLACED BY MRS. HALIBURTON!!
EH?!
?
TEN YEARS AGO, SHE LOST HER SON, DAUGHTER-IN-LAW, AND GRAND-DAUGHTER IN ONE FELL SWOOP!!
DEAD OR ALIVE, $$20,000,000!!
UNDERSTAND?!
THAT'S RIGHT. IN JULY.
NO HARD FEELINGS!!
OKAY, YOU?

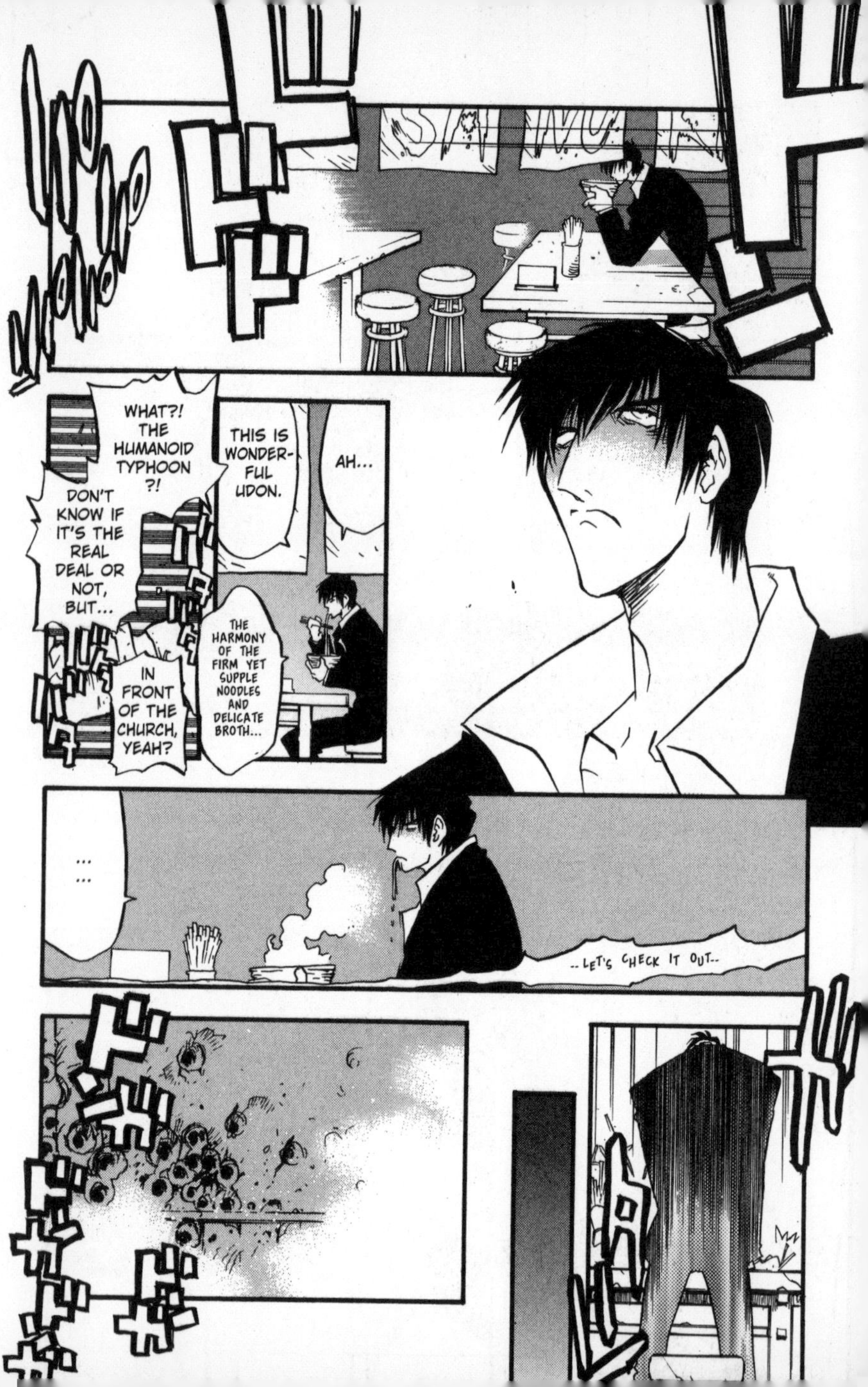
AH...
THIS IS WONDERFUL UDON.
THE HARMONY OF THE FIRM YET SUPPLE NOODLES AND DELICATE BROTH...
WHAT?! THE HUMANOID TYPHOON ?!
DON'T KNOW IF IT'S THE REAL DEAL OR NOT, BUT...
IN FRONT OF THE CHURCH, YEAH?
--LET'S CHECK IT OUT--
......

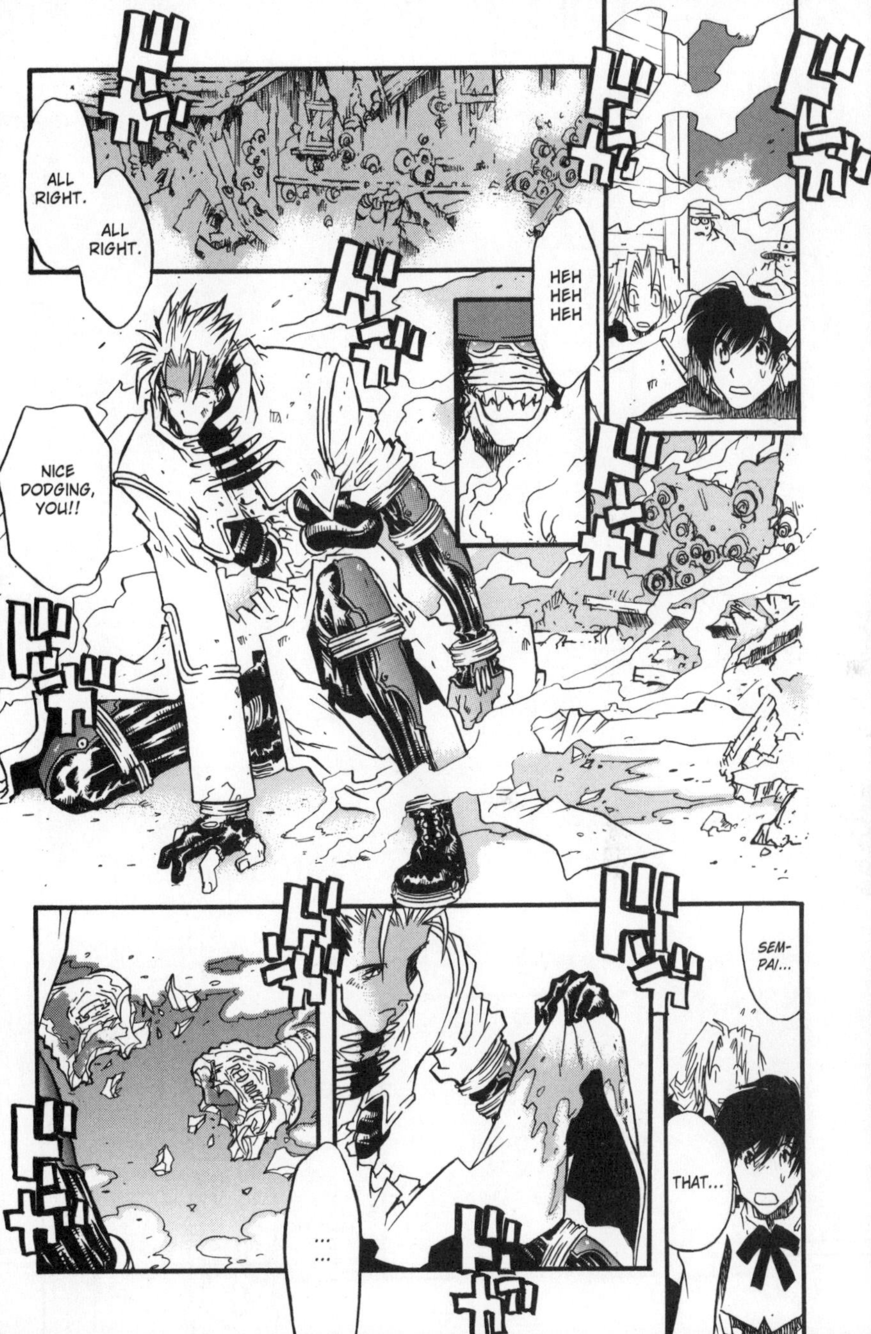
ALL RIGHT.
ALL RIGHT.
HEH HEH HEH
NICE DODGING, YOU!!
SEM-PAI...
THAT...
... ...

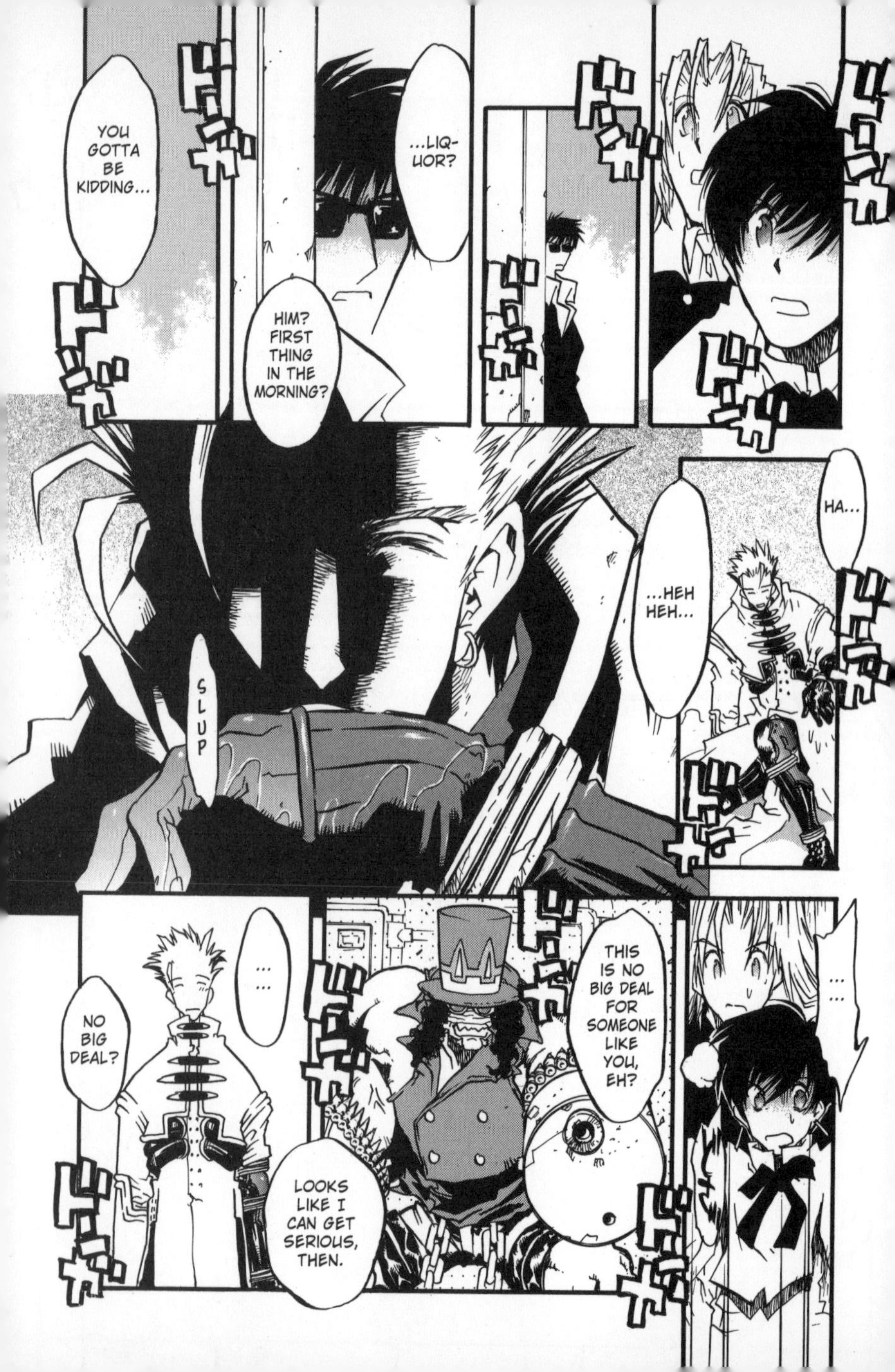
...LIQ-
UOR?
HIM? FIRST THING IN THE MORNING?
YOU GOTTA BE KIDDING...
HA...
...HEH HEH...
SLUP
... ...
THIS IS NO BIG DEAL FOR SOMEONE LIKE YOU, EH?
LOOKS LIKE I CAN GET SERIOUS, THEN.
... ...
NO BIG DEAL?

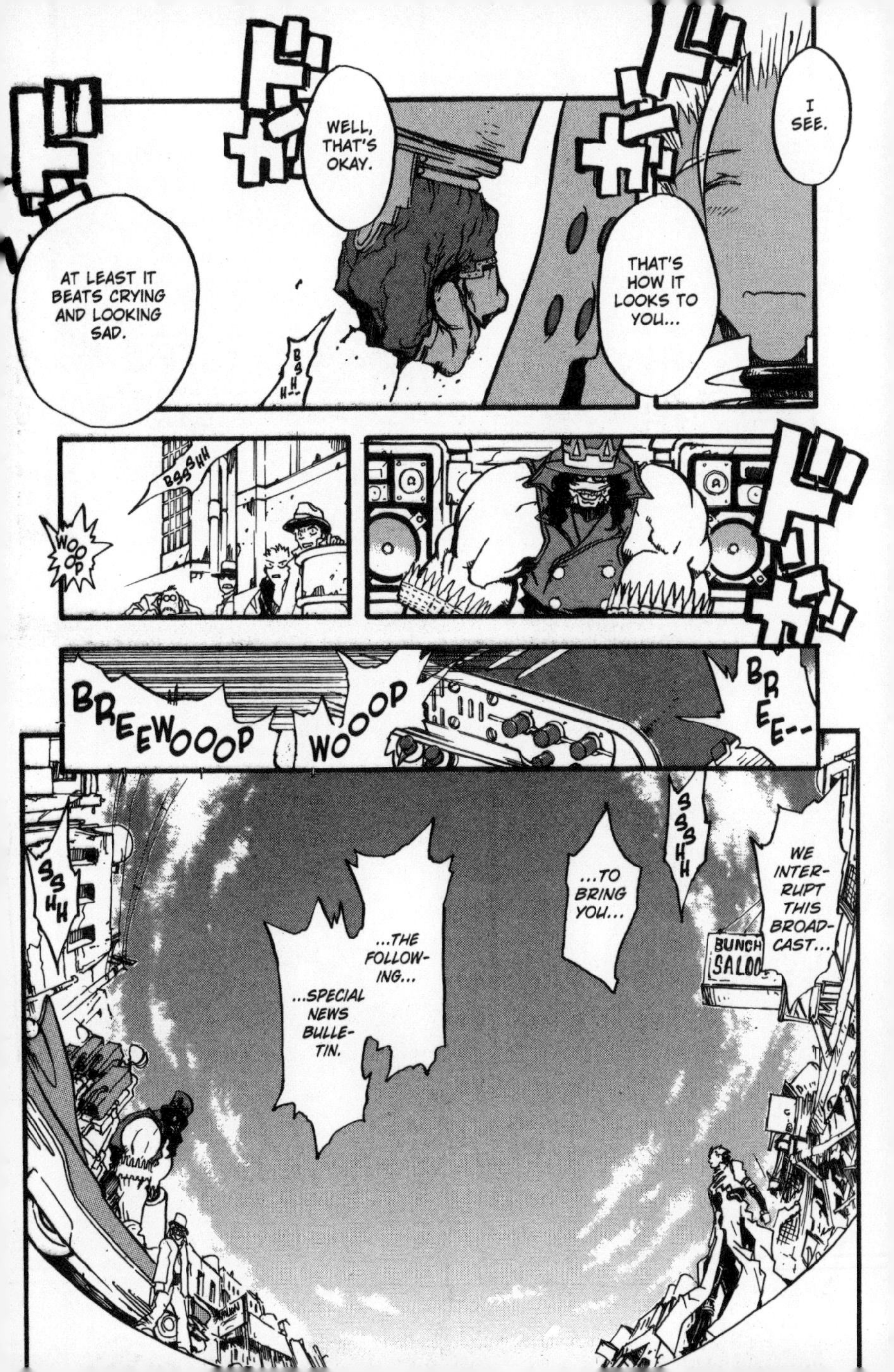
I SEE.
THAT'S HOW IT LOOKS TO YOU...
WELL, THAT'S OKAY.
AT LEAST IT BEATS CRYING AND LOOKING SAD.
BSHH--
BSSSHH
WOOOP
BREE--
WOOOP
BREEWOOOP
WE INTERRUPT THIS BROADCAST...
BUNCH SALOO
SSSHH
...TO BRING YOU...
...THE FOLLOWING...
...SPECIAL NEWS BULLETIN.
SSHH

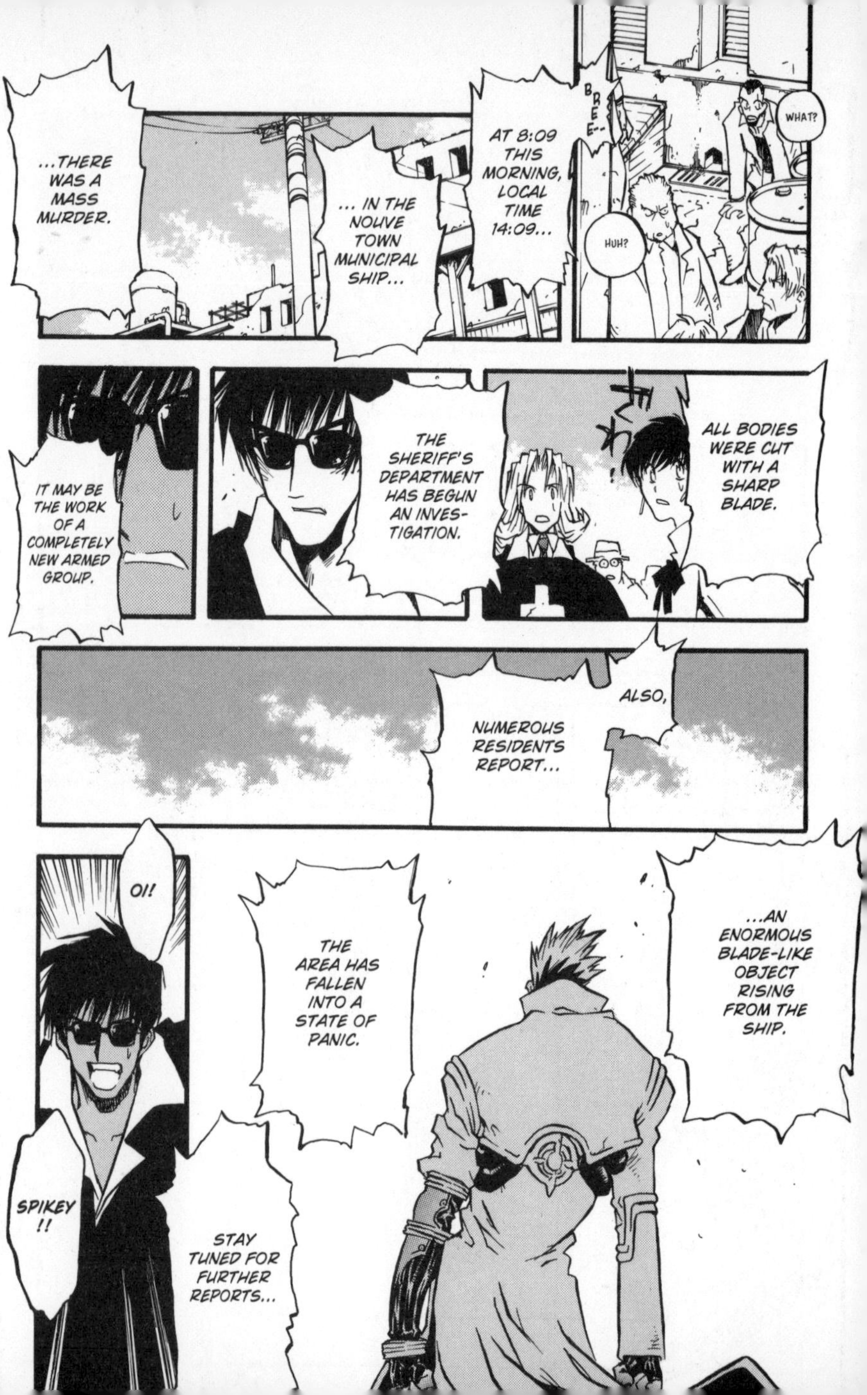
BREE--
AT 8:09 THIS MORNING, LOCAL TIME 14:09...
WHAT?
HUH?
... IN THE NOUVE TOWN MUNICIPAL SHIP...
...THERE WAS A MASS MURDER.
ALL BODIES WERE CUT WITH A SHARP BLADE.
THE SHERIFF'S DEPARTMENT HAS BEGUN AN INVESTIGATION.
IT MAY BE THE WORK OF A COMPLETELY NEW ARMED GROUP.
ALSO,
NUMEROUS RESIDENTS REPORT...
...AN ENORMOUS BLADE-LIKE OBJECT RISING FROM THE SHIP.
THE AREA HAS FALLEN INTO A STATE OF PANIC.
STAY TUNED FOR FURTHER REPORTS...
OI!
SPIKEY !!

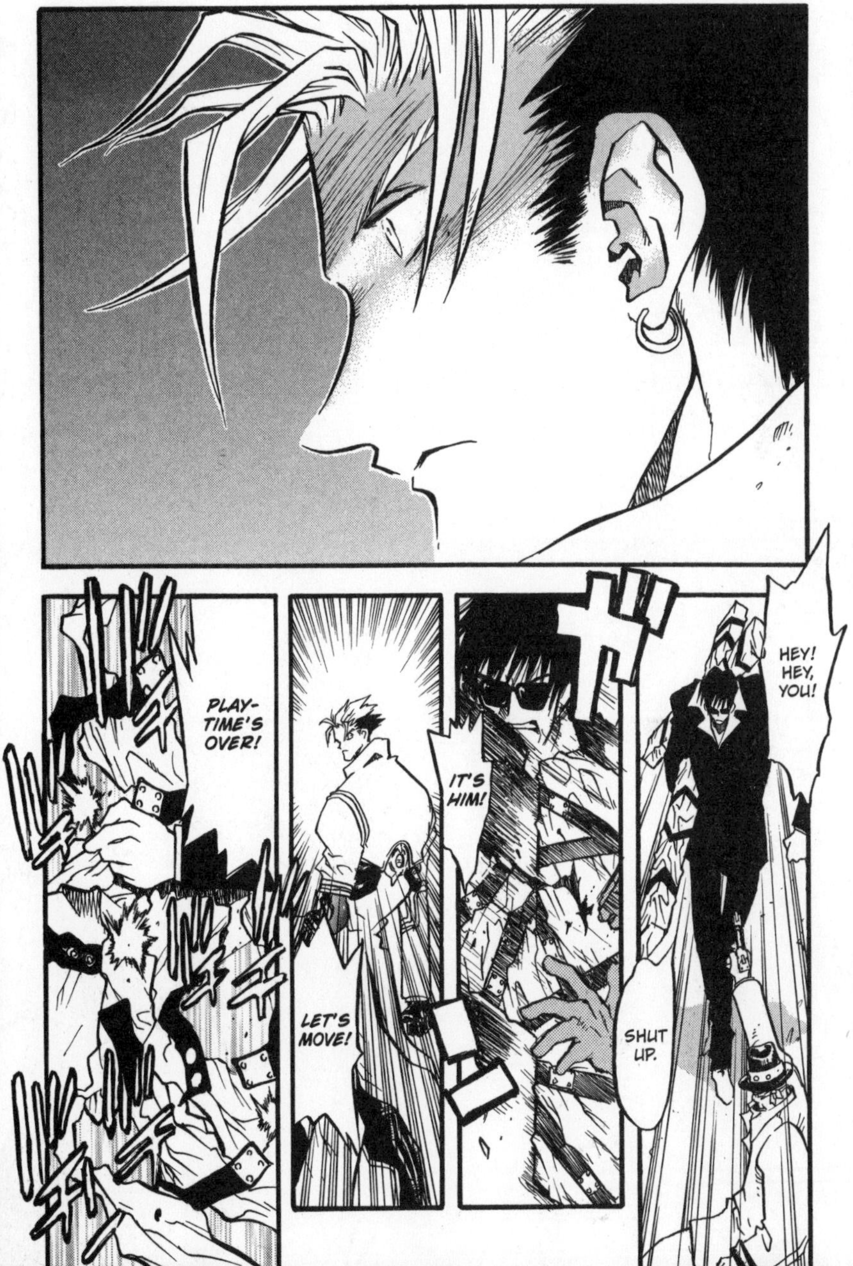
HEY! HEY, YOU!
SHUT UP.
IT'S HIM!
LET'S MOVE!
PLAY-TIME'S OVER!

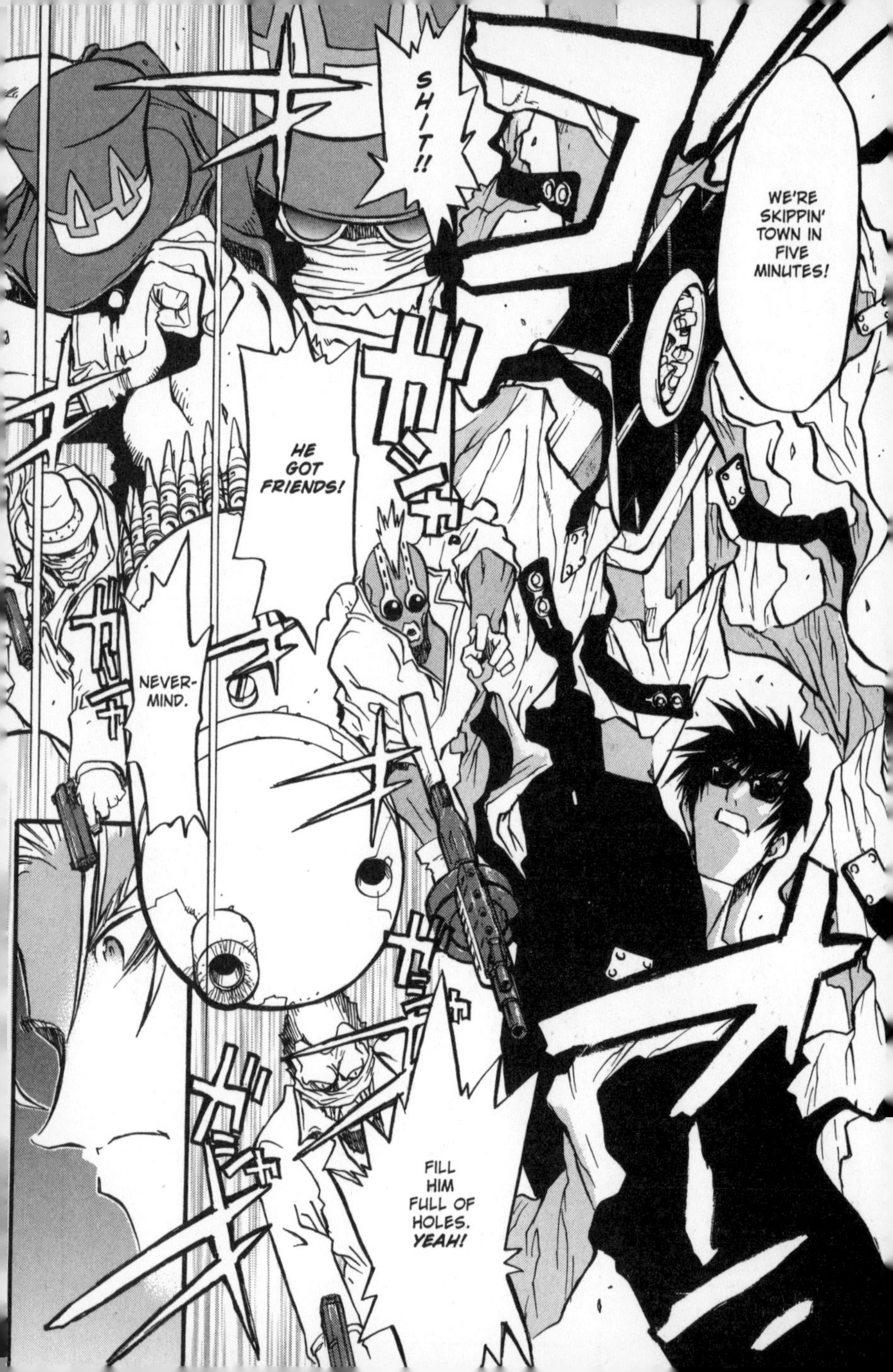
WE'RE SKIPPIN' TOWN IN FIVE MINUTES!
SHIT!!
HE GOT FRIENDS!
NEVER-MIND.
FILL HIM FULL OF HOLES. YEAH!

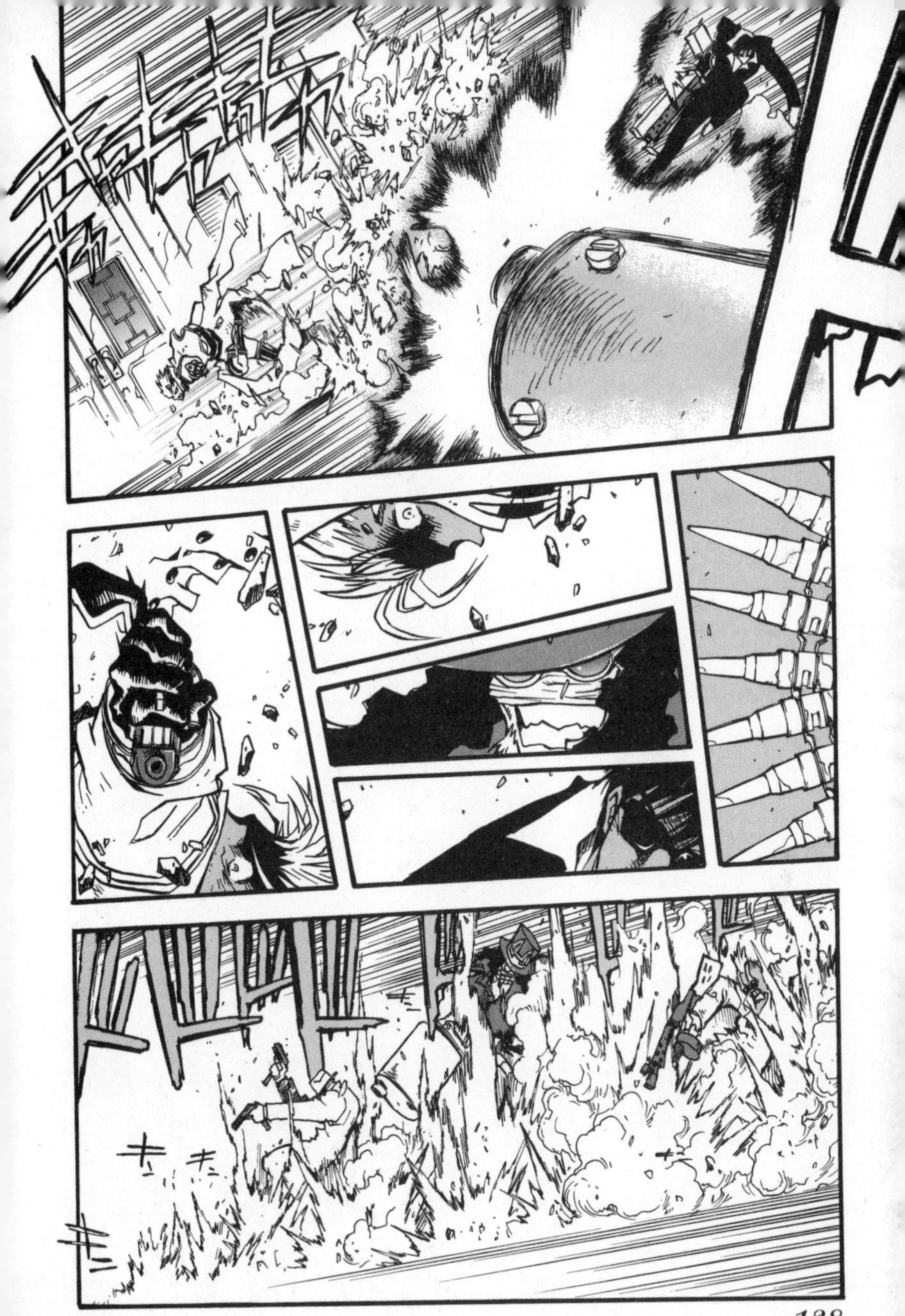

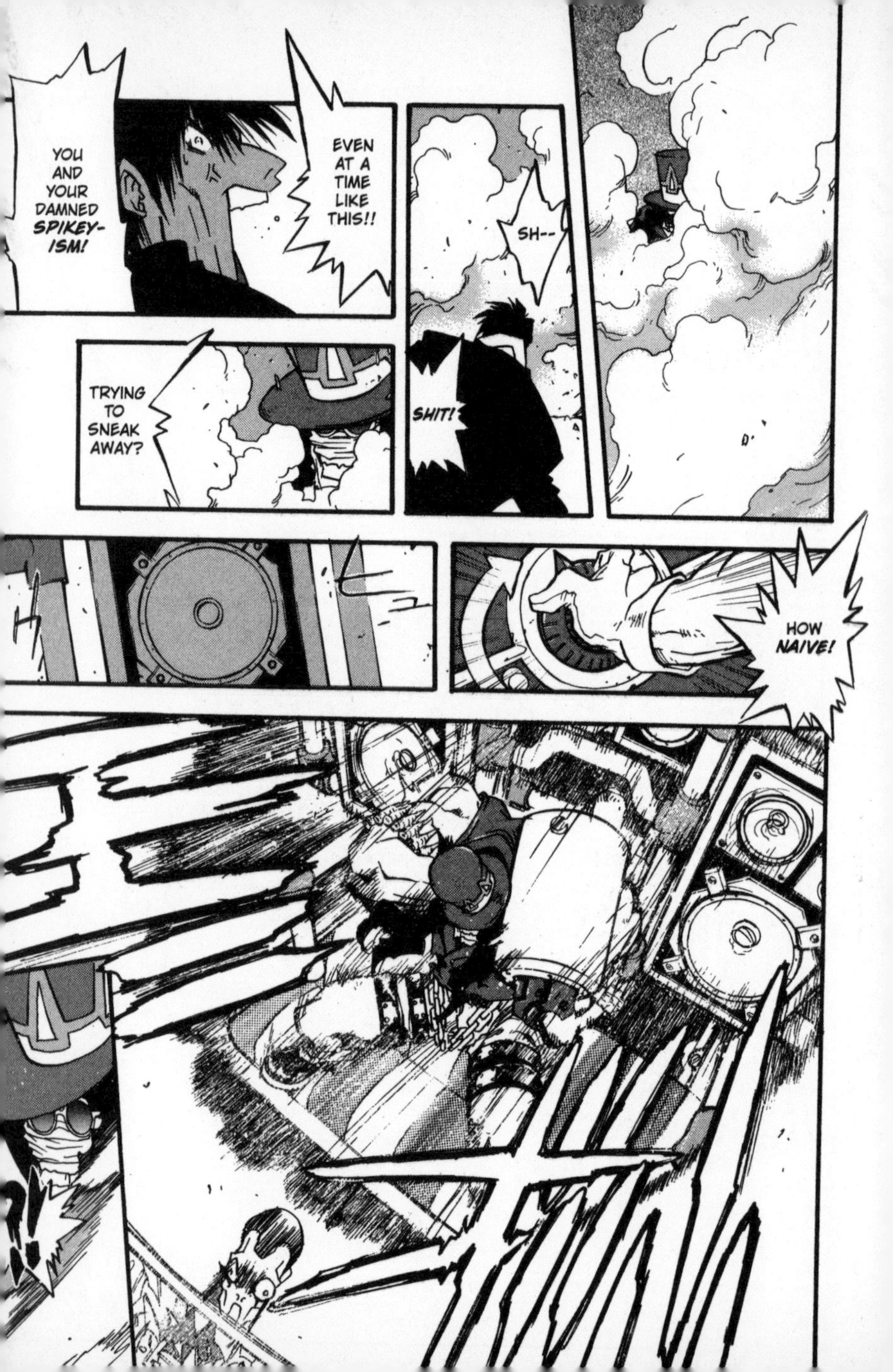
SH--
SHIT!
EVEN AT A TIME LIKE THIS!!
YOU AND YOUR DAMNED SPIKEY-ISM!
TRYING TO SNEAK AWAY?
HOW NAIVE!

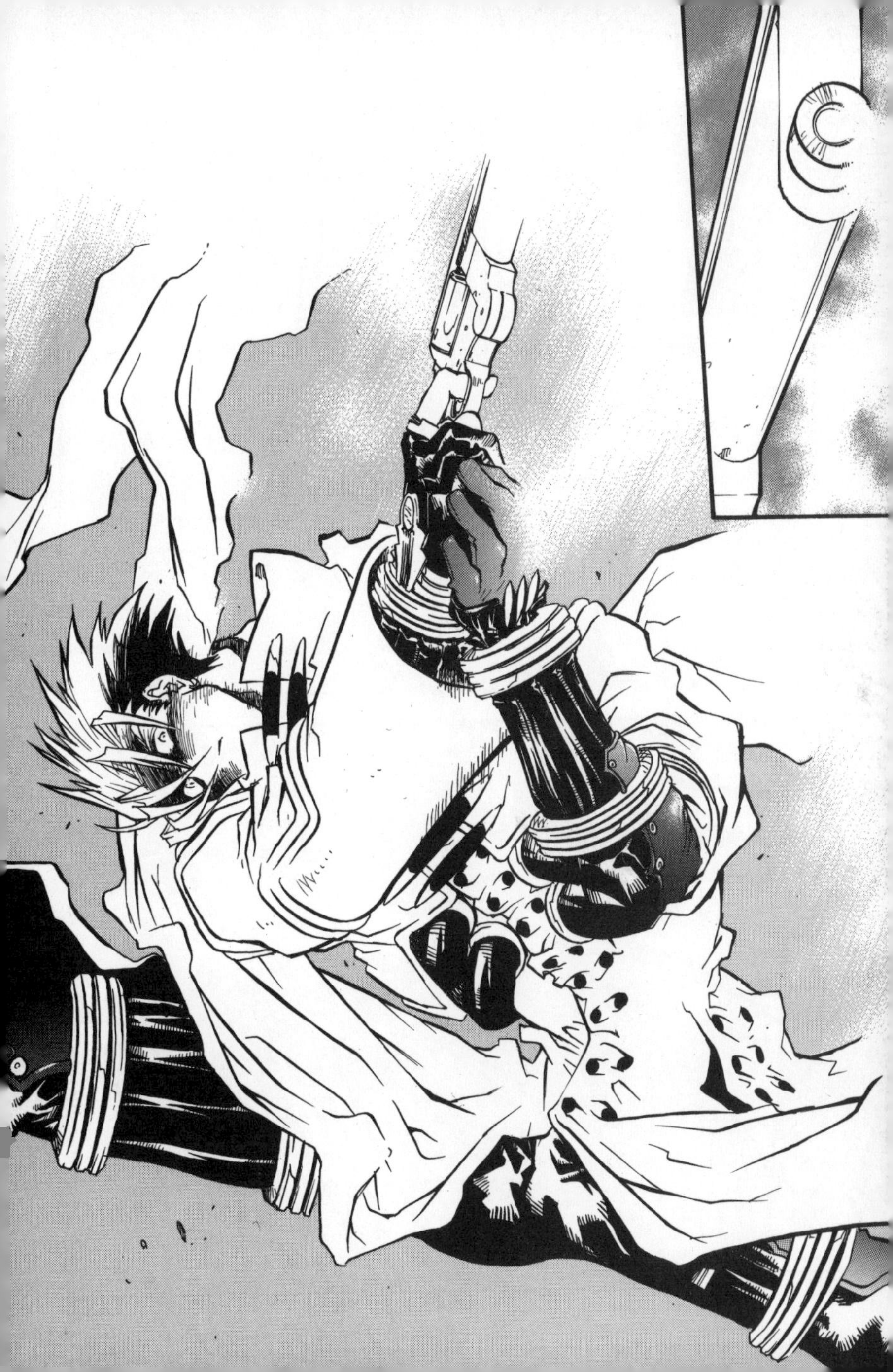

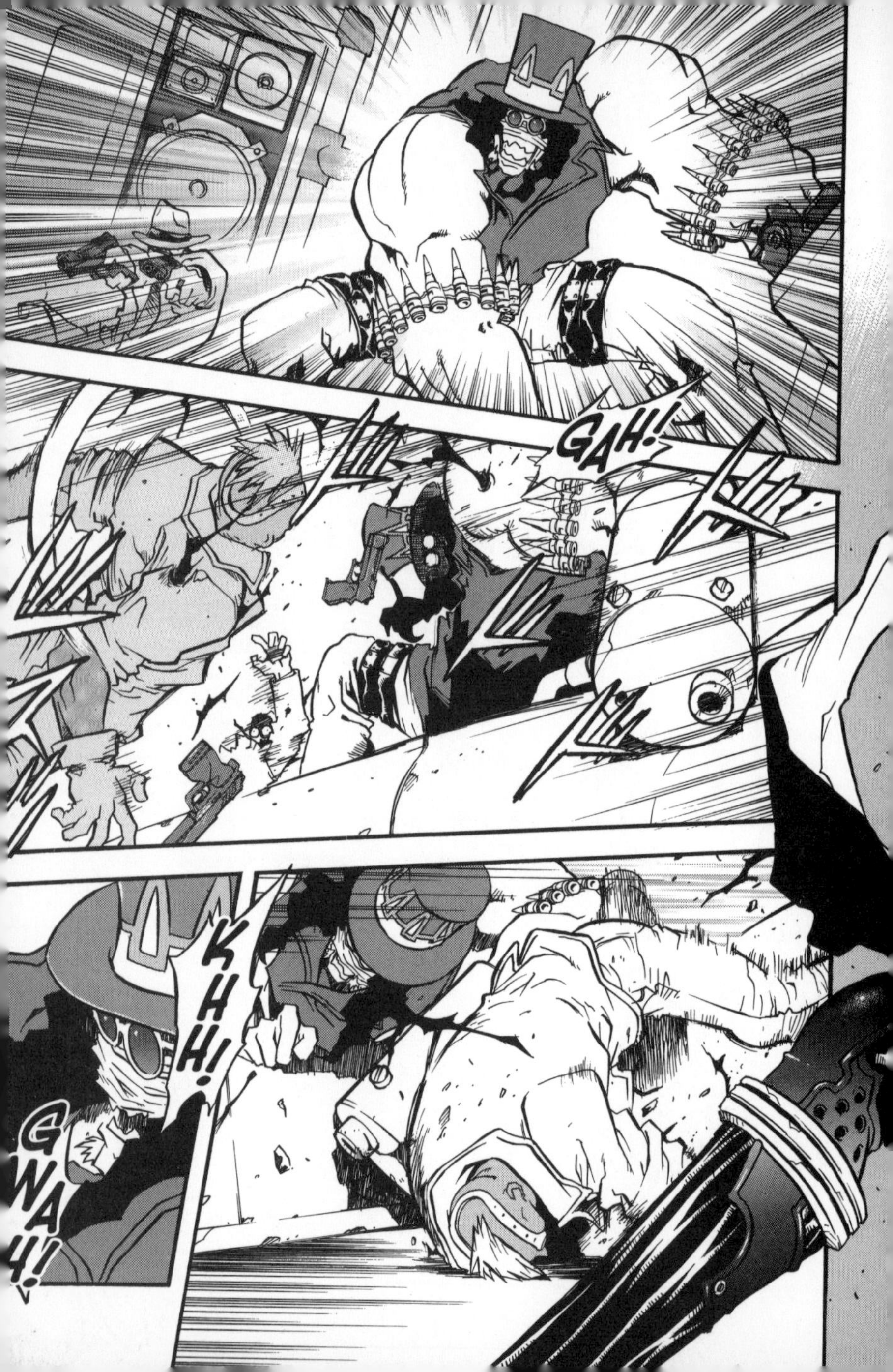
GAH!
KHHH!
GWAHH!

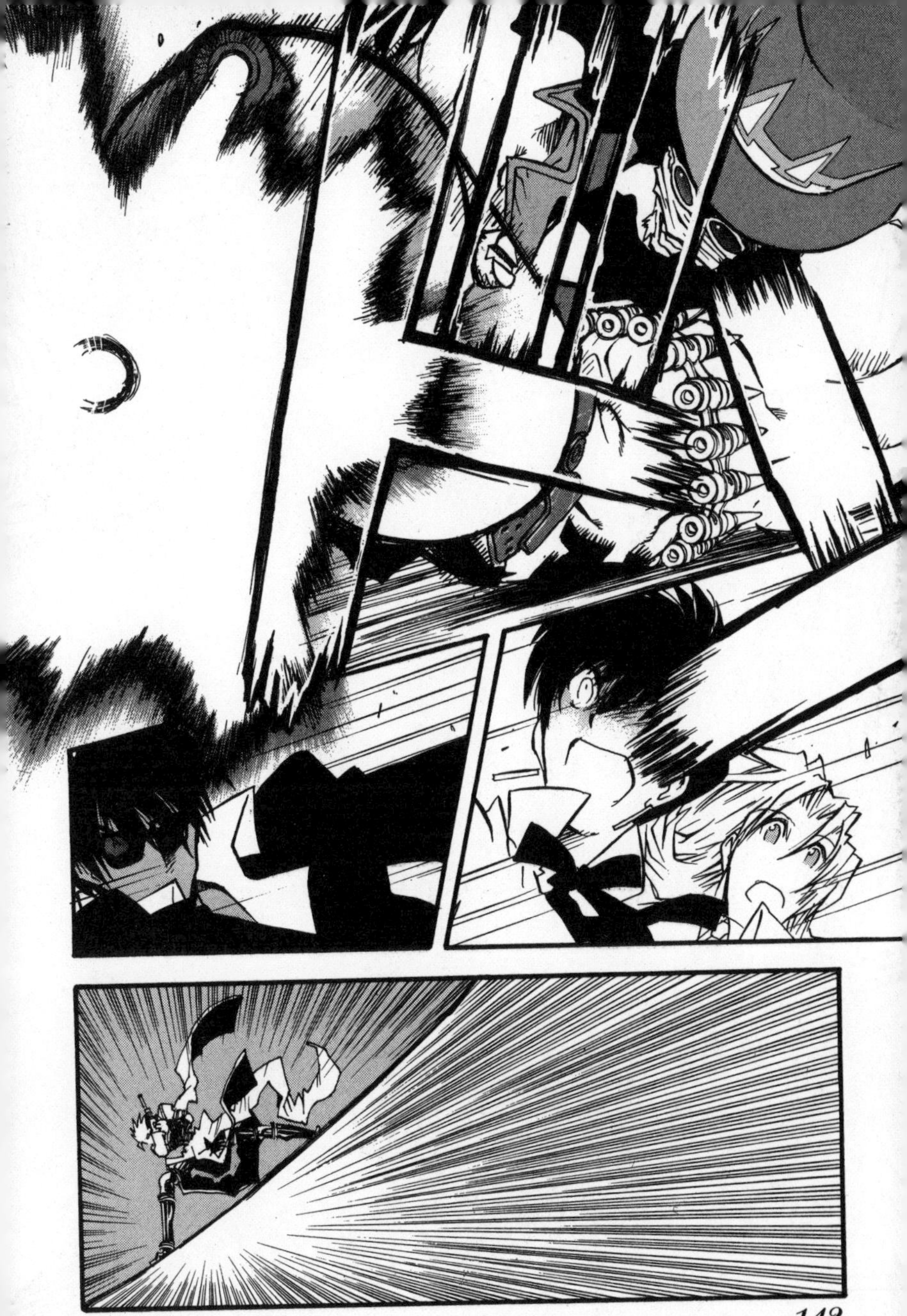

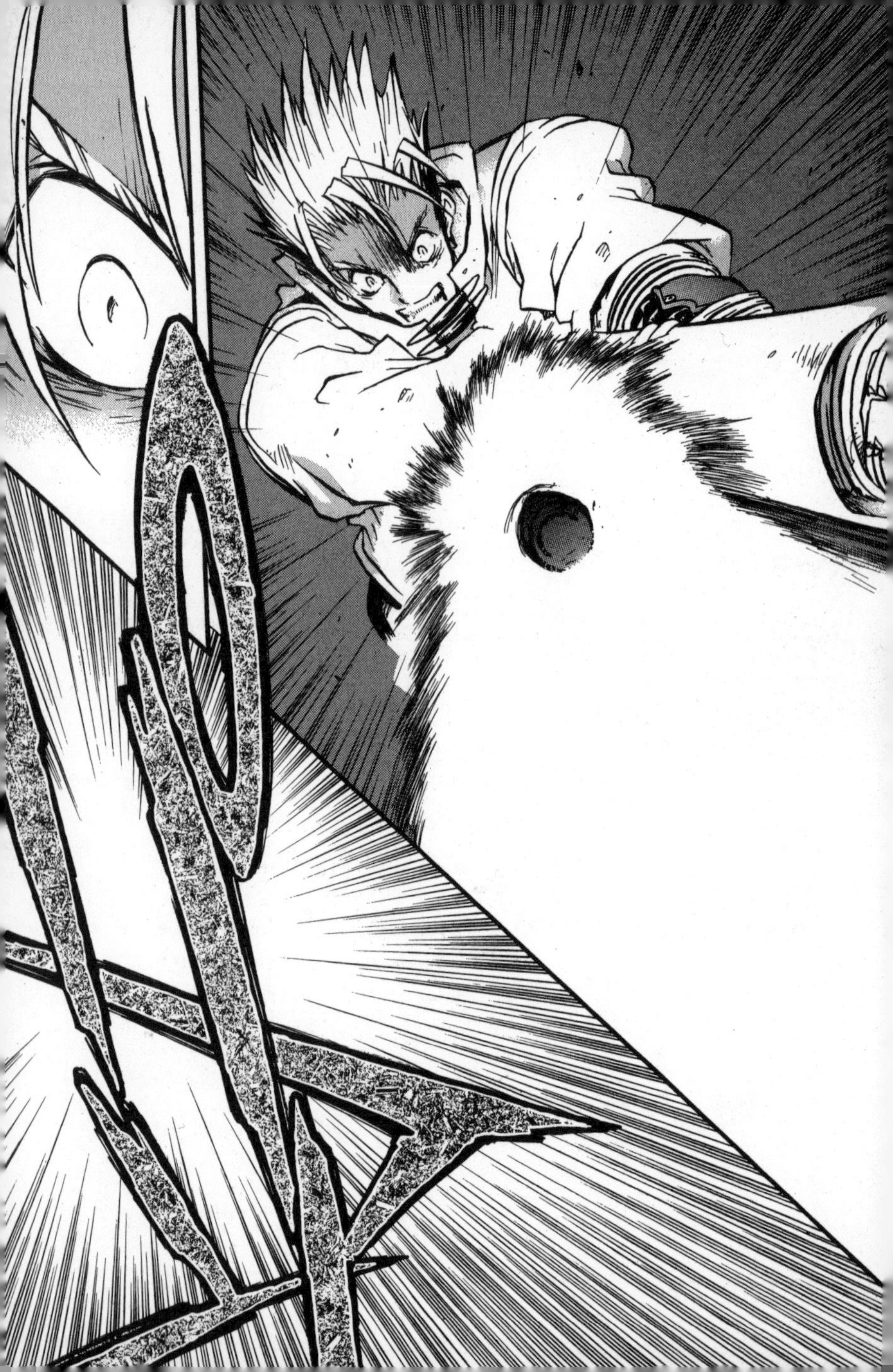

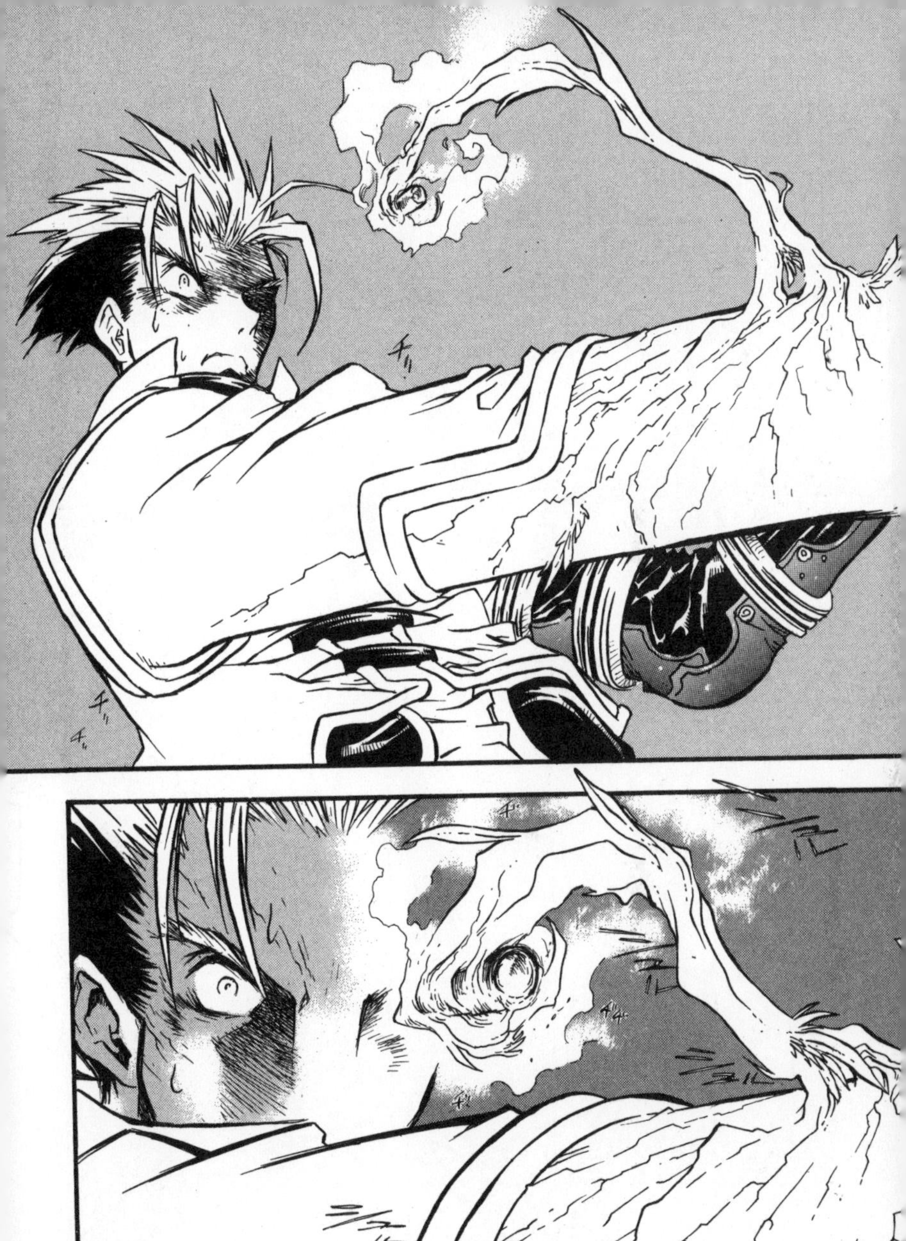

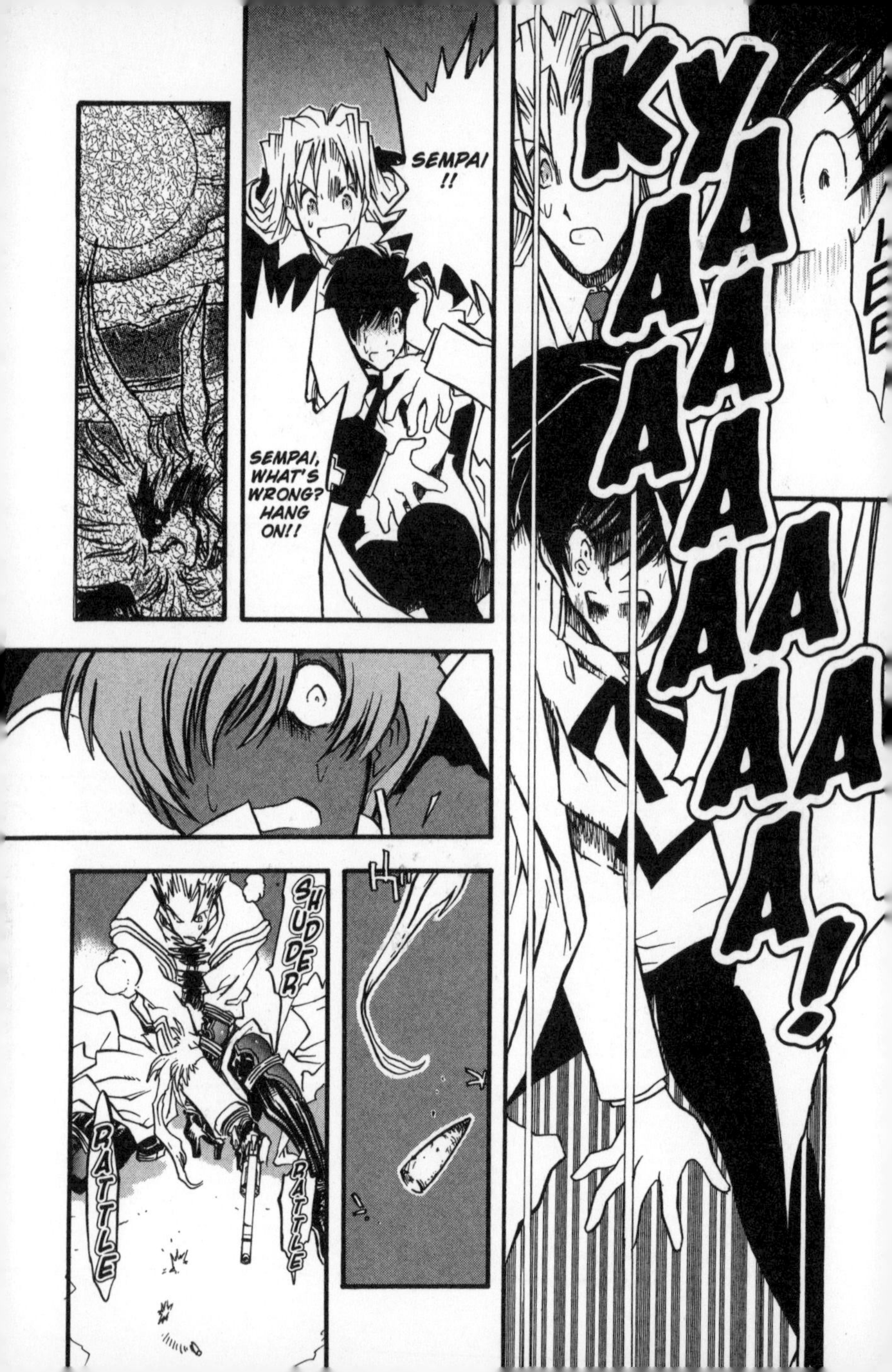
HEE
KYAAAAAAAAAAAA!
SEMPAI!!
SEMPAI, WHAT'S WRONG? HANG ON!!
SHUDDER
RATTLE
RATTLE

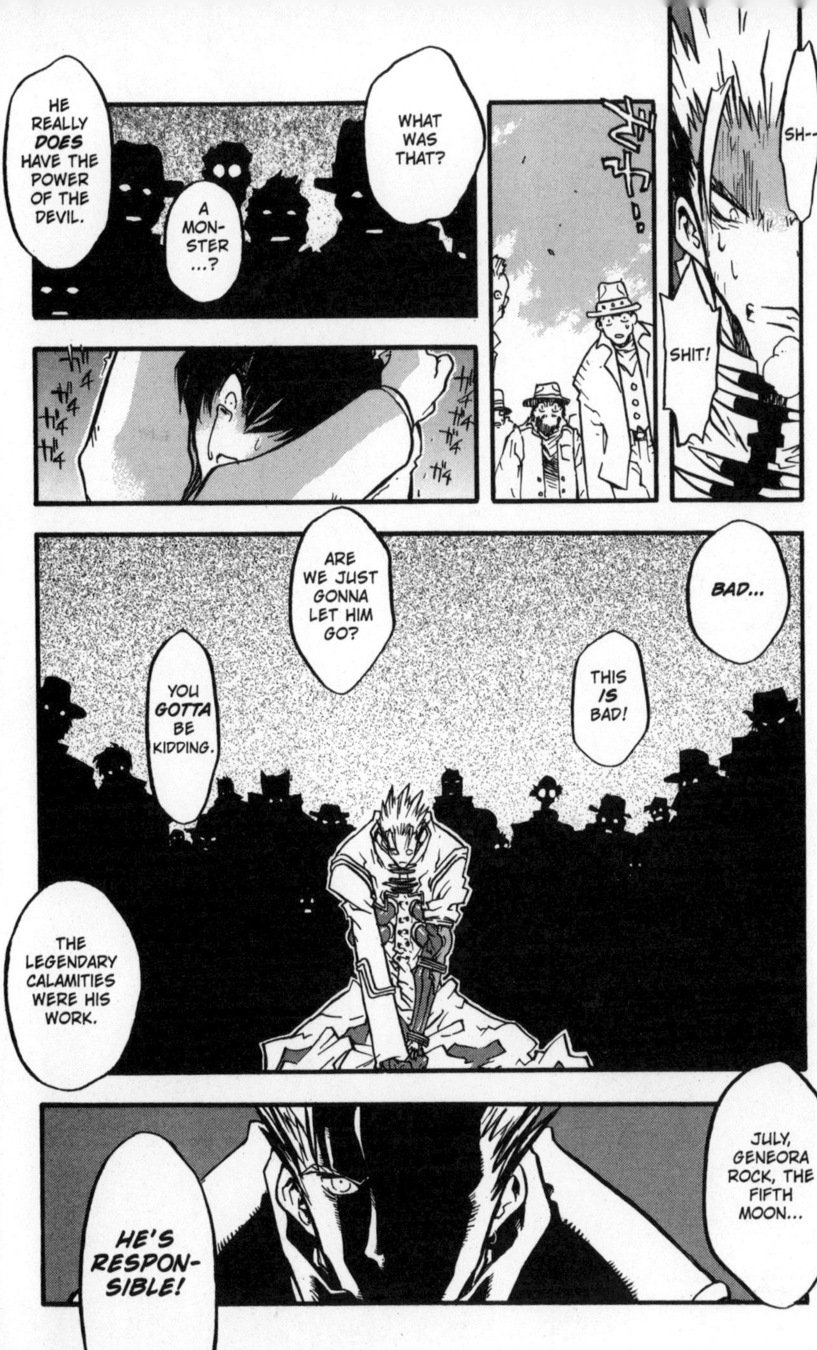
SH--
SHIT!
WHAT WAS THAT?
A MONSTER...?
HE REALLY DOES HAVE THE POWER OF THE DEVIL.
BAD...
THIS IS BAD!
ARE WE JUST GONNA LET HIM GO?
YOU GOTTA BE KIDDING.
THE LEGENDARY CALAMITIES WERE HIS WORK.
JULY, GENEORA ROCK, THE FIFTH MOON...
HE'S RESPONSIBLE!

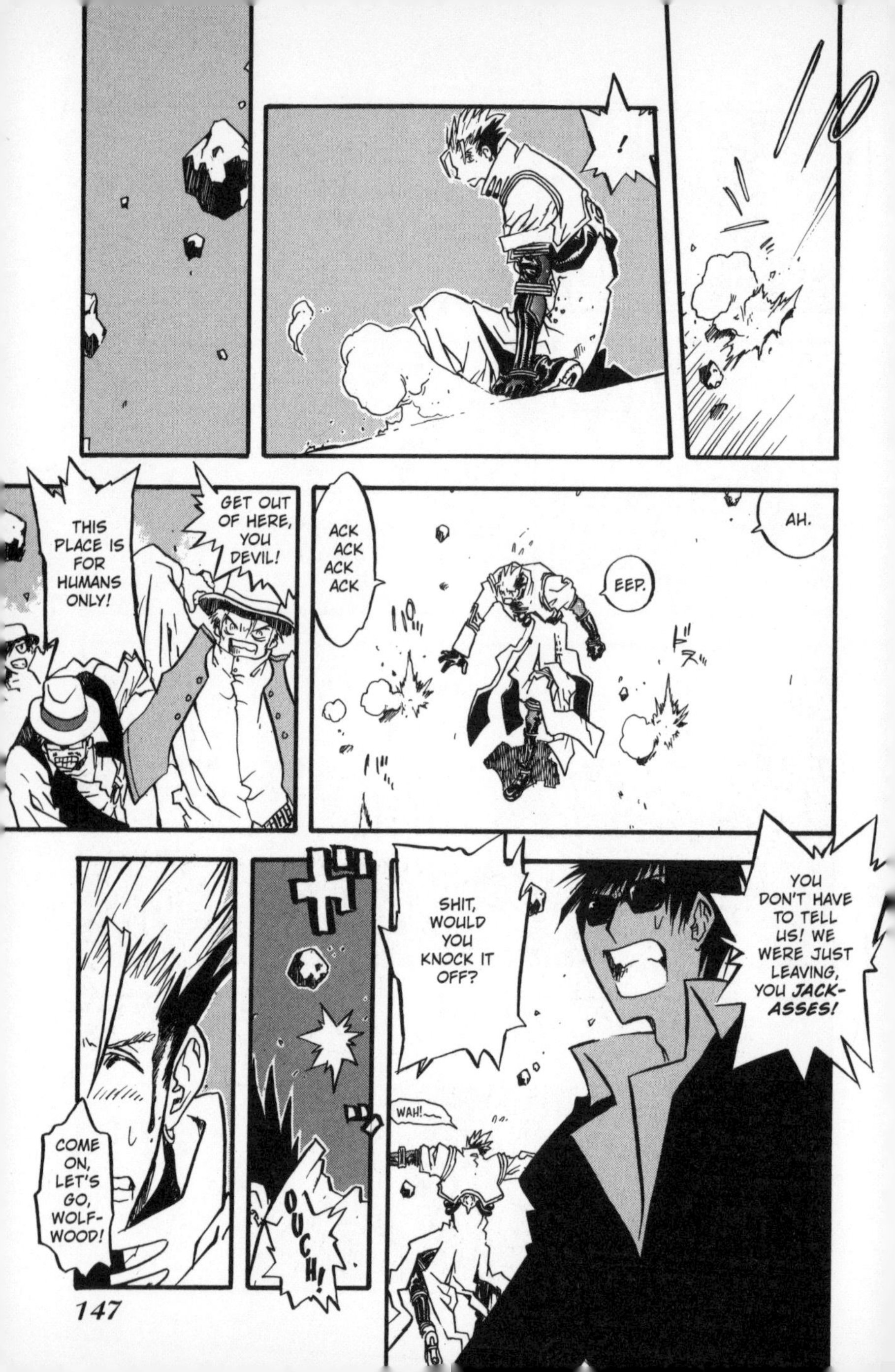
!
AH.
EEP.
ACK ACK ACK ACK
GET OUT OF HERE, YOU DEVIL!
THIS PLACE IS FOR HUMANS ONLY!
YOU DON'T HAVE TO TELL US! WE WERE JUST LEAVING, YOU ***JACK-ASSES!***
SHIT, WOULD YOU KNOCK IT OFF?
WAH!
OUCH!
COME ON, LET'S GO, WOLF-WOOD!

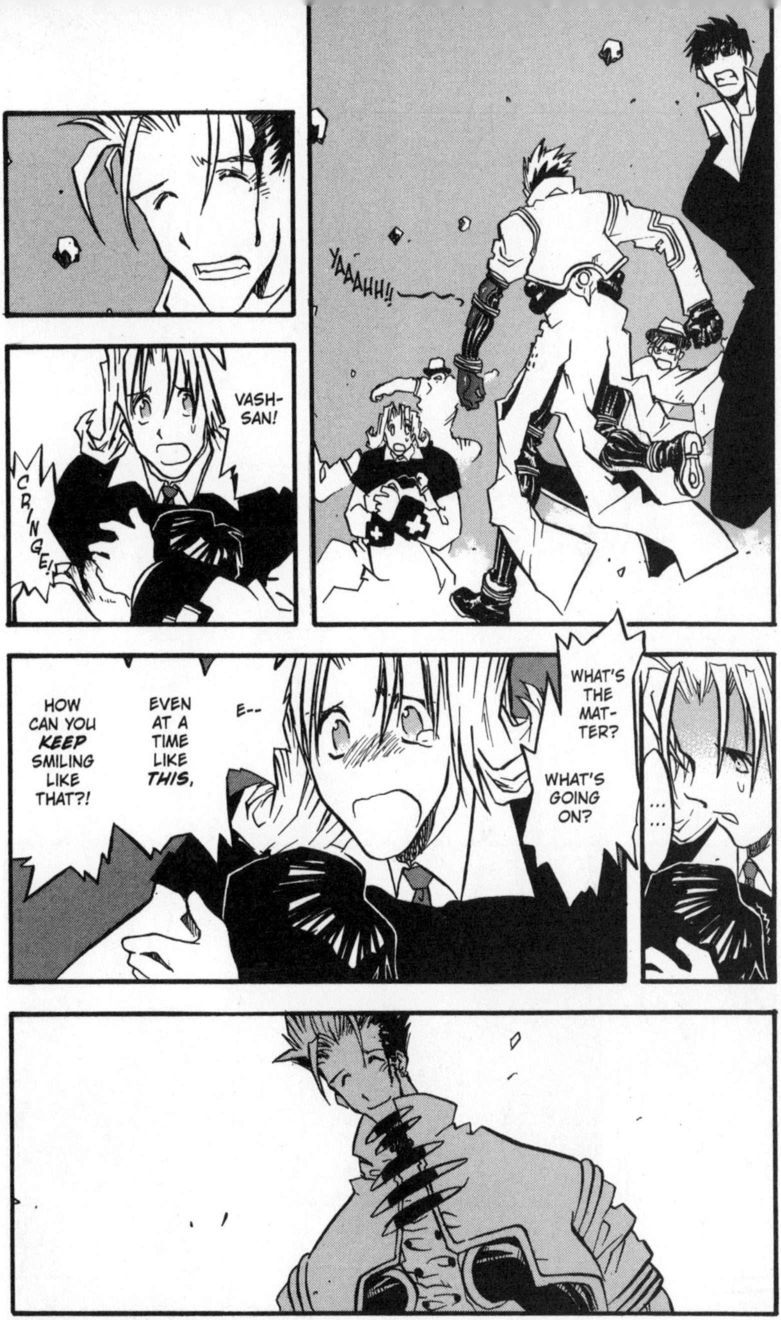
YAAAHH!!
VASH-SAN!
CRINGE!
......
WHAT'S THE MATTER?
WHAT'S GOING ON?
E--
EVEN AT A TIME LIKE *THIS*,
HOW CAN YOU *KEEP* SMILING LIKE THAT?!

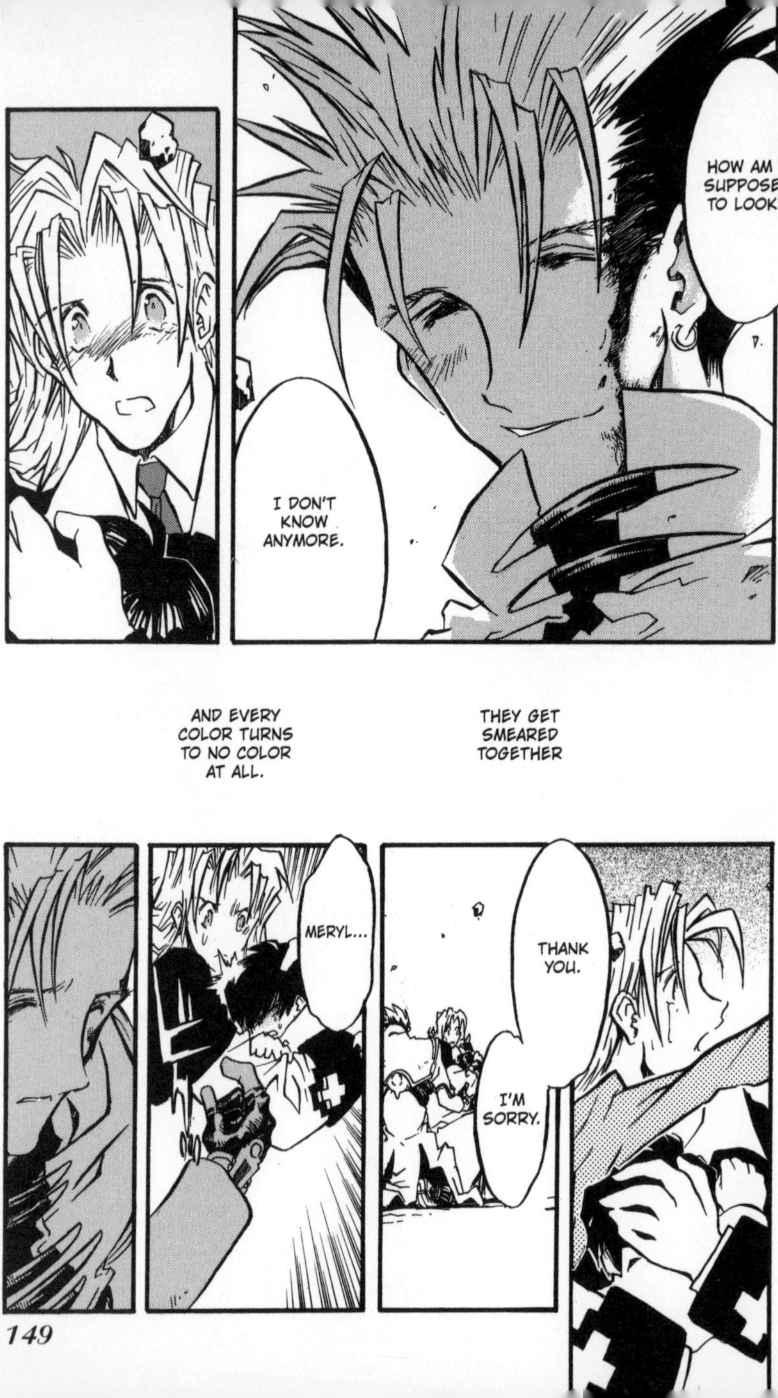
HOW AM I SUPPOSED TO LOOK?
I DON'T KNOW ANYMORE.
THEY GET SMEARED TOGETHER
AND EVERY COLOR TURNS TO NO COLOR AT ALL.
THANK YOU.
I'M SORRY.
MERYL...

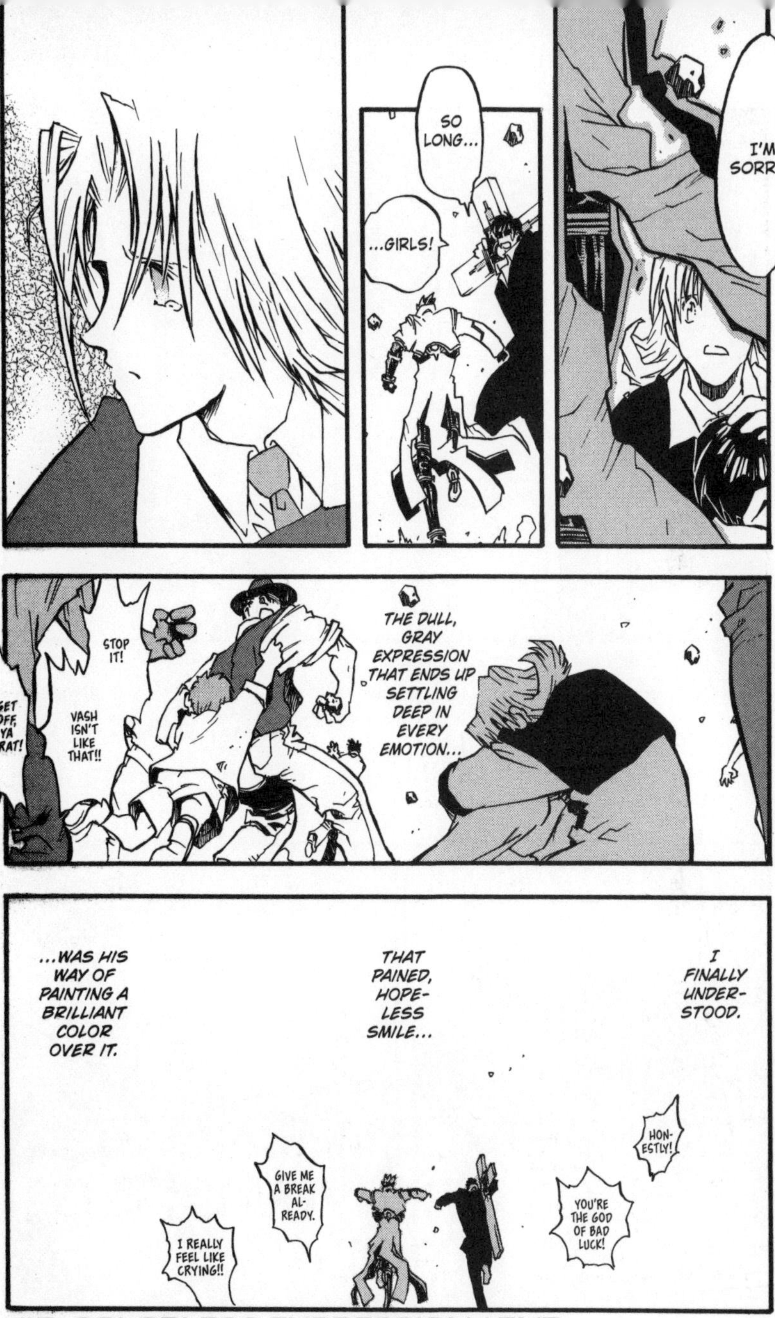
I'M SORRY.
SO LONG...
...GIRLS!
THE DULL, GRAY EXPRESSION THAT ENDS UP SETTLING DEEP IN EVERY EMOTION...
STOP IT!
VASH ISN'T LIKE THAT!!
GET OFF, YA BRAT!
I FINALLY UNDER-STOOD.
THAT PAINED, HOPE-LESS SMILE...
...WAS HIS WAY OF PAINTING A BRILLIANT COLOR OVER IT.
HON-ESTLY!
YOU'RE THE GOD OF BAD LUCK!
GIVE ME A BREAK AL-READY.
I REALLY FEEL LIKE CRYING!!

#5. COLORLESS EXPRESSION / END

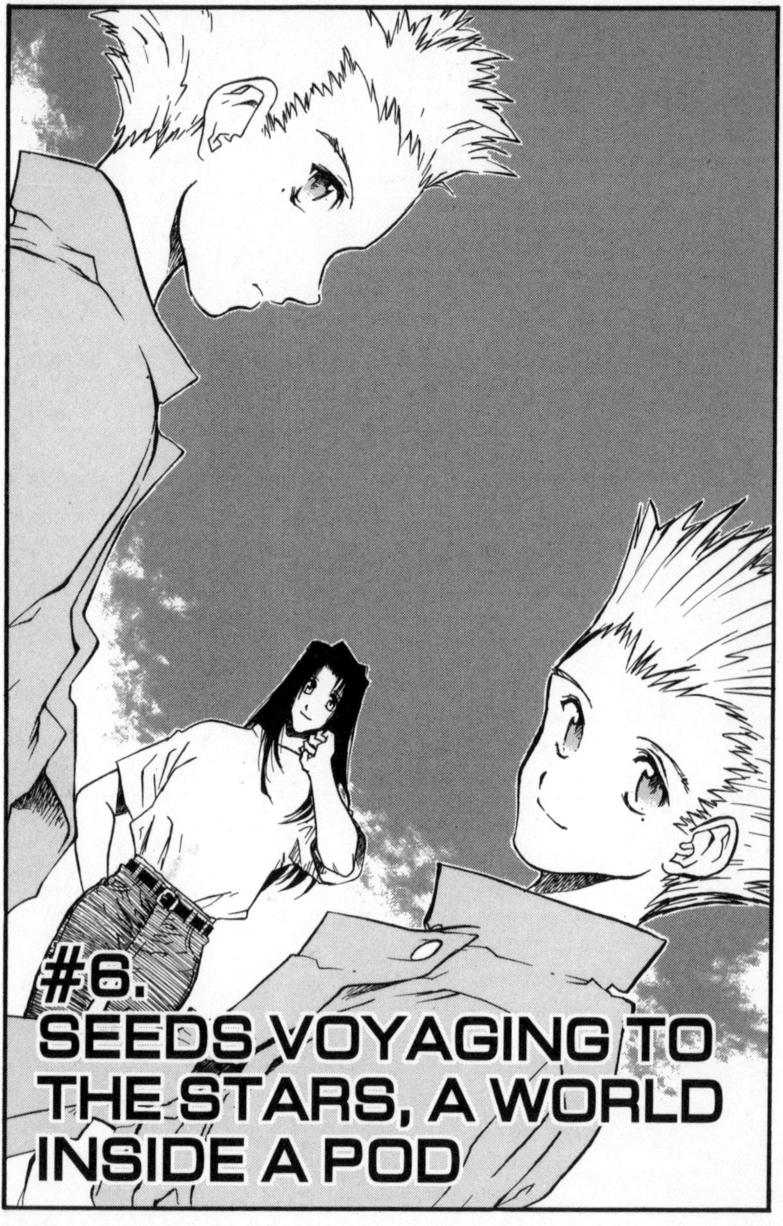
#6.
SEEDS VOYAGING TO THE STARS, A WORLD INSIDE A POD

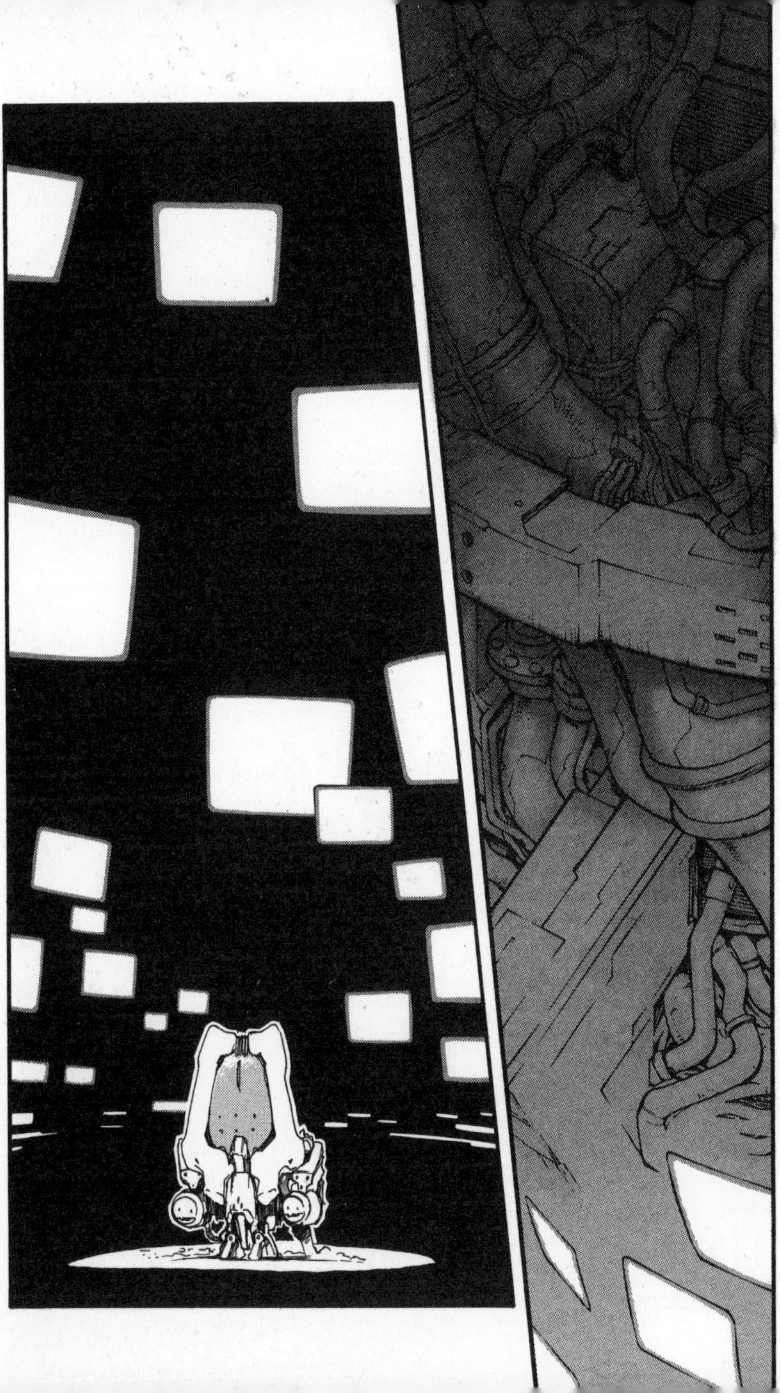

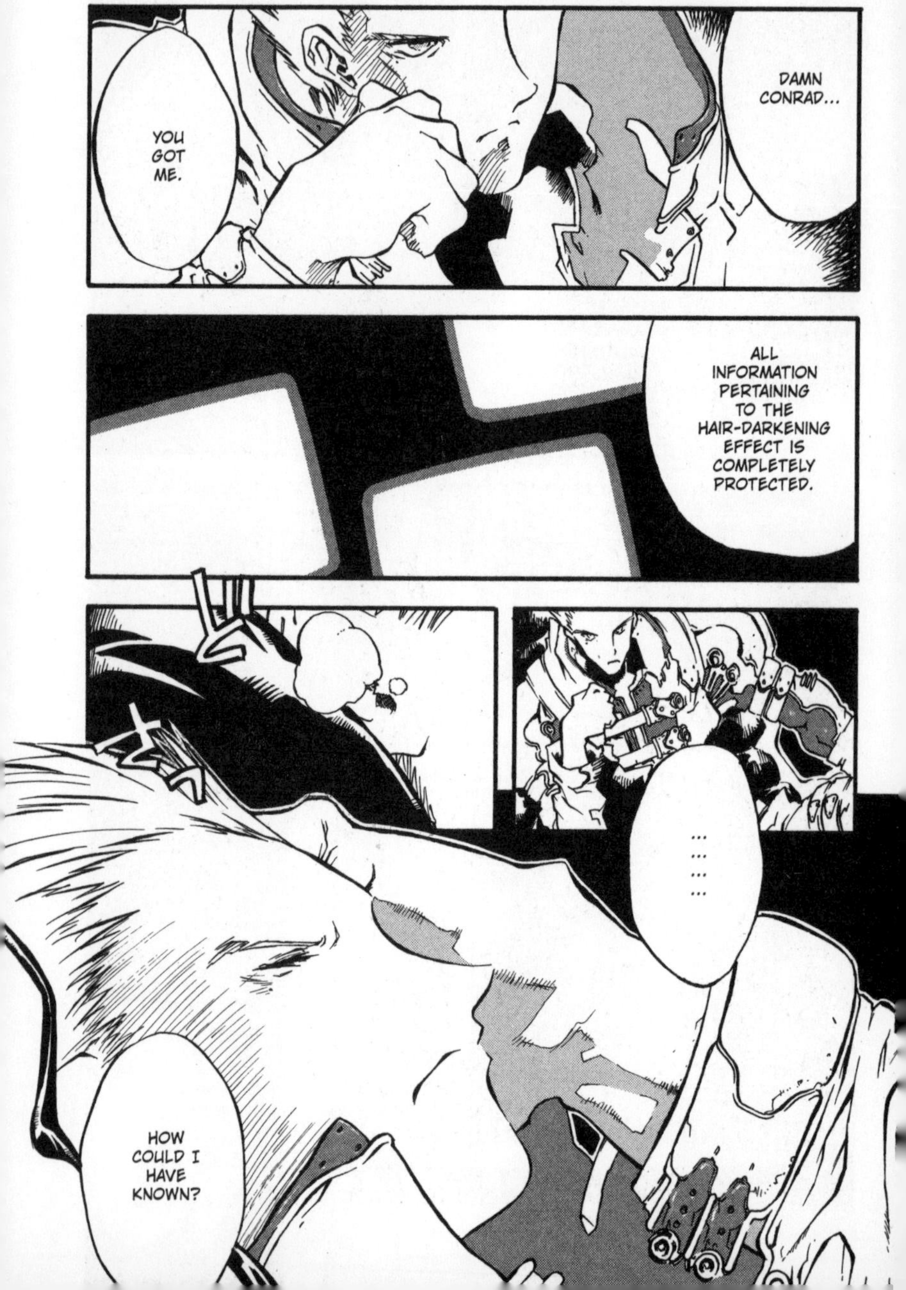
DAMN CONRAD...
YOU GOT ME.
ALL INFORMATION PERTAINING TO THE HAIR-DARKENING EFFECT IS COMPLETELY PROTECTED.
....
HOW COULD I HAVE KNOWN?

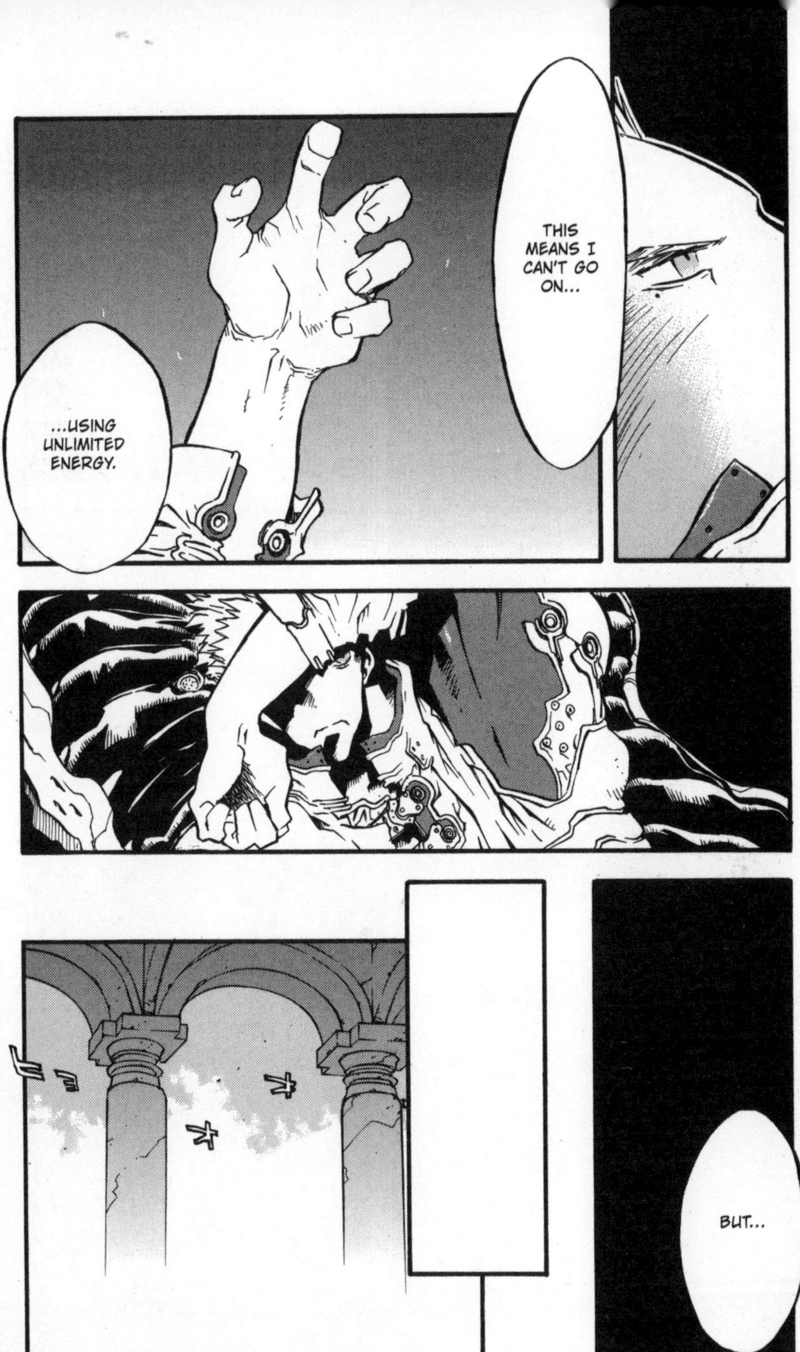
THIS MEANS I CAN'T GO ON...
...USING UNLIMITED ENERGY.
BUT...

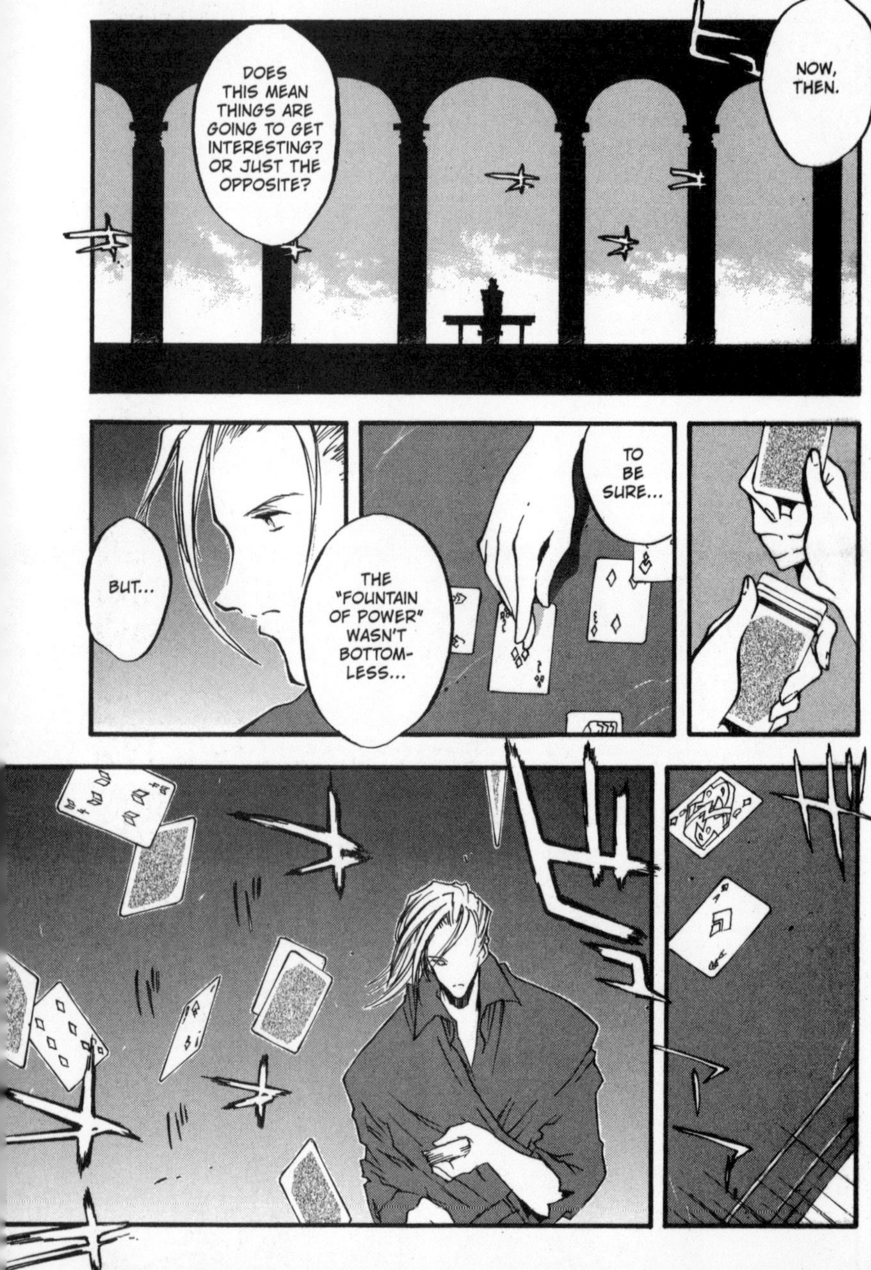
NOW, THEN.
DOES THIS MEAN THINGS ARE GOING TO GET INTERESTING? OR JUST THE OPPOSITE?
TO BE SURE...
THE "FOUNTAIN OF POWER" WASN'T BOTTOMLESS...
BUT...

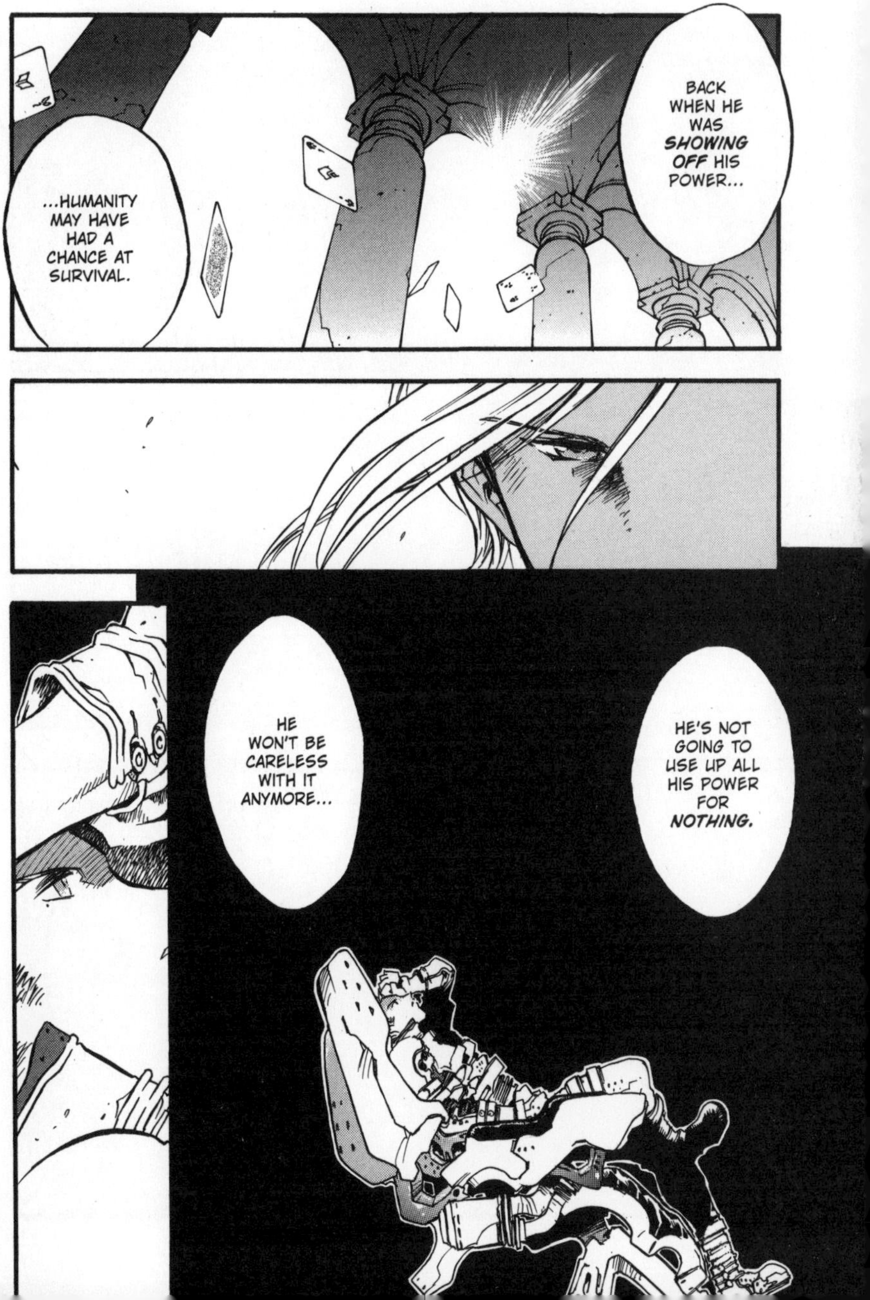
BACK WHEN HE WAS SHOWING OFF HIS POWER...
...HUMANITY MAY HAVE HAD A CHANCE AT SURVIVAL.
HE'S NOT GOING TO USE UP ALL HIS POWER FOR NOTHING.
HE WON'T BE CARELESS WITH IT ANYMORE...

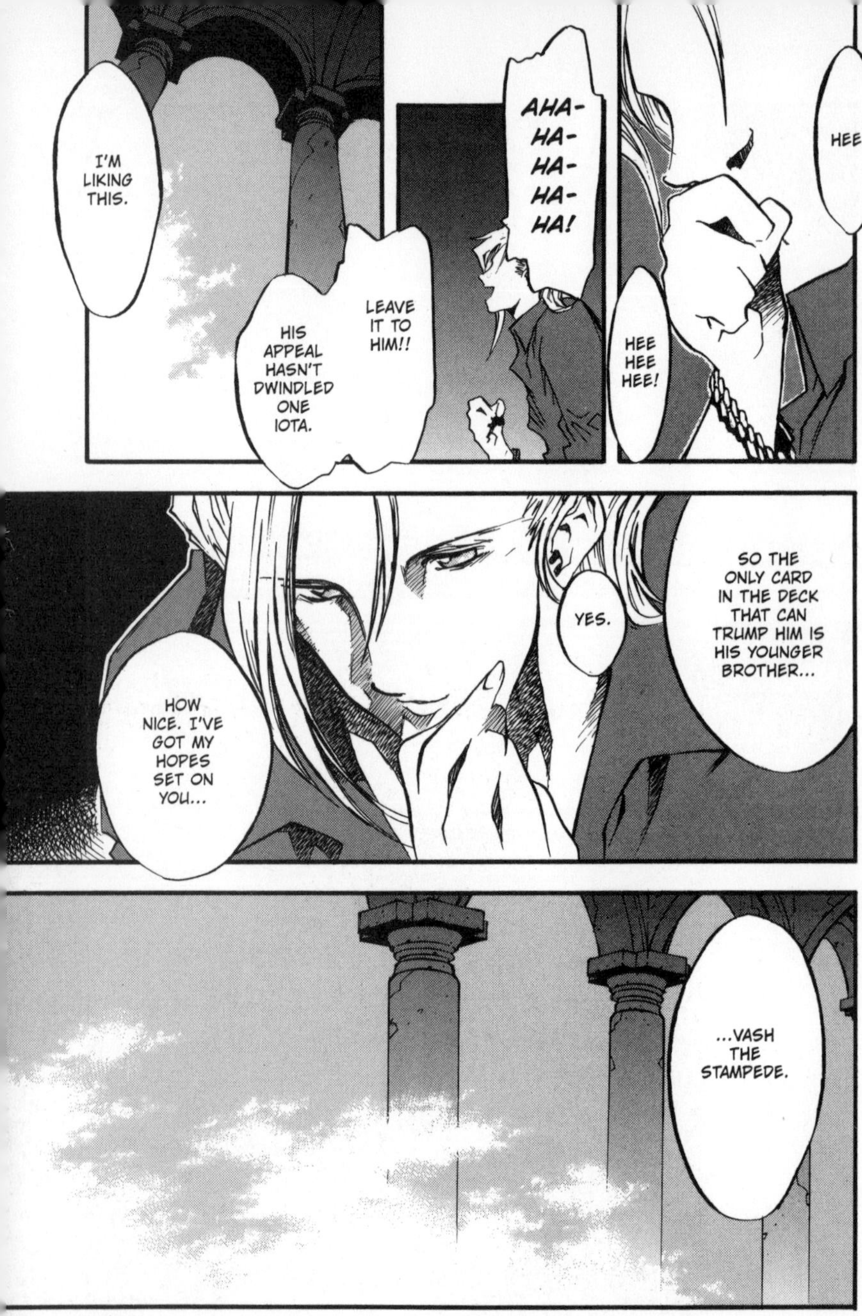
HEE!
HEE HEE HEE!
AHA-HA-HA-HA-HA!
LEAVE IT TO HIM!!
HIS APPEAL HASN'T DWINDLED ONE IOTA.
I'M LIKING THIS.
SO THE ONLY CARD IN THE DECK THAT CAN TRUMP HIM IS HIS YOUNGER BROTHER...
YES.
HOW NICE. I'VE GOT MY HOPES SET ON YOU...
...VASH THE STAMPEDE.

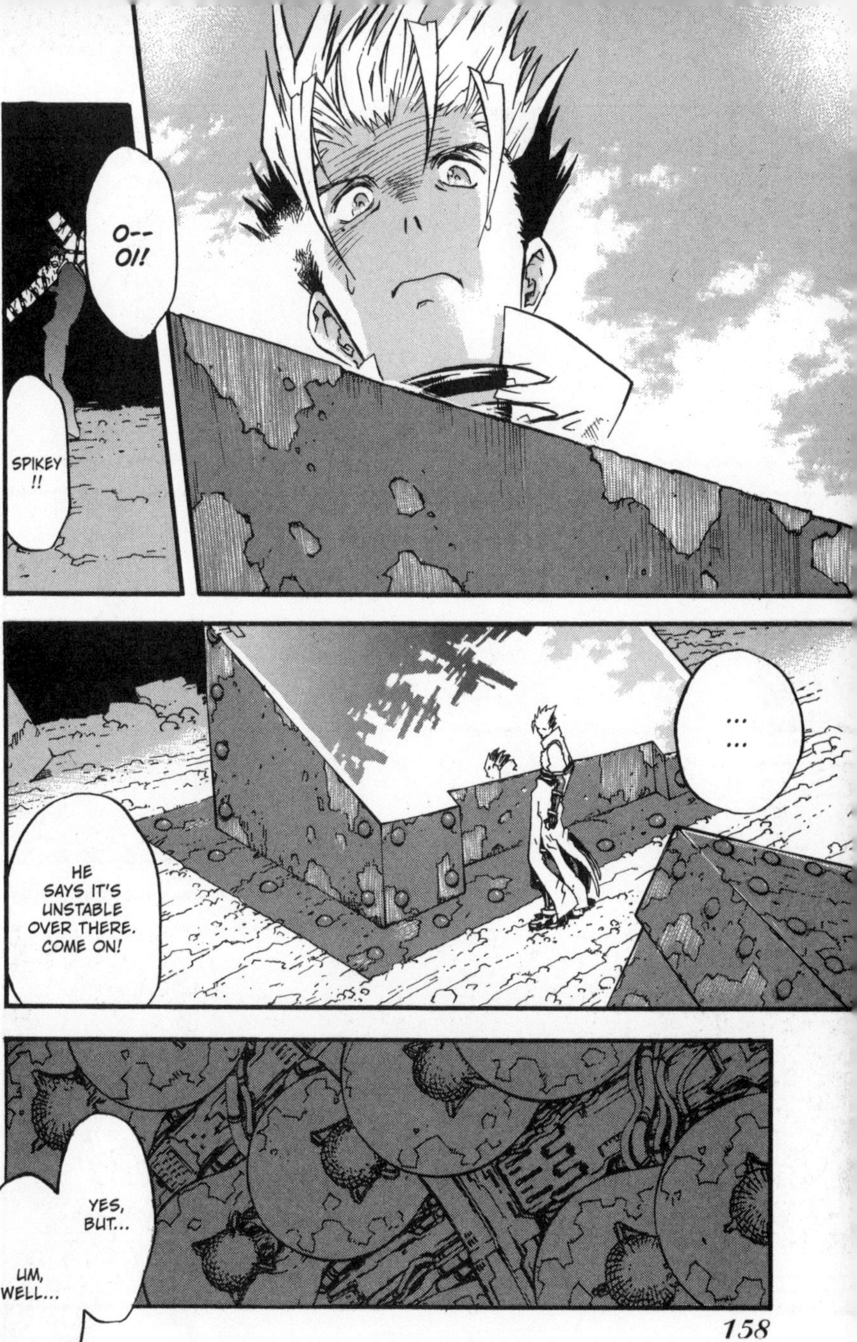
O--OI!
SPIKEY!!
......
HE SAYS IT'S UNSTABLE OVER THERE. COME ON!
YES, BUT...
UM, WELL...

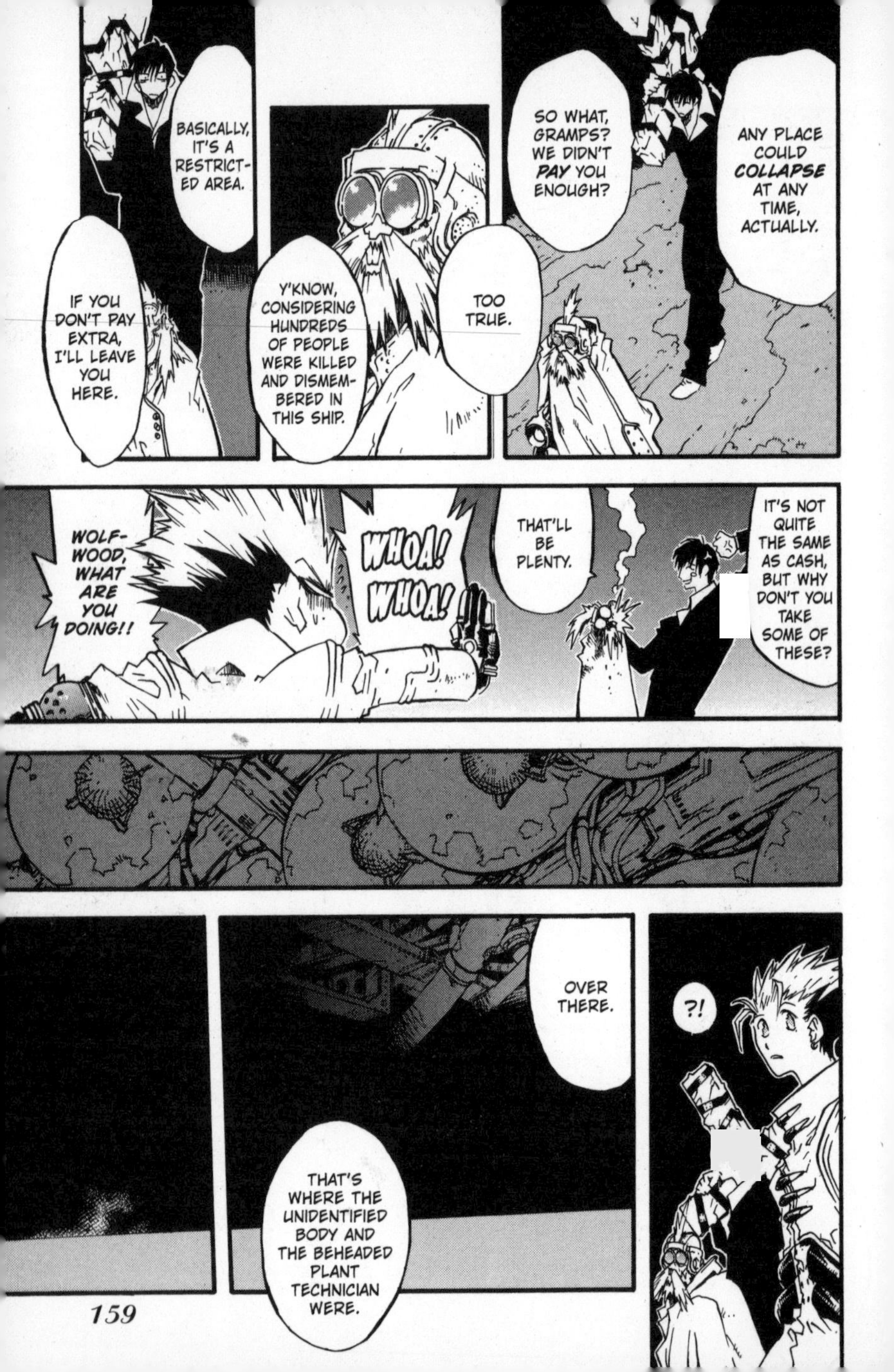
ANY PLACE COULD **COLLAPSE** AT ANY TIME, ACTUALLY.
SO WHAT, GRAMPS? WE DIDN'T **PAY** YOU ENOUGH?
TOO TRUE.
Y'KNOW, CONSIDERING HUNDREDS OF PEOPLE WERE KILLED AND DISMEMBERED IN THIS SHIP.
BASICALLY, IT'S A RESTRICTED AREA.
IF YOU DON'T PAY EXTRA, I'LL LEAVE YOU HERE.
IT'S NOT QUITE THE SAME AS CASH, BUT WHY DON'T YOU TAKE SOME OF THESE?
THAT'LL BE PLENTY.
WHOA! WHOA!
WOLFWOOD, WHAT ARE YOU DOING!!
?!
OVER THERE.
THAT'S WHERE THE UNIDENTIFIED BODY AND THE BEHEADED PLANT TECHNICIAN WERE.

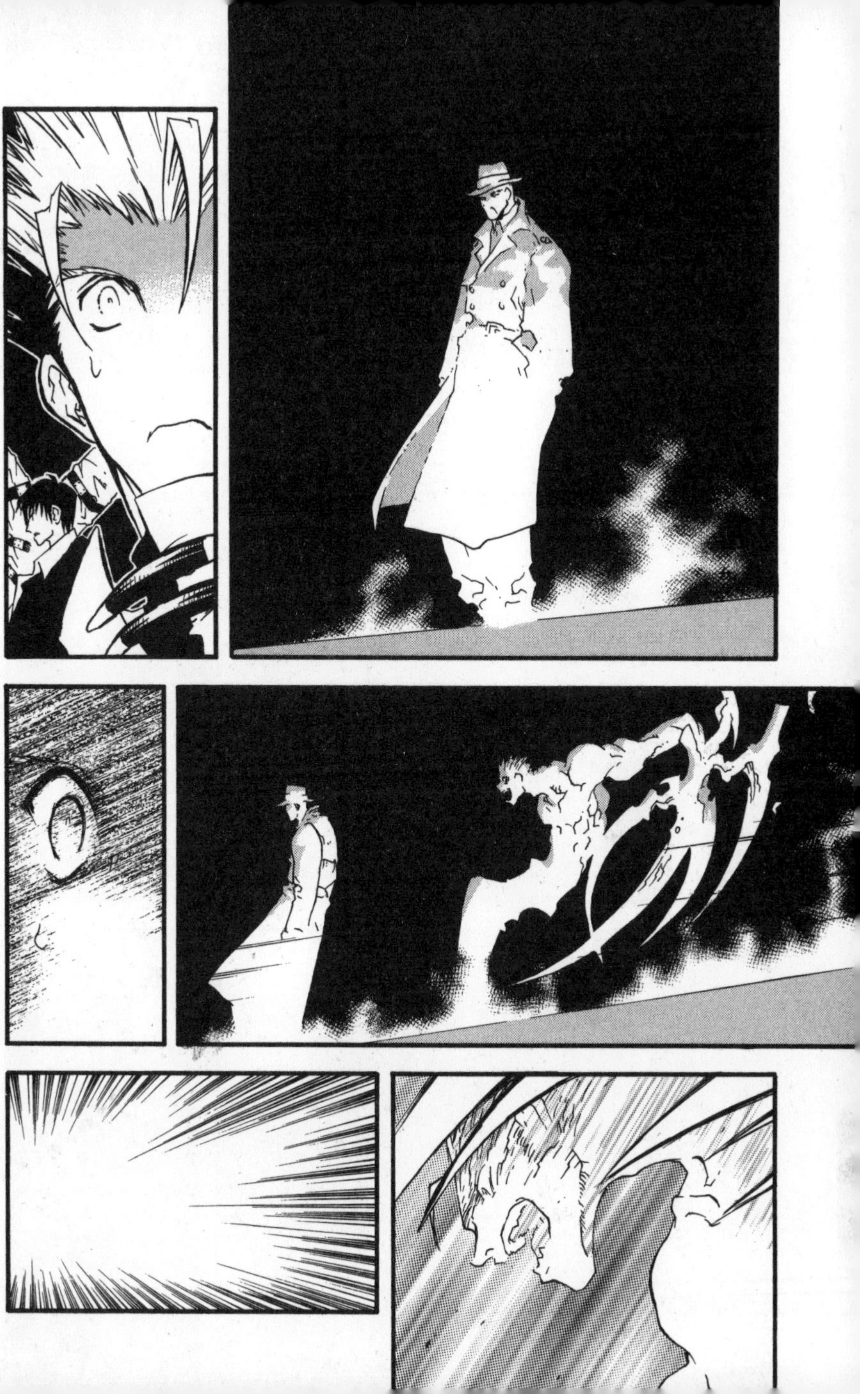

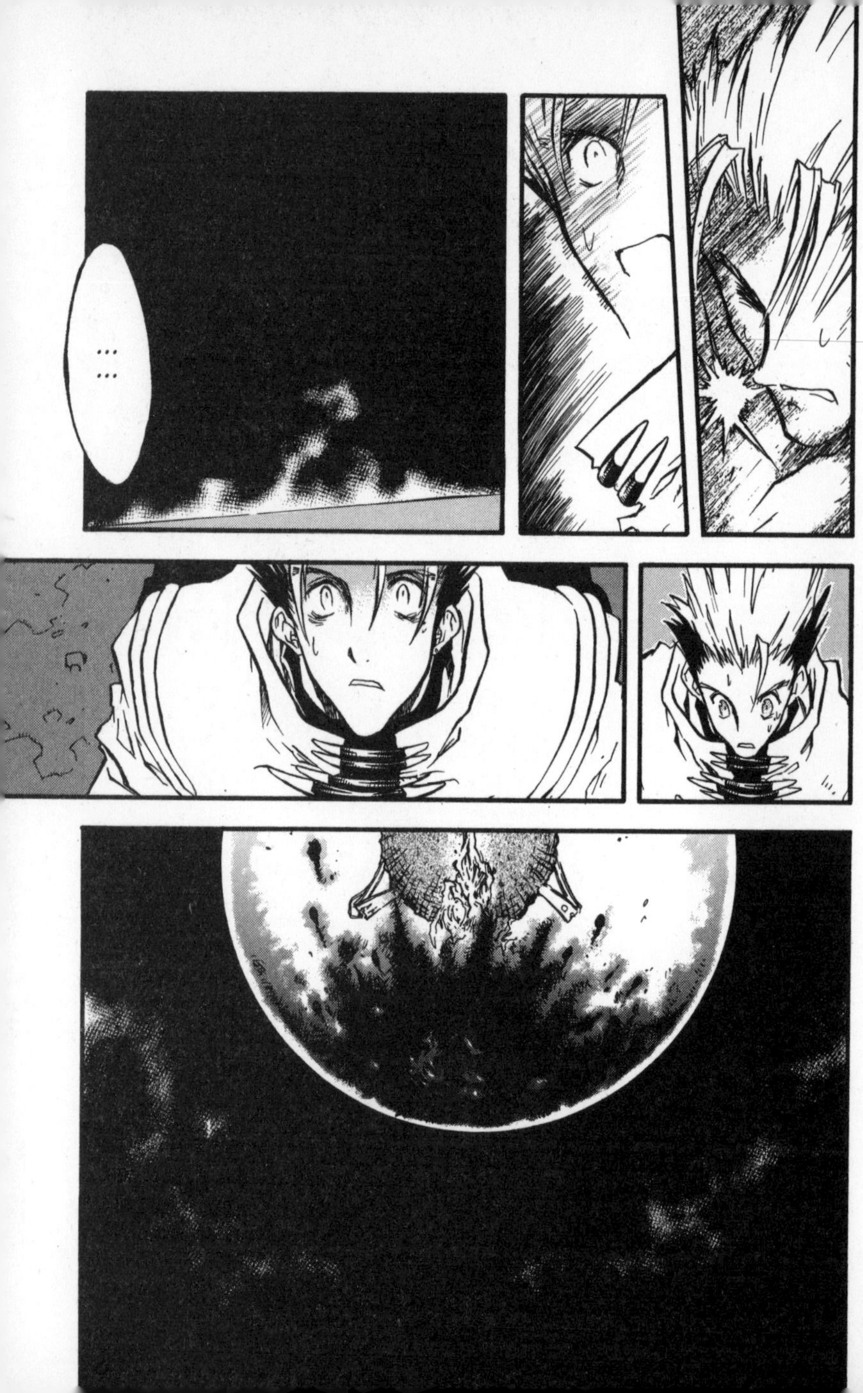
......

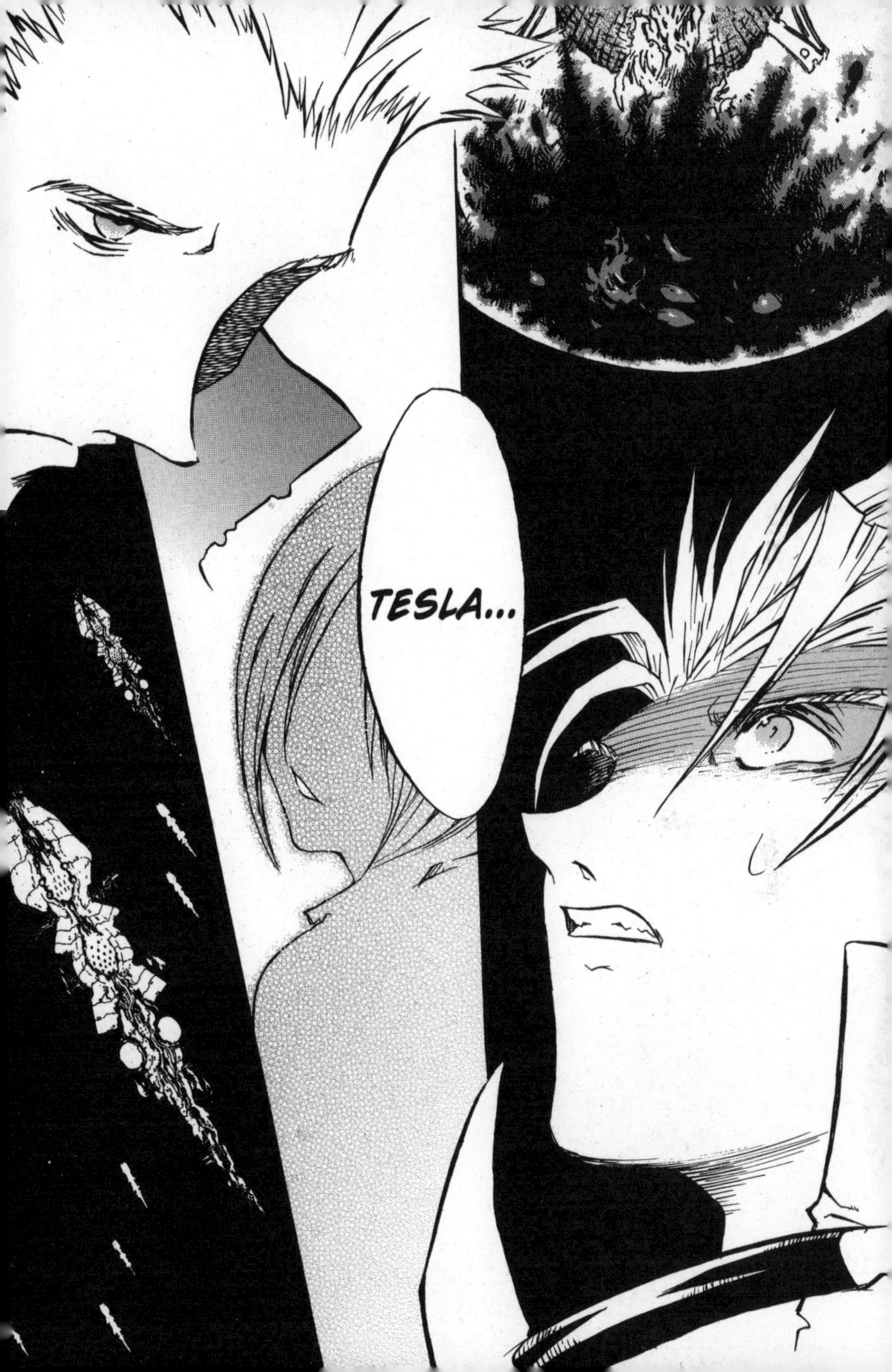
TESLA...

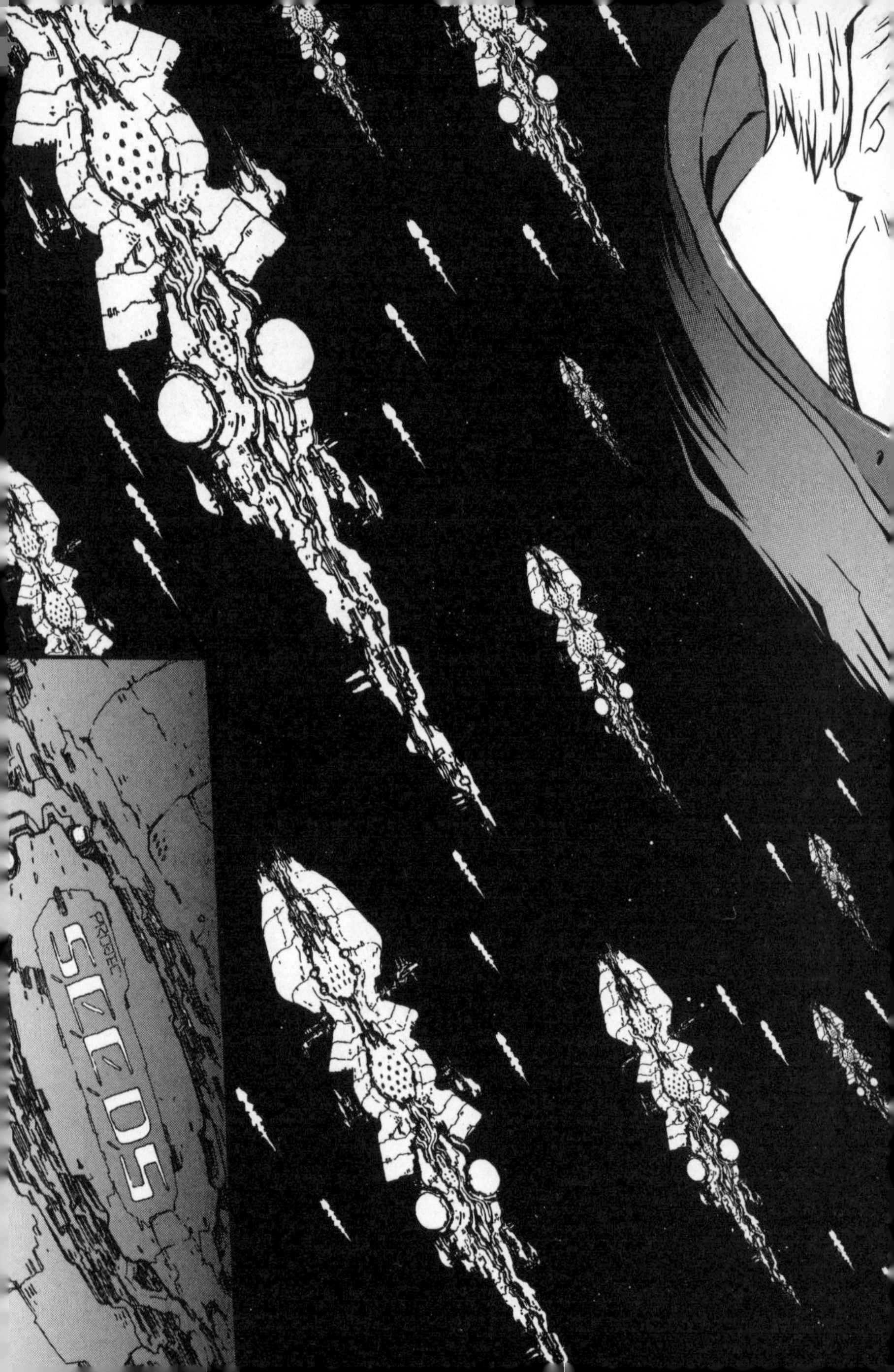
PROJECT
SEEDS

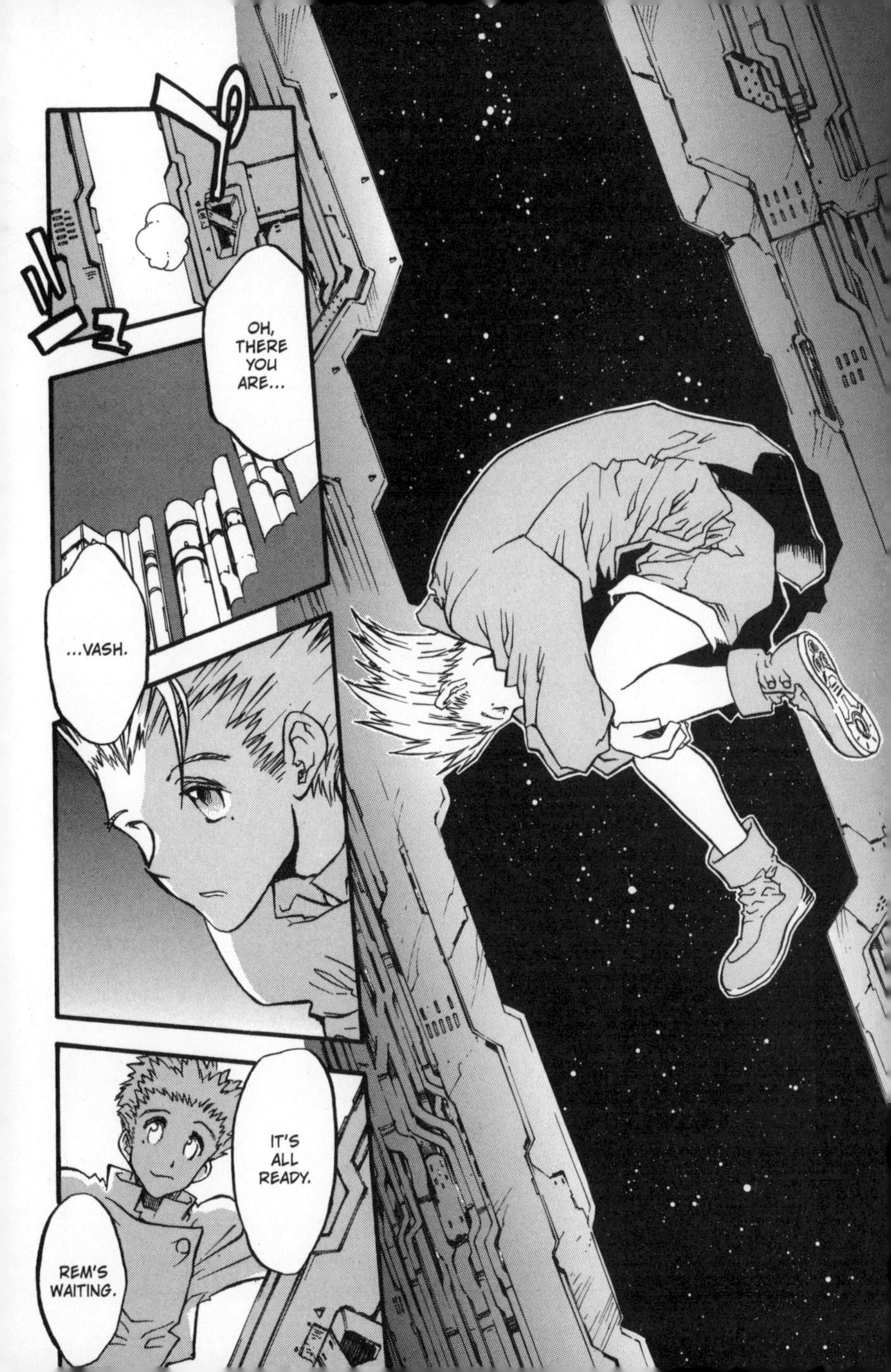
OH, THERE YOU ARE...
...VASH.
IT'S ALL READY.
REM'S WAITING.

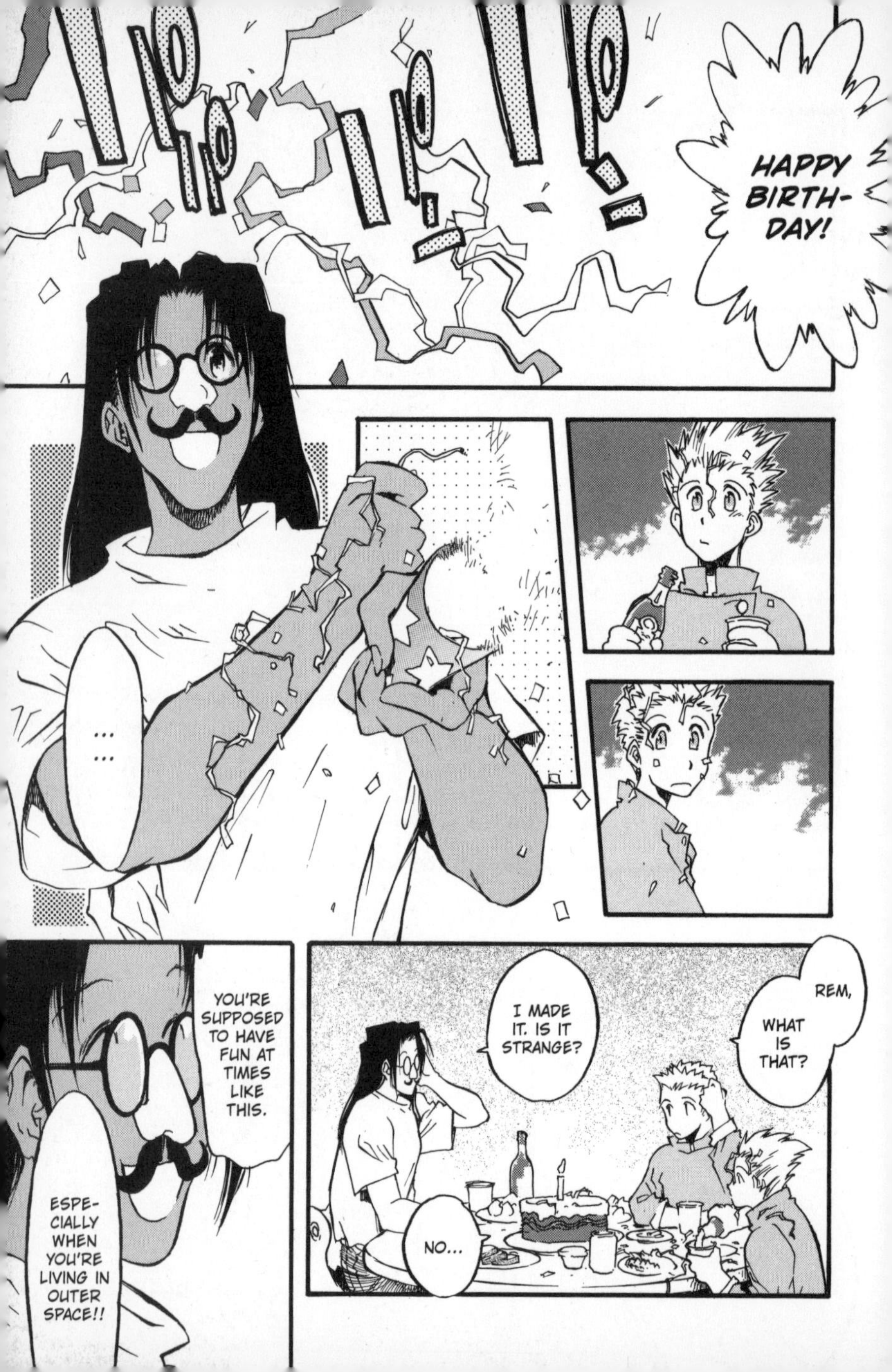
HAPPY BIRTH-DAY!
...
...
REM, WHAT IS THAT?
I MADE IT. IS IT STRANGE?
NO...
YOU'RE SUPPOSED TO HAVE FUN AT TIMES LIKE THIS.
ESPE-CIALLY WHEN YOU'RE LIVING IN OUTER SPACE!!

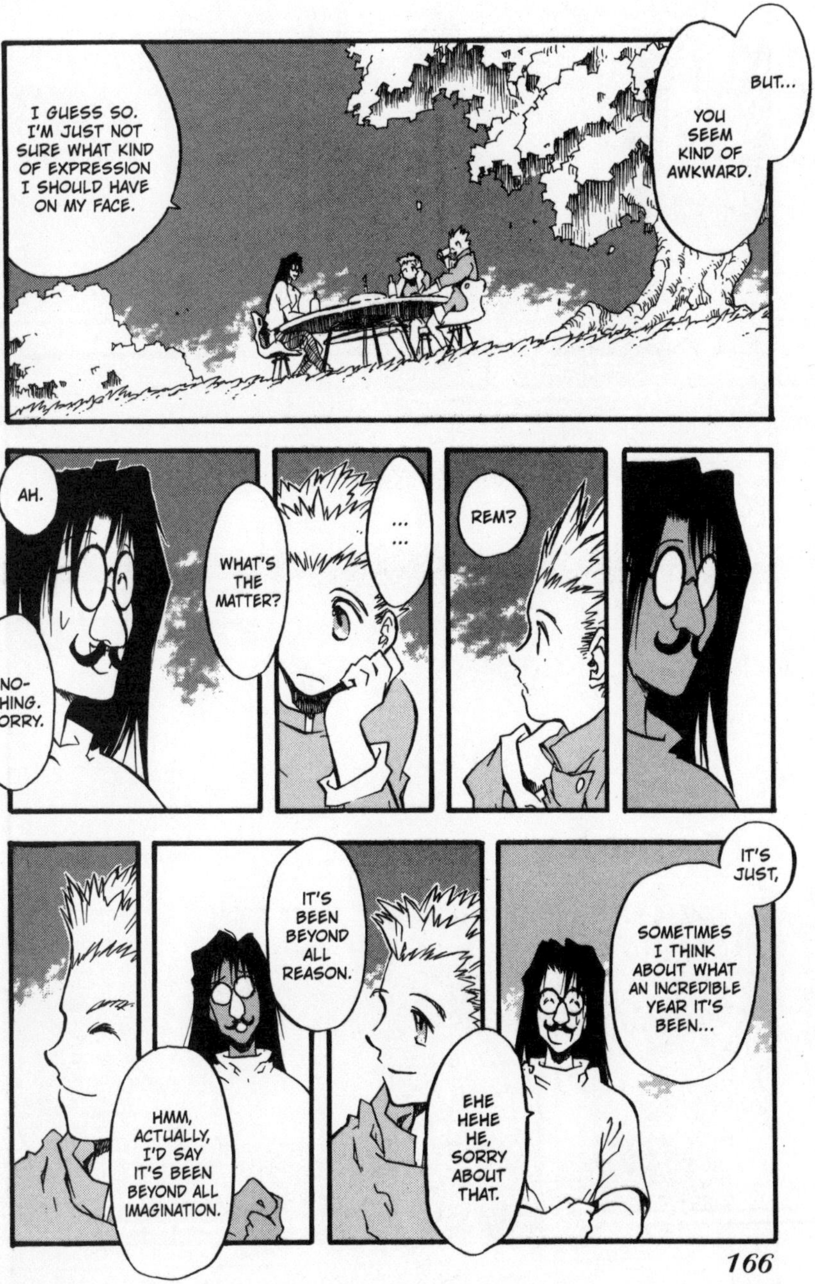
BUT... YOU SEEM KIND OF AWKWARD.
I GUESS SO. I'M JUST NOT SURE WHAT KIND OF EXPRESSION I SHOULD HAVE ON MY FACE.
REM?
... ...
WHAT'S THE MATTER?
AH.
NO-THING. SORRY.
IT'S JUST,
SOMETIMES I THINK ABOUT WHAT AN INCREDIBLE YEAR IT'S BEEN...
EHE HEHE HE, SORRY ABOUT THAT.
IT'S BEEN BEYOND ALL REASON.
HMM, ACTUALLY, I'D SAY IT'S BEEN BEYOND ALL IMAGINATION.

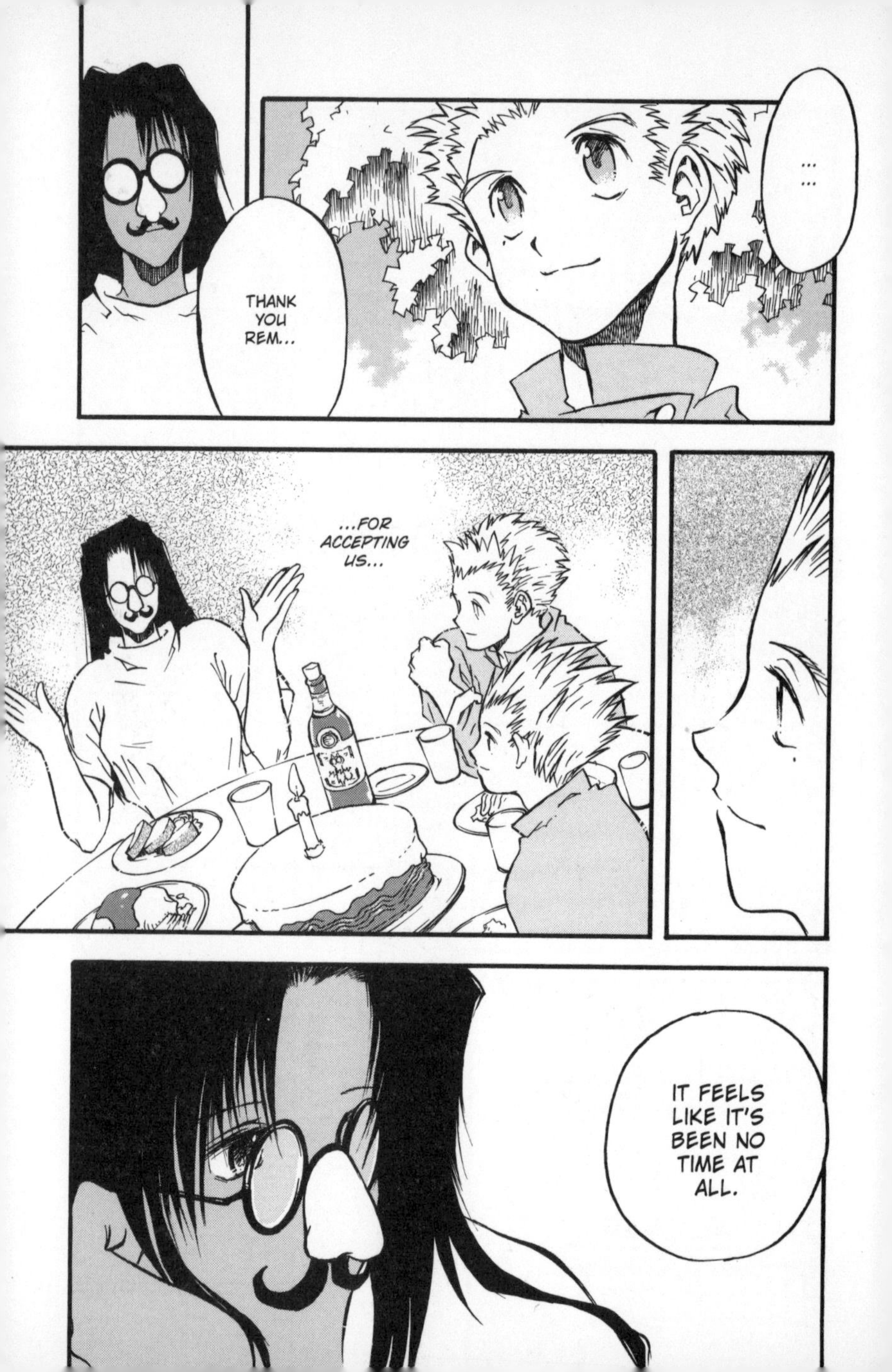
... ...
THANK YOU REM...
...FOR ACCEPTING US...
IT FEELS LIKE IT'S BEEN NO TIME AT ALL.

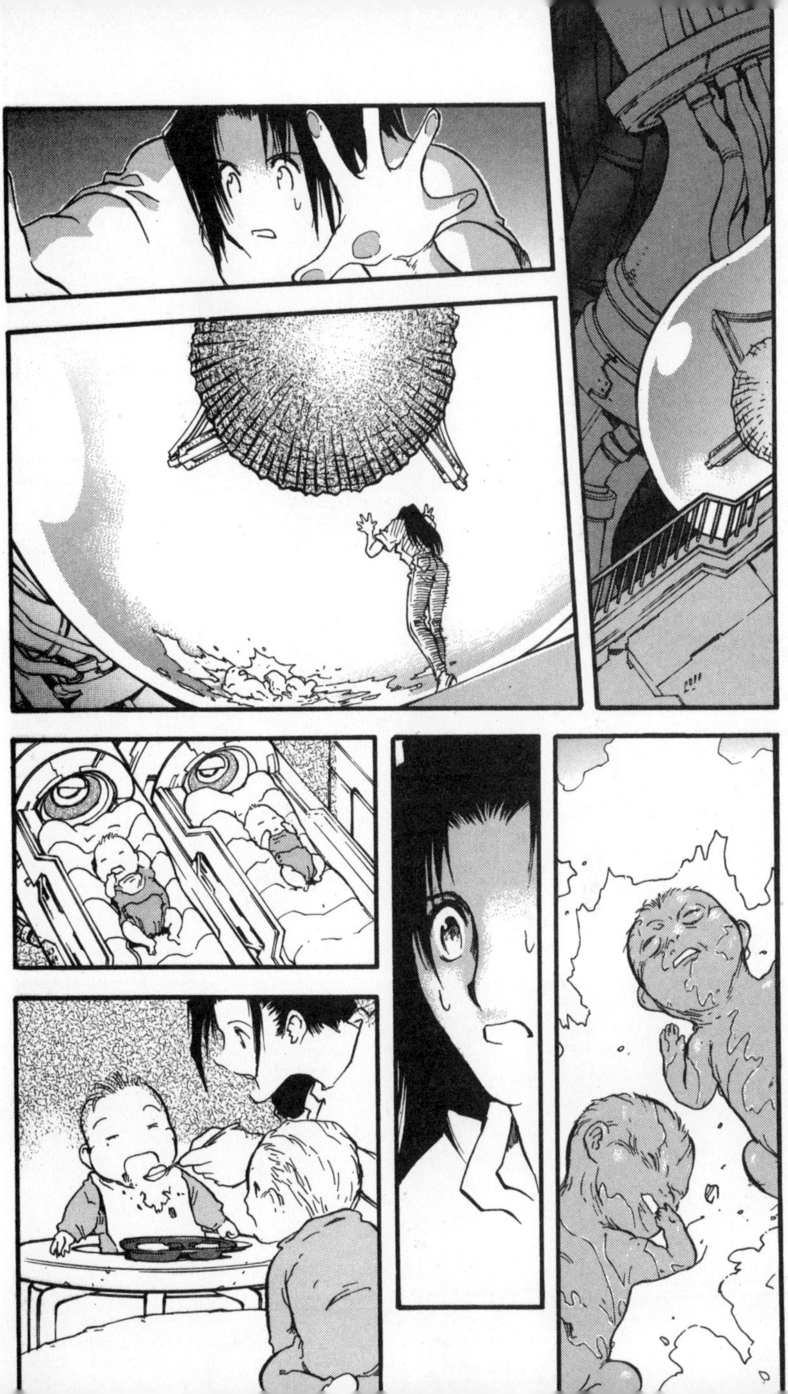

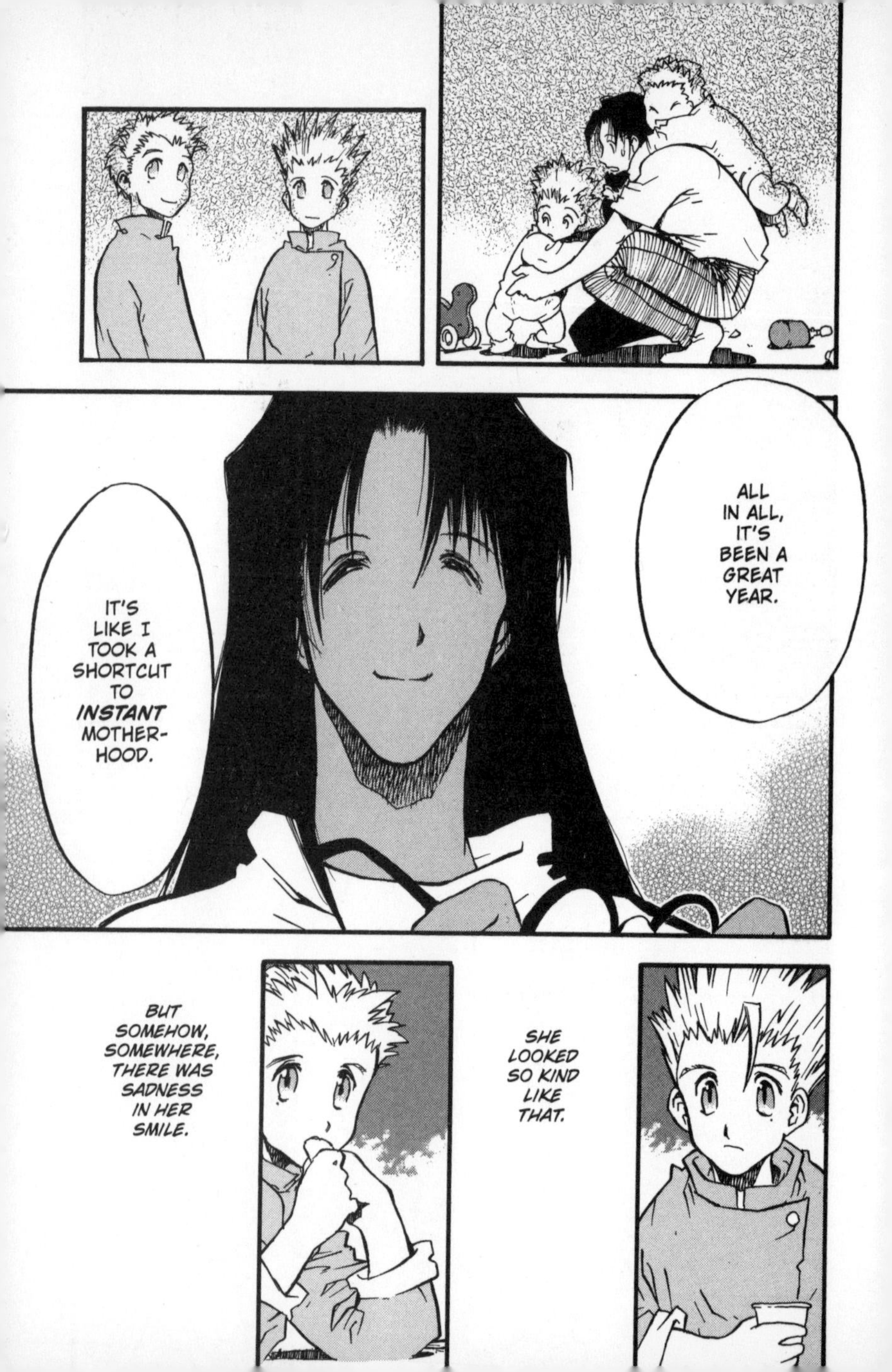
ALL IN ALL, IT'S BEEN A GREAT YEAR.
IT'S LIKE I TOOK A SHORTCUT TO *INSTANT* MOTHERHOOD.
SHE LOOKED SO KIND LIKE THAT.
BUT SOMEHOW, SOMEWHERE, THERE WAS SADNESS IN HER SMILE.

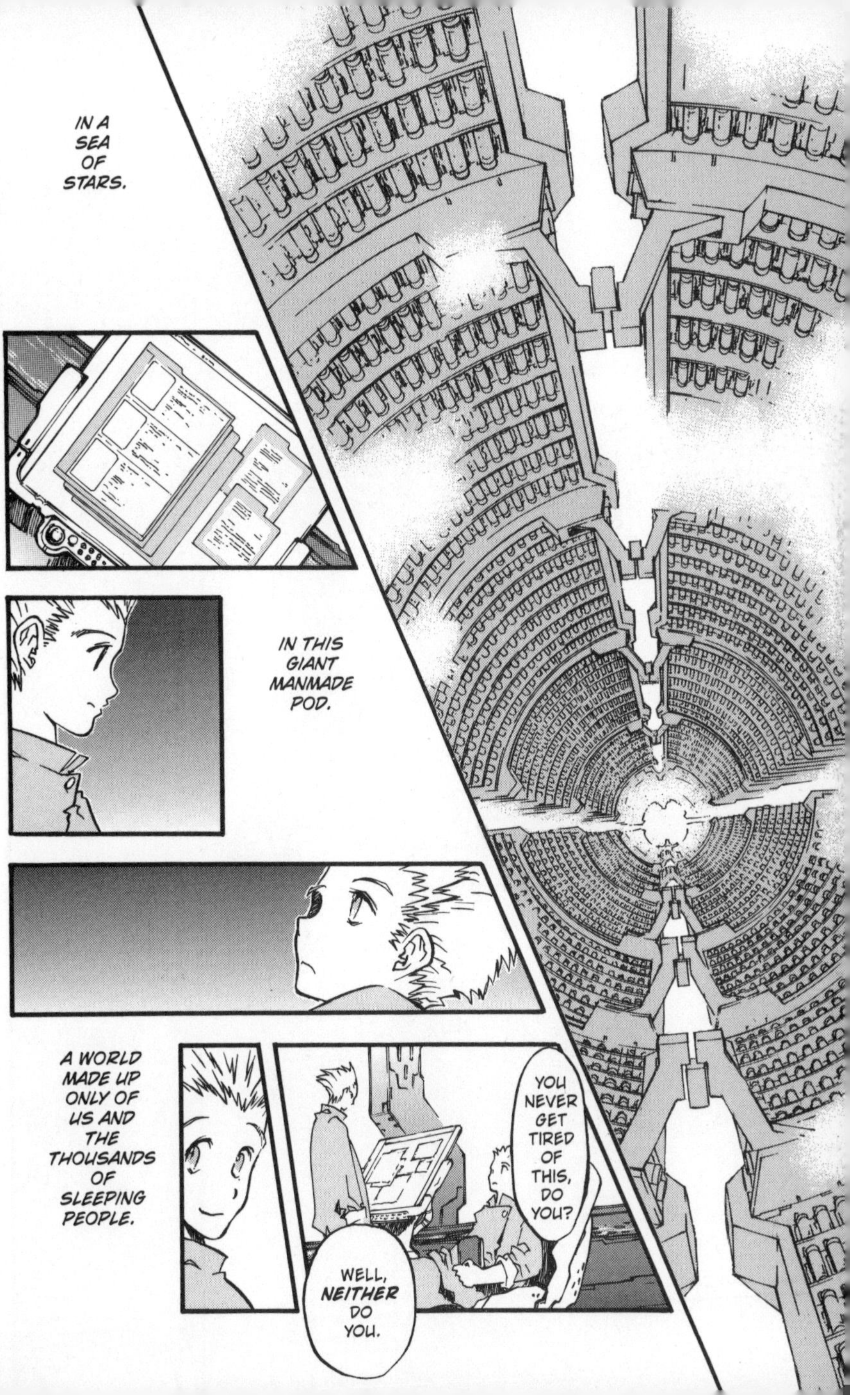
IN A SEA OF STARS.
IN THIS GIANT MANMADE POD.
A WORLD MADE UP ONLY OF US AND THE THOUSANDS OF SLEEPING PEOPLE.
YOU NEVER GET TIRED OF THIS, DO YOU?
WELL, **NEITHER** DO YOU.

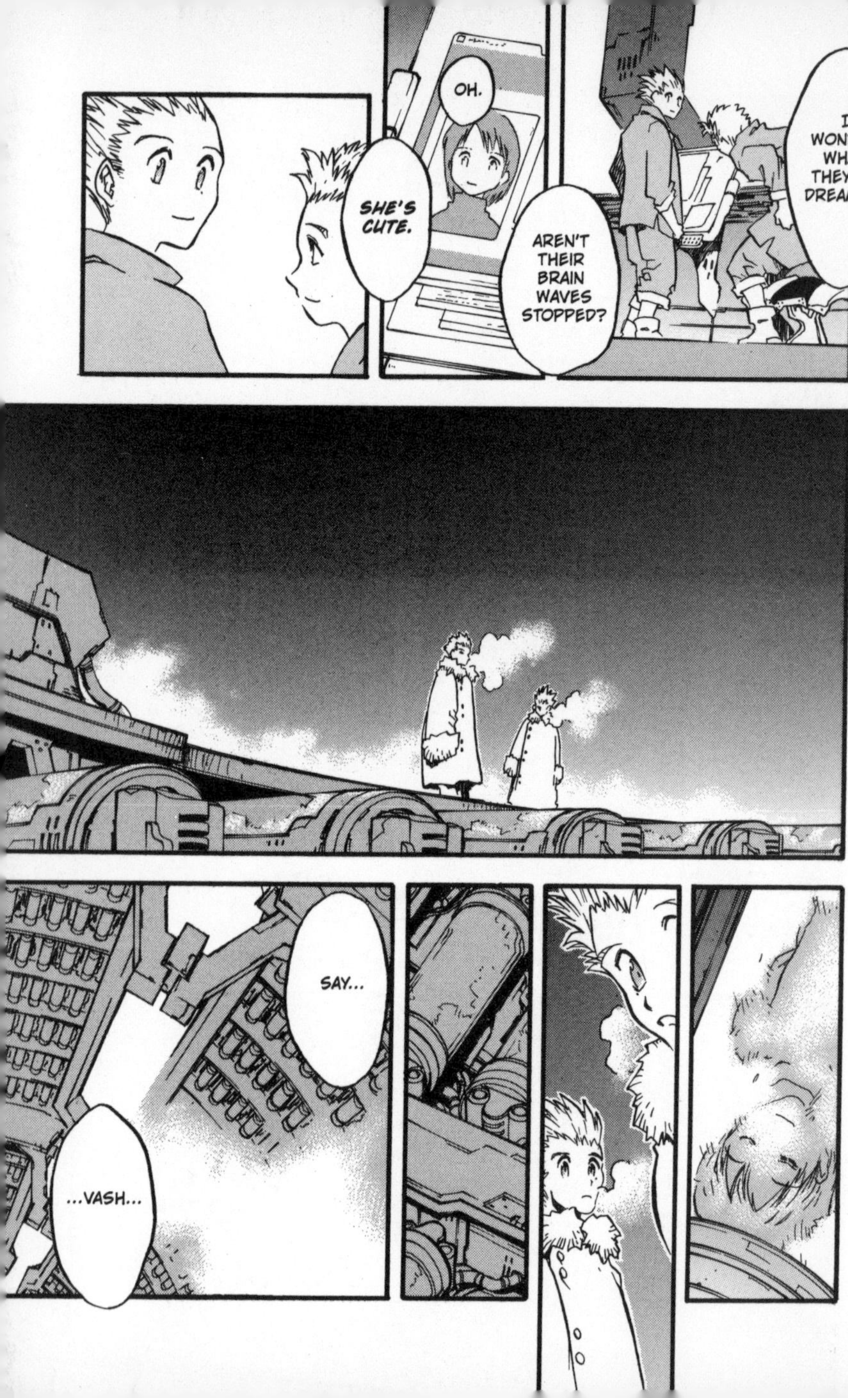
I WONDER WHAT THEY'RE DREAMING.
AREN'T THEIR BRAIN WAVES STOPPED?
OH.
SHE'S CUTE.
SAY...
...VASH...

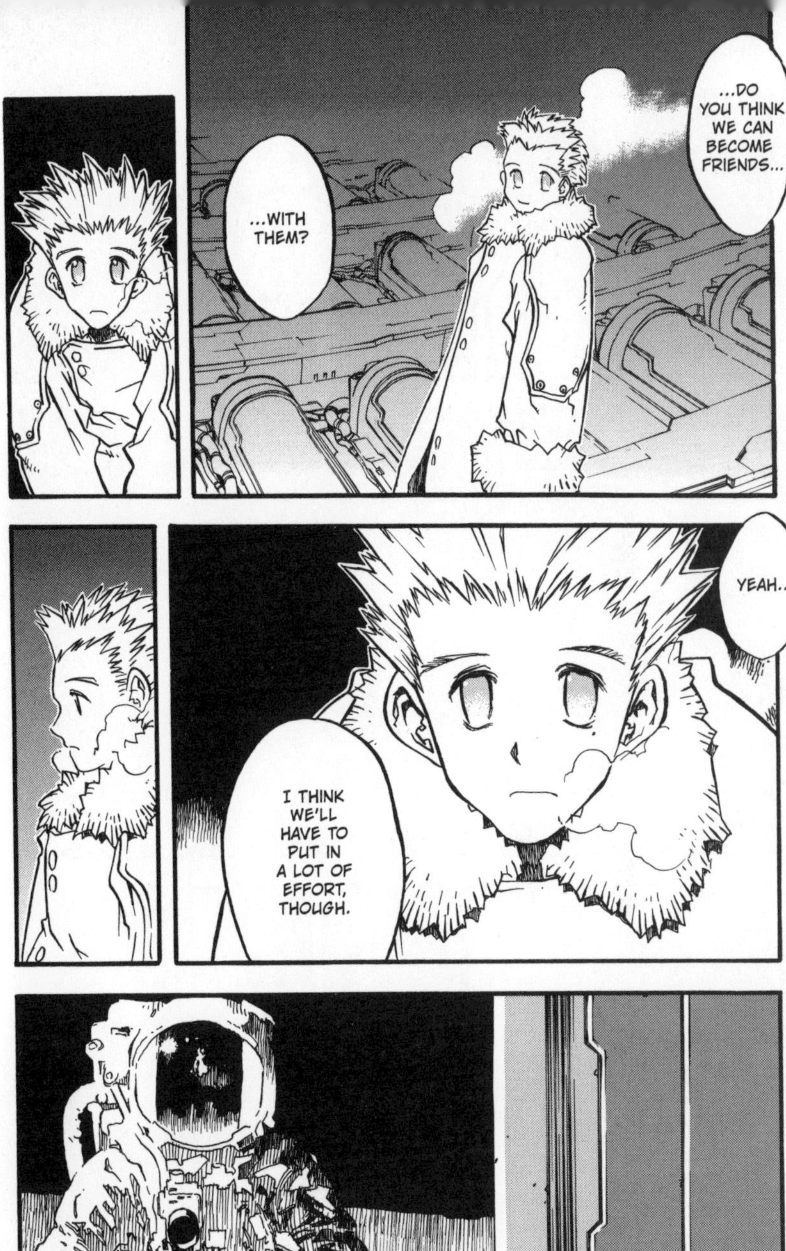
...DO YOU THINK WE CAN BECOME FRIENDS...
...WITH THEM?
YEAH...
I THINK WE'LL HAVE TO PUT IN A LOT OF EFFORT, THOUGH.

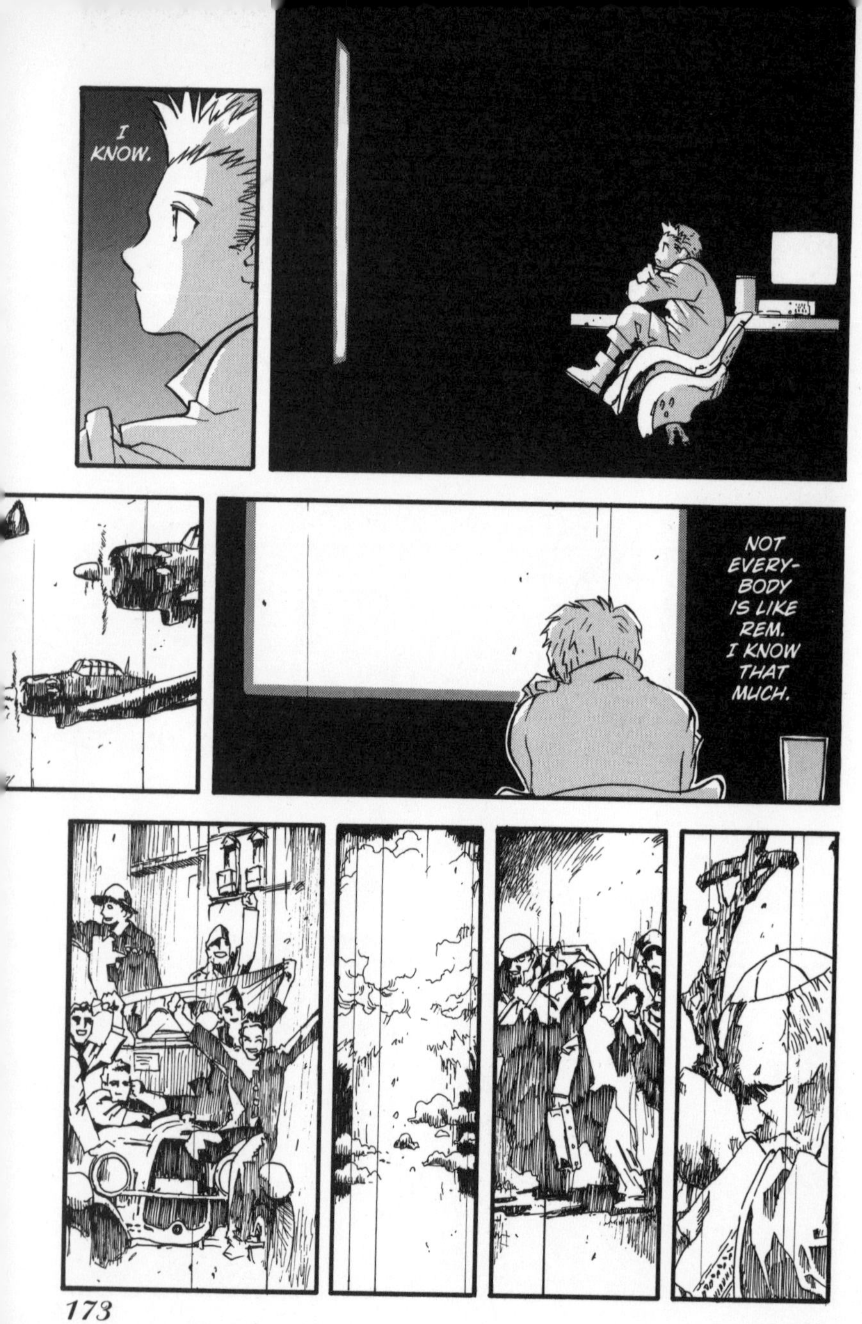
I KNOW.
NOT EVERY-BODY IS LIKE REM. I KNOW THAT MUCH.

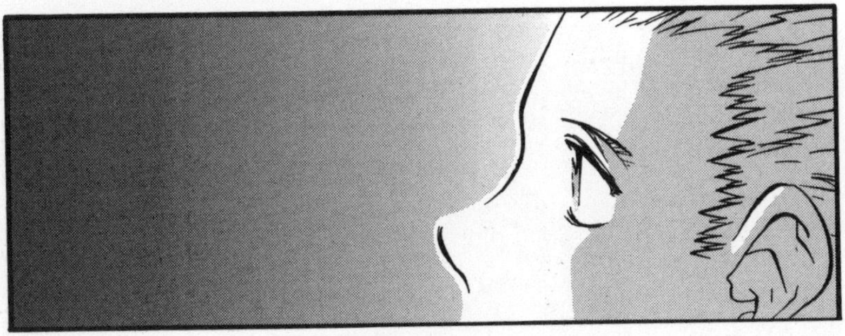

BUT THEY'RE THE ONES WHO CREATED PLANTS.

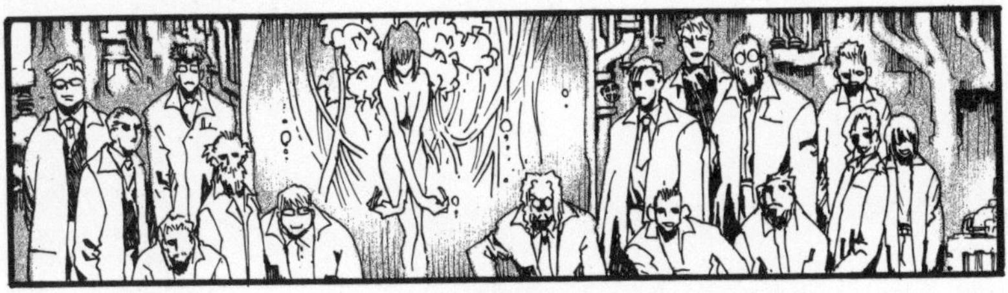

I WANT TO BELIEVE THAT THEY'LL ACCEPT US.

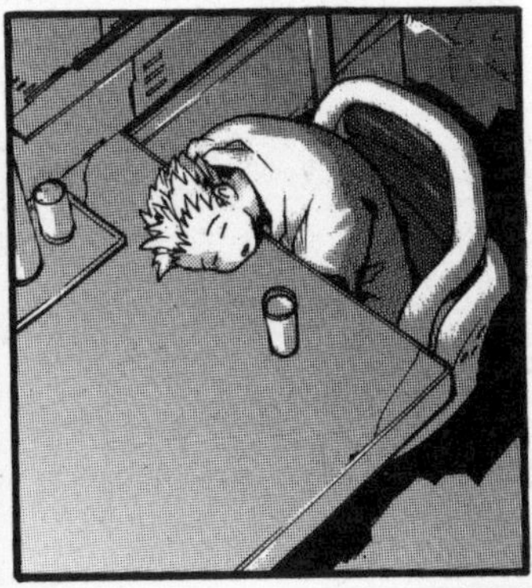

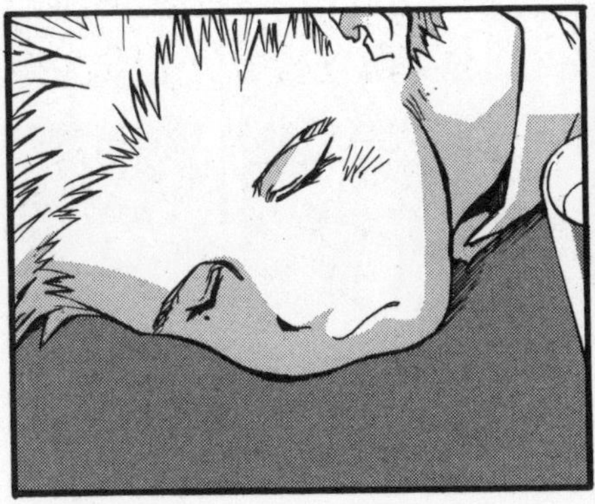

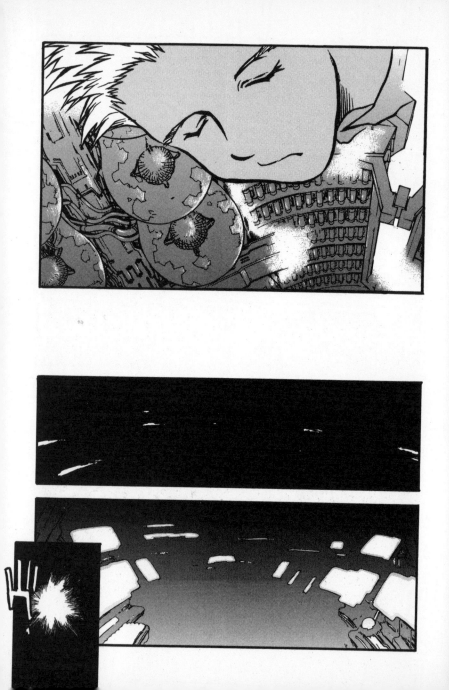

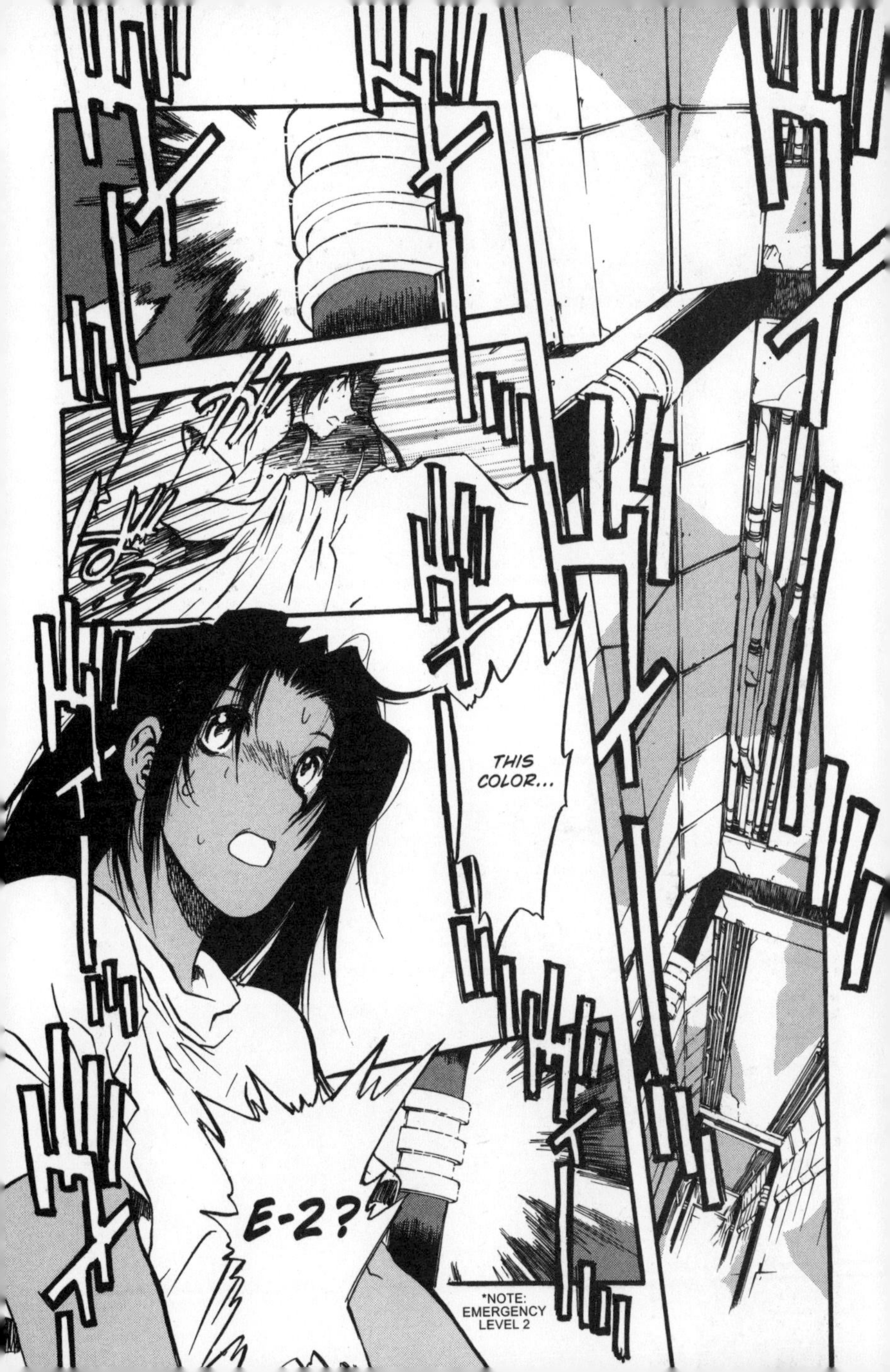
THIS COLOR...
E-2?
*NOTE: EMERGENCY LEVEL 2

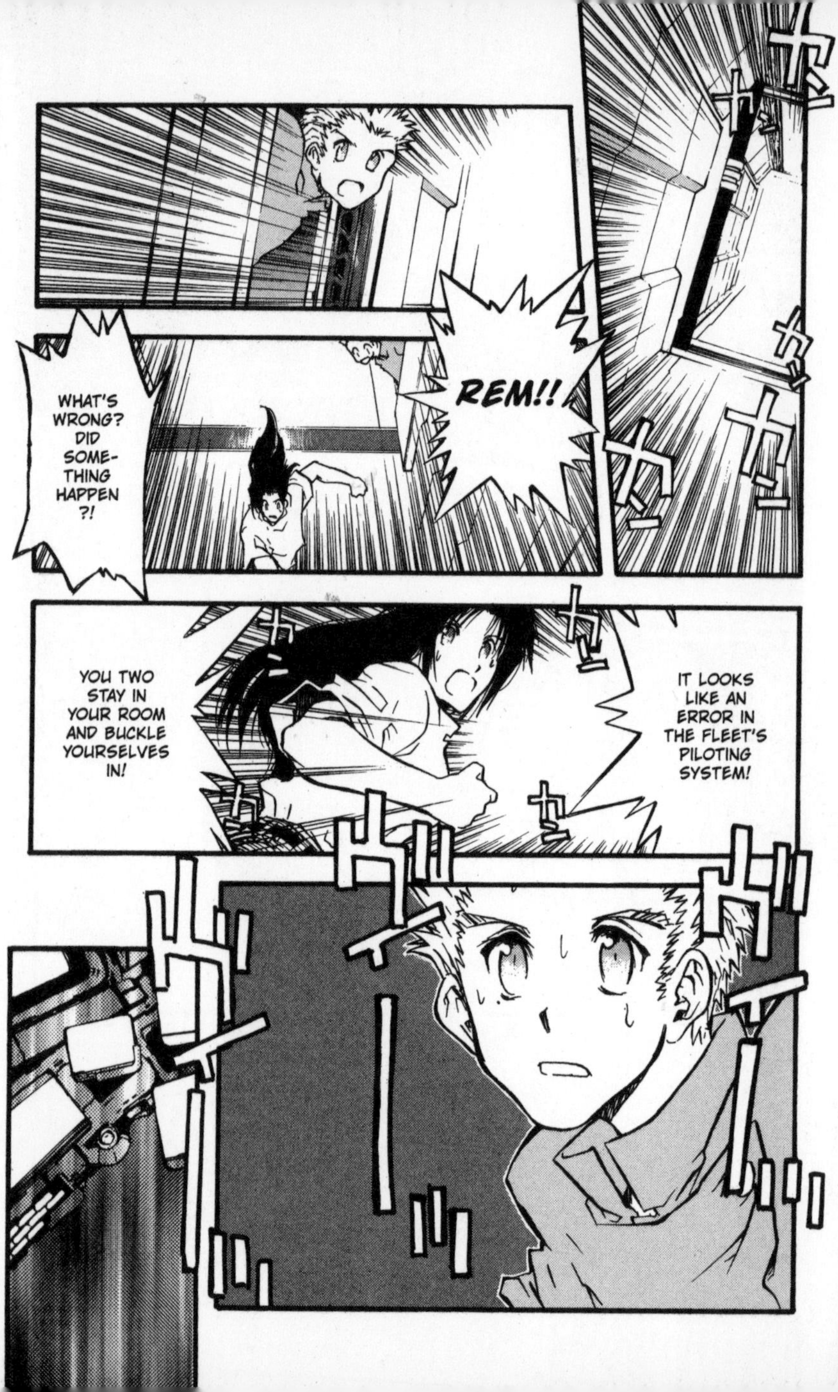
REM!!
WHAT'S WRONG? DID SOMETHING HAPPEN ?!
IT LOOKS LIKE AN ERROR IN THE FLEET'S PILOTING SYSTEM!
YOU TWO STAY IN YOUR ROOM AND BUCKLE YOURSELVES IN!

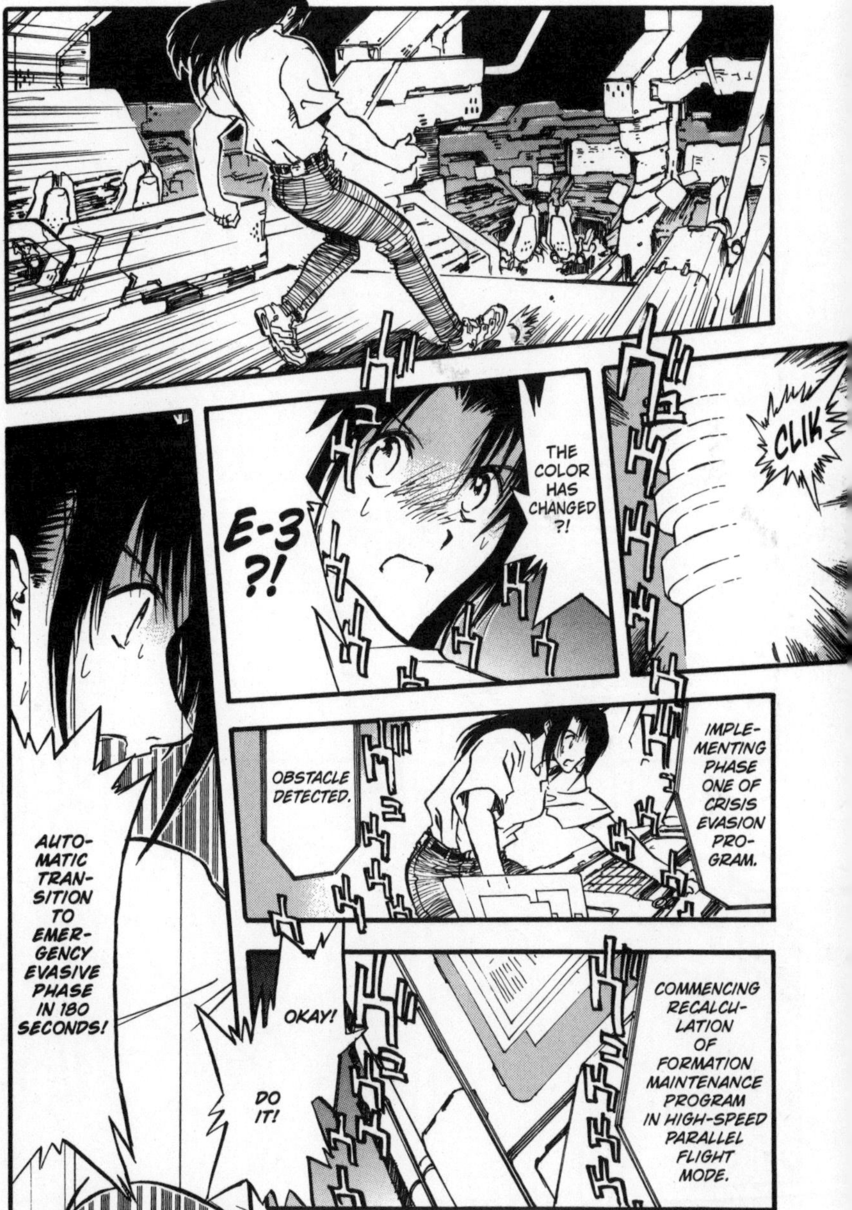
CLIK
THE COLOR HAS CHANGED?!
E-3?!
IMPLEMENTING PHASE ONE OF CRISIS EVASION PROGRAM.
OBSTACLE DETECTED.
COMMENCING RECALCULATION OF FORMATION MAINTENANCE PROGRAM IN HIGH-SPEED PARALLEL FLIGHT MODE.
OKAY!
DO IT!
AUTOMATIC TRANSITION TO EMERGENCY EVASIVE PHASE IN 180 SECONDS!

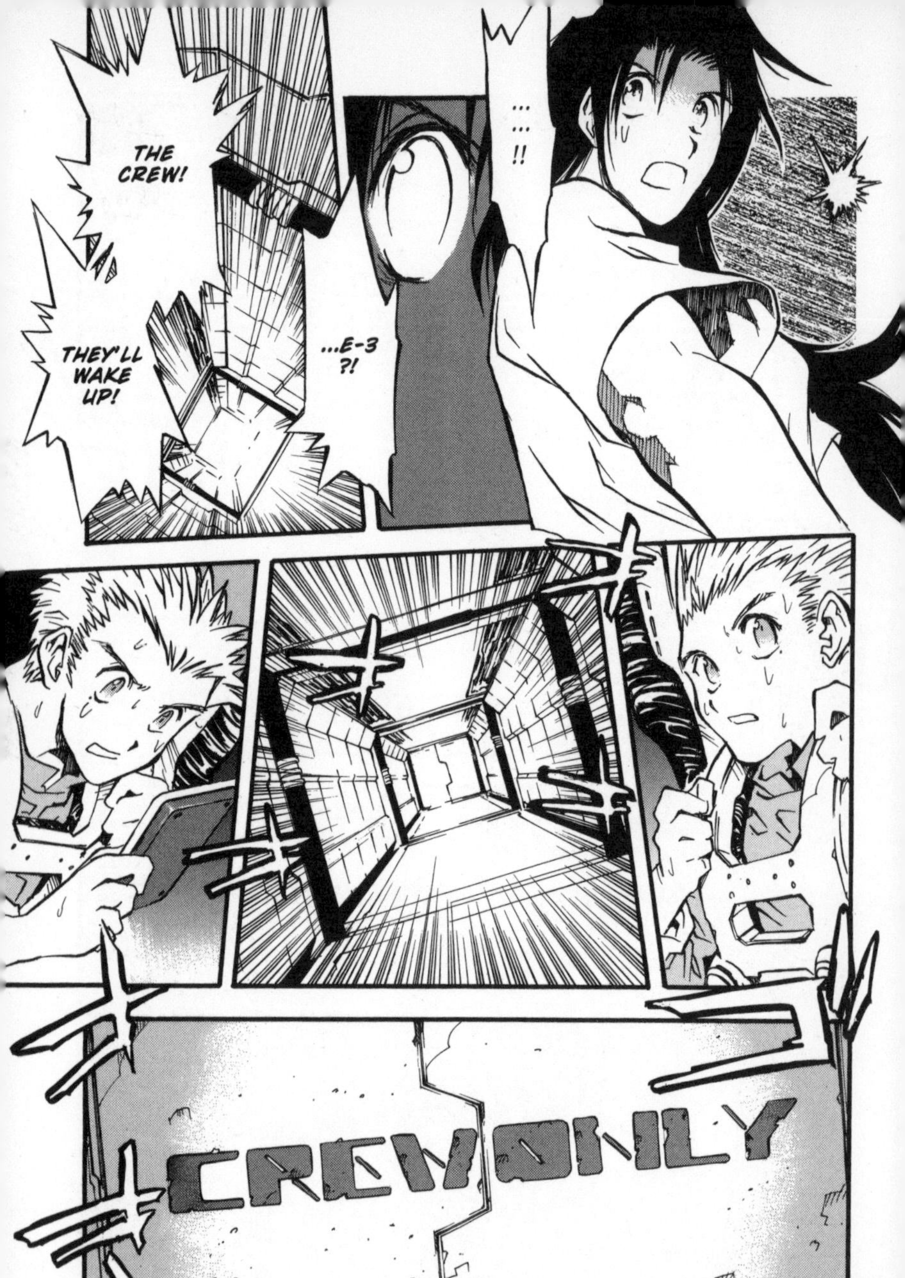

......
!!
...E-3
?!
THE CREW!
THEY'LL WAKE UP!
CREW ONLY

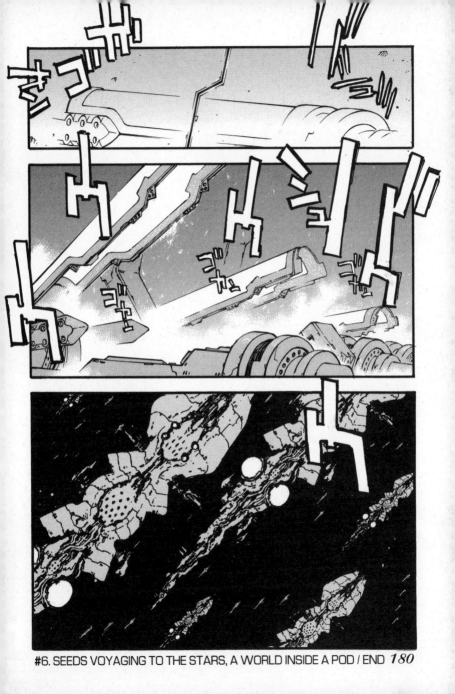

#6. SEEDS VOYAGING TO THE STARS, A WORLD INSIDE A POD / END *180*

TURN TO THE NEXT

TRIGUN MAXIMUM
YASUHIRO NIGHTOW

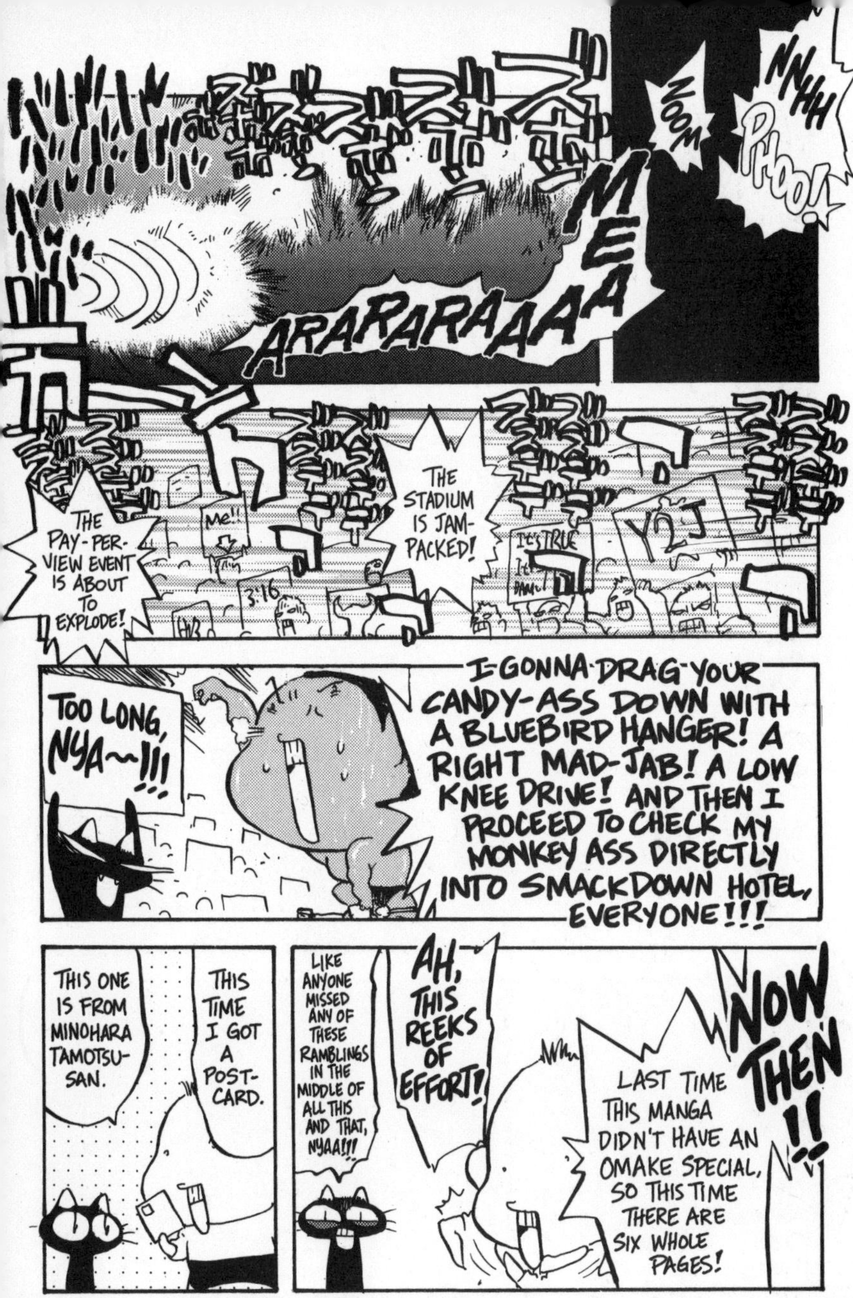
NNHHH PHOO!
VOOOM
MEAAA ARARARAAAA
THE STADIUM IS JAM-PACKED!
Y2J
IT'S TRUE
Me!!
3:16
THE PAY-PER-VIEW EVENT IS ABOUT TO EXPLODE!
I-GONNA-DRAG-YOUR CANDY-ASS DOWN WITH A BLUEBIRD HANGER! A RIGHT MAD-JAB! A LOW KNEE DRIVE! AND THEN I PROCEED TO CHECK MY MONKEY ASS DIRECTLY INTO SMACKDOWN HOTEL, EVERYONE!!!
TOO LONG, NYA~~!!!
NOW THEN!!
LAST TIME THIS MANGA DIDN'T HAVE AN OMAKE SPECIAL, SO THIS TIME THERE ARE SIX WHOLE PAGES!
AH, THIS REEKS OF EFFORT!
LIKE ANYONE MISSED ANY OF THESE RAMBLINGS IN THE MIDDLE OF ALL THIS AND THAT, NYAA!!!
THIS TIME I GOT A POST-CARD.
THIS ONE IS FROM MINOHARA TAMOTSU-SAN.

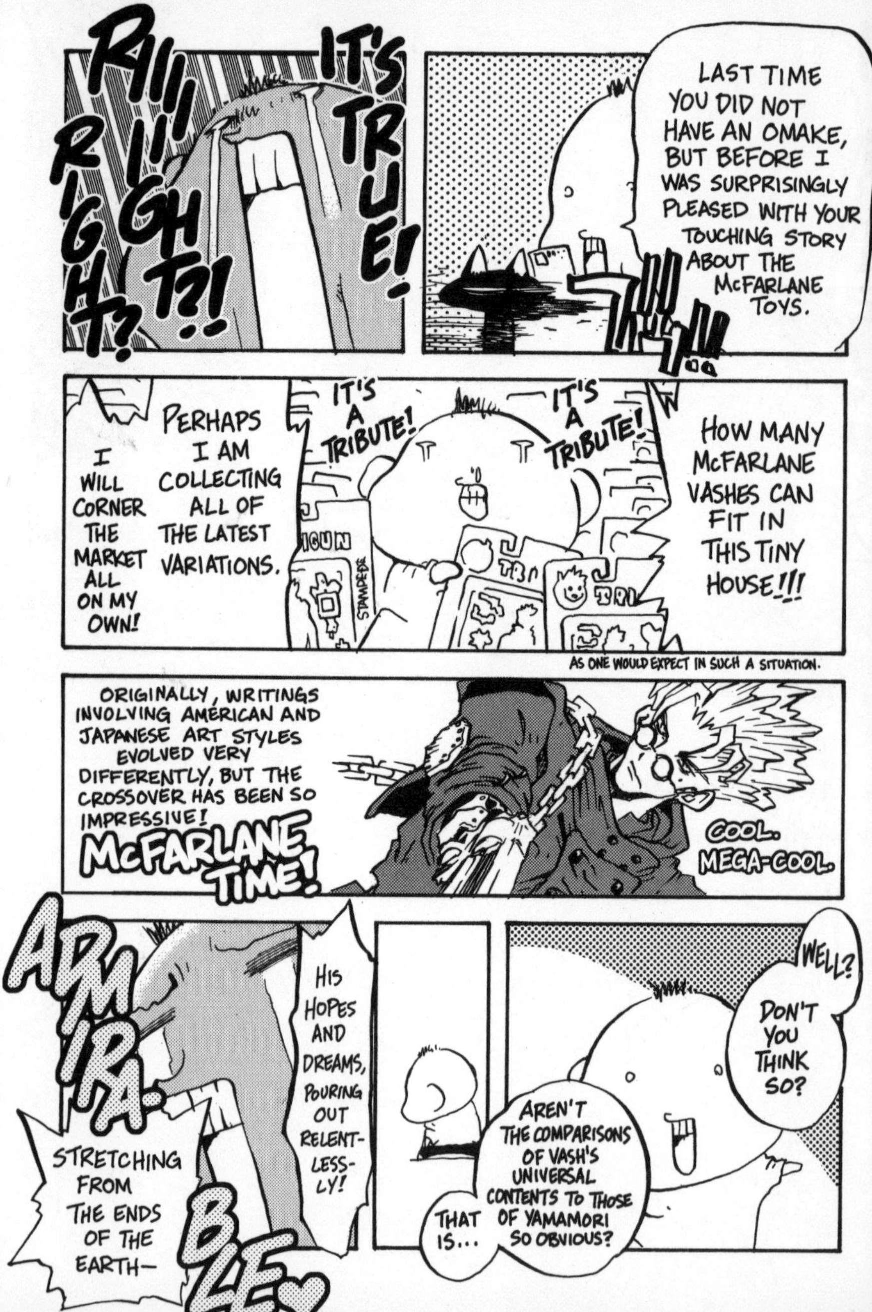
LAST TIME YOU DID NOT HAVE AN OMAKE, BUT BEFORE I WAS SURPRISINGLY PLEASED WITH YOUR TOUCHING STORY ABOUT THE McFARLANE TOYS.
IT'S TRUE!
RIIIIGHT?!
RIGHT?
HOW MANY McFARLANE VASHES CAN FIT IN THIS TINY HOUSE!!!
IT'S A TRIBUTE!
IT'S A TRIBUTE!
PERHAPS I AM COLLECTING ALL OF THE LATEST VARIATIONS.
I WILL CORNER THE MARKET ALL ON MY OWN!
AS ONE WOULD EXPECT IN SUCH A SITUATION.
COOL. MEGA-COOL.
ORIGINALLY, WRITINGS INVOLVING AMERICAN AND JAPANESE ART STYLES EVOLVED VERY DIFFERENTLY, BUT THE CROSSOVER HAS BEEN SO IMPRESSIVE!
McFARLANE TIME!
WELL?
DON'T YOU THINK SO?
AREN'T THE COMPARISONS OF VASH'S UNIVERSAL CONTENTS TO THOSE OF YAMAMORI SO OBVIOUS?
THAT IS...
HIS HOPES AND DREAMS, POURING OUT RELENTLESSLY!
ADMIRABLE♥
STRETCHING FROM THE ENDS OF THE EARTH—

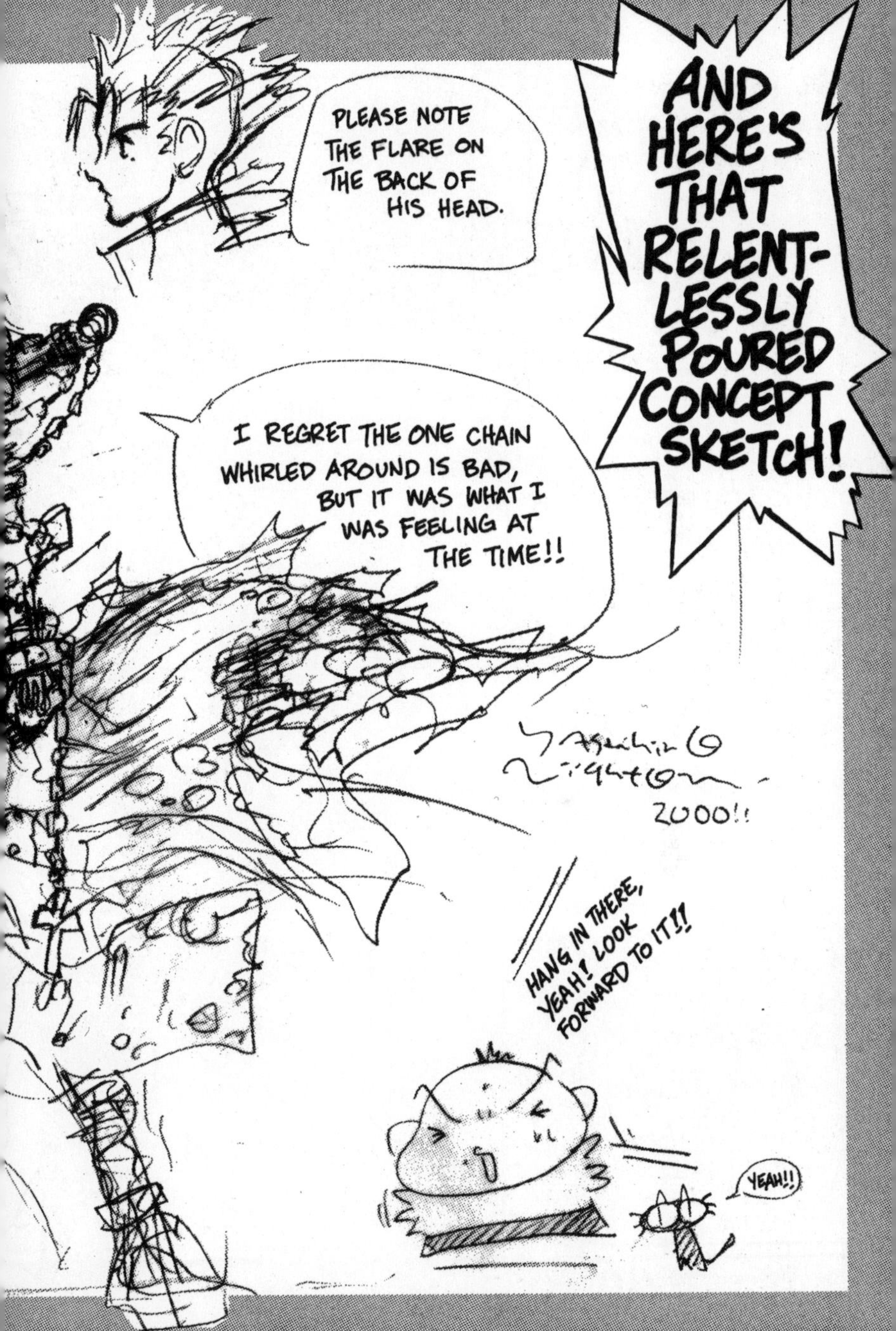

AND HERE'S THAT RELENT-LESSLY POURED CONCEPT SKETCH!
PLEASE NOTE THE FLARE ON THE BACK OF HIS HEAD.
I REGRET THE ONE CHAIN WHIRLED AROUND IS BAD, BUT IT WAS WHAT I WAS FEELING AT THE TIME!!
2000!!
HANG IN THERE, YEAH! LOOK FORWARD TO IT!!
YEAH!!

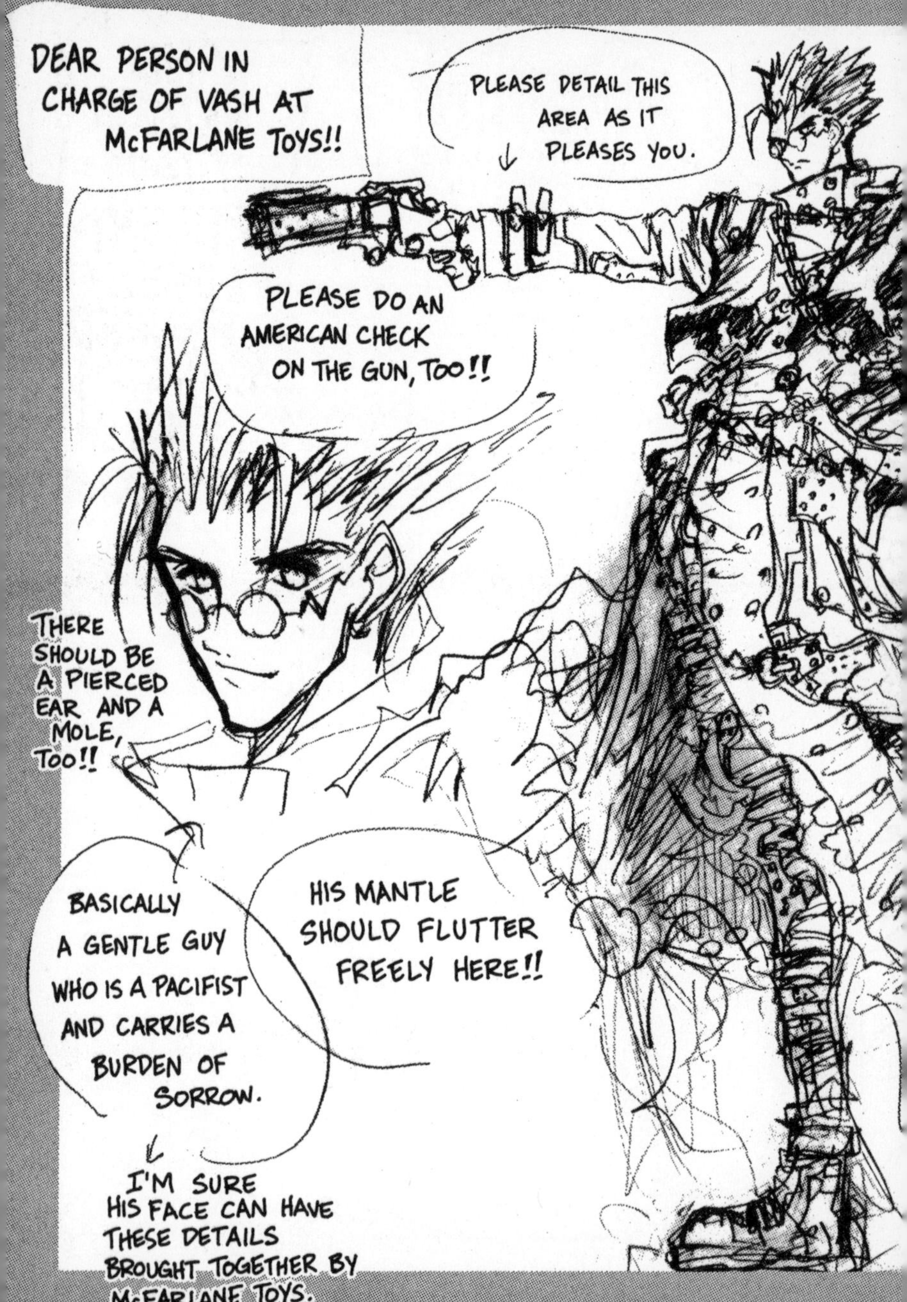
DEAR PERSON IN CHARGE OF VASH AT McFARLANE TOYS!!
PLEASE DETAIL THIS AREA AS IT PLEASES YOU.
PLEASE DO AN AMERICAN CHECK ON THE GUN, TOO!!
THERE SHOULD BE A PIERCED EAR AND A MOLE, TOO!!
HIS MANTLE SHOULD FLUTTER FREELY HERE!!
BASICALLY A GENTLE GUY WHO IS A PACIFIST AND CARRIES A BURDEN OF SORROW.
I'M SURE HIS FACE CAN HAVE THESE DETAILS BROUGHT TOGETHER BY McFARLANE TOYS.

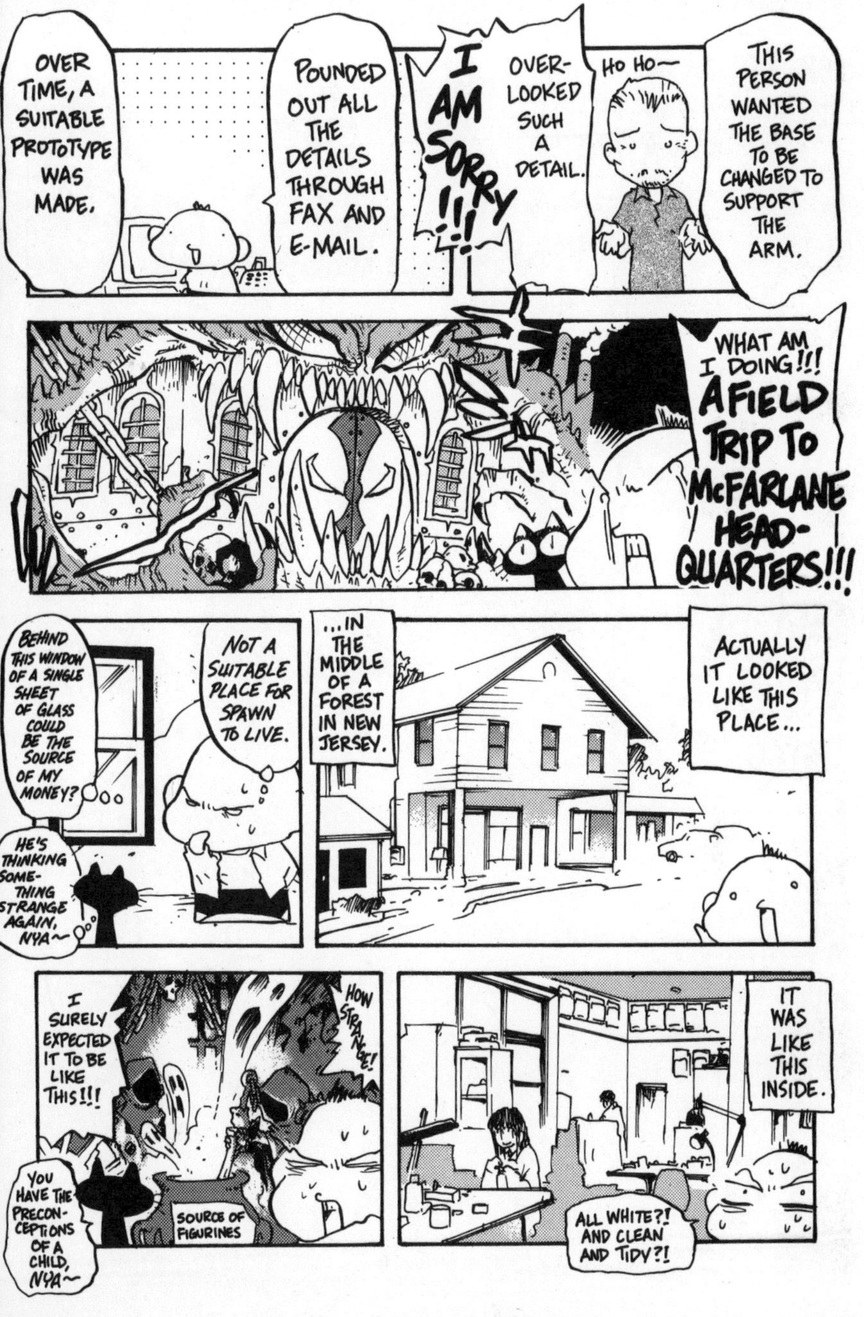
THIS PERSON WANTED THE BASE TO BE CHANGED TO SUPPORT THE ARM.
Ho Ho~
OVER-LOOKED SUCH A DETAIL.
I AM SORRY!!!
POUNDED OUT ALL THE DETAILS THROUGH FAX AND E-MAIL.
OVER TIME, A SUITABLE PROTOTYPE WAS MADE.
WHAT AM I DOING!!! A FIELD TRIP TO McFARLANE HEAD-QUARTERS!!!
ACTUALLY IT LOOKED LIKE THIS PLACE...
...IN THE MIDDLE OF A FOREST IN NEW JERSEY.
NOT A SUITABLE PLACE FOR SPAWN TO LIVE.
BEHIND THIS WINDOW OF A SINGLE SHEET OF GLASS COULD BE THE SOURCE OF MY MONEY?
HE'S THINKING SOME-THING STRANGE AGAIN, NYA~
IT WAS LIKE THIS INSIDE.
ALL WHITE?! AND CLEAN AND TIDY?!
HOW STRANGE!
I SURELY EXPECTED IT TO BE LIKE THIS!!!
SOURCE OF FIGURINES
YOU HAVE THE PRECON-CEPTIONS OF A CHILD, NYA~

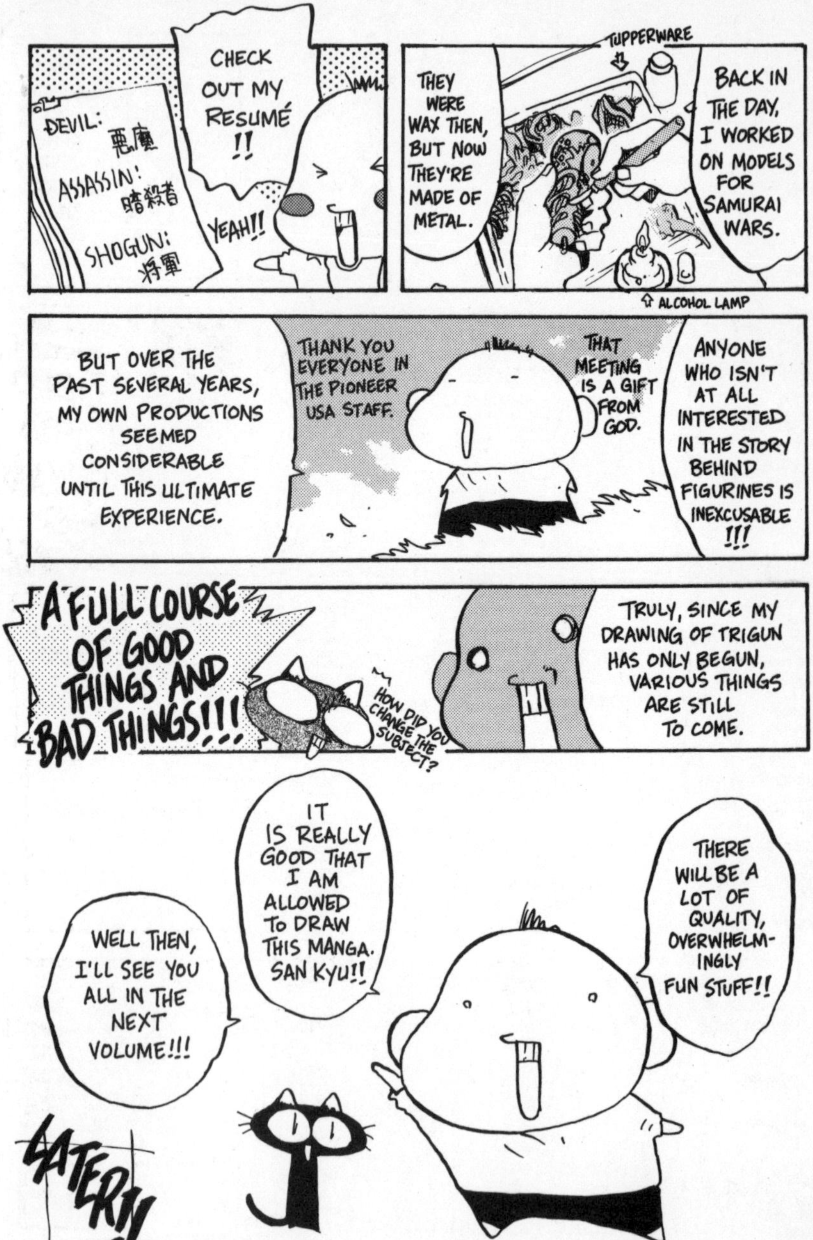
BACK IN THE DAY, I WORKED ON MODELS FOR SAMURAI WARS.
TUPPERWARE
THEY WERE WAX THEN, BUT NOW THEY'RE MADE OF METAL.
ALCOHOL LAMP
CHECK OUT MY RESUMÉ!!
YEAH!!
DEVIL: 悪魔
ASSASSIN: 暗殺者
SHOGUN: 将軍
ANYONE WHO ISN'T AT ALL INTERESTED IN THE STORY BEHIND FIGURINES IS INEXCUSABLE!!!
THAT MEETING IS A GIFT FROM GOD.
THANK YOU EVERYONE IN THE PIONEER USA STAFF.
BUT OVER THE PAST SEVERAL YEARS, MY OWN PRODUCTIONS SEEMED CONSIDERABLE UNTIL THIS ULTIMATE EXPERIENCE.
TRULY, SINCE MY DRAWING OF TRIGUN HAS ONLY BEGUN, VARIOUS THINGS ARE STILL TO COME.
HOW DID YOU CHANGE THE SUBJECT?
A FULL COURSE OF GOOD THINGS AND BAD THINGS!!!
THERE WILL BE A LOT OF QUALITY, OVERWHELMINGLY FUN STUFF!!
IT IS REALLY GOOD THAT I AM ALLOWED TO DRAW THIS MANGA. SAN KYU!!
WELL THEN, I'LL SEE YOU ALL IN THE NEXT VOLUME!!!

SPECIAL THANKS▶▶▶KAWASE TADASHI, SOHARA TOMOKAZU, KUO TAKAKO, KANNAMI SHINJI

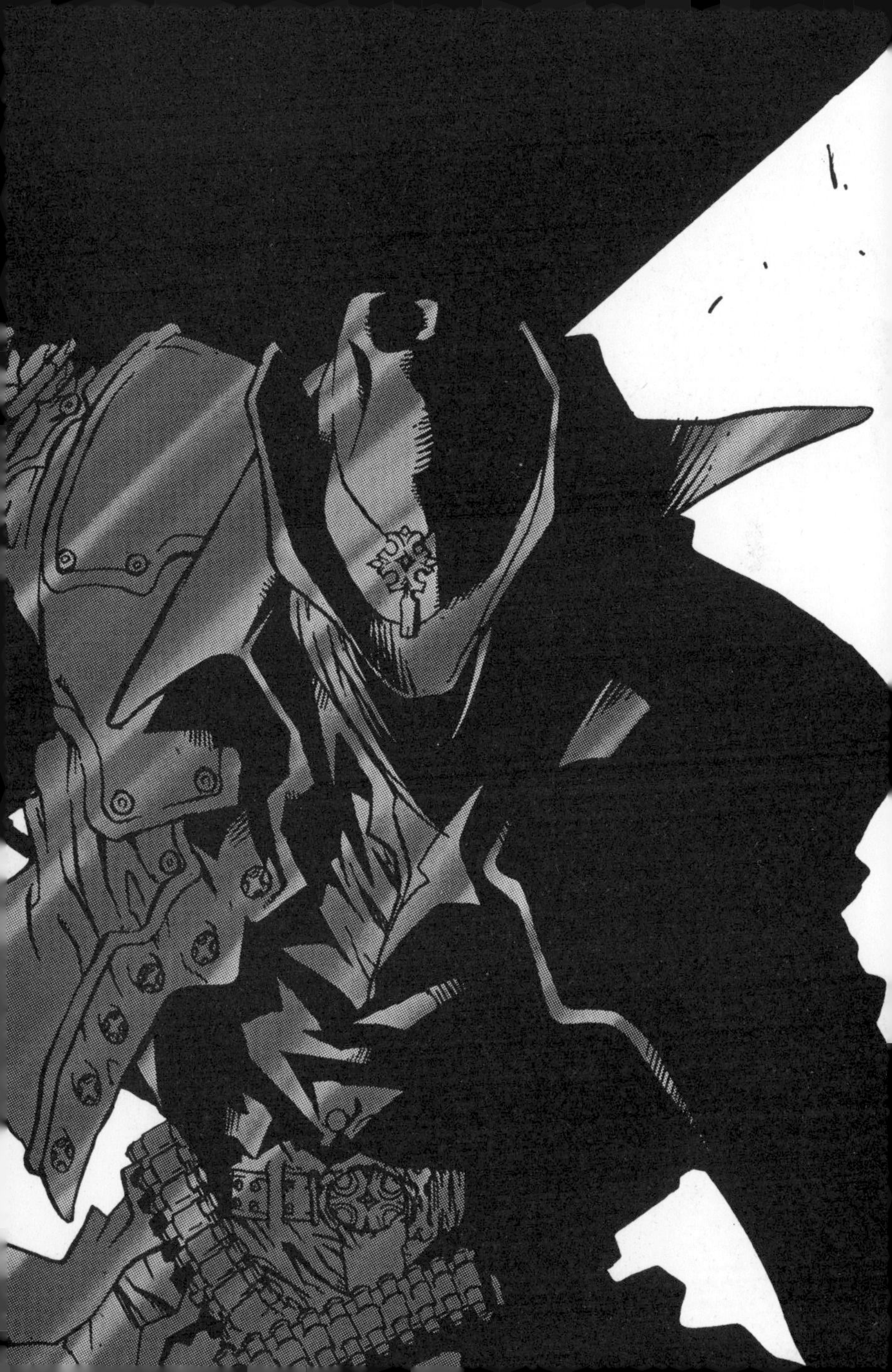

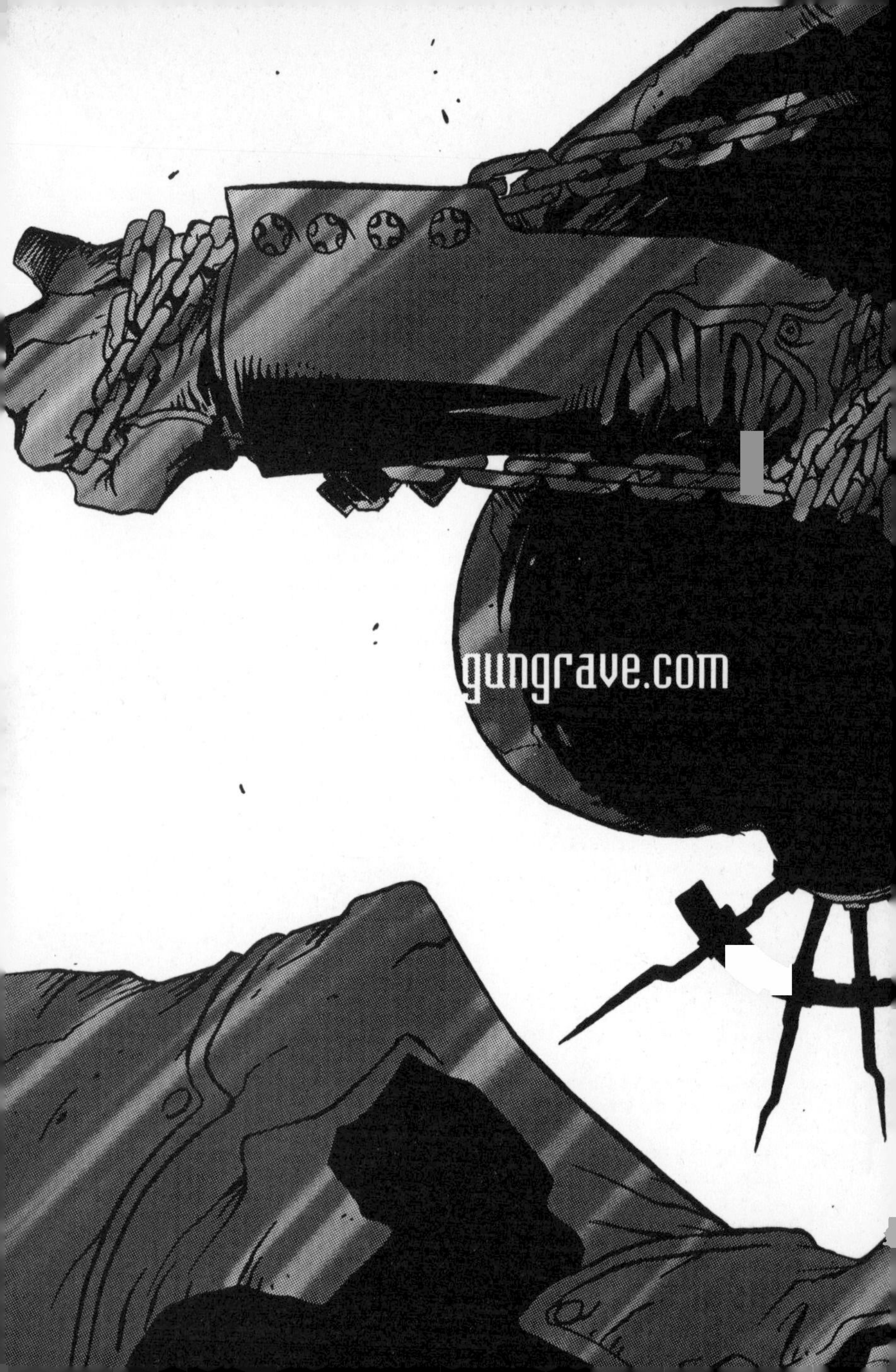

publishers
MIKE RICHARDSON and **HIKARU SASAHARA**

editors
TIM ERVIN and **FRED LUI**

collection designers
DAVID NESTELLE and **JOSHUA ELLIOTT**

English-language version produced by DARK HORSE COMICS and DIGITAL MANGA PUBLISHING.

TRIGUN MAXIMUM vol. 6

published by

Dark Horse Manga
a division of Dark Horse Comics, Inc.
10956 S.E. Main Street
Milwaukie, OR 97222
darkhorse.com

Digital Manga Publishing
1123 Dominguez Street, unit K
Carson, CA 90746
dmpbooks.com

To find a comics shop in your area, call the Comic Shop Locator Service
toll-free at 1-888-266-4226

First edition: August 2005
ISBN: 1-59307-351-8

10 9 8 7 6 5 4 3 2 1
Printed in Canada

BERSERK

KENTARO MIURA'S MANGA EPIC

Presented uncensored in its original Japanese format

Created by Kenturo Miura, *Berserk* is manga mayhem to the extreme—violent, horrifying, and mercilessly funny—and the wellspring for the internationally popular anime series. Not for the squeamish or the easily offended, *Berserk* asks for no quarter—and offers none!

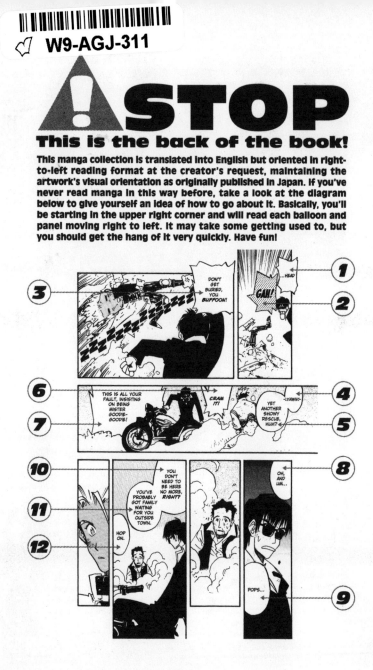

STOP

This is the back of the book!

This manga collection is translated into English but oriented in right-to-left reading format at the creator's request, maintaining the artwork's visual orientation as originally published in Japan. If you've never read manga in this way before, take a look at the diagram below to give yourself an idea of how to go about it. Basically, you'll be starting in the upper right corner and will read each balloon and panel moving right to left. It may take some getting used to, but you should get the hang of it very quickly. Have fun!

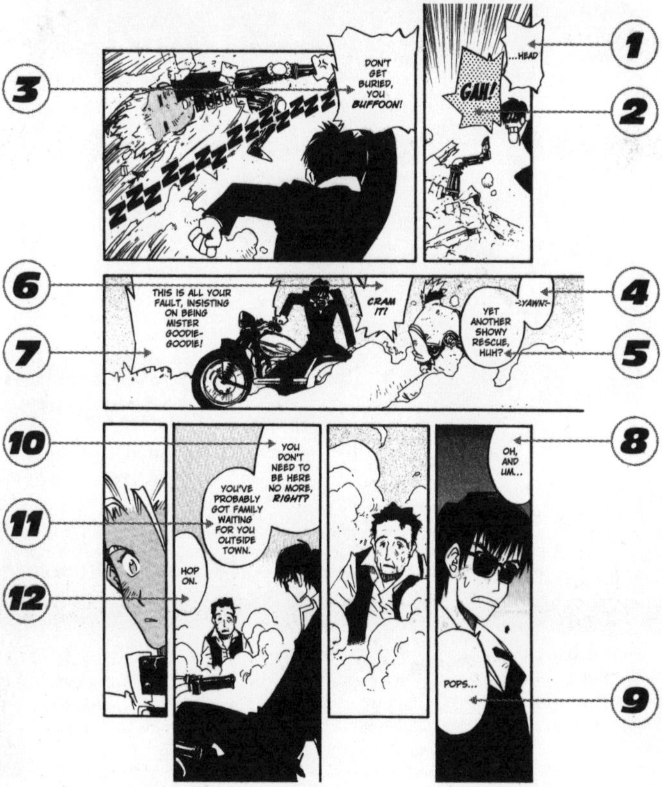
...HEAD
GAH!
DON'T GET BURIED, YOU BUFFOON!
~YAWN~
YET ANOTHER SHOWY RESCUE, HUH?
CRAM IT!
THIS IS ALL YOUR FAULT, INSISTING ON BEING MISTER GOODIE-GOODIE!
OH, AND UM...
POPS...
YOU DON'T NEED TO BE HERE NO MORE, RIGHT?
YOU'VE PROBABLY GOT FAMILY WAITING FOR YOU OUTSIDE TOWN.
HOP ON.